PENGUIN BOOKS

MULTI-AMERICA

Ishmael Reed, one of America's most renowned African American writers, is the author of plays, poetry, and novels, which include *Japanese by Spring*, *Mumbo Jumbo*, and *The Last Days of Louisiana Red*. He has been nominated for the Pulitzer Prize and two National Book Awards. He lives in Oakland, California.

MultiAmerica

Essays on Cultural Wars and
Cultural Peace

Edited by Ishmael Reed

PENGUIN BOOKS

In memory of Toni Cade Bambara
and Kathleen Chang

PENGUIN BOOKS
Published by the Penguin Group
Penguin Putnam Inc., 375 Hudson Street, New York, New York 10014, U.S.A.
Penguin Books Ltd, 27 Wrights Lane, London W8 5TZ, England
Penguin Books Australia Ltd, Ringwood, Victoria, Australia
Penguin Books Canada Ltd, 10 Alcorn Avenue, Toronto, Ontario, Canada M4V 3B2
Penguin Books (N.Z.) Ltd, 182–190 Wairau Road, Auckland 10, New Zealand

Penguin Books Ltd, Registered Offices:
Harmondsworth, Middlesex, England

First published in the United States of America by Viking Penguin,
a division of Penguin Books USA Inc. 1997
Published in Penguin Books 1998

1 3 5 7 9 10 8 6 4 2

THE LIBRARY OF CONGRESS HAS CATALOGUED THE HARDCOVER AS FOLLOWS:
Multi-America: essays on cultural wars and cultural peace / edited by Ishmael Reed.
p. cm.
ISBN 0-670-86753-5 (hc.)
ISBN 0 14 02.5912 0 (pbk.)
1. Pluralism (Social sciences)—United States.   2. Multiculturalism—United States.
3. United States—Ethnic relations.   4. United States—Social conditions—1980–
I. Reed, Ishmael. 1938–
E184.A1M8   1996
305.8´00973—dc20   96–9130

Printed in the United States of America
Set in Bembo
Designed by Junie Lee

Grateful acknowledgment is made for permission to reprint the following copyrighted works:

"A Chicano in Spain" by Rudolfo Anaya. Copyright © 1989 by Rudolfo Anaya. First published in *Before Columbus Review*, Fall/Winter 1989, Volume 1, Numbers 2–3, from a lecture presented at the Third International Conference on Hispanic Cultures of the United States, Barcelona. Reprinted by permission of the author and Susan Bergholz Literary Services, New York. All rights reserved.

"Multinational, Multicultural America versus White Supremacy" by Amiri Baraka. First published in *Disembodied Poetics: Annals of the Jack Kerouac School* edited by Anne Waldman and Andrew Schelling, University of New Mexico Press, 1995. By permission of the author.

"A Countryless Woman: The Early Feminista" from *Massacre of the Dreamers: Essays on Xicanisma* by Ana Castillo. Copyright © 1994 by Ana Castillo. Published by Plume, an imprint of Dutton Signet, a division of Penguin Books USA Inc. Originally published by University of New Mexico Press. Reprinted by permission of Susan Bergholz Literary Services, New York. All rights reserved.

"Rashomon Road: On the Tao to San Diego" by Frank Chin. First published in *The San Diego Reader*. By permission of the author.

"Multiculturalism and the Media" by Jack Foley. First published in *Konch* magazine. By permission of the author.

"Multicultural Europe: Odds, Bets, Chances" by A. Robert Lee. First published in *Konch* magazine. By permission of the author.

"Cultural Work: Planting New Trees with New Seeds" from *Claiming Earth: Race, Rage, Rape, Redemption: Blacks Seeking a Culture of Enlightened Empowerment* by Haki R. Madhubuti, Third World Press. By permission of the author.

"Beyond Multiculturalism: Surviving the Nineties" by Bharati Mukherjee. First published in *The Journal of Modern Literature*. By permission of the author.

"Blacks, Browns, and Yellows at Odds" by Brenda Payton. First published in the *Oakland Tribune*. By permission of the author.

"Being Mixed in America" by Tennessee Reed. First published in *The Baltimore Sun*. By permission of the author.

"The Border Patrol State" from *Yellow Woman and a Beauty of the Spirit* by Leslie Marmon Silko (Simon & Schuster). First published in *The Nation*. Copyright © 1996 by Leslie Marmon Silko. Reprinted by permission of The Wylie Agency, Inc. and Simon & Schuster.

"The Possibilities of a Radical Consciousness: African Americans and New Immigrants" by Amritjit Singh. Published in an abbreviated form in *The Chicago Tribune*. By permission of the author.

"Where's the Revolution?" (originally titled "Queer Politics: Where's the Revolution?") by Barbara Smith, *The Nation*, July 5, 1993. Reprinted by permission of *The Nation* magazine. © 1993 The Nation Company, L.P.

"Sexism in Asian America" by Hoyt Sze, *The Daily Californian*. By permission of the publisher.

"Multiculturalism means that in order to understand the nature and complexities of American culture, it is crucial to study and comprehend the widest possible array of the contributing cultures and their interaction with one another."
—*Lawrence W. Levine,* The New York Times, *August 21, 1996*

". . . History denied or distorted takes on a power that poisons and eventually becomes the cancer at the heart of personal, family, and group survival."
—*Lois Mätt-Fässbinder*

ACKNOWLEDGMENTS

■ ■ ■

Thanks to Sun Ra and "Poison" Junior Jones Ishmael.

For help with this book, my thanks to Don Fehr, Michael Hardart, and Beena Kamlani at Viking Penguin.

CONTENTS

■ ■ ■

3 ■ TO PASS OR NOT TO PASS

4 ■ IS EUROPEAN AMERICA DEAD?

5 ■ FRICTION: INTER-ETHNIC, INTERNECINE, FRATRICIDAL

6 ■ IMAGE DISTORTION DISORDER

7 ■ WHAT'S AHEAD FOR ETHNIC STUDIES?

8 ■ THE PARIAH SYNDROME

xiv • Contents

9 ■ THE FUTURE: NATIONALISM OR INTERNATIONALISM?

INTRODUCTION

■ ■ ■

The response of the northeastern media, punditry, Beltway political community, and corporate-financed think-tank intellectuals to the Los Angeles riots in 1992, which followed the Simi Valley jury's decision acquitting four policemen who had been charged with beating Rodney King, a black motorist, was convincing proof that the traditional establishment is blind to the multicultural realities of American society. Since it has become the field theory of some segments of the media to explain all of America's social problems and disruptions as being the result of the breakdown of the black family, this predictably became the response to the riots by the northeastern intellectuals who dominate the discussion of social issues in this country. This explanation, however, ignored the fact that the typical person arrested during the riot was of Latino background and probably from a two-parent family. It also ignored the participation of whites in the riot, a typical attitude of the media toward white social deviant behavior, which doesn't get as much play as that of blacks and Latinos.

The response to the riots is one more indication that the analysis, driven by a post–civil rights thinking which divides the society into hardworking whites and blacks whose problems are a result of their personal behavior, is inadequate. As a contributor to this anthology, Elaine H. Kim, has said, the black/white paradigm of American race relations is obsolete.

But this paradigm is difficult to dislodge, due to the generous access that its advocates have to the media and the huge sums of money that back their point of view. Moreover, the media have made little progress in integrating their personnel, and so those who might contribute fresh points of view on social issues are denied the opportunity to engage in a fair debate with those who have a dated, monocultural view of American society.

African Americans and Latino intellectuals who mimic the politically correct line promoted by conservative newspaper publishers and television producers are brought in to deflect their critics' charge that some of their arguments smack of racism. These Talented Tenth intellectuals, who serve the right, and who are now engaged in a power struggle over which ones will benefit from "progressive," neoconservative, and right-wing patronage, are rewarded for denouncing the black populist writers of the 1960s, or for opposing Afrocentricity (though they know very little about African civilization). They win praise from their sponsors when they locate all of America's hedonism, anti-Semitism, misogyny, and homophobia among the African American population.

But as an example of how biased the media are when discussing multiculturalism and race, rarely do you see an Afrocentric scholar brought in to debate their critics (this book, however, includes essays by two prominent Afrocentrists: Haki Madhubuti and Maulana Karenga, the founder of Kwanza).

The McIntellectuals and their black and brown Talented Tenth auxiliary insist that we embrace a common culture, and their consensus seems to be that this culture is Yankee, or Anglo. A genuine Englishman and scholar, A. Robert Lee, of the University at Kent, might dispute the notion that the culture of England is an Anglo culture. Anglos were only one tribe, he would claim, but the Anglo model for the American common culture persists, and it is the model that Latinos, Asian Americans, African Americans, and even European Americans are required to embrace. Contributor Daniela Gioseffi quotes Richard Robertiello: "Although a nation of ethnics, our established ethic is WASPishness, the standard by which assimilation is judged, while WASP conduct, for its part, was early on patterned on the model of the British upper class. Altogether, this has proved to be a very bad thing, making Americans WASP-worshipers, with an attendant devaluation and dilution of ethnic pride." One might add that the WASP ideal is also unfair to those Americans with Anglo heritage. They must abide hurtful stereotypes and suffer the resentment of those who resist the Anglo model, even though they had very little to do with the establishment of the WASP ethic.

Some would suggest that the invocation of the glories of Greece, Rome, and Britain as models for the common culture merely masks an effort to Keep America White, and that just as a past glory of common culture is romanticized, the same has been done for white history (though the defenders of the common culture often accuse Afrocentrists of creating a false history, they never challenge bogus European history). So vast are the media resources for what amounts to a white nationalist point of view of American culture that a non-historian, Lynne Chaney, who reaches millions through her regular appearances on entertainment television talk shows, was able to overturn new standards for teaching American history established by a committee of qualified historians. Eric Foner, DeWitt Clinton Professor of History at Columbia University, in a letter to the *New York Times* dated January 30, 1995, detected the implicit McCarthyism in the criticism made by the new standards' opponents: "Evidently, historians who draw attention to instances where the United States contributed to the increase of tyranny (such as the growth of slavery in the 19th century or the military occupation of numerous Western Hemisphere nations in the 20th) are to be declared lacking in patriotism."

Monoculturalism, then, is essentially an anti-intellectual coalition. It says that we shouldn't learn this, we shouldn't study that, we should only speak English, we shouldn't study the African continent. Though Portuguese, Spanish, British, German, Dutch explorers, capitalists, scholars, and students have been studying the African continent for generations, when African Americans do it, they are accused of engaging in self-esteem exercises. Monoculturalism says that we should revere and study Plato, though monoculturalists seem to be against a dialogue with their adversaries, and that the Enlightenment should be our model for pristine intellectual standards when the Enlightenment promoted at least as much intellectual rubbish as that promoted by some of the Afrocentrists with whom they seem obsessed. Dr. Leon Poliako, author of *The Aryan Myth*, suggests that the bizarre racial anthropology of the Enlightenment thinkers may have prepared the way for the scientific racism of the next century. Voltaire in his *Traité de métaphysique* (1734) wrote of "fuzzy negroes, the long-maned yellow races and beardless men [who] are not descended from the same man." In the same work, he wrote that whites were "superior to these Negroes, as the Negroes are to the apes and the apes to oysters." Voltaire and Diderot would have called their contemporary champions on the black ultra right, monkeys.

Obviously, as long as white supremacy is the goal of the monoculturalists, there's going to be a fight. Not only from Latinos, African Americans, Asian Americans, and Native Americans, but from a growing number of "whites" who are beginning to challenge that designation and to disavow the privileges that go along with white supremacy, and from Europeans who are now beginning to realize that abandoning ethnic cultures for whiteness was too high a price to pay.

Though the critics of multiculturalism may suggest that resistance to the white supremacy standard is something new in North America, something that began in the 1960s, the resistance in fact began very early.

One of the reasons for the Pueblo Revolt of 1680, which took place in New Mexico, was a feeling on the part of the indigenous peoples that the friars and the Spaniards were depriving them of "their idols, their dances, and their beliefs." This resistance continues. The novelist Rudolfo Anaya writes in an essay in this book: "Our first declaration of independence was from Anglo-America, that is, we insisted on the right to our *Indohispano* heritage." On May 1, 1996, it was reported that the Mayan Indians had seized a radio station in Mexico as part of the Indian war against the Mexican government. The African resistance to Westernization began as soon as the first African captives fell into the hands of their Portuguese captors. After centuries of repression, African-derived culture in this hemisphere is stronger than ever, and with the arrival of Caribbean peoples and peoples from South America, African-based religion is burgeoning within the United States, attracting adherents of all races.

Again in this book, Haki Madhubuti, a leading Afrocentrist, responds to the one-sided depiction of Afrocentrism; but lest the reader believes that Afrocentrism is a lonely outpost in a sea of political incorrectness, his views are similar to those of other contributors to this anthology. Using Juan Felipe Herrera's image, Madhubuti shows how one community is dealing with, in Herrera's words, the shattering of its cultural vertebrae. Mr. Madhubuti has been a member of the Independent Black School movement for twenty-five years, which is his way of dealing with the condition of blacks being "caught between a hurricane and a volcano when it comes to the acquisition of life-giving and life-sustaining knowledge," as he puts it here.

Ana Castillo echoes Madhubuti's frustration, saying: "The feminista also wanted a bicultural and bilingual system of child care that would validate their children's culture and perhaps ward off an inferiority complex before they had a chance to start public school; traditionally, monolingual and anglocentric schools had alienated children, causing them great psychological damage."

The resistance to the common Anglo culture isn't merely happening among coloreds, which is what the critics of multiculturalism claim, the kind of black-obsessed people who see blacks as responsible for every social and cultural evil from illegitimacy to hip-hop. Because of my Irish heritage, I've been invited to Irish cultural events. In March 1995, I attended an Irish American writers conference at New College in San Francisco. During the question and answer period, I asked the Irish American audience, had assimilation been worth it? To my surprise, not a single member answered in the affirmative. They complained that they had to change their names to Anglo names, and that they had to marry Anglos in order to get a good job. They all agreed that they had lost something. Perhaps James T. Farrell was correct when he said that when the Irish left Chicago for the suburbs, they left Ireland.

The Irish Americans are not the only restless European American group. On February 24, 1994, I attended an exhibit organized by the American Italian Historical Association, entitled *Una Storia Segreta*, described in the program accompanying the exhibit as a "special exhibit of photographs, posters, internment letters, government documents, artifacts, and news articles which for the first time gather together details of the time when thousands of Italian Americans were subject to registration, curfews, and evacuation from coastal areas, while still others were interned or excluded from California entirely."

This exhibit exposed one of those hidden and shameful episodes in American history when naturalized Italian Americans were rounded up and placed in interment camps in the West; when the Italian American community was harassed for their alleged disloyalty by J. Edgar Hoover and a congressional committee, and defamed by the liberal President Roosevelt, who used provocative and insulting imagery in speaking of Italian Americans.

Not only was I surprised by this exhibit, but I could tell that this information was new too to some of the Italian Americans who were there. Since then, I've talked to Italian Americans who'd never heard of the internment. I was struck especially by a passage from a letter from the Italian Cultural Society. Speaking of Italian Americans, it said, "We are a people that has not only lost our way, we are a people that has forgotten where we come from." This sentiment reminded me of one expressed by Malcolm X, who in the pre–African American Studies period of the 1960s described African Americans as "lost in the wilderness of North

America." Clearly, the revolt against the white supremacist Anglo standard of common culture is wider than public McIntellectuals would have us believe, and no amount of free advertising from the media or millions of dollars of corporate sponsorship through non-profit monocultural fronts will change this.

Another revisionist myth promoted by common culture advocates is that as soon as American Europeans passed through Ellis Island, they abandoned their heritages and rushed into the suburbs. American European contributors to this anthology argue differently. They write about American Europeans who were coerced into assimilating away their identities, sometimes because of extra-national considerations. It was not a good idea to be a "hyphenated" German American during World Wars I and II, when Germany was considered the enemy, writes Lois Mätt-Fässbinder, nor was Irish American chauvinism desirable when the United States policy was pro-British, or Italian American when Mussolini—who was a darling of segments of the American establishment until he invaded Ethiopia—became the enemy. But the white ethnics could be considered lucky. Native Americans in Alaska and in the Southwest were sometimes beaten if they persisted in practicing their language and customs. Some people argue that the differences between white ethnics have disappeared, and that identity is an obsession of Asian Americans, African Americans, and Native Americans. Eugene Genovese, an ex-Italian American, has said that Italian America is dead. Is European America dead? Lawrence Di Stasi, Helen Barolini, and Daniela Gioseffi engage in a debate with those who believe that an American European literature is nonexistent. They are part of a new European American ethnic Renaissance. And they insist that European American traditions, which have been denied by those who insist upon a common culture, are still intact.

Americans, even the public intellectuals, also believe that American whites are the descendants of an uninterrupted line of white ancestors. Lucia Chiavola Birnbaum challenges this myth.

As a result of the militancy of African Americans, Latinos, and Asian Americans, the universities of the 1960s instituted ethnic studies programs, the rocky history of which are covered in this book by William M. Banks and Stephanie Kelly, as well as by Gerald Vizenor—who in the only fiction piece in the book lends us one of his Tricksters to assess the state of multiculturalism on campus. Because of new interest in white ethnic studies, pioneered by the MELUS movement, universities have begun courses in Irish American and Italian American history and culture.

The Italian Americans at City College invoked Affirmative Action to institute Italian American courses. The renewal of white ethnicity is a response to the growing discontent with what has been touted as the common culture.

Today's immigrants are not under the same kind of pressure to assimilate as those white ethnics of a former period. In 1995, as a guest of Quebec's Writers Union, I was struck by how similar the nationalism of the French Bloc Québecois was to those of the Chicanos of the Southwest, who view that part of the country as northern Mexico where indigenous people are united in language and culture. In Montreal, I sat through a reading of French Canadian poets during which not one single word of English was spoken. One can experience the same thing in Albuquerque, where the language is Spanish.

Just as a definition of the common culture, or monoculturalism, seems to depend upon the definer, so a precise definition of multiculturalism seems to have been lost in the din of sound bites of performance intellectuals. Gerald Horne speaks of a "superficial multiculturalism," which for him means a conservative president appointing two black cabinet members with corporate connections, in order to give the appearance of a rainbow administration. Manning Marble has referred to a "radical multiculturalism," which means people of different backgrounds cohering around left-wing political causes. Diane Ravitch distinguishes between "pluralistic multiculturalism" and "particularistic multiculturalism." The pluralists seek a richer common culture; the particularists insist that no common culture is possible or desirable.

In his essay "American Literature and Language" in *To Criticize the Critic*, T. S. Eliot wrote:

When we read a novel of Dostoevski, or see a play by Tchehov, for the first time, I think we are fascinated by the odd way in which Russians behave; later we come to recognize that theirs is merely an odd way of expressing thoughts and feelings which we all share. And though it is only too easy for a writer to be local without being universal, I doubt whether a poet or novelist can be universal without being local too. Who could be more Greek than Odysseus? Or more German than Faust? Or more Spanish than Don Quixote? Or more American than Huck Finn? Yet each one of them is a kind of archetype in the mythology of all men everywhere.

Another example of a "local" endeavor, that of Alex Haley's *Roots*, became an archetype for men everywhere, because Haley tapped into the anxiety of American Europeans, based upon their not knowing where they came from.

If Bharati Mukherjee is right when she says that the mosaic theory of multiculturalism means an American culture divided by separate cultural entities, then this certainly doesn't describe the intellectual experience of this anthology's contributors. They don't write in Cantonese, Aztecan, or Yoruba, but in English, a language which though having Indian origins is considered a "white" language. As Rudolfo Anaya says, "While my parents' generation still communicated only in Spanish, my generation converses almost completely in English, a function of our professional lives."

I am a typical multiculturalist. I studied European history, art, and politics formally for the first fifteen years of my life and often did better than my white classmates. In high school, I performed in a string quartet devoted to the works of European composers. Like most African Americans of my generation, whatever efforts I made in discovering African and African American history were extracurricular. Asian American, Latino, and Native American contributors to this anthology can make the same claim.

So multiculturalists are by no means separatists. As Sam Hamod writes in a forthcoming issue of *Konch* magazine, "Our dual vision as 'ethnic' and American allows us to see aspects of the U.S. that mainstream writers often miss; thus, our perspectives often allow us a diversity of visions that, ironically, may lead us to larger truth—it's just that we were raised with different eyes." Those who say that the standard of an American common culture should be European are in fact the separatists. And few of them know the European culture which they champion, for anybody who has traveled to Europe will discover that there is no monolithic European culture. Although historians like Arthur Schlesinger, Jr., discourage the learning of African Amerindian cultures, it is quite possible that Americans can benefit from some of their examples. The English introduced racism in New England, but it was the Spanish who introduced racism into the Southwest with their strict color guidelines, which placed whites at the top and blacks at the bottom. Before their arrival, the Pueblo people, according to Leslie Silko in her book *Yellow Woman and a Beauty of the Spirit*, "looked at the world differently; a person's appearance and possession did not matter nearly as much as a person's behavior. For them, a person's value lies in how that person interacts with other people, and how that person behaves toward the animals and the earth." The Pueblo people believed that all creatures emanated from Mother Earth.

The singling out of black Americans and sometimes Latinos as the unassimilatables serves to limit the discussions of the divisions within the American society. Not only do divisions exist between ethnic and racial groups, but within. Fractures between foreign-born and American-born Asians have led to violence in San Francisco high schools. K. Connie Kang develops this theme in her essay about conflicts between American-born Asians and foreign-born Asians. There are similar conflicts between American-born Chicanos and Mexicans. The northeastern media and some African American and Jewish literary mercenaries may cast the conflict between blacks and Jews as the major ethnic conflict of the moment, addressed here by Martin Kilson. But this hyperbolized conflict seems like a lover's spat in comparison with the fight between African Americans and Latinos. As Roberto Rodríguez and Patricia Gonzales put it, "The violence over the past few years between the two groups in Los Angeles—particularly in Compton, the mid-city area, and Venice—has been particularly deadly. It has ranged from random drive-by shootings to full-scale gang wars. There have also been dozens of racial brawls at area middle and senior high schools, and hundreds of violent incidents in one jail facility alone, including upward of one hundred full-scale racial riots between the two groups."

The fact that the media sensationalizes a quarrel between blacks and Jews while ignoring a much more serious fight between blacks and browns indicates the value that the media place upon black and brown life.

Brenda Payton, Amiri Baraka, and Maulana Karenga all address this ethnic conflict. William Wong talks about a redistricting fight in Oakland during which Latinos and Asian Americans were pitted against African Americans and Latinos. Ana Castillo tells of divisions within the Latino community. "There is a universe of difference, for example, between the experience of the Cuban man who arrived in the United States as a child with his parents after fleeing Castro's revolution and the Puerto Rican woman who is a third-generation single mother on the Lower East Side. There is a universe of difference between the young Mexican American aspiring to be an actor in Hollywood in the nineties and the community organizer working for rent control for the last ten years in San Francisco." And she cites a study by the University of Chicago which she says shows that "deep divisions based on race exist between black Hispanics and white Hispanics in the United States."

Not only are there inter-ethnic, interracial, internecine conflicts, but gender, class and sexual conflicts as well. Though Hollywood, television, National Public Radio, and *The Village Voice* have ordained the black male as the universal symbol of sexism, a sort of effigy figure for women of different ethnic backgrounds and a source of billions of dollars of revenue reaped from his scapegoating, Hoyt Sze writes about sexism in the Asian-American community.

Elaine H. Kim describes the fears of Asian immigrants and explores the myth of the model minority—a myth that has led to Asian Americans being subjected to hate crimes, the typical perpetrators of which are young white males. This must come as a surprise to readers of the *New York Review of Books*, who were told by the two-nations theorist Andrew Hacker that American whites don't engage in violence—a remark that might be interpreted as Eurocentric myth making.

But despite these differences, there *are* some mutual experiences that Latinos, Asian Americans, Native Americans, and other colored minorities can identify. We have all been subjected to hostility and rudeness from anonymous whites, of the kind that Frank Chin and his son Sam encountered while traveling through certain western states. As another example of how the media hides white pathology while playing up that of other groups, it was only when blacks came into conflict with Korean Americans in Los Angeles, during riots in which no Korean or black killed one another, that the media discovered hate crimes against Asian Americans. Meanwhile, Helen Zia is one of many Asian American intellectuals who complain that year-round hate crimes against Asian Americans are ignored. Maybe it's because the typical perpetrator is a white male.

We can identify with the humiliation meted out to Leslie Silko and her companion Gus, as they were hassled by white law enforcement officials. Many Latinos and African Americans can endorse Ms. Silko's remark that "injustice is built into the Anglo-American legal system." Though the kind of white public intellectuals who get their information about multicultural people from other whites may dismiss these experiences as paranoid, whites who've actually done empirical research produced the same results.

Recently, Joshua Solomon, a student at the University of Maryland, used a chemical to change his skin color and was received with such hostility by whites that he curtailed the experiment. He was following an experiment by the late John Howard Griffin, author of *Black Like Me*, who was also struck by the hostility that he'd received from whites.

Though frictions do exist within the multicultural community, the thing that unites these various factions is an opposition to white supremacy and to the one-sided discussion of ethnicity and multiculturalism by the national media. These monoculturalists must feel right at home when they appear on network shows to engage in colorful sound-bite dismissals of multiculturalists as engaging in political correctness, or disuniting and balkanizing the country.

During the Unity 94 Convention in Atlanta which assembled Asian American, Native American, and African American journalists, a newspaper carried the headline: "Minorities See the Media As the Enemy." The media, according to their own professional organizations, have done little to diversify their staffs, so that the discussion of multiculturalism is conducted by the same faces from the same class and racial background. How can the kind of national discussion of race that Lani Guinier calls for, or the discussions about the common culture requested by Sheldon Hackney, be conducted when wealthy white men talking to each other, or to themselves, are what constitutes a "dialogue" about multiculturalism and race these days? When it's not them, it's their rainbow surrogates who carry the fight against bilingualism, a diversified canon, and so on. They use their power to denigrate blacks, idealize Asians, and marginalize Hispanics. If the conflict between monoculturalists and multiculturalists constitutes a cultural war, then how can there be peace talks without bringing both parties to the table? Every other book blasting political correctness mentions Dr. Houston Baker, Jr., but whereas the authors of these books receive generous and friendly media attention, Dr. Baker is barely known beyond academic circles.

This anthology provides a forum for members of these groups to talk back. Drs. Michael LeNoir and Nathan Hare write about the psychological impact upon Latinos, Asians, and blacks of media which seem resistant to any kind of change urged by black, Latino, and Asian American critics. Marco Portales discusses the portrayal of Asian Americans, Latinos, and blacks in the media, and Gerald Horne discusses the power that a few men from similar backgrounds have for setting the agendas for various ethnic communities. These contributors are joined by those whom I would consider to be New White intellectuals—those who, instead of glibly and ignorantly dismissing the arguments of multiculturalists, have studied Latino and African American history and culture. Few white mass media public intellectuals who earn a living denouncing Afrocentrism, multiculturalism, etc., have the range of the white and ex-white contributors to this anthology like Bob Lee, who knows his way around Latino, Asian American, and Native American literature; or Bob Fox, who spent years teaching and studying in Africa; or Werner Sollors, the former chairperson of Harvard's African American Studies Department or other new intellectuals who no longer need whiteness as a self-esteem crutch, a whiteness that former Europeans had to adopt in order to succeed in the American mainstream.

As Lawrence Di Stasi has pointed out, the Italians began to pass for white as a way of fitting into the common culture, which, as Toni Morrison has pointed out, was forged by hostility toward black people. As Morrison said in *Time* magazine in Fall 1993, ". . . Black people have always been used as a buffer in the country between powers to prevent class war, to prevent other kinds of real conflagrations. . . . In becoming an American, from Europe, what one has in common with that other immigrant is contempt for me—it's nothing else but color. Wherever they were from, they would stand together. They could all say, 'I am not that.' "

If white monoculturalists would make the same intellectual effort as the New White intellectuals whose essays appear in this book, then perhaps serious talk could get under way about a new, inclusive definition of the common culture. Rarely mentioned in the whitewashed patriotic version of the common culture promoted by the right and by liberal historians like Arthur Schlesinger, Jr., are the violent confrontations between white ethnics in the eastern United States. Pre–white ethnic Europeans fought it out in the streets of northern cities during the eighteenth and nineteenth centuries over ethnic and religious differences, and Grady McWhiney, in his *Cracker Culture*, writes that the Civil War was a continuation of a European ethnic feud. It is his thesis that the Civil War—one of the bloodiest conflicts in world history—involved a struggle between Welsh, Irish, and Scots on one side and Anglos on the other. After the Civil War these groups began a reconciliation, so that those who might have been considered war criminals, like Jefferson Davis and Robert E. Lee, have regained their citizenship and are honored. Harvard University is now debating whether to honor Harvard alumni who fought on the side of the Confederacy.

If reconciliation can come about after the Great White Inter-ethnic fight that occurred in the nineteenth century, certainly the mostly paper skirmishes between monoculturalists and multiculturalists can be reconciled. What impedes the peace talks that would lead to a more peaceful co-existence is the monopoly that performance intellectuals arguing for a monocultural standard have in the debate. Print is still one way to talk back. I had suspected this for many years, but it was really driven home to me after the publication of my critical work about the media, *Airing Dirty Laundry*. The publication and the controversy that ensued placed me face-to-face with some of those who have a virtual monopoly over the dissemination of information—anchor persons, talk show hosts, and print journalists. It was as though I had entered the television set in my living room and taken my place at a forum, voicing opinions that I had usually blurted at my set in the privacy of my living room.

The intention of this book is to give others the same opportunity. It is, in a sense, an intellectual anti-trust action against the tyranny that communications oligopolies hold over the public discussion. We would hope that these fresh voices will engender a genuine debate, and maybe even stimulate those minds that daily furnish us with what amounts to propaganda and that have grown indolent in having no one to oppose their opinions. The contributors to this anthology are not likely to make the lists of minority intelligentsia compiled by the *Atlantic Monthly*, *The New Yorker*, and *The New Republic*, publications whose record of minority inclusion is not good. One powerful mediaperson gave it all away when he said of a current designated black hitter of black culture and values: He says what we say in private.

The contributors to this anthology are not designated McIntellectuals. They are scholars, students, journalists, a physician, and a psychiatrist, all of whom are concerned about the future of the United States in which one "race" or ethnic group is no longer dominant and where the pressures to assimilate are not as demanding as they were in a former time. The multinationals who back monocultural stars might also know that 30 million Americans negotiate trade in languages other than English. (Maybe this is why *Fortune* magazine, in its January 1991 issue, declared multiculturalism one of the most exciting ideas of the 1990s.)

I think that a new definition of a common culture is possible, and that because of their multicultural status, Latinos, African Americans, and Asian Americans with knowledge of their own ethnic histories and cultures as well as those of European cultures are able to contribute to the formation of a new, inclusive definition.

What lies ahead? John A. Williams sees multiculturalism as the successor to the "melting pot" and "rainbow" theories of American society, all of which failed before what he calls "the unmovable force" of racism. Ortiz Walton is optimistic that common ground might be found among the competing interests. Bharati Mukherjee recommends that the disputants conduct a reasoned discussion and not resort to demagoguery, and Amritjit Singh encourages arriving immigrants to learn from the experience of African Americans. Maulana Karenga believes that the most pressing ethnic conflict, that between African Americans and Latinos, can be resolved.

What is the common culture? Gundars Strads, a Latvian American;

Rudy Anaya, a Chicano; and Juan Felipe Herrera of Mexico all returned to the countries of their ancestors' origins and found that they were different from the people they encountered there. Gundars is no longer a Latvian, Anaya no longer an Indian or Spaniard, and Juan Felipe Herrera isn't Mexican. That difference—whether it be a matter of style or aesthetics—is something that foreigners have noticed about Americans, be they black, white, yellow, or brown. Defining the difference may provide the key to our common culture. The thing that makes us all in this together may ultimately be defined by a foreigner, as Gunnar Myrdal and Alexis de Tocqueville have done previously.

Maybe someone like Ingo Hasselbach, a former neo-Nazi, can provide some clues. In his *Memoirs of a Former Neo-Nazi* (1996), he recounts how, after breaking with the Nazi Party, he traveled to Paris and began to experience the "multicultural" world that he had denounced. He decides that he likes it.

> Paris was the most amazing thing I'd ever seen. . . . We were surrounded by people of every race and color—many of them black Africans and Arabs. . . . People were friendly to me. . . . This was a cosmopolitan world, and they were used to seeing people from all over. The splendid diversity of the world was brought home to me in a way that it never had been before, when foreigners had been like cartoon characters. . . . Here they were real people—an entire world taking place in many languages and skin colors. It was as though I'd stepped out of a cartoon universe into real life and was seeing before me its staggering complexity.

When I asked another European, Michel Fabre, Professor of African American Literature at the Sorbonne, how he saw our culture, he replied simply, "We see the United States as a civilization."

—Ishmael Reed

1

THE UNBEARABLE
WHITENESS OF BEING

How Americans Became White: Three Examples

■ ■ ■

WERNER SOLLORS

> All persons not included in the definition of "negro" shall be
> deemed a white person within the meaning of this article.
> —*Willson's* Criminal Statutes of Texas, *1906, §347*[1]

1. Invention of "Whiteness" in Analogy to "Nobility"

In 1809, Friedrich Alexander von Humboldt observed an aristocratic
sense among whites as a constitutive feature of the American continent:
"In a country dominated by whites those families of whom it is assumed
that they are least intermingled with Negro or Mulatto blood are the ones
most highly honored; just as it is considered a kind of nobility in Spain to
be descended neither from Jews nor Moors." Humboldt adds that a barefoot white man who mounts a horse believes he belongs to the aristocracy
of the land, and that this color-consciousness even generates a sense of
equality among whites: thus a common man may address one high above
him with the question, "Do you believe that you are any whiter than
I am?"[2]

2. Immigration

One of the earliest and most detailed "America letters" by Swedish immigrants was written by two maids, the sisters Catharina and Charlotta Jonsdotter Rÿd from Moline, Rock Island County, Illinois, who sent it on March 15, 1856 (a few months before the *Dred Scott* decision), to an uncle and aunt in the area of Vetlanda. In the letter, America is praised as a country "where every *white* person is free" (in the original, "ty här är *hwit* menniska fri"—"hwit" underlined in the letter). Here is Ulf Beijbom's partial translation; the original document is at the House of Emigrants in Växjö, Sweden:

> We feel well and are working in American families here in Moline for $2 a week. In this country, the servant is not bound by a yearly contract. . . . Here the servant can come and go as it pleases her, because every white person is free and if a servant gets a hard employer then she can quit whenever she likes and even keep her salary for the period she has worked. A maid in America doesn't have to toil in the fields and not even feed the animals or milk the cows, which all is menfolk's chores. What a maid must do is to wash, make the beds, cook, lay the table and assist the mistress in the home. A woman's situation is as you can imagine much easier here than in Sweden and I Catherine feel much calmer, happier and more satisfied here than I used to do when I attended school in Nässjö. Everything in this country [seems praiseworthy]— to describe all benefits would take a lifetime![3]

3. Passing

A journalist of the 1940s told the story of Gladys (whose skin "is tan smooth, as if she had but recently returned from vacation") and her much lighter college beau Jerry, to whom Gladys expresses the following feeling: "I'm like a blouse dyed to match a skirt and coming out a few shades too dark, but enough to spoil the whole thing. Off color." After a cousin of Gladys's dies in a Pennsylvania hospital because she receives inferior medical care, they decide to get married and pass. "When it came to having a nice home and decent medical care and happy children who would receive, without *question* or *legal fights,* the benefits of our country, we took the step," Gladys argues; and at the Municipal Building in

New York City, Jerry "for the first time wrote their lie. In unhesitating strokes . . . he wrote the word that did it—'White.' " They lead a successful urban life; when pressed, they explain their backgrounds simply by saying that they are from the South and that their parents are dead; they are well-to-do church members and Rotarians; and their two children attend the best schools. Yet the account concludes on a different note:

> There is one hitch! Most of the local help is colored, and Gladys will not hire a Negro. "Maybe because I'm afraid of being found out."
>
> This complex becomes a boomerang when the members of her bridge club criticized Gladys on the grounds that she is intolerant! These members must have been more than puzzled, since Gladys vouchsafed no answer to their accusation but stubbornly continued refusing to employ a Negro maid.[4]

■ ■ ▦

NOTES

1. Albert E. Jenks, "The Legal Status of Negro-White Amalgamation in the United States," *American Journal of Sociology* 21 (March 1916), p. 678.
2. *Versuch über den politischen Zustand des Königreichs Neu-Spanien*, vol. 1 (Tübingen: Cotta, 1809), p. 193. The original reads: "In einem, von Weißen beherrschten, Lande sind die Familien, von welchen man annimmt, daß sie am wenigsten mit Negern- oder Mulatten-Blut vermischt seien, am geehrtesten; so wie es auch in Spanien für eine Art von Adel gilt, weder von Juden noch von Mauren abzustammen."
3. Ulf Beijbom, "The Swedish Maid," delivered at Växjö on June 2, 1991. A copy of the letter is in the Växjö Emigrant Insttute. See also Beijbom, "The Promised Land for Swedish Maids," in *Swedes in America: New Perspectives*, ed. Beijbom (Växjö: Swedish Emigrant Institute Series, 6, 1993), pp. 110–125.
4. Nanette Kuttner, "Women Who Pass," *Liberty* (March 1949), p. 44.

Becoming Post-White

■ ■ ■

ROBERT ELLIOT FOX

I got the whiteboy blues and I can't be satisfied.

Only when white people can become indifferent to the risks of their full (and, perhaps, possible) immersion in a broad range of meanings produced by race, will there be a transformation in white/black interactions.[1]

We began to see race as a verb and not a noun.[2]

Is post-whiteness a possibility, or is this another ploy in the seemingly endless play of theory, always seeking new scenarios of liberation, more always-already apparatuses to deconstruct?

Or, as Noel Ignatiev puts it, in a brief but provocative essay, "Can the white race be dissolved? Can 'white' people cease to be?"[3]

When Ishmael Reed invited me to contribute to this anthology, he suggested I address my Polish American heritage, asking, "Is it still alive for you?" It's a question that certainly would be worth addressing if I *were* Polish American; yet this is something I've never considered myself to be, despite having some Polish Catholic ancestry on my mother's side of the family. Maternally, I'm also descended from German Protestants. My father's side of the family is Jewish, with Austrian and Russian roots.

(Polish friends I made in Africa when we were expatriates together argue that the Russian part of my heritage is due to partition and actually is Polish. From the various conflicting tales I was told by my father, aunts, and others, I conclude that the generations born in America didn't feel compelled to record all the details of their family histories, which they remembered differently and imprecisely; so, who knows?)

I was born and raised in Buffalo, New York, home of one of the largest Polish American populations, but I had nothing to do with these or any other "ethnics," who, in my view, were an anachronism, incompletely assimilated communities left over from the heyday of European immigration. Today I know that while there are present-day ethnic enclaves, such as South Boston, that remain insular, even in the old days the ghettoishness of immigrant communities was scarcely impermeable. My Russian grandfather, an Orthodox Jew, used to converse in Hebrew with a Catholic priest in their Brooklyn neighborhood of Greenpoint, and the public school my father went to was attended by children of widely varying backgrounds. But *my* only ethnic experience was, intermittently, culinary (the potato pancakes and pirogis my grandmother made for us from time to time when she visited) and linguistic (the occasional admonitory Polish phrases, as unintelligible to us as Martian, that Grandma snapped at my siblings and me).

Basically, my roots aren't dead for me because they never were alive (at least, not overtly). I knew my ancestors had come from elsewhere, but my accessible past was *here,* in the USA, and whenever I added up the various parts of my background, they always equaled "American." I felt no nostalgia for any reality prior to the Atlantic crossing my predecessors had made, although there was curiosity, buoyed by perhaps a touch of Europhilia, concerning life in the "Old World." My study of German literature, for example (it was my undergraduate minor), had nothing to do with the fact that I was part German but a great deal to do with my artistic and intellectual impulses. I didn't feel the "pull" of a German identity; indeed, I was highly ambivalent about Germany because of my Jewish heritage and my knowledge of the Holocaust. Yet I'm not aware of any relatives who were victims of the Nazis. My Jewish ancestors were victims of nineteenth-century Russian pogroms, which finally drove many of them to emigrate to various parts of the Americas.

By virtue of my love for literature, I was also an anglophile—English literature, for a long time, being what I knew best. What I really was drawn to was words and the worlds within words. Through all of my far-flung literary and cultural engagements I have never lost a certain feeling of Americanness, which, for me, has been a source of freedom: the freedom of the crossroads, of intersecting possibilities. This sense of liberation (which some would term "rootlessness") remained, even when I entered into strong emotional, intellectual, and moral opposition to much of what America had become, to the degree that I felt like an internal exile. For those of us who came of age in the 1960s, America, an immense, inchoate thing, had in many respects grown monstrous; but our dream of America, our love of the often-betrayed American idea of freedom and justice for all, inspired us—licensed us, in fact—to try and right the mess. Still, there were times, so many times, when I could have echoed Derek Walcott's Shabine: "I had no nation now but the imagination."

The imagination has no color. But in imagining a nation, nationalists too often have based it on an imagined purity of "race" or ethnicity. America has not been exempt from this dogmatism of identity—in the view of certain groups, the United States equals *us*—but if there ever was a nation that gave the lie to this dream of homogeneity, it is America, a highly polymorphous polity. America interfaces with the rest of the planet and has done so since its inception. Its vital "output" has been fed by many different "inputs." Borrowing a tasty metaphor Ishmael Reed has used so effectively to describe our cultural "mixology," I'd argue that the only nationalism that makes sense in the American context is gumbo nationalism (many varied ingredients).

What does it mean to become "post-white"? Marxists talked (do they still?) of the need for intellectuals to commit class suicide in order to side with the masses and therefore ensure their "salvation" on the "correct" side of history. Racists view "amalgamation" as "race" suicide. Today, there is a certain vogue in academic circles for citing the need to undo "skin" and gender privilege—articulated for the most part by people who never would do without their own privileges as tenured elites.

Is a condition of post-whiteness one of post-privilege? It often has seemed to me that I've been privileged, in a way most people I knew were not, to be a chameleon of sorts, to dream myself into other selves; to cloak myself, sometimes, in the aura of difference and imagine that it was mine. I didn't feel I had any advantages *because of color,* although I knew that, precisely because of color and the burdens it was made to bear, other people did experience disadvantages.

Some will argue that my freedom from ethnicity was no freedom at all but rather a loss of identity. On the contrary, I see it as the inheritance of a space in which to claim an identity. It's true that my "ethnic" friends and neighbors knew who they were—or, more accurately, knew who they were supposed to be. But I, too, knew who I was—someone in the process of making himself, which is what America is supposed to be about. The fact that I had no vested interest in a particular given identity was one of the things that made my move toward post-whiteness possible. Indeed, I now understand that I *needed* to become post-white, because too many people insisted that my whiteness made it impossible or intolerable for me to do what my heart and mind told me to do, such as enter into an intimate engagement with other cultures, especially those of Africa and its diaspora.

It also is argued that the "whiteness" of whiteness is unacknowledged by most white people because of the degree to which whiteness has been established as the norm from which all else departs. In this sense, whiteness is colorlessness, and it is precisely this sphere of colorlessness which constitutes the realm of privilege. Those who are critical of the deconstruction of race claim that it's relatively easy for white people to engage in such deconstruction because they have never been especially conscious of having a racial being, a "privilege" they ought to acknowledge and refute. There's a double bind here typical of the claustrophobia and combativeness of today's identity politics: white people are unduly privileged to be "raceless," but they are perverse if they manifest "race" consciousness—unless it's a consciousness of the culpability of being white.

But it isn't only white people who are engaged in deconstructing race. And privileges aren't inherently obscene; they can provide opportunities for the exploration and mapping of what privilege in the bad old sense would never subject to scrutiny. Thus some of us privileged to spend time "thinking things through" have begun to understand the degree to which "the 'whiteness' of whiteness" is blindness—indeed, darkness—even as some of the more desperate and deluded in our society have seized upon "the 'whiteness' of whiteness" as a key to their presumptive salvation. Such extreme, fundamentalist whiteness—which one could characterize as "the white bizarre," though its milder manifestations are, alas, widespread and harder to combat—forms a solidarity among Know Nothing whites. As for the rest of us, "Many of us can remain white only by splitting our psyches and feeling great unhappiness."[4]

In an apparent irony, I was able to begin "escaping" from whiteness in Africa, even though, chromatically speaking, I was more visible there. After all, Nigeria, where I invested the better part of a decade, has the world's largest black population, in which I was a distinct minority. Yet Africans were willing to consider me a "brother" in a way that many black Americans could not or would not. History has to bear the burden here, not history's "victims." And the extent to which history has been inscribed on our skin (one can't help thinking of the punishment device in Kafka's penal colony), mixed in with our color, is terrible, exercising tyranny over our freedom to be.

Ultimately, when we "raise race"—bring it up as an issue—we must recognize that "raising race" can mean praising, promoting, reclaiming it; yet to "raise race" also can mean suspending it, lifting race off of us as an imposition, a form of siege mentality ("us," in the castles of our skin, against "them"). Psycho-politically speaking, to praise what has been powerfully and badly prejudged, defamed, may be a necessary step in the undoing of the exclusionary project of a false universalism (what "we" possess is meaning; all else is gibberish), since to dispense suddenly with race in a context of inequality results in an apparent circumstance of winners and losers.[5] Nevertheless, this step of dis-closure, or proclamation, requires a further step ("keep on steppin' "), for it's difficult to see how we can do away with race by insisting upon it. True humanism can't be based on colorism. But post-whiteness must come first, because people of color won't have to "raise race" in the assertive sense if we "erase race" as an impediment and a desire. The hegemonic must level itself; otherwise, it's foolish to expect the oppressed to give up their resistance, to forgo the need to "rise."

Color is no determiner of consciousness—but too often it has been a determiner of one's destiny. This is an affront to decency and the common good we must continually strive to undo. Color has no "merit"—although we have made it out to have—and groups such as the so-called White Aryan Resistance clearly wish to cling to this (false) construct, which for many of them is the mark of chosenness, but which I read as a reflection (only skin-deep) of a desire that dare not look below the surface to see the chaos there.

We know about the minstrels, white and black, who put on blackface, but—apart from the "black" people who "passed," and who, by so doing, emphasized the absurdity of the color line—what about those who, identity-wise, have put on whiteface? To what extent is whiteness a performance? To what extent is it a con/formance, a deceptive act and/or accommodation?

Whiteness *is* a constructed identity, not a racial characteristic. In its overdeterminations, its blank assertions, it's a pathology; indeed, all "race" thinking is a form of dementia, a dull, desperate dreaming into sameness. Recently I read of a poster proclaiming the Ku Klux Klan's desire to "keep the dream alive." Nightmare would be more accurate. Or whitemare.

On the opposite side of this "whitemare" from the hard-core caucasoids are people who seek absolution from "racial" guilt by embracing the "weird science" of melanin theory, or what I call Yacoubism, after the Nation of Islam fantasy about a black Dr. Frankenstein whose desire for difference led him to create a "white devil." I'm thinking of those agonized individuals involved with Caucasions United for Reparations and Emancipation (CURE), an organization whose white female founder was a follower of the late Elijah Muhammed (but who couldn't join the Nation of Islam precisely because she is white), and who agrees with the Black Muslim doctrine that white people are genetically recessive, exceeding in wickedness, but otherwise inferior (and presumably doomed to extinction).

Loony-Toon theorists to the contrary, there is no such thing as genetic guilt or skin sacrilege, though there are perverse prejudices. What is necessary, therefore, is an assault on "white" ideology, not on white people. The damage done by history certainly needs to be repaired (insofar as it can be repaired), but self-flagellation, self-hatred, is no "cure." And reversal is not redemption.

Frankly, I don't recognize myself in the gospel of whiteness set down by those for whom "whiteness" is tantamount to a religion, nor do I recognize myself in the Satanic portrayal of whiteness emanating from certain non-whites. I'm not into the "skin" thing, the "nation" thing, or the "domination" thing. If I belong to any tribe, it's that of the dissenters, the border-crossers, the rainbow breed. We're radioactive—raised on rock 'n' roll, a hybrid music with black roots, performed by contra/bands. (There's a strong case to be made for the claim that rock 'n' roll was the medium through which Africa spoke to white America—and thereafter, to the world—in the second half of the twentieth century.) We're interactive (miscegenative), cultural mulattos—and this is not a postmodern characteristic, it's a result of the cross-cultural development of America from the jump, its "mumbo-jumbling."

Post-whiteness isn't a theory, it's a shift in consciousness. Post-white means pan-human.

In the 1960s, the "normality" of whiteness began to be seriously challenged. As Noel Ignatiev notes, this was occasioned by the counterculture's "break with the conformity that preserves the white race."[6] Members of perhaps the most privileged (at any rate, affluent and pampered) generation in the history of the United States "turned on" to drugs and different vibrations, "tuned in" to messages from the outer limits of experience from which we had been insulated, and "dropped out" of the "race" for excess accumulation and status. We became (or imagined ourselves to be) the people our parents warned us against. (Some of us, alas, have come to resemble the people we warned ourselves about.) We aligned with the Third World, here and abroad—and, indeed, one factor in the radicalization of many an innocent young person was the discovery that there was a Third World within the United States, a nation that prided itself on being the richest and most developed on the planet. We saw the system of our education as socialization for servitude (*The Student as Nigger*), even if it was a "masterly" servitude—though the appropriation of the term "nigger" by children of the middle and upper middle classes was as much a presumption and a hyperbole as it was an index of genuine shock and disillusionment. We had tribal longings (identifying now with the Indians instead of the cowboys), inner-space leanings (drugs, spiritual "technologies"), interracial relationships (1967 was the year the Supreme Court finally overturned all laws against interracial marriage). We were "freaks," post-atomic agers mutating in the neon of overabundance and the shadow of apocalypse.

This is the time (again) of the nomads, of cultural "itinerancy," to use Paul Gilroy's term. It isn't necessary to have a fixed "center."[7] The boundaries of our being are fluid, marked by what Wilson Harris calls "numinous inexactitude."[8] The truth of identity is that it's complex and contingent, not simple and set. I am "American," but this is a multiply-centered, multifaceted "ground."

A currently popular bumper sticker reads: "The World's Most Endangered Species: The White Race."

The truth is, the white race is the world's most fictional species. And it hasn't been a benign fiction for those outside the privileged "text" (and maybe not for those inside, either). The beginning of post-whiteness comes with a recognition of the fact of this fictionality.

Since whiteness is not an "essence" but a construct, it isn't given but has to be acquired; therefore, one can refuse to (seek to) acquire it. If whiteness must reproduce itself each generation, as Noel Ignatiev argues,[9] then one can refuse to reproduce it. I can't become black, but I can become post-white.

Ruth Frankenburg writes that "it may be more difficult for white people to say, 'Whiteness has nothing to do with me—I'm not white,' than to say, 'Race has nothing to do with me—I'm not racist.' "[10] This difficulty may not be the result only of an unwillingness or an inability of white people to disclaim whiteness—although "diswhitening" surely hasn't become a mass phenomenon; the difficulty also exists because identity politics as currently construed won't *allow* one to disavow color.

In my own case, it primarily has been white people—those, for example, who refused to hire me to teach black literature because I'm not black—who reinscribed my whiteness and used it as a cause for exclusion, even as my whiteness became porous as a result of living engagedly in Africa for seven years and of living emotionally and intellectually in the worlds of black writing and black art for a much longer period. (Ironically, or perhaps predictably, many whites for whom the self-remaking of people like myself has proved troublesome or inconvenient are also products of the sixties, who still see themselves as the anointed "patrons" of the underdog, necessarily holier than thou.) It is instructive that black people have been among the staunchest supporters of my participation in the field of Black Studies. This is in part because they understand the marginalization that can result when so-called minority studies are relegated to insular academic ghettoes, in part because they resent being automatically typecast as minority studies specialists (whether they have trained for this role or not) by the "logic" of identity politics.

On the other hand, the white people who set the agendas in academia frequently view transculturalists as a threat to their statistical designs and categorical arrangements, wherein select individuals are valued chiefly for their supposed ability to "represent" their respective groups. White people who control the game and therefore are immune from its consequences will, when it serves their agenda, play the race card against other white people who lack the same immunity. This demonstrates that while whiteness has been a costume of privilege, it never has been a uniform one. Some of us always have been can(n)on fodder.

Thus, after an era of genuflections and mea culpas before the altars of unending critique, the attacks from divers directions on "the white male," another overdetermined species, have at last provoked my resistance. I balk at being herded into the internment camp of theory as a historical villain. But this doesn't mean clinging to "whiteness"; it simply means refusing to be a fixed category. If I'm lashing back, it isn't against the actual victims of our general inhumanity and systemic malignancy; it's against victimology, tribal politics, circumscribed agendas of the self that masquerade as revolution.

Already I anticipate some oppression specialist arguing that the advocacy of post-whiteness is just a ploy to evade "judgment" or to undo the disadvantages that being white now can sometimes bring. "You wanted to be white when it was cool. Now that it's uncool, you want to sneak out of your skin." There always seems to be a need, in the academic arena, to score points against your opponent by submitting his every move to an ideological litmus test, or by targeting her for what Ishmael

Reed would call an intellectual drive-by shooting. The inevitable falli-
bility of one's efforts to move in the direction of greater humanity wins
little or no sympathy when measured against the theoretical cutting edge
of idealism.

Today, everyone is allowed to talk about race except white people;
that is, white talk of race automatically is construed as racist, while non-
white talk of race is accepted and even appropriate (for reasons of self-
esteem, nationalism, or postcolonial power shifting). White people
certainly have monopolized the topic of race, and "it's our turn now"
would seem a fair assertion on the part of those who have been the
"objects" of race rhetoric and its essentializing message. I'd be one of the
first to say that white people should have shut up long ago when it comes
to race talk—then maybe we could all dispense with it. But race talk on
the "other" side has not only made the deconstruction of race suspect, as
I've already noted; worse, it has reinvigorated a racist reaction on the part
of the most race-conscious whites—people whose sense of self-worth is
so shaky that they see the growing assurance of "the other(s)" as a threat.

One of the most depressing aspects of race, in fact, is the degree to
which it becomes a final refuge against worthlessness for many marginal
groups—including whites. The call for "white power," ugly as it is,
nonetheless is understandable when one realizes the falseness of the assertion that white (without differentiation) automatically equals power.
(This is not only a reification of whiteness from both the street and the
bureau of political correctness, it's an illusion that white elites frequently
have employed to distract and diffuse the revolutionary potential of poor
whites.) The current in-your-face promotion of what we could call the
White Trash Nation is precisely a bid for a share of attention, if not of
power, driven not only by others' assertions of group rights but also by
the sense of powerlessness felt by the white underclass. This shouldn't be
interpreted as blaming non-whites for a racial backlash. All I'm suggesting
is that an overheated climate makes it very hard for anyone to be cool.

Ishmael Reed correctly notes that "so-called white studies dominate all
our experience."[11] (Even the most blatant cultural conservatives find it
injudicious to talk of "white studies"; they prefer to call it "civilization.")
The outer limits of this Eurocentric self-absorption are satirized in Don
DeLillo's novel *White Noise* (1985), the narrator of which is chairman of
the Department of Hitler Studies at a liberal arts college whose chancellor
was "quick to see the possibilities." "White noise" is Western culture's
sustained broadcast of hegemonic desire and narcissistic identity on the
"Universal" network. (For many listeners, "white noise" is not exactly

the music of the spheres.) But the racial madness of Hitlerism in all its kinky manifestations is "white noise" of the most atrocious kind—a noise that unfortunately has not been totally tuned out, that is in fact being rebroadcast today by neo-Fascists here and abroad. Clearly, the ghost of Hitler hasn't been exorcised; it keeps possessing "white"-wing weirdos. The memory of Hitler cannot be erased because it's history, and we still need to learn from history—desperately, it seems.

Whiteness itself has a history, and therefore requires understanding, which requires study. "Whiteness" may become the next growth industry in academia; it's certainly a hot topic currently.[12] Will this lead to the harmonizing of "white noise" or a reduction in its volume?

The inquiry into the history and character of whiteness is not just the brainchild of oppositional coalitions of color. Rather, it's an inside job, a requisite next step in the alternative tradition of the West, which is one of self-doubt, self-scrutiny—a practice of critique that provides a necessary counterpoint to the West's front of self-assurance, its sense of destiny and supremacy.

Is the deconstruction of whiteness a precondition for the eventual elimination of all identity politics, or will the deconstruction of whiteness simply leave more room for the (re)inscription of color?

Post-whiteness, among other things, describes a situation wherein color is in the majority; thus post-whiteness is our demographic destiny in the United States. (The world itself never has been white.) Whiteness no longer will "submerge" color, at which point color, too, will need to rethink itself.

I am married to a Yoruba woman from Nigeria—something viewed as a racial transgression by certain people on both sides of the needless color chasm. So be it.

As I write this, we are expecting our first child, who clearly will be of shared heritage: African *and* American. A child of color(s).

The rise in the number of people of "mixed race"—another demographic shift of significance—not only contributes to post-whiteness, it also aids in the erosion of fixed categories of "color." *Mestizaje*—Creolization—is the future; it's also an insufficiently acknowledged part of our past (especially culturally). Post-whiteness may enable us finally to see the extent to which America never was "white."[13]

■ ■ ■

NOTES

1. Timothy Maliqalim Simone, *About Face: Race in Postmodern America* (Brooklyn, NY: Autonomedia, 1989), p. 13.

2. Phyllis Palmer, et al., "To Deconstruct Race, Deconstruct Whiteness," *American Quarterly* 45.2 (June 1993), p. 286.

3. Noel Ignatiev, " 'Whiteness' and the American Character," *Konch* 1.1 (Winter 1990), p. 38.

4. Palmer, et al., "To Deconstruct Race," p. 289.

5. It's argued that legacies of deprivation make equality a hollow promise without efforts at remediation, but the institutionalization of such remedies and their attainment of entitlement status guarantee that they will never "complete" their task. People have said, "We have to start somewhere," and there is truth in this; but has anyone given thought to the other side of the equation, namely that "we have to stop somewhere"? That "somewhere" ought to be at the point of "balance," whenever and however that might be achieved. But when you are dealing with machines that go of themselves—which, for good or ill, is what governmental apparatuses are—what prevents them from driving on through to imbalance once more?

   It should be understood that I'm not condemning the search for solutions to undeniable problems. I merely point out here that our solutions often generate new problems—a dilemma for which I don't have an answer.

6. Ignatiev, " 'Whiteness' and the American Character," p. 39.

7. See Karen J. Winkler, "Flouting Convention," *Chronicle of Higher Education* (September 28, 1994), pp. A8, A15. Gilroy's work—particularly *There Ain't No Black in the Union Jack* (1991) and *The Black Atlantic: Modernity and Double Consciousness* (1993)—makes very important contributions to the reconstruction of blackness *and* whiteness, which is precisely why it is both celebrated and controversial.

8. Wilson Harris, "Imagination, Dead, Imagine: Bridging a Chasm," *Yale Journal of Criticism* 7.1 (1994), p. 187.

9. Ignatiev, " 'Whiteness,' and the American Character," p. 36.

10. Ruth Frankenburg, *White Women, Race Matters: The Social Construction of Whiteness* (Minneapolis: University of Minnesota Press, 1993), p. 6.

11. See Keith Antar Mason, "Ishmael Reed Talks About Multiculturalism, the Media, and Fighting Back," *High Performance* (Fall 1989), p. 35.

12. In addition to Ignatiev, Frankenburg, and Palmer, et al., cited above, a selective list on the topic would include Virginia R. Dominguez, *White by Definition: Social Classification in Creole Louisiana* (New Brunswick, NJ: Rutgers University Press, 1986); David Roediger, *The Wages of Whiteness: Race and the Making of the American Working Class* (New York: Verso, 1991); Vron Ware, *Beyond the Pale: White Women, Racism and History* (New York: Verso, 1992); Toni Morrison, *Playing in the Dark: Whiteness and the Literary Imagination* (Cambridge: Harvard University Press, 1992); Cheryl I. Harris, "Whiteness as Property," *Harvard Law Review* 106.8 (June 1993); Theodore W. Allen, *The Invention of the White Race* (New York: Verso, 1994); Harryette Mullen, "Optic White: Blackness and the Production of Whiteness," *Diacritics* 24.2/3 (Summer 1994); Lisa Bloom, "Con-

structing Whiteness: *Popular Science* and *National Geographic* in the Age of Multi-culturalism," *Configurations* 2.1 (Winter 1994); *RACE TRAITOR: A Journal of the New Abolitionism*, and "The White Issue" of the journal *Lusitania* 7 (Winter 1994). Some of these titles are reviewed by Judith Levine in "The Heart of Whiteness: Dismantling the Master's House," *Village Voice Literary Supplement* (September 1994), pp. 11–16.

13. The foregoing meditations of a self in process constitute first thoughts on a topic I expect to be addressing at greater length elsewhere.

2

■ ■ ■

STRANGER IN A
STRANGE LAND

Multicultural Europe: Odds, Bets, Chances

■ ■ ■

A. ROBERT LEE

In summer 1991, the Sunday edition of the London daily, *The Independent*, carried a feature about why so few images of pastoral Britain showed any Afro-British or Asian-British people. The point, in quick contour, was to emphasize how, despite a growing multicultural population, essential Britishness, island-garden Britishness, was still one of fortress Anglo-Saxonism (Celts, Jews, immigrant Poles, Cypriots, or Italians and others notwithstanding). Shakespeare's *As You Like It* to Wordsworth's Lake poems to *All Creatures Great and Small*—is not this the true lineage of "England," one with its usual aggregation of Scotland, Ireland, and Wales, and despite whatever citizenry of color, ever custodially "white."

This, then, was "England." But what the piece did not tackle was: how true is this of Western Europe? Do not each of the main players—whether Germany, France, the Benelux, Scandinavia, Italy, Spain, or Portugal—equally harbor a residual (and at source "rural") self-image as a "white" civilization, one which, despite all the historicities of colonialism, also remains somehow still inviolate, still "our" Europe? To be sure, there are the cities, "African" or "Arab" Marseilles, "Bajan" or "Chinese" London, "Moroccan" Barcelona, "Turkish" Bremen, "Mulaccan" or

"Indonesian" Amsterdam, or "Ethiopian" Rome. But, runs the standard line, the cities have always, one way or another, been imaged as pits, dens, staging posts.

So the question arises, what real credibility attaches to all the talk within the Common Market, now the European Union, of Europe as a multiculture to embrace peoples of black, Asian, and Arab ancestry in equal part with its residual "white" cultures and citizenries? And, to add a further (and pejorative) twist, for many Europeans has not a term like "multicultural" on the evidence of pre-apartheid South Africa or the Balkans meant only fracture, hatred, one human encampment set against another?

Europe may, self-evidently, be no America, no voluntary or involuntary "immigrant" mosaic. But, even so, some hard questions need to be pressed. How committed is Brussels, Strasbourg, or Luxembourg (the sites of the three EU parliaments) to a true, and thereby non-Balkan, multicultural Europe? Is there not always an unstated preference to enlarge the Common Market (presently Austria, Norway, Finland, etc., are among the applicants, and ahead has to be "slavic," and so white, ex-Eastern Europe) at the expense of safe residency, jobs, quotas, training, and often enough actual citizenship for "European" people of color? Never mind, then, just the "pastoral" image—why no black or Asian European commissioners, no black or Asian heads of the European banks and universities, no black or Asian cabinet members, no black or Asian justices in the European Court at The Hague?

Why, in sum, no inclusion within all the "European" fanfare (not least at the recent D-Day celebrations where barely a soldier or sailor of color seemed in evidence) of the historic "European" interface with Arab and sub-Saharan Africa, with the Caribbean or Antilles, and with the countries which make up the once colonially designated Indochina?

The issue grows in complication at each bead one takes. In one sense, for instance, the neo-Fascist menace, by being explicit, is relatively easy to spot and contest. In the case of German's "Republicans," Italy's reborn Mussolini-ites, Britain's BNP, France's Le Pen–led "Front National," the Flemish Aryan groups, or Spain's "Frente Nacional," the terms of reference take on a familiar look: old-time, strong-arm supremacism in the name of the patria, the "corporate" or nationalist state. Ultimately, however, the more insidious danger may well lie in the implicit consensus building up that Europe is, and should remain, essentially a self-approving "liberal" white order.

Germany, while hosting the largest immigrant population in Europe, even so still refuses full citizenship to its Turkish *gastarbeiters* and rushes to incorporate former East Germans. Italy, one would hardly ever know from TV and the newscasts, has almost a million black residents—many homeless and increasingly pushed into the poorer south of Calabria and Sicily. France habitually refuses entry, even for the proverbial day trip, to Britons of Caribbean stock, a tie-in, no doubt, with its treatment of, among others, Algerians, Moroccans, or francophone Africans, in northern Paris or portside Marseilles. Spain's daily toll of dead Moroccans on the Mediterranean beaches as they seek economic hope from onetime colonizers barely merits a footnote. Among Lisbon's white exile population there still festers anti-independence feeling against Angola and Mozambique.

The British, for their part, have long shown themselves inconsistent and selective in matters of "race," from preferential treatment given to white then-Rhodesians to the initial refusal to admit Kenyan Asians at the time of Idi Amin, and (not unlike the U.S. Immigration Service) from white-favoring immigrant "quotas" to the divisive policy by which certain "professional" Hong Kong Chinese, but not other population, will have access to a British passport in the light of 1997.

Where, it might well be asked, is the Common Market in all of this? Has it not proved better, or at least more conveniently "European," to dwell (however ineffectively) upon ex-Yugoslavia, or the return from Sovietism of "European" Russia, or the prospect of welcoming the Baltic states back into the European fold? Who needs more of black or Asian Europe if, as for America, the West has essentially ditched Africa (hunger south of the Sahara, human rights in Zaire) and with it much of Indo-Pakistan (poverty in Bangladesh, dictatorship in Burma) in favor of block trade with the States, Japan, and the Pacific Rim? Who, from Sweden to Belgium, from The Netherlands to Portugal, really, as it were, needs reminders of the underside of colonialism?

"Empire," even so, shows two recent faces. On the one hand there is indeed the nostalgia, among Gaullists and former Pieds Noirs in France, ex-India or ex-Africa "hands" in Britain, one-time Mozambique or Angola farmers in Lisbon, returnee expatriates from the Congo in Belgium, or Italians once the power brokers in Ethiopia or Somalia. On the other, there is a new stew of racial purity, of Aryanism, brought on not only by "immigrant," or to invoke German, "guest" minority presences within the "host" culture (the usual terms say plenty), but as the generations evolve, by an increasing inter- and biracial population, whether Arab-French, Caribbean-British, Turkish-German, or even African-American-Swedish.

One speaks, for sure, in broad political-demographic terms. Ironically, however, in cultural and especially literary terms, matters take on a more encouraging look. First, a modern Europe without black and Asian music, foodways, dance, carnival, speech, TV presenters and (increasingly) programs, sports figures (a soccer star like John Barnes in the UK, a tennis player like Noah Yannick in France), places of worship, an ever-rising student population, and, much to present purposes, a postcolonial literature would be unthinkable.

And to come back to the country of my own origins, the United Kingdom: consider the following. The usual phrase for multiculturally written Britain is "The Empire Writes Back." But, mantralike as it has become, it does anything but best service, tending to confirm that, somehow, "real" Englishness or "real" Britishness remains inviolate. Writers like V. S. Naipaul, Salman Rushdie, Sam Sevlin, Ravinder Randhawa, or Buchi Emecheta can thus conveniently be termed "immigrant," or the more modish "migrant," with the evasive, all-purpose "commonwealth" ever ready in the wings.

But what of a still younger literary generation? In this, names like the Pakistani-English Hanif Kureishi, the Chinese-English Timothy Mo, the Afro-Guyanese Mike Phillips, the Japanese-English Kazuo Ishiguro, the Caribbean-English Caryl Phillips, or the Indo-Guyanese-English David Dabbydeen (whose art-historical study *Hogarth's Blacks* makes model reading) come to the fore. Each, I suggest, both speaks out of, and to, the absolute center of England/Britain, not "immigrant" or "guest" voices, but endemic, full-fledged voices in the realm. In a 1986 interview, Kureishi properly observed: "People think I'm caught between two cultures, but I'm not. I'm British; I can make it in England. It's my father who's caught." The UK offers but one instance or case study.

The same process holds across France and Germany, Italy and the Benelux, Europe south and north and everywhere. Here, literally, is a multicultural writ, with behind it a lived multicultural reality and a changing regime of languages-within-languages. As usual, thereby, the writers set the going rate. It remains for "political" Europe, whether through its Common Market and bureaucratic institutions, its workplaces and seats of learning, to recognize, and act on (not to say welcome), the same reality. For, to adapt James Baldwin, Europe, too, is indeed "white no longer."

A Yoruba American in Germany

■ ■ ■

NGOZI O. OLA

The room smells of lye and nicotine. Beside me a woman in a green dress is getting her hair curled. Across the room a man in a brown sweater and blue jeans is getting a haircut. I'm sitting with my head bent back getting my hair washed. If I cock my head a bit to the left and let my eyes roll back and focus high up on one corner of the room, I see a small TV set. For a few seconds I catch a glimpse of Salt 'N' Pepa singing and posing and reminding me of who I am. Someone turns down the sound when R.E.M. appears on the screen and pops a cassette into the stereo. Two beats later Ice Cube is singing "Perfect Day." My hairdresser starts to sing along. He's not alone, for just about everyone in the room seems to know the words.

A plastic cap is put on my head. I'm ushered over to a hair dryer which looks like a relic from Dr. Frankenstein's laboratory. My hairdresser flips a switch. Within seconds my head's baking. From this seat I have a perfect view of the TV screen, which now shows Neneh Cherry and Youssou N'Dour singing "Seven Seconds." I can't hear the words but I recognize the video. I motion to one of the hairdressers to give me a magazine. She hands me two. I glance through the magazines, whose names both begin with "E," and choose the one with Vanessa Williams on its cover. Before I start searching its pages for a hairstyle, I look around the room.

I think to myself: "This could be New York." Just another typical Saturday afternoon at the hairdresser's. But if Martians invaded the salon on this Saturday afternoon, they'd have cause to think they'd found the Tower of Babel. They'd hear French, Portuguese, Spanish, and English. They'd see black faces and not the white ones which appeared on their TV screens when they watched the Earth soap operas picked up by their satellites. They would also hear snatches of Yoruba and Igbo. But if the Martians don't have any of the above programmed into their Universal Language Translator, then they'd better at least have German on file because this multi-Black clientele, though multilingual and multicultural, uses German for universal communication.

My eyes stop at the shop window, which is cluttered with a display of hair products, wigs, and posters. The tiny chunk of street beyond the cluttered glass is dark gray. The building across the street is a lighter gray. Every few seconds a car whizzes by, interrupting the gray on gray with a flash of color. Yes, this could be New York. But it's not. My eyes have stopped at the shop window not because of the gray on gray, for that has become standard scenery like the scaffolding outside my apartment window; my eyes have stopped at the shop window because of a white face pressed up against the glass. A staring white face, which reminds me that I am not in New York.

I am in Berlin, where after five years it still appalls me to receive rude, penetrating stares from strangers. In New York, where I was not born but raised, a stare is simply asking for trouble. Only an insane person, a lecher, or a tourist would risk casting a longer than appropriate look at a stranger. The offending party could expect to receive a cold look, a crisp remark, or a well-aimed bullet. In New York, when a staring person receives a stare in return, he or she will most often look away. In Berlin, this basic rule of behavior in public places seems not to exist for a good many Germans. I've learned that a well-aimed remark *auf Deutsch* can shame even the most insistent of eyes. But since a typical day in Berlin for me means being constantly subject to intrusive stares, and responding to every one of them—be they of curiosity, fascination, repulsion, or hostility—would keep my mouth running longer than that of a World Series commentator, I most often opt to save my breath and look through or over the heads of the crowd.

Thirty-one years ago, John F. Kennedy, standing upon a platform positioned over the heads of an attentive crowd, uttered a sentence which since then has been quoted to death in admiration and in ridicule: "Ich bin ein Berliner." The word *Berliner* has two definitions. It can either refer to the hole-less donuts which are a popular Berlin pastry, or it can refer to those persons born and raised in Berlin. Given the unlikelihood of JFK claiming brotherhood with donuts, his statement is generally interpreted as an affirmation of Berlin being a city of the world, a metropolis which welcomes all foreigners with open arms. Sort of a German version of New York City, but without the Statue of Liberty, skyscrapers, yellow cabs . . .

Well, not really. Berlin isn't like New York City. New York City, where after taking enough verbal punches and learning how to deliver a few jabs oneself one can say, "I am a New Yorker," and—regardless of accent—know that every other New Yorker acknowledges and accepts him as one of their own with a polite "Who gives a shit?" The joy of New York is that no one gives a shit. In general, people do mind their own business, and as long as you don't jump into anyone's face, people will leave you alone. No one will scream at you for walking against the light. Correction. No fellow pedestrian will scream at you; a taxi driver, perhaps.

In contrast to the daily concerns of the average New Yorker, there is a sense of civic responsibility among Germans in Berlin which sometimes seems boundless. Fellow pedestrians might just censure you for crossing even the narrowest of streets without a car in sight, while they dutifully wait for a green walk signal. This sense of civic responsibility also inhibits most Germans from littering the streets, although upon seeing a candy wrapper on the ground some will pause to shake their heads, mutter *tja, tja,* and then continue on their way. However, this sense of civic responsibility does not include intervening when skinheads try to throw a Ghanaian from a train. *Gott sei dank* that there are limits to civic responsibility, even in a cosmopolitan city like Berlin.

Evidently Berlin's open arms are only reserved for U.S. presidents, for my experience, as well as that of most foreigners in this city, has shown the incorrectness and idealism of Kennedy's statement. The reality is that one can never *become* a Berliner, one is or one isn't. (Not that I'd want to become a Berliner; for Berliners, similar to New Yorkers, are regarded by their fellow countrymen as a rude and aggressive lot who are civil, if not friendly, only when treated with the same rudeness and aggression they so readily dish out.) Berliners don't accept other Germans—let alone foreigners—as one of them, even if the person can boast twenty years of residence behind the Wall, for a true Berliner is born in Berlin and—for those of non-German descent who fulfill the first criterion—can claim German forefathers. However, even in Berlin authentic Berliners are a rare species in a city where an overwhelming number of residents are transplanted Germans from what Berliners derisively refer to as *Wessiland*, as well as from former East Germany.

I first visited West Berlin in 1987 when the city was an island surrounded by watchtowers, barbed wire, and the Wall. After having spent several days yawning in Munich, I felt myself experience the figurative adrenaline shot upon my arrival in Berlin. What impressed me back then was what at first glance reminded me of New York. Unlike Munich, where everything and everyone was clean, proper, and painted either in pastels or whites, Berlin was dingy and dirty, its landscape of gray on gray made colorful by an abundance of graffiti and multicultural humanity. My favorite pastime became riding the subway lines. On a Saturday night I'd jump on the *Linie 1* at Nollendorfplatz and head for Kreuzberg, the predominantly Turkish section of the city. During the twenty minutes I needed to get to Kottbusser Tor, I'd just have to look around me and see a man reading a Turkish newspaper, a group of French teenagers, an Ethiopian couple and their two children, and three men speaking in Tamil. From Kottbusser Tor I'd walk to Oranienstrasse, where purple mohawks, blond dreadlocks, and veiled heads were nothing unusual. I decided then that if I ever lived in Germany, I'd make Berlin my home.

In October 1989 I did just that. One month later the Wall came down. I witnessed the tears and embraces and the popping of champagne bottles. It didn't take long for the shouts of joy to turn into chants of *Deutschland den Deutschen* (Germany for the Germans). Two years after the German reunification I spent a year riding the S-Bahn, the elevated train line, from Bahnhof Zoo to my office in the East. It had already taken me two years to realize that I'd been experiencing culture shock in West Berlin with my daily confrontations with petty bureaucrats, surly cashiers, and rude waitresses. But that whole period was nothing in comparison with the mornings and evenings I spent shuttling between East and West. East Berlin was gray and beige without a trace of color. I felt as if I were traveling every day to a foreign country where the custom was to be as hostile as possible to visiting strangers. I tried to escape the frosty stares of other passengers by choosing a seat where all that would meet my eyes was a wall.

One morning I went to my prized corner of the train car and found a young Vietnamese woman sitting in what would have been my spot. Over the next few days I began to notice that the few recognizably foreign foreigners who were traveling in East Berlin also chose seats facing walls. So I was far from alone in my discomfort. On another morning I took my usual seat and automatically opened a book which would absorb my attention for the next forty-five minutes. But a stop later my routine was interrupted when a group of schoolchildren boarded the train and stood in a huddle before me. They were as loud and unruly as six-year-olds on an outing can be. It took a while for their teacher to bully them into silence. Suddenly a boy's voice started chiming out *"Ausländer Raus"* with a very familiar melody. My look of surprise alternated between the boy who averted his eyes, his other schoolmates who simply stared at me, and the teacher who smiled awkwardly. The teacher told the boy to be quiet, but to no avail, for he continued chanting away. As the group filed out at the next stop, I noticed for the first time the graffiti on the wall across from me. Scribbled several times in black ink were the words *Ausländer Raus.*

Ausländer Raus. Just a couple of words. But the combination of words meaning "Foreigners, get out!" has turned into the ugly battle cry of conservatives and right extremists. One would think that the word *Ausländer* (foreigner) when uttered alone would have a neutral meaning. But like so many other words used to refer to foreigners in the German language, *Ausländer* has developed a negative connotation. Words such as *Asylant* (a person seeking asylum) and *Neger* (Negro) have been uttered so often with a tone of disdain and contempt that they are now commonly used as ethnic slurs.

Berlin is a city of *Ausländer.* No other German city possesses such a mixture of cultures. Yet despite the great many Europeans, stemming from nations such as Italy, Great Britain, and the former Yugoslavia, who reside in this city, the attacks against foreigners have been launched against Africans, Turks, Vietnamese, and *Romas*—identifiably foreign foreigners who don't quite fit into the European Community family's photo album. What's foreign is easy to identify. It's as simple as black and white when one reads the recent headlines which tell of skinheads attacking and throwing Blacks off trains. I can only shudder when I recall my year of daily travel on the S-Bahn. I was lucky. However, one doesn't have to be Black to think twice about using this means of public transportation or about avoiding certain parts of the city. I know a young Italian man who won't travel to the East because with his dark, curly hair he feels himself to be an easy target. The same self-imposed travel restriction goes for a Persian friend whose dark locks and brown skin also put him at risk for attacks.

But anti-foreign sentiment is neither restricted to the eastern part of the city nor to young men with shaven heads, combat boots, and a button which reads: "Ich bin stolz, ein Deutscher zu sein" (I'm proud to be a German). One can live in the middle of West Berlin, have a full head of hair, wear a gray suit, and still tighten one's lips at the sight of a black face or a brown hand. Then again, one could also live in the middle of Boston and react the same way. One can complain that there are too many foreigners living in Germany when one Black person moves into one's building. I live in a West Berlin neighborhood which isn't particularly hospitable to non-white faces which are not sweeping up or carrying trays. But, at least my German neighbors didn't pick up their bags and take flight to another part of town when I moved in.

I've met Germans who look like people I knew back in NYC or at my alma mater Harvard, but unlike their white American counterparts they were willing to get to know me. I've developed friendships with people, German and non-German, who are genuinely interested in who I am and what I think. And these friendships have destroyed many of my own prejudices against white people.

Being Black in Berlin, more specifically, being a Black woman in Berlin means having people assume you're either a singer, a dancer, a prostitute, or even someone's mail-order bride. Other than having a love of dance, I am none of the above. Being Black in Berlin means that people assume you can't speak the language. People see Black and think English. Sometimes they think French and, in rare instances, they think Spanish. Despite years of high school French and a brief stay in Madrid, I'm far from proficient in either Spanish or French. I do speak German. And I'd even dare to say that I'm fluent. Being Black in Berlin can mean saying "guten Tag" to a fellow Black person upon crossing paths on the sidewalk. Sometimes it can also mean looking through each other. Being a Black woman in Berlin means receiving dirty looks from elderly German women. Being Black in Berlin means being observed while observing. Sometimes it means laughing at oneself and other times at the other, like when German children try to rub off the color from your skin. And then there are times when neither laughter nor a shrug will do.

Nonetheless, I like Berlin. I like Berlin because I can walk into a store without being followed by a salesperson who pre-labels me a criminal. I like Berlin because I can stand on any sidewalk and hail a cab and not suffer the insult of a progression of empty yellow cabs whizzing by me. I can walk down a street without having white hands constantly pull their purses away when I approach, without having some white female voice scream if I choose to run for a bus. I can see an interracial couple, a homosexual couple, an interracial homosexual couple and smile because they can walk the streets, hold hands, and exchange a kiss without receiving derisive remarks or cringes from the rest of the world. Yes, I like Berlin. And even with its minuses I'm grateful that it's not New York.

Minorities in England:
A Report

■ ■ ■

CALVIN HERNTON

1

The term "minorities" is not used the same way everywhere in the world.

In the United States, "minorities" is used to designate smaller groups of people who are singled out in society, and claim to be treated unfairly, on account of their ethnicity, race, sex, national origin, physical disability, or other identifying differences. In England, however, the term "minorities" is not used as much as it is in the States.

But certain references to "minority groups" are commonly used, however differently, both in America and in England. For example, in England not one but two terms for racial bigotry and discrimination are frequently employed; one is "racialism," and the other is "racism." A British attorney, a West Indian, and two Asian collaborators—Ian Macdonald, Gus John, Reena Bhavnani, and Lily Khan—define and distinguish between the terms.

Racialism. Refers to prejudiced beliefs and behavior based on race, colour or ethnicity. Someone who acts in a racially prejudiced way based on those beliefs is a racialist.

Racism. The doctrine that an individual or his or her behavior is determined by stable inherited characteristics deriving from separate racial stocks. . . .

Racism is more than just a set of ideas or beliefs. When these become systematised into a philosophy of "race" superiority, and when this then becomes a part of the way in which society as a whole is organised, then the term "racism" is used. A society whose most powerful economic and social institutions are organised on, or in effect act on or reflect, the principle that one race is superior to another is racist.[1]

Although several generations of black people have been born and bred in England, when English people refer to an "Englishman" or "Englishwoman," the man or women is automatically thought of as being white. In the United States the term "Asian" most likely means Chinese, Japanese, Korean, Vietnamese, and other people from the Far East. But in England, references to "Asians" most often mean people of Indian descent. The terms "coloureds" and "immigrants" have been traditionally understood to mean all dark-skinned people, and refer specifically to people of Africa and Indian descent, including West Indians and also Pakistani, Bangladeshi, and other Afro-Caribbeans and East Indians. Compared with the United States, there are differences in the way these "minorities" are treated in England and how they get along with each other. These differences may be related to the different historical relations that have existed between dark-skinned people and white people of each country.

For example, while the United States colonized and enslaved Africans *within* the territory boundaries of North America, England has ruled over a vast empire of colonies stretching from the East Indies to West, East, and Southern Africa. England's empire included, moreover, the West Indies and Ireland, as well as the land, resources, and people destined to become the United States of America. The point is that the historical relations between English people and the people colonized by England have taken place *outside* of England. The relations took place in the lands of the conquered people.

On the other hand, the Africans in the United States were brought out of Africa to America. The Africans became Negroes, or African Americans. They are historically the largest minority group in the United States. Within the territorial boundaries of the United States, this minority has been subjected to nearly three hundred years of slavery, and another one hundred and fifty years of "Jim Crow" segregation and discrimination, plus a draconian ideology of racism that continues even today.

The historical relations between England and people of color have taken place in India, Nigeria, Ghana, and in other lands to which the English came and to which they transported mainly Africans and Indians. These two groups, African West Indians and Indians, are the major minorities of color in England today. The islands of the Caribbean were foreign to the English and to the Africans and Indians. But since only the English colonizing groups of planters and poor whites came to the foreign lands, the original minority peoples of African and Indian descent eventually became the majority. This happened in Barbados, Trinidad and Tobago, Jamaica, Guyana, and smaller islands of the Caribbean, such as St. Kitts, St. Lucia, St. Croix, Anguilla, and so forth.[2]

The prosperity of an empire that made England the most powerful nation in the world was built on the slave trade and West African colonization. Ghana was the source of so many slaves and precious resources that the British named it the "Gold Coast." But it was the West Indies in particular that supplied the wealth of the British Empire. Eventually, though, the West Indian colonies, and those in Africa, wrested their independence from the English.

Direct English rule in these colonies was overthrown. Rather as the North American Revolutionary War against England resulted in the creation of the United States, the Africans and West Indians claimed, or reclaimed, titles to their own lands. Official power was taken from the British, and often they had to move back home to England.[3]

But for those of African descent in the United States, the overthrow of white people and driving them from North America was not possible. From slavery until now, white people have remained the majority. Unlike the Africans, Indians, and West Indians who fought for and won their independence and assumed power over their countries, the African Americans are a "trapped minority." They are trapped *inside* the very country that holds them at bay.

Thus, the historical struggle of African Americans has been not so much for independence. Rather—except for two nineteenth-century small migrations from the United States back to Sierra Leone and Liberia—the sole quest of North America's largest minority has been to win equal rights within American society and culture. Because the vast majority of Africans colonized in North America were forced to give up their cultural heritages, the African Americans—unlike Africans, West Indians, and Indians in England—do not have the option of remaining in the States or going back home. For African Americans, there is no home but the States. They speak no language but the American language.

African Americans remain aliens in a land from which there is no escape. In this land, they have been degraded and rejected, and, according to one of the time-honored Negro spirituals, have always felt like "motherless children . . . a long ways from Home." On the other hand, the Indians, Africans, and West Indians were in lands which were, or which they came to regard, as their own. They were socialized, moreover, to feel that England was their mother country. Barbados, for example, is traditionally referred to as "Little England." Again, unlike the blacks in the United States who were brought there against their will as slaves, West Indians, Africans, and people of Indian descent have themselves migrated to England. They come and remain—or depart—by choice. Of course, rather than pure choice, other dynamics are involved, such as the political and economic forces of local and worldwide import.

2

The British were forced to abolish slavery in 1838. Mass migration from the Caribbean to England, however, did not get under way until the 1950s. The first instance of migration was motivated by reciprocal economic interests on the part of England and Barbados. World War II, 1939–45, and the labor shortage that the war caused in Britain, played a significant part. In 1955, the government of Barbados and London Transport negotiated a deal whereby England's labor shortage in the transportation industry would be aided by employing Barbadians. In turn, the unemployment problem in Barbados would be assuaged. A dozen years later, in 1967, a report was issued by the West Indian Standing Conference (WISC). The report noted that "Barbadians have been employed . . . as bus crew, caterers, underground [subway] workers and maintenance staff. . . . The standard of recruits is very high. . . . London Transport has told the Barbados High Commission that they [the workers] are above average . . . steady, reliable and trustworthy. . . ."[4]

Back in 1958, the first major social disturbances between West Indians and London whites took place in one of the "immigrant"-populated areas, Notting Hill. The West Indian Standing Conference had been formed in the heat of battle with racists and Fascists who perpetrated the Notting Hill riot. It consisted of numerous associations organized on a neighborhood basis. Nine years later, in 1967, WISC issued its report, which was entitled *The Unsquare Deal: London's Bus Colour Bar.*

The report asserted that after more than ten years of high performance by West Indian workers, when it came to promotions and wages, West Indians were subjected to racism. London Transport management and the Transport union were opposed to racial prejudice and discrimination. It was therefore strange and inexplicable that racism had been blatantly practiced over the last decade by the white union rank-and-file membership and the white workers of London Transport. In 1967, there was not a single West Indian bus inspector. The majority of workers were West Indians; all of them were doing bottom-level jobs.

Born out of the Notting Hill riots of 1958, the WISC sought to protect and improve the condition of West Indians in London, who at the time numbered 150,000. Through a sustained program involving such actions as demonstrations and picketing, black bus inspectors are commonplace today. But, as the 1967 report points out, race prejudice and discrimination exist not just in the transportation system, but in all types of employment, education and the schools, housing, labor and business, government, politics, the justice system, in art and culture, and among the police. In 1986, in a multiracial society such as England, there were no black policemen.[5]

3

The rise of racism in Britain began in earnest during the 1960s. In addition to discrimination and random attacks against people of color in general, organized hate groups sprang up. The most reactionary and violent of such groups was and is the National Front, which is similar to the Ku Klux Klan in the States, but without the white hoods and sheets. Also, the 1960s witnessed for the first time in England the rise of an avowed racist politician. Enoch Powell became a member of Parliament on the basis of his program of racial hatred and a "Keep England White" campaign. Powell's racism and the racist-Fascist groups such as the National Front, were directed toward Jews as well as Asians, Africans, and West Indians. The National Front, and the political party that inspired the Front—the British National Party—are active today. Near the beginning of the Ireland versus England football game in Dublin during February 1995, a bloody riot ensued, which had been planned and was deliberately provoked by National Front Fascists and other followers of extreme right-wing groups chanting "Sieg Heil" and "No surrender to the IRA." One neo-Nazi splinter group takes its name (C18) from the initials of Adolf Hitler (A equals 1 and H equals 8).[6]

The response of the British government has included the enactment of anti-racist laws and the creation of governmental bodies. Such measures, however, have been contradicted by other enactments of the government. The 1961 Immigration Act and the 1979 Nationality Act, for example, place severe restrictions on the flow of black people into England and make for easier deportation of people of color already in the country. The perception on the part of colored people in Britain is that government measures are gainsaid by the persistence of the British colonial attitude. Since 1960, John La Rose has been a leading West Indian intellectual and activist. Of the Commission for Racial Equality and the Community Relations Council (both established in 1976), La Rose expressed the view held by many blacks: "We see these [government bodies] in this struggle and campaign as a colonial office for blacks in British society. Their purpose is to undermine the independent struggle of blacks."[7]

People of Indian descent view government anti-racist initiatives much as West Indians view them. Tarlochan Gata-Aura, an organizer and activist for racial justice in Britain and Scotland, says that the Race Relations Act of 1976 "is a totally useless piece of legislation, and it allows the authorities to always say: 'Look, if you are experiencing racism, why don't you use this legislation?' The reality," Gata-Aura continues, "is when that legislation is used, hardly any cases come to any fruition."[8]

The spontaneous rioting, insurrections, and organized struggle against discrimination, injustice, and racial violence by the police and organized hate groups also began during the 1960s. The civil rights *cum* black power movement in the United States inspired its counterpart in England. Martin Luther King, Jr., Malcolm X, Rosa Parks, Huey Newton, and many others served as role models for West Indians. Then, too, many of the outstanding figures of the historical black struggle in the States were West Indians, for example, Marcus Garvey and Stokeley Carmichael. Carmichael electrified his audience at the 1967 London international conference on the Dialectics of Liberation, held in the Camden Town Round House and organized by anti-psychiatrists R. D. Laing, Joseph Berke, and David Cooper, among others.

Swept along by the worldwide social upheaval of the 1960s and 1970s, colored people in England rose up in spontaneous riots and insurrections, organizing on community, regional, and nationwide levels. In addition to the West Indian Standing Conference and the various local community-based West Indian associations, newsgroups and movements were formed, such as the Pan African Congress movement, the Alliance of the

Black Parents movement, the Black Youth movement, the Race Today Collective, and many others. A sparse group of Black Panther and black power advocates even emerged. After a visit to London by Malcolm X, a West Indian hustler donned the hat of a black power advocate and changed his name from Michael Defratis to Michael X.[9]

4

Racism was not an unfamiliar experience for the Caribbean immigrants. They came to "Mother England" with a history of prejudice and discrimination back in their home countries. People of East Indian descent, for example, were brought to Trinidad with the indentureship system and the Africans were brought as slaves. The majority population consisted of these two groups. Because they were poor and colored, they faced discrimination in education, health, and the use of public facilities.[10] But the struggle that brought about the abolition of slavery in 1838 did not bring an end to white domination and racism. The movement against social injustice and for independence continued in the West Indies.

The people of East Indian and African descent came to England with a consciousness of being a majority in their home countries. They also came with a history of struggle against slavery, racism, and colonialism. These struggles were largely successful in their home countries. The new arrivals in England were no doubt shocked, but they were already familiar with racism. Thus, they were not undone by the hatred, discrimination, and rejection they encountered. Nor were they overwhelmed by a pattern of physical violence against them.

The 1958 riot in Notting Hill was merely one instance in a continuing cycle of racial warfare in London and other large cities throughout England—Leeds, Birmingham, Manchester, Liverpool among them. The upheaval in Notting Hall has been repeated many times, including 1964, 1976, and 1981. Racists acts of intimidation and violence have been perpetrated against West Indians and East Indians in London neighborhoods where they form a large part of the inhabitants, such as New Cross and Tottenham. Brixton is the equivalent of a "sprawling" American ghetto like Harlem or South Side, Chicago. The area has witnessed a cycle of physical confrontations between its black inhabitants and hate groups, on the one hand, and the police, on the other.

Throughout the neighborhoods where people of color live, they have been the victims not only of physical abuse, but of murder as well. In

Southall, for example, some 35,000 Asian people—Indian, Pakistani, and various other people of Indian descent—live in about six square miles. In 1976, an Indian taxi driver, Kuldip Singh Sekhon, was murdered by forty-five stab wounds from the knife of a racist white man named Steven Coker. Like other such communities, Southall is an embattled colonial outpost in West London. At a 1990 conference in London on "Racism Nazism Fascism and Racial Attacks," Suresh Grover made the following observation: "Then they have these Territorial Support Groups stationed permanently in Southall in their armoured vehicles, which is the Special Patrol Group. . . . Then they have the Anti-Terrorist Squad . . . the Bomb Squad in Southall. They've got the Fraud Squad . . . the Customs and Excise. They've got the Drug Squad. They've got the Riot Training School three miles from Southall. They've got a Territorial Army in Southall. And yet they've got a Gang Squad." The report goes on to say that "something like 30 to 40% of young Asians, of young black people in Southall have been either stopped or searched. In eight years there were 25,000 stop-and-searches in Ealing," another largely black-populated community.[11]

5

The 1985 riots in Brixton and Tottenham marked a new phase of urban insurrection in Britain. In Brixton, police broke into the home of Cherry Groce. They were looking for her son, but shot and crippled her for life. A week later, during a search of Cynthia Jarret's home, the police pushed over the middle-aged Jarret and she died. The cry went out, "They are killing our mothers!" Some 271 premises were searched, 350 people were arrested; and 160 were charged. Guns were fired in the Broadwater Farm Housing Estate (equivalent to the "projects" in the States) and a policeman was killed. An army of police lay siege to the housing estate. Defense campaigns sprang up both in Brixton and in Tottenham. More than three thousand people marched from Brixton to Hyde Park in the center of London. Both events—permanent injury to Cherry Groce and the death of Cynthia Jerret—were the result of police actions.[12]

In 1986, a seven-year Brixton resident, Joseph A. Hunte, published a report entitled *Nigger Hunting in England?* It asserts that police brutality is a common experience and that most complaints suggest "policemen are like other members of the host community . . . averse to members of the coloured population in this country."[13] Like other English people, the police view all "immigrant areas" as being inhabited by criminal types. Policemen believe a battery of racial stereotypes about dark-skinned people—that all immigrants are dishonest, that they are "cheeky" and have come from jungles, are boisterous creatures, untrained in and alien to the niceties of living; and that immorality and prostitution are their way of life. Immigrants are indolent and show resentment when spoken to; immigrants grin and behave like little children.[14]

When a West Indian was involved in an automobile accident, he sought assistance from two policemen, one of whom asked, "What do you black bastards want?" Similar epithets are spoken frequently to people of color by the police. The investigation and report by Hunte brought to light that in neighborhoods where people of color live, policemen go out of their stations on the beat claiming that they are going "nigger hunting." When charges are brought against the police for brutality and unfair charges, the police frequently lose the cases.[15]

Perhaps the largest mass demonstration to date of black people in Britain took place on March 2, 1981. The demonstration was in protest of the "New Cross massacre." On January 17, a fire raged through the home of a West Indian family in New Cross Road, South London, killing thirteen young people who were having a birthday party. Rather than looking for the culprits who fire-bombed the house, the investigating police built a case blaming certain young people at the party themselves. This fabrication of evidence was motivated to avoid admitting that the incident was a racist attack. The police themselves had originally said (in private) to surviving family members that the house had been fire-bombed. The New Cross Massacre Action Committee was organized, a Black Peoples Day of Action was declared, and on March 2 some 20,000 to 25,000 blacks demonstrated through the streets of London. In an interview, one of the organizers, John La Rose, said that "there had not been any kind of demonstration of this nature in Britain in the 30 years since the black community . . . had arrived from the Caribbean. We crossed Blackfriars Bridge [which] had not been crossed by a major demonstration since the Chartists in the 1830's. . . ."[16]

La Rose claims that New Cross was a historic event in the history of British society. Like the national struggles in Scotland, Ireland, and Wales, and like the workers' struggles, La Rose says that after New Cross the black struggles became center stage in British politics. Following the 25,000-strong demonstration, other riots and insurrections broke out in Brixton, Southall, and Toxteth in Liverpool. ". . . For the first time we saw British Prime Minister [Margaret Thatcher] . . . in a state of speechlessness and perplexity . . . because with that movement came the insurrections in about 60 cities."[17]

6

England is a modern society made up of various black and white minority nationalities, races, and ethnic groups. The twenty-odd thousand demonstrators in the March 2, 1981, New Cross Black Peoples Day of Action included thousands of white supporters. The Irish and Jews were well represented. A history of British anti-Semitism, anti-Irish sentiments, and acts of violence have frequently inspired mutual support between white minorities and people of color in England. The various colored minorities themselves tend to cooperate in Britain rather more than African Americans and similar minorities—such as the Vietnamese, Koreans, Indians, and, of late, Jews—in the United States do. At least, a more friendly attitude seems to exist between the various people of color in England. The colonial strategy was to import Indians as cheaper labor to displace the Africans who were in almost constant rebellion against domination and exploitation. This strategy fostered bitterness and conflict between Indians and Africans in the West Indies. The lack of hostility and the frequent mutual support between these two major minority groups in Britain is therefore all the more remarkable.[18]

Perhaps the experiences of collective racism in British society encourage unity and cooperation between Indians and West Indians, rather than division and rivalry. At the 1990 European Conference on Racism Nazism Fascism and Racial Attacks, different nationalities of people of color attended, including Indians, Pakistanis, Africans, West Indians, and Arabs, along with those of French, and West and East German nationality. The American expatriate and leading feminist of Wages for Housework in the States, Wilmette Brown, along with Clotil Wilcott, was in attendance, representing the multiracial King's Cross Women's Center. Multicultural anti-racist educational policies and pedagogy have been instituted in schools throughout England. The fact that the policies and instructional philosophy have on the whole been ineffective is due more to faulty application than to any flaws in the measures themselves. The investigation known as the Macdonald Inquiry into racism and racial violence in Manchester schools, which examined the murder at Brundage School of a Pakistani pupil by a white racist schoolmate, was conducted by a cross-section of races.

In 1994, the African National Congress came to power in South Africa with the election of Nelson Mandela. During the decades that this multi-racial organization was banned in South Africa, its international head-quarters was in London. The West Indian Student Center in Earl's Court plays host to a highly diverse group of patrons, one of which is the International Book Fair of Radical Black and Third World Books, an annual two-week festival. Writers, poets, publishers, agents, and audiences come from Britain, France, and Holland, from Africa, Asia, the Americas, the Caribbean, and from Third World countries generally. John La Rose, England's long-lasting West Indian publisher and bookseller (New Beacon Books), is founder and organizer of the book fair. The longevity and ambiance of the fair speaks to the sense of multicultural, multiracial unity and cooperation in England. La Rose writes that

> Britain is a society of nationalities and ethnic communities: English, Scots, Welsh, Irish nationalities as well as the West Indian, Asian, and other ethnic communities. Inside both the nationalities as well as the ethnic communities. . . . We stand for a horizontal alliance across classes to change British society. . . . We stand with those sections for change in British society, and obviously it's a multi-national state, a multi-ethnic state.[19]

■ ■ ■

NOTES

1. Ian Macdonald, Reena Bhavnani, Lily Khan, and Gus John. *Murder in the Play-ground: The Burnage Report* (London: Longsight Press, 1989), p. 43.
2. During the 1960s through the 1990s, the author has lived in England for more than ten years.
3. See Eric Williams, *Slavery and Capitalism* (London: Andre Deutsch, 1964).
4. *The Unsquare Deal:London's Bus Colour Bar.* Prepared by the West Indian Standing Conference, 1967. Quoted in *New Beacon Review* 1 (July 1985), pp. 45–46.
5. *Documents from the Black Struggle.* Quoted in *New Beacon Review* 2/3 (November 1986), p. 36.
6. *Sunday Times* (London), February 19, 1995.
7. Ibid., p. 8.
8. John La Rose, ed., *Racism, Nazism, Fascism and Racial Attacks: The European Response.* (Book Fair of Radical Black and Third World Books, European Action for Racial Equality and Social Justice, 1991), p. 21.
9. Michael X, *From Michael Defratis to Michael X* (London: Andre Deutsch, 1968).
10. La Rose, ed., *Racism, Nazism, Fascism and Racial Attacks*, p. 31.
11. Ibid., p. 26.

12. *Documents from the Black Struggle.* Quoted in *New Beacon Review* 2/3 (November 1986), p. 15.

13. Joseph A. Hunte, "Nigger Hunting in England?" *New Beacon Review* 2/3 (November 1986), p. 23.

14. Ibid., pp. 42–51.

15. *Documents from the Black Struggle,* op. cit., *New Beacon Review* 2/3 (November 1986), pp. 23–34.

16. *The New Cross Massacre Story: Interviews with John La Rose* (London: The Black Parents Movement, Black Youth Movement and the Race Today Collective, 1984), pp. 5–6, 16.

17. Ibid., p. 18.

18. Amon Saba Saakana, *The Colonial Legacy* (London: Kanak House, 1987), p. 23.

19. *The New Cross Massacre Story,* pp. 26–27.

A Nuyorican in South Africa:
South African Diaries

■ ▓ ▪

MIGUEL ALGARIN

Johannesburg, July 15

After an uneventful yet nonetheless grueling fourteen-hour flight, Amiri and Amina Baraka and I are taken to the Windybrow Arts Center, where the conference on creating a South African writers' organization is nearing the end of its afternoon session. Nadine Gordimer, the chairperson, is pressing the business to a close so that progress can be made toward the goal—an organization of writers. Mr. Ronald Hardwood, the keynote speaker and president of PEN International, urges the panel and writers gathered to use "organizational models" so that the work will yield fruit, namely, an organization capable of "plenary sessions," "steering committees," whose reports, properly organized, could be submitted to the new body.

It was immediately apparent that "parliamentary procedure" would be the tool with which to carve the writers' "central organized union." It reminded me of the early 1960s, 1970s, and 1980s, when the "left" in North America would parliamentarily invent new educational and teaching approaches to public schooling and to university educational programs. Well, none of it worked. Not one iota of progress has been made in the USA to teach better, to read better, or to do arithmetic with more precision.

To listen to the noble Dennis Brutus speaking, when it was clear the session was closing, was heartwarming as he moved the gathering of writers to hear Baraka and myself speak. Yes, black people find it hard to kill the spirit in the name of a "rule." The Pablo Neruda poem I read from my translations of *A Song of Protest* established what the writer's mission is to be. He must be defiant, clever, a trickster, and above all, a historian—for where there is no acceptable historical account, the writer, be he essayist, novelist, or poet, must provide the story and the invention for growth. The means for growth is upon us, meeting us at this threshold. It is important to know that the book I read from, a book written from the heart of a people in struggle, has been read by millions. Yet we, the contemporary poets, have a hit on our hands when we sell ten thousand copies of a book. This is not acceptable. We must move on. Now, the question is: where?

Well, the answer is simple: we must move on to the electronic frontier. We must grab ahold of the awesome speed of today's communication. After all, when Mandela is burdened by the stranglehold of bureaucratic governmental procedure, what better tool can he have to sustain his vision than the public opinion of South African writers arriving through his E-mail system? With discs of direct electronic communications and faxes in his hands, he can combat the most entrenched opponent in Parliament. And please here notice how *parliamentary* procedure is for Parliament to claim the voice of the people without direct communication. But direct electronic communication provides for the people to impress, affect, and change those rules; which, in effect, have been used to keep "democracy" more consistent with the will of the powerful than the needs of the individual voter from the middle and poor classes.

If South African writers want never to be cut off from the world again, they must coalesce and become united. If being individual writers is not enough, or effective, then let your president know that if he arms you with the communicative forces of the electronic frontier, you will, in turn, from the most rural township of South Africa, communicate to him through his E-mail what he needs to know to ensure that he is caring for the needs of the people, who fought so hard to bring about the heroic struggle that achieved a peaceful change in leadership.

Organizational structures and constitutions have been put in place only to be quashed by the opposition. But a fully equipped communications center right here in Hillbrow, where we are meeting today, at the Windybrow Cultural Arts Center, set up by the government but owned and administered by the writers, will be a historic beginning. For if a coup upturns your present progress, the people and writers with access to a telephone line can speak out to the world against whatever infamy is being perpetrated at home. South Africa must never be severed from the world and its communication centers again.

It struck me that in thinking about South Africa, I became intensely aware of the absence of minority representation in the United States at the congressional and senatorial level. Minorities are no better off in letting our congressional representatives know what we want than are the South Africans. Multiculturalism has become a buzzword for an empty rhetorical effort to speak about the correction of inequities in North America. What words like "relevance" and "empowerment" indicate is that we in the United States are looking for what the South Africans have just done for themselves. It is as if the proverbial stone is rolling back down the hill after we pushed it all the way up during the late sixties, seventies, and part of the eighties. South Africans now stand proudly at the top of a clearer mission.

The South African writers must prepare a long shopping list that will put this nation "on-line." And Mandela must be taught to understand how such communicative access can enlighten the weight of leadership. How, in fact, he can use it to marshal public opinion and the collective pen of writers to support his moves in governing South Africa into the twenty-first century, with all its writers and people organized and on-line. This is the effort now afoot in Cuba, El Salvador, Nicaragua, and anywhere there is a telephone line reaching into the future where writers are arming themselves with computers. Care should be taken not to let "government" control electronic communication.

So now it is the turn for South African writers to organize and to acquire the money for the long list. It becomes necessary for the writers to say to President Mandela, "We will keep your people informed and your leadership honest as long as we are on-line reporting to the world how 'our democratization' is doing at home."

July 16

The stories of individuals in exile were the most fascinating and disturbing encounters. Everywhere I turned there was a story of loneliness, homesickness, and loss. So I found myself dedicating whole pages in my diaries to different stories, oftentimes handing the book over to newly made friends so that the story would be related in their words:

> This is Blackman Ngoro's page. I'm from Zimbabwe and am a journalist. Do you know how I got my name? My particular full name is Freeblackman. I shortened it so it could fit onto my T-shirt. In my eyes being in a freedom train is all that makes my eyes bright. The more I feel this way the more I know I'm not wrong.

> Ray Choto—a Zimbabwean novelist and journalist
> Please give my warm regards to
> fellow comrades in your country
> We are together in the struggle.

Immediately after arriving by plane, we were taken to Windybrow Cultural Arts Center. Work had started. I was moved by the vigorous cool weather and the determination of the delegates to arrive at a consensus. Two working morning committees were formed. The first was to work on the language of the constitution. The second was "the models" committee. Amina, Amiri, and myself were on the second committee. Our charge was to investigate the models that would give us guidance toward framing the working structure of the Organization of South African Writers. Maishe Maponya began the discussion by suggesting that two position papers be prepared. The first was that existing writers' organizations be studied and identified, so that their accomplishments and needs would be both recognized and provided for wherever necessary. The second position was to find a constitution that could be used as a model for a South African Constitution. Much discussion followed, with the eventual accord that the two suggestions be adopted.

However, Dennis Brutus made the point that the "models" we were looking for were in fact delineated in the material already submitted by the organizing committee. He further urged us to understand that we were capable right-in-the-there-and-now of adopting a working model and not ending up with empty hands, with no structural model at the end of our session. Another member on the committee felt the need to create an umbrella organization that would regulate, yet leave all existing writers' organizations autonomous; this was an amendment to what the committee had already passed. He felt the word "interim" should be inserted so that we would end up proposing at the planning session an interim umbrella organization that would research and prepare two or more studies of existing South African writers' organizations. This interim umbrella organization should take all the findings and make recommendations that would lead to the actual, not interim, formal South African Writers Organization.

We broke for tea. Yes, tea. I asked Nadine Gordimer if she spoke Afrikaans. Nadine said, "Not a word." She had attended an all-girl Catholic school and all instruction was conducted in English. At this point a tall, bleach-blonde woman interrupted with, "Look, racism in South Africa has always been severe among the whites. The English absolutely refused to mix with the Afrikaans. It was unheard of for a proper English girl to speak Afrikaans." Nadine broke in to say, "All I've ever spoken is my mother tongue. I'm rather limited as a linguist." I was surprised, so I asked her how it was possible to avoid the language of the streets. Well, apparently, there was no mixing between "classes." So it was not just a matter of black and white, it was also a matter of distinguishing the "Queen's English" speaker from the ordinary white folk, who speak an unwieldy mixture of Dutch-Portuguese-German-Malaysian. Afrikaans was not "purely" anything. But the separation did yield the measured, gorgeous Gordimer prose that we know. I suppose "ethnic-linguistic purity" is exercised in some potent yet apparently subliminal exorcism or "language cleansing" in South Africa. Immediately after this pure English versus Afrikaans discussion, Amina, Amiri, and myself left for Soweto. We were on our way to eyeballing the icon of segregation.

July 17

En route to Soweto we will visit the regional offices of Azapo, the political party that sprang from Steven Biko's South African student organizations. The Azanian civilization is noted particularly for its smithing, mainly gold. Azania is the original name of South Africa.

The political line of Azapo maintains that Nelson Mandela was released into a "new settlement" that was already "prepped up" before his freedom, so the regional director of Azapo, Tiyani Lybon Mabasa, asserts that the political line of the Mandela party is not keeping its focus where it needs to be. Azapo maintains that not enough is being done to assure the South African people of the state of the disposition of land. No promises for distribution of land have been kept and none seem to be forthcoming. The control of wealth is entirely out of the hands of the Mandela people and should be put into the hands of the South Africans. As far as political power goes, the Azapo Party feels that "the Black

Africans have become the new managers of their own oppression." The united front is no longer united and a call for reunification is imperative. The leaders of Azapo tirelessly reiterate that Nelson Mandela was released into a "new settlement" that was already "done up." However, the "new arrangement" is cosmetic.

On the way to Soweto, we are told that we will meet with the leadership of the party. At the entrance of the ghetto, we are asked to get out of the car and searched at gunpoint, with soldiers' fingers on triggers and ready for operation. "Why are you searching me?" asks Amiri. "You are the one with the gun." Nervous glances are exchanged. We are released. We drive on to the Sowetan offices of Azapo, where we meet Strike Thokoane, national organizer, and are then introduced to Jairus Kgokong, secretary general of Azapo. Amiri is talking up support for Mumia Abu-Jamal—we find ourselves pleading in South Africa for support for an Afro-American on death row. What Amiri feels is the loss of the struggle at home, the mainstreaming of the Afro-American bourgeoisie. What the Azapo Party feels is that the African National Congress (ANC) has fled the very ground from which it sprung. It is made clear, however, that prior arrangements would have been needed to reach "high into ranks" in order to catch Mandela's attention.

In the evening we are taken to the Witwatersrand University Press, back in Johannesburg. The session has been called for a discussion on exile and the return to the homeland. The stories that *were* told need to be heard around the world if we are to learn the lessons of the South Africans who fled the oppression of apartheid and enslavement. Many of the writers during this roundtable discussion spoke feelingly and often in tears about what it means to be exiled, how the memory of home begins to fade and only a gray vestige remains after many decades of separation from the homeland.

The sharing begins with Barolong Seboni from Botswana. He speaks of the literature of Botswana as deeply influenced by the writings and writers from South Africa. The heart of their writing is "protest." Poetry written in English has become very popular and performance becomes the theatrical way in which the spoken word is used. Seboni returns to an almost palpable hurt when he speaks of Namibia, Mozambique, and Angola. They are all at war. Botswana is surrounded by violence and destruction, and so the literature is affected; the writers become more introspective. Domestic issues are at the heart of the poetry and prose. The plight of the economy and ecology of Botswana is the driving content. Then Seboni pulls back from the table, wipes his brow, looks around and says that by the late eighties and nineties, the writing became more retrospective and popular, so that it now occupies the central pages of newspapers and journals.

Ray Choto from Zimbabwe speaks with urgency about independence, and how with it came a writing that sought to reveal whether or not the "promises" of the revolution were being delivered. People had determined that as long as they had fought, they were going to make the new leaders pay attention to the issues of education and the distribution of land. Choto says that in Zimbabwe, literature became a call for government carrythrough. In short, the moral and principal call were for delivery on promises made. Choto demands that the new South African writer be "independent," and that the concern of the new South African literature never forget the promise of land distribution, access to information, and an insistence that the government deliver the goods: land, employment, health, work, and involvement in how "money gets spent."

South African Mirriam Tlali spoke passionately about censorship and the hunger that she felt for suppressed literature. She calls on women in South Africa to remember that they are the mental nourishment of the nation. Tlali speaks of her decision to write about the system's repression of "us"—not the self, not the individual family, but the overall family. She recalls how her hometown was disassembled. Instead, she was moved into Soweto—into isolation, into emptiness. She looks around the table, breathes hard, and reveals, "After the publication of my first manuscript, the police raids started." Her life became invaded by repressive forces; finally she decided to leave and follow her mother to Lesotho. Tlali has touched the room and those present have reached a new level of sensitivity and empathy with what made this woman choose exile in lieu of home.

Mandla Langa speaks about the hurt the South Africans experience as they leave the motherland. He also feels, however, that the absence from home gives him a distance from which to look at what is happening. He maintains that fiction does not need invention. The South African reality is so extreme that fiction needs to stay clear-eyed and detail the injustices that are perpetrated. "Exile," he says, "helps to bring out the questions that needed to be addressed." Then, in a long pause, he turns inward, before adding that the return to the land—a land from which you have been separated for so long—is a new experience, a new beginning.

Keora-Petae "Willie" Kgositsile speaks about his return in 1990 after thirty years of exile. Painfully, he reminds us that he has lived outside Johannesburg longer than inside. He pauses, then says, "After a while, only street names remain." Then a longer pause, and he adds that to return is to find that "all has changed, and your memory has to begin to remember that you are 'home.' " Kgositsile speaks of the fright of exile. He says that after the first few years, people, places, homes begin to fade. Then, by the fifth year, everything comes back to you sharply, so sharply that it is almost like a documentary, and it is at this point that the return of the memory spurs the need to write. The return of memory makes for writing. In a sudden realization, Kgositsile looks at all of us around the table and says, "You know what? The return to Johannesburg is so strange that it is more distant to me now than New York."

Reading Richard Wright's *Black Boy* taught Willie Kgositsile that he can write in English without being "a white boy." In his newfound world, it is music and New World writers who feed him: Baraka, Ted Joans, the blues, Langston Hughes, jazz, Gwendolyn Brooks, Sterling Plumpp, Aime Cesaire. For Kgositsile, life is a creative affirmation, it is the use of the truth. Then, in an almost shocking moment of self-revelation and profound truth, he says, "Why the return? It was problematic. We'd been talking about seizure of power and engaged armed struggle." Never did he expect to come back to the South Africa he had left. After the agreement to cease armed struggle, Kgositsile says we were asking questions about the truth of this agreement and whether or not it in fact had been an instrument of surrender. Because, he affirms, when the enemy comes from the same womb as you, there is a physical breakdown. "I felt like not writing at all."

Sterling Plumpp, African American, has been in touch with South Africa since the sixties. His first feelings of mutual identification with South Africa came through Miriam Makeba and Hugh Massakela. Dennis Brutus kept him knowledgeable and moving on the political issues of South Africa. Plumpp spoke about the process of collecting the two anthologies that he put together on South African writers, asserting that South African literature deserves a world audience and that attention should be paid to the indigenous languages. Then, in a turn from the talk of literature, he begins to outline the need for literary theory, which has to be developed and applied in order for the work to be taken seriously. He appeals to the women of South Africa to write, and promises that when they are ready, "we will publish you when the manuscript is in hand." The women in the room bristle silently.

July 18

Jo'burg, as it is popularly referred to, still reflects the separation of people, some incorporation, but mostly multicultural and racial integration as rigidly fixed by dividing lines as in New York's El Barrio on East 96th Street and the Upper East Side silk-stocking district that stops right at the border between poverty and poor education on the southeast side of 96th Street and the progressive and well-prepared teachers of the northeast side.

The united front is split. Mandela is being made into a saint. Not a good sign, if we judge by what happened to the saints in Christianity. It is, to be expected that if he is canonized and crowned, he will become an ancient figurehead, too saintly to criticize but too old and out of touch to rule. Mandela is often encircled by civil servants who will not let the people through. Since our arrival in South Africa, we have been surrounded by the ANC. They have brought us here, and it should be up to the ANC to assure that Mandela will remain vital and not canonized into isolation.

Later in the afternoon, Nadine Gordimer, Dennis Brutus, Willie Kgositsile, Ray Choto, Amina and Amiri Baraka, Lilia Momple, myself, and many more demonstrated in front of the Nigerian Embassy to urge that the jailed Nigerian author Ken Saro-Wiwa be released from jail immediately. The slippery and cunning diplomat who came to us wanted to know why we were making such a demand.

"Because there is no due process being practiced," we shouted. The conversation was courteous. Two policemen arrived, demanding to know whether or not we had gotten permission to gather. Nadine Gordimer quickly told the officers that she had asked her lawyers and that no regulation existed prohibiting our congregating to demonstrate peacefully. Willie Kgositsile asked what "injunction" existed on the books. Could the officer cite it and give particulars? The white officer began retracting, speaking about a phone call, that we should not block street traffic. As he walked away, I noticed the black South African officer who was sheepishly standing there almost wanting to be transparent. Injustices still prevail; yet South Africa is dealing in building a new democracy. Let us hope democracy comes to South Africa more quickly than our own United States. We in the USA are still hesitantly inching toward it, while the South Africans are taking giant steps.

Witwatersrand University
July 19

Amiri Baraka addresses a liberal arts class. He talks of the old Greek legend of Sisyphus, who rolled the stone up the hill only to have it roll down again. Afro-Americans are now in the Sisyphus syndrome: For the last thirty years Afro-Americans have rolled the rock up the hill, but it kept coming down swiftly. Now South Africa has pushed the rock up; yet, if it falls asleep, South Africans will find themselves in jail or carrying passes once again. The monster of apartheid will have reared its decapitated head once more. Baraka speaks of a United States where people of color are losing access to power and equality everywhere. He predicts a time when black South Africans will be accused of reverse racism and will be called racists. Baraka urges that money for education not be cut. He affirms that Newark, New Jersey, is today in the place that Johannesburg was prior to 1991. He warns that Affirmative Action will be the quicksand mud puddle of Johannesburg in less than a decade. He warns that real heroes become "amoral comics," and that the media shows the life of the lumpenproletariat, not the real revolutionary. And then, in an astonishing turn, Baraka looks up at a packed-to-capacity auditorium and says that in a few years, "black people" will bring the death penalty back to control and safeguard the new interests of the black bourgeoisie.

In the question and answer session, Maishe Maponya asks whether or not multiculturalism works in the United States, and Amiri states that it is mostly cosmetic. In answering Maponya, Baraka divides people into three general slots: The first are the small, backward people, who hold power; the second is the mass of society, as in "the middle"; and third is the small group of revolutionaries who seek to redefine the terms of governance. And it is the middle, according to Baraka, that we must make strong in order to destroy all disease. Blacks in office must be held accountable. Then, in a rhetorical mode, he poses a series of issues concerning doing away with "all pests." Vigilance, struggle for democracy, self-determination, self-reliance, these are the tools with which to do away with "pests." He looks at the audience and says, "You are at step one, South Africa; you must keep to your socialist purposes."

Later that afternoon, I meet with Thundi Booi, a thirty-year-old Xhosa woman who is intelligent, sensual, and learning to live in an ever-expanding universe since 1991. Nothing in my fifty-three years has prepared me for the cynicism, sarcasm, equivocation of a Xhosa woman seeking her way on South African soil. Thundi has left her two-year-old daughter, born in exile, with her mother in Cape Town so that the mother can raise the daughter she never had, because exile had drawn the curtain of make-believe and survival between Thundi and her own mother. Xhosa women in Johannesburg with the street smarts of Nuyorican women around the planet. She has never felt so alone. She claims that if she learns to love herself, she will then be able to love others. *Thundi* means "patience." *Xhosa* means Cape Town people—a liberated, civilized city. "In Jo'burg I'm in Africa, but in Cape Town, I'm in the world," says Thundi. "Its environment makes for futuristic thinking."

I returned to the Holiday Inn to find Amina and Amiri having dinner with Willie Kgositsile. The conversation was heated. Earlier, Nadine Gordimer had attacked Baraka and all participating readers for not giving Mandela enough recognition, enough respect, enough devotion. Baraka had in fact made a direct plea for Mr. Mandela to intervene in the execution of Mumia Abu-Jamal. Baraka said movingly that he stood on South Africa soil pleading that Mandela stand up against the death penalty newly reintroduced in many American states.

"It is ironic," says Baraka, "that we [Afro-Americans] come to Johannesburg to ask for your help in order to save a freedom fighter from legal murder." The reading proceeded vigorously. However, I still fear that the deification of Mandela continues. Baraka had in fact recognized the worldwide importance of Mandela by directing his pleas to the President of South Africa. In response, Mandela has written to the Honorable Governor of the State of Pennsylvania a letter requesting that on humanitarian grounds the governor commute the death sentence imposed upon Mumia Abu-Jamal:

President　　　　　　　*Republic of South Africa*
Dear Governor:

MUMIA ABU-JAMAL

On humanitarian grounds I urge you to use your power as Governor of the State of Pennsylvania to commute the death sentence imposed upon Mumia Abu-Jamal. The Constitutional Court of South Africa has recently declared that the death penalty is inconsistent with the right to life, the right to dignity and the right to be protected from cruel and unusual punishment as enshrined in the Bill of Fundamental Rights in the South African Constitution, Act No 200 of 1993.

In accordance with these views I ask for your compassionate reconsideration of the sentence imposed on Mr. Abu-Jamal.

Yours sincerely

"It Happens All the Time"— or Does It?

■ ■ ■

KATHRYN WADDELL TAKARA

It happens all the time, even in Hawai'i, especially if one is an African American. Stereotypes, selective memory. Even in Hawai'i, where I have lived now for almost twenty-seven years, bell hooks speaks of "talking back." Bessie Head speaks of the man who came to the realization that "I am just anybody." Somehow I combine these two points of view and reflect on my experience as an African American immigrant to Hawai'i.

After graduating with an M.A. in French from U.C. Berkeley, leaving behind the turbulent black power revolution, the Black Panther movement, the anti-war movement, and radical organizations like Students for a Democratic Society (SDS), the Weathermen, the hippies, and the peaceniks, I arrived in Honolulu with my Caucasian husband, our baby daughter, lots of energy, yet few preconceived notions about the islands, except that I had listened to melodious strains of Hawaiian music when I was young since my dad enjoyed it. I had heard that it was a place of racial harmony—good for people with interracial marriages, nurturing for children—a kind of paradise with fragrant air, balmy weather, beautiful beaches, and full of romance. Being an Alabama girl, of course all this was alluring. I had been raised in a time and place where fear hung like a razor's edge, where Jim Crow and prescribed behavior was the status quo, where it was against the law for me to marry my former husband, where my closest cousin, a civil rights worker, was shot and killed trying to use a whites-only bathroom, and the accused was acquitted, in spite of convincing evidence against him. I became bitter, enraged, carried my recollected racial experience to the East Coast where I received my private education, to Europe where I lived and studied, and finally to West Africa.

Still, I was somewhat utopian in my philosophy, artistically inclined. I had long worn flowers in my hair and loved to go barefoot, even though my mother hated the latter and thought it was a "country" way to act. So when we deplaned in Honolulu one balmy evening marveling at the sweet air and exotic flowers, I hardly noticed the black porters at the airport. In fact, it didn't immediately strike me that I saw no other blacks around for several weeks, as we hustled and bustled and got settled in at the elite private school where my husband had been recently hired to teach. What I did notice was, whenever I was not with my husband in a public place, friendly local people would inevitably ask me if I or my husband (whom they assumed was black) was in the military.

After a few months, I began to substitute-teach at public and private schools and soon began to realize, by the curiosity of the students, that there were few if any African American teachers in the community. The more I read the local newspapers and watched television in those days, the more I was offended and embarrassed by the sensationalized stories about blacks: riots, unemployment, welfare, and crime. And there were few counter stories or role models to make people think we were not all in some way stigmatized. I began to feel anger and pain that even outside of the continental shores of America, people were still learning how to be prejudiced.

My second year, I was offered a job teaching French at a small private college, where I worked for two years, and then I was hired in the university system in the new Ethnic Studies program to teach a course on African Americans. The following year I enrolled in the Ph.D. program in political science, prompted by my recent divorce, and my desire to teach and inform the public on our neglected history and contributions to society. As a single mother who now had to support my daughter, I realized that I would need a Ph.D. to advance in my profession and to gain the respect of my colleagues. I also remembered the words of my father, who had constantly reminded me since I was in elementary school that I had to always do more and be better than anyone else in order to be considered equal.

I chose to study political science for a number of reasons: (1) the university did not offer a doctorate in French; (2) my cousin had been slain in the civil rights movement; (3) I knew that to gain tenure in Ethnic Studies, I would need a doctorate; and (4) political science seemed relevant to Ethnic Studies and the political science department had an excellent national reputation at that time. When I began my coursework, there were no African American professors in the College of Social Sciences, and only one tenure-track, full-time African American professor out of more than two thousand faculty members. There were no more than five or six black graduate students at that time.

Moreover, as a mother I realized that the local community did not offer information about African Americans in the public schools, mainly because the majority of teachers were not informed, had little if any contact with blacks, and had not been exposed to any academic courses taught by or about blacks. Indeed, there seemed to be little knowledge or understanding of the historical African American experience beyond the public and often demoralizing fictions. I was surprised that the Hawaiian Islands and local community did little to encourage, support, or sustain a noticeable African American presence or community, which could in turn develop and promote cultural awareness, business interests, political power bases, and intellectual forums. As I actively searched for African Americans, I found a few black churches, social organizations, and entertainers in town, and of course athletes at the university. (Out of 20,000 plus students at the university, about 100–200 African Americans were full-time students, and about 80 percent of those were athletes. Unfortunately, the statistics at the university have not changed very much.)

Of the approximately 29,000 African Americans living in Hawai'i when we arrived, the military was by far the largest representative group, numbering perhaps around 20,000. The several thousand permanent residents were living and working throughout the islands, and many had assimilated into the local community and culture through intermarriage. This was fine; but when other ethnic groups had a visible economic and cultural presence, it made me want to promote the same in order to enhance the self-esteem and dignity of our children and our group. I also knew that we had many positive qualities and talents to share with the world. Therefore, whenever there was an opportunity, I had my daughter do a report on an outstanding African American or African to instruct the class and teacher.

I slowly began to meet other African Americans, and after a small racial riot at the marine base, I began to work as a mediator between black G.I.'s (who were often incarcerated in the brig) and the predominantly white officers. Perhaps what struck me the most was how alienated these young black men felt here. Of course, much can be said about socio-economic factors predetermining their attitudes, but many said it was the most prejudiced place they had ever been. I certainly never felt this way, although in retrospect perhaps part of their complaint was the lack of a feeling of the support and understanding that comes from a visible, supportive, and representative community. As a result of racial problems in the military during this period, several people of diverse ethnic groups created a black cultural center featuring food, music, books, and discussion groups in downtown Honolulu, which catered to the military. However, many longtime black residents no longer felt the need for an active African American community center since they had assimilated into the island lifestyle.

Meanwhile, my daughter seemed to be accepted into the local community since she looked "local," and unless/until I showed up with my afro and obvious continental connection, most assumed she was another ethnic mix like a majority of the children in these islands. But even here in "paradise," *hapa* (half) black children can be maligned as a result of the stereotypes, institutional and interpersonal racism, historically generated fears, and racialist ideologies which have come to the islands with the missionaries, the plantation owners, the military, tourists, and of course the media.

Yet on an individual level, my daughter and I soon felt quite at home here, comfortable without the constant tension between black and white, secure in a community where the majority were many minorities, where an individual could be rewarded by his/her contributions and not only because of skin color or ethnic affiliation.

Of course I would be lying if I did not say that people of darker hue— the Hawaiians, Filipinos, Samoans, Fijians, Tongans, and more recent immigrants, including African Americans—have fewer connections, advantages, and privileges than do the whites, Japanese, Chinese, and Portuguese, to mention a few with obviously lighter skin color, better jobs, and more power. Nonetheless, there is considerably more diversity, mingling, and opportunity for anyone who is well trained, prepared, and willing to compete as an outsider, that is, someone who was not born and reared in the islands.

For several years I worked hard and went to school, and eventually remarried, this time to a "local" man. We had a daughter and struggled to buy a home in the country (where we could afford one), raise the children, and later send them to private high school and college.

In 1976, I began to work on an oral history project on African American women in Hawai'i, and to my surprise I discovered that a few black men and women had been in the islands since the late 1700s and early 1800s. However, due to the great amount of intermarriage and the various and erratic historical methods of categorizing black people in the islands, research was very difficult and tedious, not helped by locals who seemingly found it disturbing to learn not only of our small yet long and consistent presence, but also the institutional discrimination which discouraged our coming and staying. Unlike the process on the mainland, where persons of African descent were automatically classified as "Negro," "Colored," "Black" or "Afro-American," the census takers often labeled blacks as Portuguese, Puerto Ricans, part Hawaiian, part something else, or "other."

Even in 1995, perhaps because of our small numbers (3 percent of the population), we are still often categorized with Samoans, Tongans, and other small minority groups as "other." I also discovered that there were other African American immigrants, some as early as 1913, who were well educated and of light complexion, who wanted to forget their haunted heritage and who preferred to pass for white, thereby escaping the restrictions, handicaps, and stereotypes of being born "black" in America. Amongst these were a few outstanding women who contributed actively to the Hawaiian community in politics, art, entertainment, and business. For example, some blacks who called themselves part-Negro in the 1910 census found it easier to become part-Hawaiian in 1920.

I learned that the earliest settlers of African ancestry arrived in the islands well before the missionaries came in 1821. One man, called Black Jack or Mr. Keaka'ele'ele, was already living on Oahu when Kamehameha conquered the island in 1796. It is said he helped to build a store house for Queen Ka'ahumanu in Lahaina, and probably made his living in the maritime industry.[1]

Another individual, known as Black Jo, was a longtime resident, trader, and the sailmaster for King Kamehameha II, working with his trading vessels and acting as an adviser and interpreter for the king. He died in 1828.[2]

In 1811, an ex-slave, Anthony D. Allen, came to the island of O'ahu from New York. In 1813, he took a Hawaiian wife, had three children, and was granted six acres of land in Waikiki by a high priest, where he prospered and was much respected in the community.[3] He established a boardinghouse, a bowling alley, a "dram shop" (saloon), and the first hospital for American seamen in Pawa'a. He was also a dairyman, farmer, and blacksmith, supplying vegetables, livestock, and service to residents and ship captains. His popular boardinghouse was widely known for its excellent cuisine and entertainment. Allen is given credit for building one of the first schools in the islands and the first carriage road to Manoa Valley. He was so highly respected by Hawaiian royalty that they gave him land to hold and pass on to his descendants. That land is the present site of the Washington Intermediate School near King and Kalakaua. Allen's son was a *paniolo* (cowboy). Allen died in 1835.[4]

Other African American men were also active in early Hawaii business matters. "William the Baker" was the king's cook and sold his place in 1833. Joseph Bedford, known as Joe Dollar, had a boardinghouse from 1826 for almost twenty years. Spencer Rhodes operated a barbershop in 1838, Frederick E. Binns had his barbershop by 1845, and Charles Nicholson, a black tailor, was sewing from the 1840s until 1861. William Johnson also had a barbershop in 1863.[5]

African Americans starred in the musical world of early Honolulu. Four African Americans formed a royal brass band for Kamehameha III in 1834, and he hired America Shattuck as first master and David Curtis as second master. Another black, George W. Hyatt, organized a larger band in 1845 with Charles Johnson as band leader.[6]

One can imagine my surprise when I discovered in the archives the first available history of a black woman in Hawai'i, Betsey Stockton, who arrived in 1823 with the second company of Christian missionaries. She was an ex-slave and one of the earliest foreign women settlers in the islands.

Born in slavery in 1798 in Princeton, New Jersey, into the family of Robert Stockton, Esquire, Betsey Stockton was presented as a gift to the Stocktons' eldest daughter and her husband, Mr. Green, who was then the president of Princeton College.

Although her new master did not favor educating his servants beyond a proficient training as a domestic nurse, seamstress, and cook, his son, perceiving the thirst for knowledge and the innate intelligence of Betsey Stockton, gave her books and encouraged her to use the family library, thereby helping her in her studies. She later attended evening classes at Princeton Theological Seminary, where she proved especially brilliant in English and theology.

A friend of the family, a certain Charles Stuart, also learned of her exceptional character and that she was a devoted Christian. It was not long before Betsey Stockton expressed openly to him her great desire to be useful in a mission and her interest in going with Charles and his new bride into the foreign mission field. She was granted her freedom and accepted by the American Board of Commissioners for Foreign Missionaries. On November 20, 1822, she sailed for Honolulu on the ship *Thames* from New Haven, Connecticut. There were twenty people in this second group of missionaries to sail for the Hawaiian Islands. They arrived in Honolulu on April 27, 1823, and in Lahaina, Maui, on May 31.

Mr. Stuart's plan was to establish a mission. However, Betsey Stockton was interested in starting a school for *maka'ainana* (common people) and their wives and children. It was the first school of its kind on Maui, and probably the first of its kind in all Hawai'i, since most missionaries were occupied exclusively with the instruction of chiefs and their families.

I was pleased to learn that Miss Stockton was always seen in a turban and moved in a dignified and regal manner. She was reported to be well trusted, and her advice and opinions were often sought in many matters, even those of personal and family concern. She was intelligent, industrious, and frugal, aptly described as a devoted Christian. She took part in church services, supported the temporal interests of the church, and often procured clothes for her students as well. Besides all this, Miss Stockton performed domestic services.

Miss Stockton's stay in Hawai'i was ended after only two years because of the illness of Mr. Stuart and their subsequent return to the mainland. Nevertheless, her efforts at education and her school set a wonderful example of a new direction in education in the islands, and the school was commended for its proficiency.

After my research project on black women in Hawai'i in 1977, I wondered how the contributions of this remarkable black woman had strayed so far from the history books. Yet I must add that as recently as 1978, very little Hawaiian history was offered in the schools, and what was included was about the monarchy and *ali'i* (royalty). The time was just arriving for Ethnic Studies and oral histories.

Between 1820 and 1880, descendants of black Portuguese men from the Cape Verde Islands off the coast of West Africa arrived on whaling ships (80 percent of the whalers were black during this period). Some stayed and became residents, working as musicians, tailors, cooks, barbers, and sailors.[7]

Because of the great slavery debate in the United States, blacks were intentionally excluded from the proposed lists of immigrant groups sought in the 1850s to provide contract labor by the Kingdom of Hawaii by local missionaries and abolitionists opposed to contract labor.[8] At one point, U.S. Secretary of State James G. Blaine urged the importation of blacks and not Asians to help replenish the dwindling Hawaiian population, only to meet resistance and aversion to Negro immigrants.

Although individual African Americans were accepted into the community, mass immigration was discouraged by legal restraint as early as 1882, when sugar planters wanted to import large numbers of blacks to relieve their labor shortage. Hence there were no significant numbers of black immigrants until after Hawai'i became a territory in 1900.

In the late nineteenth century, Booker T. Washington, the famous educator from Tuskegee Institute in Alabama, came to Hawai'i to investigate the possibilities of African American plantation workers being used to supplement the growing Japanese, Chinese, Filipino, and Portuguese workers. To his surprise, he found the working conditions on the islands in many ways worse than in the South.

However, by 1901, the first group of about two hundred African American laborers was brought over by the Hawaiian Sugar Planters' Association from Louisiana and Alabama to join the other Asian plantation workers on the islands of Maui and Hawai'i. Many later returned to the South, but some were amalgamated into the local community.[9]

The Puerto Ricans who came to Hawai'i in about 1901 were in the main also of Negro, Indian, and Spanish descent, although in the census they were listed as Caucasian until 1940, probably due to the Spanish part of their heritage. In 1907, another small group of twenty-five to thirty families came to Maui, recruited from Tennessee, Mississippi, and Alabama, including the lawyer Crockett family and a Mr. Maple, a chemist. The Maple School on Maui is named for the family.

Just before and after annexation in 1898, several African Americans from the United States participated in politics and government and made the islands their home. Among them were T. McCants Stewart, an attorney, who was in the cabinet of King Kalakaua and helped in drafting the Organic Act of the territory, and on several occasions aided Hawaiians in regaining their lost *kuleanas* (property, titles, etc.). His daughter, Carlotta Lai, arrived in 1898 and graduated in 1902 from what is now Punahou School; she later became a principal at Kauai's Hanamaulu School.

I next learned of another family who distinguished themselves in the islands. In January 1901, twenty-one blacks, including six women, arrived from Tennessee to work. Among them was a lawyer, William F. Crockett, who came to Hawai'i in 1901, became a district magistrate of Wailuku, Maui, a judge, and territorial senator. His wife, Annie V. Crockett, and his mother were outstanding women, and their son became deputy county attorney of Maui.

Annie V. Crockett, also known as "Mother Crockett," distinguished herself as an outstanding teacher; and her daughter Grace in 1918 received a master's degree in education at the University of Michigan, an unusual accomplishment for a black woman in that period. Both mother and daughter were responsible for the education of many fine women and men who later became principals and leaders of Maui.

Mrs. Crockett had a fondness for plants, especially flowers, and she was in fact the creator of many of the hybrid hibiscus flowers that now enhance the beauty of the islands. I was saddened that few people knew of her contributions and thought once more, "It happens all the time."

Other black pioneers included James Oliver Mitchell, born in Koloa, Kauai, in 1893, a teacher for forty-six years on Oʻahu and Maui, principal, coach, and finally athletic director at Farrington High School; and Nolle R. Smith, a resident of Honolulu who, in the early part of this century, was an engineer, a fiscal expert in Haiti, Ecuador, and Puerto Rico, and a member of the territorial House of Representatives. The family also acquired a considerable amount of land.

Eva B. Jones Smith, known as Eva Cunningham, was the first woman to have a radio show in Hawaiʻi and her piano school was "the place to go" before 1920.

It was some years later, after I had had my second child, that I renewed my research and read about Alice Ball, a Negro chemist at the University of Hawaiʻi, who in 1915 started research on a leprosy serum that was later used at the leprosy colony at Kalaupapa, on the island of Molokaʻi.

I wondered why there were so few black residents in Hawaiʻi for so many years, and I discovered some amazing facts. It seems that although individual blacks were readily accepted and assimilated into the community, mass immigration was discouraged as early as 1882, when the Honorable Luther Alolo introduced in the legislative assembly a resolution that efforts to repopulate the islands with Negroes be discouraged (the Hawaiians had been largely decimated by diseases). In 1913, there were strenuous efforts to keep the U.S. Army's 25th Negro Infantry Regiment from being stationed in Hawaiʻi. Yet they did come, made quite a favorable impression, and again, some stayed on to marry, have families, and create more daughters and sons, most of whose descendants were subsequently also classified as "part" or "other." These people gradually faded into the local community, most never learning African American history or culture, many not even knowing that they had a rich black heritage.

During World War II, several thousand black men and women came to Hawaiʻi as soldiers and civilian defense workers. In this period, there was reportedly much friction between the races, perhaps due to the seeds of prejudice planted previously by those missionaries and planters who came or returned from the mainland, as well as by the military population itself. To balance flaring tempers and incidents, the military largely maintained segregated housing during the 1940s, called "Little Americas" for its personnel.

At Hickham Air Force Base, black women were housed separately until a petition was filed. During this time, their barracks were neglected, habits of visitors and guards became lax, and finally two black women were attacked by unauthorized visitors. An investigation followed, and eventually segregated housing was abolished.

The Navy was also flagrant in its discriminatory treatment toward those of African descent, even in the islands. In an interview, Clarissa Wildy said she joined her military husband in the islands, only after a long and inexplicable delay in California, even though white women and their families were constantly being sent on to Hawai'i to join their husbands. Finally, after as much as months of waiting in some cases, the black women registered a complaint with an admiral, who assumed no responsibility for the delay. However, a few days later, a freighter with thirty black women aboard set sail for Honolulu. Had they in fact been waiting to have enough black women from around the country so that they could ride together in segregated accommodations across the Pacific? The structural patterns of racism and oppression seemed to spread over land and sea, but I was philosophic the more I learned, and again noted, "It happens all the time."

Like many others who have chosen to settle in the islands, Wildy commented that after the initial adjustment in segregated housing (two streets on base where only blacks were permitted to live), and after the war when many returned to the mainland, she had no particular problems, and grew to love her home in a multiethnic, multicultural environment.

Through the years, a few blacks have been active in public life and politics. Helene Hale arrived with her husband, both educators, in 1947 to escape the racial discrimination on the mainland and to raise her family in a place with less discrimination. In 1954, she was elected head of the board of supervisors for West Hawai'i, and in 1962, she astonished everyone by being elected Democratic county chairperson, the executive officer of the island of Hawai'i, a position comparable to mayor now. Thus, Mrs. Hale became the first woman "mayor" in island history.

Meanwhile, I struggled with my part-time job at the University of Hawai'i and became active in civil and human rights issues, gender issues, and race relations. For a while I worked with and taught blacks in the military, became involved with the literary arts council, coordinated events featuring African American scholars and artists, and began to use public speaking and poetry as a forum for black history and culture. The longer I lived in the islands, the more I realized how isolated the local inhabitants were from a spectrum of African American reality. The stereotypes persisted, although the number of African Americans not affiliated with the military began to increase with each passing year.

In addition to the NAACP, there were other social groups: the Wai Wai Nui, the Eastern Stars, several sororities and fraternities, an African American Association, and most recently an African American Chamber of Commerce. Moreover, there are two black newspapers, several black businesses, a Black Pages publication, several large annual social events including the Martin Luther King, Jr., dinner dance at the Hyatt, which has featured such outstanding speakers as Martin Luther King III and the Reverend Louis T. Farrakhan.

There are also more black tourists. However, rarely are blacks included in the tourist industry, which caters to Caucasians from the mainland and Japanese from Japan—both groups that often hold negative stereotypes about African Americans.

Many African American women would agree that there is a sense of alienation here in the islands, especially for the new arrival. There is no geographic community, although African Americans often settle in centers near the numerous military installations around the islands. Some have observed that the cultural sensitivity, traditions, music, and events so easily found in communities on the mainland are lacking here. But also significantly lacking is the crisis of violence, poverty, and the deterioration of our communities. There is an optimism, especially among those with creative ideas or those who are well prepared in their fields, as doors sometimes open more readily than one would find on the mainland. In other scenarios however, the many local minorities—Filipinos, Hawaiians, Pacific Islanders, Chinese, Japanese, and even Caucasians—are the ones who are able to benefit from economic opportunities for "underrepresented" groups, sometimes at the expense of African Americans, who are a less visible, more highly suspect minority.

So, if this be paradise, a place of racial and ethnic harmony, a haven for interracial couples, it is also a place where prejudice is overlooked, discrimination is subtle, and corporate ceilings are clear as glass. Overt discrimination is rare, dehumanization is not uncommon; yet the illusive "it" of marginalization persists—it happens all the time, but less here than in many other places.

■ ■ ■

NOTES

1. Marc Scruggs, "Black Friend of Hawaii Missionaries," *Honolulu Star Bulletin*, January 12, 1987, p. A10.
2. Ibid.
3. See the *Honolulu Advertiser* (July 1991), p. B1.
4. Scruggs, "Black Friend," p. A10.
5. R. A. Greer, "Blacks in Old Hawaii," *Honolulu* (November 1966).
6. Ibid.
7. Romanzo Adams, "Census Notes of the Negroes in Hawaii Prior to the War," *Social Process* (1945), p. 214.
8. Eleanoz Nordyke, "Blacks in Hawai'i: A Demographic and Historical Perspective," *Hawaiian Journal of History* 22 (1988), p. 244.
9. Figures from the *Hawaiian Annual* (1902), p. 164.

Catching the Rush-Hour Train—Sketches of Life in Japan

■ ■ ■

YURI KAGEYAMA

For years, for generations, young women in Japan have been groped, fondled, and violated by dirty old, and not so old, men who hide in the crowded anonymity of rush-hour commuter trains.

Known as *chikan*—literally translating to "foolish man"—these molesters are facts of Japanese life as unquestioned as deep bows, cram schools, and go-between mediated marriages.

To say these men are tolerated and forgiven would be an overstatement. They are definitely not respected. Often newspapers carry one-column snippets on corporate executives nabbed in an undercover operation, whereby the unsuspecting, high-ranking *chikan* is arrested, let's say, after looking up the skirt of a female officer standing before his train seat.

Such stories are sneered at. But I have yet to meet a real person who has professed to be a *chikan*—"real" meaning a person I know, a cousin, a coworker, some man with a real name and face. As with most Japanese women who take the trains, my meetings with the nameless, faceless ones have been numerous.

My first encounter came in fifth grade. I was standing by the train door—an area I later found out was favored by *chikan* because of the dense crowds and off-and-on movements that disguised their activities— and I still remember he was an acne-marked teenager, easily identifiable by his black militaristic high school uniform. His hands ticklishly went up and down my arms, as though chivalrously helping me stand up to the rocks and starts of the rumbling train.

When I got to school, I dashed to the restroom and washed my arms off with soap and water.

That was a mild case. In years to come, there were men who waited in line on the platform, jumped on with you, and frenziedly massaged your breasts from behind. Then there were those whose fingers inched up the skin of your leg, searching for your panties.

My American friends are aghast when they learn that this is an everyday occurrence in Japan. Even though there probably is an ironic parallel in how most of my Japanese friends are aghast at the everydayness of America's violent crime, how a child at an age when he'd be suffo- cating under the pamperings of an overprotective mother in Japan would be firing a handgun at another child in this country.

"If it happened to me or my daughter, I just wouldn't let it happen again," one American woman said of the *chikan* phenomenon. Asked what she'd do, she replied with conviction, "I don't know. But I'd do something."

That's quite a contrast from the advice given by my mother, who had her share of *chikan* growing up, who said to be careful because they may stalk you and really hurt you, should you fight back and embarrass them in public. One good tactic, according to her, was to place your schoolbag strategically between his menacing hands and your privates. Sometimes, that didn't work because there'd be more than one of them in a crowd, attacking from both sides, so to speak. One of my mother's friends, how- ever, had the gall to take the offending hand, raise it above the heads, and pronounce, "Whose hand is this?"

That *chikan* ride safe and sound on the super-efficient trains of Tokyo and Japan's other vibrant modern cities is, to me, a perverse but clear example of the two-faced nature of Japanese society. The academics refer to it as the *omote* and *ura,* or the "seen" and "unseen" duplicity that char- acterizes Japanese culture. The art of tea ceremony has the *omote* and *ura* styles, the subdued *ura* being the far more popular school, even among housewives feigning culture the same way their American counterparts flock to aerobics classes.

In Japan, nothing is what it seems. No one says what he (or she) really means. In fact, he may say the exact opposite of what he means. And the listener is supposed to know. Not read between the lines. Just know.

I am not a member of the ethnic minority groups in Japan that have suffered generations of quite blatant oppression and discrimination. And many mainstream Japanese—and remember, unlike America, almost everyone in Japan claims to be mainstream, and middle class—would say the picture I am depicting of Japan is unduly harsh and askew. But perhaps it is my past persistent encounters with *chikan* that give me the "in" so far as seeing the country for what it is: the other face, or the faceless face, of Japan.

During the past decade, Japan was increasingly viewed as an economic rival to the United States, with literate, dedicated, antlike workers, delivering right-on-time productivity under high-tech innovations. But Japan, in its darkest *ura* niches, is a society that remains ruthlessly closed to the outside.

Women—like foreigners, low-income classes, the handicapped, homosexuals, and those without the right fashion items for the season—are classified as outsiders.

While growing up on both sides of the Pacific, I was an outsider to mainstream America because of my skin color and an outsider to mainstream Japan because of my upbringing. In Japan, being fluent in English was not seen as an asset but as an aberration. Instead, my Japaneseness was constantly questioned through quizzes about my dubious mastery of the millions of characters that make up the mazelike language.

Even when I got the strokes right, that wasn't enough. My brushstrokes—and there are brushstrokes even when one writes in pencil or a ballpoint pen—weren't right. They were dead giveaways of an illiterate low-class mind, widely referred to in jest as the laid-down-nails style of calligraphy.

"People just think you're a foreigner," my best-meaning Japanese friends would say. They were trying to explain, not be critical.

Having been subjected to this, *chikan* and all, I suffered an identity crisis. But, fortunately, I was a child of the sixties, when identity crises were fairly fashionable. After a while, I gave up trying to make sense of the values behind what turns out to be a *chikan*-filled society, in the same way minority individuals in America must somewhere along the way let ourselves off the hook as far as laying the blame for racism: Whoever's fault it is, it's not ours.

Instead, I worked out a fairly effective way of dealing with Japanese—

making them part of the landscape. It's a trick of the eye that negates the individualism of the people with whom you interact, making them a big blur of faceless faces. The Japanese have an expression for it: "treating people as a pumpkin patch," generally used to comfort those who get stage fright before a speech or a performance. And it's likely the way the West has viewed Japanese all along.

Walking down the streets, I no longer saw the snickering faces or the incriminating stares that combined horrifying hatred with a mysterious envy. Japanese blended in with the signs for mom-and-pop stores written in snakelike kanji characters, the cherry trees blowing pale pink blossoms into a fragrant wind, the glowing festival lanterns bobbing to taiko drum beats. Japanese became props in a Noh theater, sacred because they had a function. They fit into the landscape, part of its beauty but robbed of their ominousness.

But making Japanese part of the landscape is an acquired skill. Naturally, newcomers tend to start out by trying to relate to Japanese as individuals. Such naivete, although human, can be risky. Allowing them to exist outside the landscape, letting their motives affect true feelings, lending validity to their feudal values can be dangerous.

Quickly, Japanese became part of the landscape. And, as I grew older, even the *chikan* stopped. Like most cowards, they prey on the young.

But moving back to Tokyo in the 1980s with a new American family brought it all back. We lived in Tokyo for eight years. It was the first visit to Japan for my Japanese American husband, as well as for my San Francisco–born son. To put it bluntly, the experience drove my husband crazy.

In Japanese eyes, he was the ultimate despicable Outsider. He did not have the white skin that puts some foreigners above others, due to an Occupation mentality that lingers on from World War II. He spoke no Japanese. A house husband, while I worked full time, he was a category that did not exist in the Japanese lexicon. He was a loser, extremely strange, possibly crazy, probably dangerous.

The treatment extended to the pettiest details. He didn't like being the only male in a supermarket, where housewives studied his purchases to calculate our salary. Most importantly, for him, Japanese had not yet become part of the landscape.

Logically enough, it was commuter trains that became a nightmare for my son. His pageboy haircut and the navy blue uniform blazer of an international school made him already different at age six. He was taunted daily by Japanese schoolchildren. For him, too, Japanese had not become part of the landscape.

It is difficult to describe how hemmed in I began to feel. It was akin to witnessing crawling, squirming creatures suddenly pop out of a canvas, no longer a hazy dull landscape. The Japanese had again become figures to be dealt with—like *chikan,* out to do me in.

I began to notice the stares on the train. I understood too well why our American neighbor, a longtime Japan resident, refused to talk to us on the buses or trains. It wasn't animosity. It was simple fear of those perked-up ears around us, listening in on every alien word.

Perhaps my depiction of Japan will confuse most Americans, especially those who have lived quite pleasant adult lives in Japan. They may find it hard to believe that Japan is a nation crawling with *chikan.* They may find it harder to believe that Japan is also crawling with police—the other side of the same coin.

The police-state aspect comes in many forms. Housewives' clubs want burnable and non-burnable garbage separated and disposed at specific spots on certain days. And pity the poor offender. Japanese society is so regulated—down to the color of socks and underwear (no kidding) one is allowed to wear in public schools—that even the most conservative elements of America offer no comparison. Neighborhood watches are a feudal tradition. Census counters are meticulous. The PTA and other volunteer vigilantism is rampant. Japanese hire private detectives to run background checks on potential marital mates to root out foreigners, or members of a former feudal underclass whose existence is supposed to be unconstitutional, as well as more mundane undesirables.

It is often said that ostracism is the number one punishment used in Japanese society. The argument given for this is that in a farming society, being shut out from the help of other families during harvest and planting was lethal. Whatever the historical reasons, it is fact that Japanese still live in mortal fear of being excluded. That helps to control behavior and keep people in their place—as the Japanese saying goes, "The nail that sticks out gets hammered in." And as the writer Osamu Dazai, an outcast of sorts before he killed himself, said, "Society is individuals."

From kindergarten to supermarkets to corporate offices, Japanese people spend a great deal of their energies studying the people around them, second-guessing what people are thinking about them, and doing what they think is expected of them. It is a claustrophobic society that operates on fear. "Conformist" is too soft a term to describe it.

Promotions in corporations depend on which faction, or *habatsu,* one belongs to—membership of which is determined often by the university one graduates from. Japanese politicians also belong to *habatsu. Habatsu* politics—be it among farmers, housewives, gangsters, or Parliament members—underlies a society of emotion and personal loyalties, rather than one ruled by competence, logic, and democracy.

Foreigners, or non-Japanese, of whatever race, color, creed, or national origin, are called *gaijin*—meaning "outside people," although the term is frequently followed by the honorific "san." With or without the "san," it is used freely, without qualms.

Even if they become Japanese citizens, *gaijin* cannot ever truly become Japanese. This is because being Japanese is defined by what the Japanese like to call "blood," rather than status or rights. Citizenship is not a birthright in Japan, as it is in the United States. Acquiring Japanese citizenship, nevertheless, is a complicated, soul-wrenching procedure, requiring proofs of Japaneseness that include taking on Japanese names, shunning one's cultural heritage; in short, assimilating.

The largest ethnic minority in Japan are the Koreans—the descendants of those who were brought into Japan during the years of militaristic expansion to work as cheap, slavelike labor in mines and factories. Many Koreans, despite their fluent Japanese and excellent scholarly records, cannot get jobs at Japan's top corporations. Many pass as Japanese, using Japanese names, enduring a life of pain and cruel loss, so fundamental is the denial.

Seiji Yoshida is an elderly, soft-spoken man who has broken the taboos in acknowledging his role in the systematic kidnapping of Korean women as sex slaves for Japanese soldiers during World War II. For this, his life has been threatened repeatedly by the ultra-right wing, who still wield considerable economic and political power in Japan.

It was only a few years ago that the Japanese government finally admitted it was involved in the sex-slaves venture, known as *ianfu* or "comfort women," in double-speak euphemism. Despite a formal apology, the government has not agreed to any redress for the women victims.

Yoshida still can't erase from his mind the sobs of children running after the truck that carried off the women—for it was mothers, not just virginal maidens, that the Japanese took. And his sense of the Japanese status quo today remains grim.

"Just imagine, they're all like the Klan wearing those sheets," he said quietly.

The Koreans are just one group that has suffered under the closed Japanese system. Newcomers include Iranians and Filipinos—welcomed, although not openly, during the boom of the eighties as cheap labor. With the economic downturn of the late eighties and early nineties, the crackdown began. The Iranians were fenced out of public parks that had grown to be their gathering place. They are shackled and deported.

Shamelessly, the Japanese police say crime has increased because of the Iranian involvement in drug deals and knife-stabbing brawls. Equally shamelessly, regular Japanese say the flocks of Iranians give them the creeps. American musicians and Israeli jewelry vendors also congregate in the parks. They say the Japanese look upon them as freakish minstrel shows. Yet, searching for the upswinging yen, the *gaijin* keep coming.

Japan's dream of postwar affluence has always been reserved for the thoroughbred Japanese. It is a system that has proven flexible enough to keep abreast of change. The streets are safe. Unemployment is virtually a non-problem.

But it is doubtful whether the Filipino bar girls—today's equivalent of the sex slaves—who strip-dance for Japanese out-of-the-closet *chikan,* will ever share in that dream. The women are brought in by underworld pimps who dominate the hostess bars, restaurants, and "soaplands"— establishments where men, many of them *gaijin,* are given baths for a fee by naked women.

The essential character of Japan emerges most beautifully in its traditional arts, such as Kabuki theater. Kabuki is rigidly stylized, extremely closed, and defiantly sexist. One must be born into one of several families even to become a Kabuki actor. Men play all the feminine roles, in a transvestite splendor that puts Western versions to shame.

The closed, sexist, stylized universe works because that's something the Japanese do well. Those traits are so inherent to the foundations of their society that no amount of modernization would ever change it.

I now live in Detroit—not exactly a city that highlights the successes of America's domestic policies. At Eight Mile Road, the line that divides the inner city from the suburbs, one crosses a border so deep and inherent to America that time has yet to change it. At that line, smooth highways become studded with potholes. Shopping malls and trimmed lawns give way to shattered homes that look as though they've been blasted in Sarajevo.

But, here in Motown, we drive to work, there being no commuter trains, only buses that barely remember their schedules. So here, at least, we are safe from those hands.

Now That the Iron Curtain Is Gone, Where Do We Build the Fences?

■ ■ ■

GUNDARS STRADS

Ethnicity and race—concepts currently being muddled together and mis-represented in the politically induced debate over multiculturalism—have become fodder for political cannons in the West, just as they have long been in the former Soviet Union. Bureaucrats and businessmen on both sides of the former Iron Curtain have rediscovered prejudice as a tool not only for preserving existing power structures, but as a means in the quest for more power. The war is no longer between the two superpowers, it is now internecine—it is in countries that used to be all the same shade of pink in the old maps of Eastern Europe and it is in the streets of America as well as its hallowed halls of government. International terrorists have given way to the rage of next-door neighbors, and the target enemy is anyone who doesn't share your culture or who expects you to share with other cultures. There is a desperate search going on for new adversaries to replace the old monoliths. In the old Cold War days, all James Bond had to do was find the people with accents to know who the bad guys were. Both sides have now expanded on that technique and diversified the opponents. The enemy is now among us—and from folk songs to rap music, language helps define the opposition. In Eastern Europe and in

America, "race" and "ethnicity" have replaced ideology as the new fighting words.

Both the former Soviet Union (with its constellation of satellites, "republics," and bloc countries) and the United States (with its island territories, reservations, and ghettoes) have had their respective versions of the melting pot. East of the Iron Curtain, there were "Russification" policies, the supremacy of Soviet culture, and political oppression from central government. In the United States, there was acculturation, the supremacy of mainstream white American culture, and political oppression from central government. In the USSR, indigenous culture was considered subversive and treasonous—local religion and language were suppressed. In America, loyalty to a dissimilar culture and language is still considered as making use of contraband, a disruptive and disorderly substance that threatens the Union. As the American-born son of Eastern European refugees, I have seen this country's welcome wagon for immigrants become increasingly more selective, racially as well as culturally. It is not just "illegal" immigrants who raise mistrust and scorn. And now that the Iron Curtain is down, even otherwise "white" Europeans are no longer looked upon so favorably—no longer the benign victims they were right after World War II. So many Americans, long separated from their own cultural histories, have been amazed to discover that the homogenous "all-white" Europe never existed—even barring the prominent political conflicts of the past century. And despite the aspirations for a common market and a common currency, despite reunifications and liberations, the now-expanded European "community" is perhaps more divided than ever—with political gains being substituted for social losses. Just as America—in the wake of the seemingly cathartic advances in civil rights over the past decades—is convulsing with racial division and cultural class conflicts, so too has Eastern Europe—with its newfound freedom and the resurgence of distinct identities—taken the knife away from the political oppressors and put it up against its own throat.

The "liberation" of the Soviet bloc has generated vicious outbreaks of persecution and genocide based not on geography and turf wars but on cultural identification. While the gunfire has been most prominent in Bosnia, Chechnya, and Armenia/Azerbaijan, the potential for ethnic conflict is pandemic. Ethnic "difference" has again become synonymous with "a threat to security," just as it had been for the once-unifying oppressor of the Soviet dynasty. Old habits are hard to unlearn. In a grand reverse imitation, America is also laying blame on race and ethnicity as the cause of all its social ills, with poor minorities the economic scapegoats. Since most Eastern Europeans have lived their entire lives under official policies of cultural disapproval, it is regrettably not surprising that victimization would so readily turn to self-destruction in the wake of political decentralization. Eastern Europe is the child abuse victim thrust into adulthood, and because it has never experienced anything else and knows no other way to live, the cycle of abuse is witnessing a new generation of perpetrators. As appalled as many Americans get when they watch reports from Bosnia to Chechnya on TV news, and when they watch people who are neighbors—who seemingly look, talk, and dress alike—go about killing each other over some vague culturally motivated political incentive, they forget how thoroughly subscribed Americans are to the same notions. Racial and cultural differences may be more visually pronounced in the United States, but to people in Eastern Europe they are no more prominent than the prejudices they partake of.

In the cultural fallout of the Cold War, a new enemy seems to be necessary to make us feel secure and validated in our selfhood—"I'm good because they're bad." And that enemy is now the specifics of cultural diversity rather than the vagaries of political distinctions. The battles are waged by neighborhoods rather than along dotted lines on a map. Both the former Soviet Union and the United States are more concerned with civil unrest (or its euphemism, "domestic strife") than with external threats. During the Cold War, the generals were the same on both sides; you could tell the difference only by their uniforms or by the direction they were facing. As the old joke went: "The difference between capitalism and communism is that under capitalism man exploits his fellow man, whereas under communism it's the other way around."

As the entire world becomes more multicultural (or "cosmopolitan," to use an earlier and less discredited term), it is also desperately seeking new ways to build fences. The more blacks, Hispanics, and Asians merge into the American mainstream, the more we see reciprocal distrust and insidious racism. The more the countries of Eastern Europe come out from the yoke of oppression, the more they are at each other's throats. Wars of political boundaries have now become wars of social boundaries, on both sides of the torn-down curtain. As the world becomes more "global," recognizing and accepting the reality of a modern multicultural society seems to be the hardest thing, and yet the only solution. But the roots of fear and resistance to change run deep.

One of the things my family first noticed about America was its cultural diversity. Europe was also quite multicultural, but the distinctions between cultures and ethnicities were more gradual, just as the political borders were vague, imprecise, and constantly changing. In the United

States, there weren't these subtle differences, there were divisions. The 1950s America my family emigrated to was big on fences and neighborhoods. Segregation was still an assumption, taken for granted as a necessary way of life. Especially in California, the privilege of the new frontier allowed for the building of fences before the building of neighborhoods. There was plenty of space to keep cultures separated, aided and abetted by a growing suburban sprawl. And if the neighborhood began to change and integrate (i.e., become more multicultural), those who felt threatened could almost always take flight to some newly sprouted subdivision with a more uniform cultural disposition. "There goes the neighborhood," was a literal as well as figurative saying. In an ironic reversal of this catch phrase, one of the main reasons my family left their home in Latvia was that their neighbors were disappearing in the middle of the night—but not by choice. Siberia (or some mass grave) was the new neighborhood for those ethnically and politically suspect. Moving into the neighborhood were freshly imported Soviet citizens, meant to dilute the local population under Stalin's Russification policies. It was curious for Eastern Europe's political refugees to come to America and now see Americans calling themselves refugees from their "old neighborhoods" or "urban refugees." Being "forced" out seemed to be a matter of cultural perspective, and ethnicity appeared to be blamed as much as guns and politicians were.

In America, my family was taught early on that where you lived helped determine how acceptable you were. You could even get away with being poor, so long as you did it in the right neighborhood. Furthermore, we learned that becoming a good American usually happened by default; you were constantly, surreptitiously, and insidiously reminded of who not to be like. Our being "ethnic" was exotic and interesting to a point, but even with white European ethnicity there was such a thing as "too much." Too much culture was akin to being from a different race. Flavoring, yes; essence, no. Too much essence meant you were still an outsider. The fact that I talked a different language to my family and to my fellow Latvian Americans was intriguing, but ultimately threatening (an experience shared by most bilingual American families). As a child, I was urged to offer up an "American" nickname for myself so that I would not only be more pronounceable but more a part of the team (and hence more acceptable). Where you were from had its charm, but what was now important was fitting in—swimming in the melting pot. Belonging necessitated sacrifice.

The Europe my parents left behind was crowded with cultures. After centuries of redrawing the maps, Europe realized that it was like one of those large families in which, when it gets together for a holiday dinner, fistfights break out. And Eastern Europe—the outcast prodigal of Western civilization—felt it had no hope of ever truly being invited to rejoin the family, so it tried to synthesize on its own family. The grand experiment of Soviet society behind the Iron Curtain was to outdo Europe by stifling the multiplicity-of-cultures problem. While the rest of Europe continued to fight among themselves, the Soviet Union felt it would triumph by exerting control, complete and total, over its own divergence. The Russification policy (which hit my family's homeland of Latvia disproportionately hard) was designed to smother the complexity of cultural diversity so that only one harmonious—and thus politically quiescent—society remained. Under Russification, indigenous populations were displaced, relocated, or otherwise "disposed of," to be replaced by culturally approved Soviet citizens—usually, Russian immigrants. (This is something the United States had also done to its indigenous population. "Russification" simply translates as a Soviet version of "manifest destiny.") In Riga, the capital and largest city in the country, the Latvian population had been shrunk to less than 40 percent.

The theory stipulates that an ethnic minority can't rebel effectively, and political stability is thus more enforceable. However, what finally brought about revolution and liberation all across the former empire that had so prided itself on the concept of "the Revolution" were multicultural coalitions, which sought independence on nationalist, economic, and geographical criteria. Amazingly, the irreconcilable conglomeration of ethnicities finally united against oppression. In Latvia, for example, there would have been no independence without support from the non-native population—those very Russians imported precisely for the opposite purpose. Similarly, "emancipation" and civil rights in the United States would not have become political realities without the support of those who came from the ranks of the oppressors. But such alliances can prove to be quite transitory. After only a few years of independence, Latvia—along with most other newly independent countries—is now experiencing ethnic divisiveness over how to divvy up the freedom pie. Old guard Communists in Moscow are wagging their fingers in admonishment, saying, "See what happens. Give them their freedom and they fight among themselves!" Strangely enough, these are the same exhortations offered by opponents of multicultural concerns and civil rights in this country.

When I first came to grips with the term "multicultural" in the seventies, it was as an adjective. Something that described. Not a philosophy, an alternative lifestyle, or an ideology. Not a political movement or counterculture or agenda. Simply a description—and an obvious but profound realization—of the social reality in this country. A multicultural America was not a matter of choice, preference, or aspiration. It is just something that American society was, like it or not. Though many (or most) did not embrace the idea, they could not logically deny it.

The primary fallacy of the so-called debate over multiculturalism is that there is no such a thing as "culturalism" for it to be in opposition to. It is not a political organization or a conspiracy. The "multiculture" is not an attack on the "monoculture"; rather, it is the monoculture that feels the need to be defensive and attempt to start a fight. It's the same as trying to say that the many religions of the world are an attack on the one religion—yet there have been countless wars throughout history based precisely on such a naive presupposition. Religious intolerance functions the same way as cultural intolerance; in fact, it is an extension of it. That's why the Soviet Union put religion on the same hit list as ethnic identity. Solving the power and control problem by eliminating religion failed miserably (people were easier to dispose of than beliefs). My grandmother told me that even long after the Russian Revolution, the underground churches were filled with adherents nevertheless willing to risk it all to be there—and among the worshipers were soldiers in uniform and government bureaucrats. In Latvia, during Soviet times, the churches were converted into concert halls. In the center of Riga, the Russian Orthodox Cathedral—otherwise emblematic of the officially dominant culture— had been transformed into a planetarium, the ceilings housed inside the onion domes covered up so that they could become a projection screen for official, scientific versions of the heavens. But all the different churches survived, and so did all the diverse cultures. Multiculturalism was politically inevitable, and an undeniable reality.

While the United States was founded with the explicit mission of providing religious freedom, the God in whom "we trust" is not allowed to have too many faces. It has long been the government's mission to protect against religious persecution, yet it remains curious to note how many religious organizations have recently felt the need to arm themselves (including the self-professed "mainstream" religious right). A quick Freedom of Information look at FBI files shows extensive policing of Jews and Muslims, followers of Voodoo and of Buddhism. And for those who think religion was never banned in this country, start by asking a Sioux ghost dancer. (Interestingly, my English-language thesaurus places "Voodoo" and "Ghost Dance" under "Sorcery," and not "Religion.")

Though cultural survival in Eastern Europe has been a constant struggle, in the United States it faces a more subtly destructive force. Acculturation can be much more effective than overt oppression. Unless there are strong religious or racial antecedents, a progressive number in the second generation of immigrants and those on down succumb to acculturation (from which the melting pot mythology), often despite strong parental and social support systems. This is an especially prevalent phenomenon among small cultures—such as the Latvians'—that get lost in the broad expanse of the United States and become geographically diffused and absorbed. In areas and cities where there are actually neighborhoods full of Latvians, the cultural survival rate is much higher. There are Latvian cultural centers, annual culture festivals, and even Latvian schools and credit unions, but the drop-off rate is quite high. Although I was raised in a Latvian society that needed to commute to get together, we were instilled with the mission that cultural survival was up to us, given its official repression back in Latvia. It imbued strong emotions and loyalty in many, but when I try to count up those fellow Latvians I knew as a child and those who remain "active and practicing" Latvians now, it seems almost as if they had been surreptitiously deported to Siberia.

When I visited Latvia, people were amazed at how well I spoke Latvian and that I knew about my people's history and culture. Their assumption about émigrés is that "you lose it over there." I told them that the phenomenon of "losing it" is not just true for Latvian immigrants, but that many of the people who have been living in America for centuries are still struggling not only with what they lost culturally, but what was taken from them. Acceptance in America requires living up to the expectation of "losing it"—the sacrifice of acculturation that must be made to gain entry to the club. America cherishes the unusual, but then insists on putting it in museums, on stages, or on television—where it's controllable. America has everything from "pop culture" to "high culture," but it skulks furtively away from anything that might approach a "shared culture" that respects all the divergence.

Language is perhaps the prime denotation of culture. It not only gives us identity but also signifies the "other," who is with us and who is against us; it reveals economic status; and it identifies the ruling culture. In Soviet times, if you wanted to get ahead, you learned how to speak well in Russian. Insisting on talking Latvian—at school, work, or a grocery store—was akin to subversion, insurrection, and cultural disobedience. "It may be your language and your culture, but take it home—it's not appropriate here." Just like in the United States, where foreign languages and accents are something to be "cured" (so that night school "American Accent" classes are offered as "therapy" for recent immigrants). In Soviet Latvia, how you spelled and pronounced your name would cost you at a job interview. In the United States, similar discrimination still goes on (unless you can afford a good lawyer). "If you want to get ahead, learn to talk proper white American." In my office, I have often joked with one of my coworkers about the "white voice" she puts on for formal business calls; family and friends get an altogether different language and intonation. If you simply listen, you can hear the effects of the cultural hierarchy.

Most Americans know only one language, and most of the rest who do learn another learn only enough to meet college entrance requirements or travel needs. Everybody in California knows ten words in Spanish, all learned from Speedy Gonzalez and Taco Bell. The concept of "bilingualism"—the simple fact of its existence—is considered threatening. The English Only movement is not an educational effort; rather, it's one based on exclusionary tactics. The call for English as an official language does not seek to stimulate widespread volunteerism in teaching English to American citizens; rather, it is meant simply to discriminate. My father learned six languages before he came to America, but English was not one of them. He learned English as well, but that did not cleanse him of his accent or his difference. On hearing his accent, people still talked slowly and loudly to him. The impression I got as a child was that education and multilingualism don't count; what matters is that if you're different, you're stupid. In English, another definition for "discrimination" is "having high culture and distinction."

In Soviet times, Russian was the official language in Latvia. Most Westerners I talk to see that as patently unfair and oppressive. (Then, if I bring up the subject of Native Americans or Spanish-speaking Americans, I get a quite different and quite qualified response.) Now that Latvia is free, the official language is Latvian. Which seems logical. Unless you're a Russian living in Latvia. Then you hear the same complaints about reverse discrimination and arguments against affirmative action that you hear in this country. The former oppressors protesting linguistic oppression—and the irony escapes everyone. The Latvian Language Law mandates only that inhabitants be conversationally proficient in Latvian—a law with as much bite in it as Speedy Gonzales. Most of the cops in Latvia are Russians; they have been given two years to learn Latvian. (How many cops in L.A. speak Spanish, or are even able to communicate with the average black teen?) Most Russians in Latvia never bothered to condescend to learn the language, even after generations of residence in a Soviet state still referred to in part as Latvia (the LSSR). Most Californians can't properly pronounce all the Spanish place names, usually mispronouncing the name of the very city in which they live. Although the schools in Latvia now operate in Latvian rather than Russian, "flexibility" remains a necessity. At best, ethnic Latvians make up only 52 percent of the population, and some schools are 95 percent ethnic Russians. Furthermore, schools in these more Russified areas have a shortage of teachers who can teach Latvian, so the classes continue to be held in Russian. Even in a democratic society, cultural sovereignty will supersede the native language. (So why is Spanish taught as a *foreign* language in the schools in L.A.?)

One of the first things I learned when I visited Latvia was "How to Spot the Russians." I thought at first that identifying the oppressors/ invaders would be difficult since everybody looks like an Eastern European white person—the old "they all look alike" syndrome. But after a while, I got surprisingly good at it. While touring about the countryside with my Latvian hosts, it was sometimes necessary to inquire for directions. Picking out a random person on the street who would respond in Latvian turned out to be not such a complex endeavor. It was as simple as detecting an attitude, an arrogance, a subtle emotive response to a question asked in the native language. People who responded in your language, in your dialect, were much more helpful and sympathetic. Just like in America: if you want directions, you can usually tell who you should ask. What disturbed me most about my newfound ability to sniff out the non-Latvians, however, was that it was the same skill used in Soviet times to discriminate against Latvians. I could now avoid giving my tourist dollar to someone who once used to deprive Latvians of their money, rights, or fair shake in life. Sweet retribution. I could taste the gratification of reverse oppression. These arrogant Russians were like out-of-work rednecks and they deserved what they got. But if I looked closer, I could also see a seething tide of resentment, just like what you hear when you listen to an interview with a white supremacist on CNN.

As a Latvian, affirmative action programs made a lot of sense to me. Mere recompense was the logical, rational, and equitable response to the need for retribution. In response to the extreme effects of the Russification policies, Latvia has been more stringent and restrictive than most about granting citizenship (and the rights and benefits thereto accruing) to non-Latvian residents. There is an annual quota. The cry and hue has been such that even the U.S. president (on a historic first presidential visit to Latvia last year) brought the house down to a pin-drop silence when he suggested that more ethnic Russians be given citizenship privileges (a political nod to the larger and more strategically significant Russian Republic, which does not want these expatriates crowding up the over-stuffed streets of Moscow any more than the Latvians want them). "Quotas" is now a dirty word on both sides of the former Iron Curtain.

As are "civil rights," "compensation," and "retribution." A solution may have to give way to paradox. The trick is not to become the oppressor yourself. Things were much more "black and white" during communism. I got this uneasy feeling of conflict in the pit of my stomach when I began to feel sympathy for some of the evil invaders/oppressors who had stolen my people's homeland and would like to do so again. On top of that, I had to remind myself that I have Russian blood in my veins as well. It's hard when you lose the grip on the definition of your "enemy." Growing up in Berkeley, I learned that identifying the invaders/oppressors in the United States was simply a matter of finding white males—and then excluding the empathetic ones (like me).

In Soviet times, there were restaurants that Latvians could not go to, clubs and ballrooms where they were not admitted, hotels and resorts they could not hope to stay at. Very much like the "Whites Only" signs in this country, or the "No Indians Allowed" signs you can still find outside bars in North Dakota. Most Latvians still cannot afford to go to certain restaurants or stores. However, the class distinctions that favored invaders and oppressors over indigenous people persist. At one of Riga's most expensive restaurants, I treated one of my hosts to a very nice dinner. With wine, it only cost me about twenty-five bucks (but that's half a month's average wage for a Latvian). The restaurant, named "Ancient Riga," has three rooms decorated in the traditional folk patterns and designs of Latvia's three regions, with the waitresses for each room dressed in their respective traditional folk costumes. There was also a band with dancing, but the only other people there on a Saturday night were members of a Russian wedding party and a Baltic-German couple's anniversary party. My host and I (the bankroll tourist refugee offspring) were the only Latvians in this très chic, high-atmosphere Latvian eatery. What bothered me was that this was not an unusual situation. It bothered me the same as being in a jazz club that doesn't allow black people in. And it bothered me that most Latvians feel, not through defeatism but through an acceptance of social and economic realities, that "that's just the way things are."

Although it would be more inspirational to view Latvian independence as a triumph over communism, in many ways it was merely a byproduct of the dissolution of Soviet power structures. It was no less hard-fought, no less a victory of liberation, but the fact remained that the master could no longer crack the whip. The empire was too big—just as it had been for the Romans, the British, and all the other empires that crumbled in the face of social diversity, the strain of trying to exert political control over a multicultural society. However, empires may die, but their architects are a tenacious breed who will remain lurking in the shadows of smoke-filled rooms until new opportunities arise.

When the new Republic of Latvia was created, citizenship was extended to expatriates and descendants of Latvians throughout the world. The goal was to create some restitution politically by allowing as many ethnic Latvians as possible to vote for an expressly Latvian government, given that World War II, the Soviet takeover and pogroms, and the Russification policies had depleted the native culture. The new Republic had stated categorically in its constitution a policy of non-discrimination against other cultures and ethnicities. Nevertheless, many non-Latvian residents now in turn felt victimized. As Latvia struggles with its political growing pains, the last election has seen the rise of expressly non-Latvian parties, including an unlikely coalition of Germans and Russians (neo-Nazis and neo-Communists, by many accounts). Since most Latvians are poor and unpracticed in political machinations, the future looks very uncertain. Having won their freedom twice in one century, they fear desperately the possibility of the loss record being evened up.

In the United States, there is a similar fear—not of losing "freedom," but of losing "freedoms," the rights gained that can still be lost. America is seething with voices of discontent that want to roll back and eliminate the hard-won gains in civil rights over the last century. White rage has rolled into Washington, and the first line of attack has been on the multicultural front. Politicians hate terms such as "restitution," "compensation," "equal opportunity," "affirmative action," and "social welfare programs." And for obvious reasons, these terms are associated with the term "multicultural" in some form or another. Political intolerance does not want cultural equalization. It wants to keep the minor in minority, it wants to keep the prefixes off the term "American." It does not want to give land back to the Indians (or Latvians); it does not want to give citizenship to Mexican farm workers (or Latvians); it does not want to see businesses bought and run by Asians (or Latvians); it does not want to see masses of blacks going to voting booths (or Latvians). It hates the concept of a multicultural society because that saps its strength and diffuses its control.

Freedom is not enough. Without an acceptance of oppressed cultures, there is no lasting peace. As backlash begets backlash in the new American balkanization, "multiculturalism" once again gets thrust into the political arena to be devoured by the lions of dissension. The legacy remains. Many Latvians remain unsure of whether they are now actually better off. For most of Eastern Europe, political freedom has created new burdens, and the past cannot be cured simply by writing a new constitution and redrawing the maps. In the United States, the 130 years since "the emancipation" have not been enough to eradicate the effects of slavery. For Native Americans, freedom is not a concept that exists outside of the repressive context of a reservation system and meaningless treaties. The fact that it has been fifty years since there were "internment camps" for Japanese American does not erase the memory. The increasingly global reality of multicultural society finds its worst enemy in the political sphere. Those in control need fences and divisiveness between cultures, ethnicities, and races as tools to keep those not in power in a state of disarray and conflict.

In the new Latvia, buildings and businesses have been repatriated and property returned to Latvian owners, an apparent symbol of triumph over the oppressors. Many of the stores in downtown Riga used to have large block letters identifying the business in both Latvian and Russian. The Cyrillic letters have been torn down, but their unfaded shadows remain, waiting for fresh paint that is still too expensive for Latvians to afford. Erasing the legacy of cultural oppression may prove impossible, but learning to live with it may not. If we can tear down the fences as well, there may still be hope.

A Chicano in Philadelphia

■ ■ ■

DANNY ROMERO

For the past few years I have lived in America, as a matter of fact where it all began: Philadelphia. When I first moved here, a friend of mine who lived in the area kept telling me about the history of the city, which is the history of the country: some buildings and streets preserved now for hundreds of years, unchanged from Colonial times.

The same friend dragged me sightseeing through them—Elfreth's Alley, Congress Hall, Independence Hall, and the Liberty Bell, in particular. I must admit that I went begrudgingly. I knew my friend had studied history in college, where we met, and he was trying to be a good host. He would tell me about this history: the Revolutionary War, winter in Valley Forge, Washington crossing the Delaware River, the Declaration of Independence, "We the people . . ." (African American slaves and Native Americans excepted).

Philadelphia history. American history.

I always did well in the subject when I was young. I could always remember a lot of those dates and names and places when the time came to say so.

I was born in a foreign land—California—a land of many different cultures and peoples, not merely black and white (if anything, the world I grew up in, in South Los Angeles, was black and brown). If you look at the state flag, you can see the colors of the people of California: black and brown and red and white and yellow, all in various shades. But if you looked at who holds power, you would never know this.

Family legend dictates that my father's great-grandmother was an Indian from Mexico. Consequently, I have come to believe that I would still have been born on this side of the world, no matter if Columbus had never gotten lost and stumbled across the "New World." If there had never been a George Washington or Thomas Jefferson, I would still have been born in "El Norte." If there had never been a Woodrow Wilson, a Nixon, or Reagan, I still would have been born in (El Pueblo de Nuestra Señora Reina de) Los Angeles. My history stems from south to north, not east to west.

Before there was a USA, Mexicans lived in the Southwest and California. In 1781, while the American Revolutionary War still raged, the city of Los Angeles was founded in the southern portion of Alta California, as it was then known. Of course, Baja California still exists as present-day Mexico. In fact, the entire Southwest (Texas, Arizona, New Mexico, Utah, Nevada, and Colorado) and California once belonged to Mexico.

Nearly two hundred years later, I grew up in a Mexican neighborhood, not far from the intersection of Compton and Florence Avenues. My mother, herself born in Los Angeles, gave birth to me in a hospital on South Hoover Street that no longer exists. My parents baptized me Catholic, like so many Chicanos before me, at La Placita, the Mission church of Our Lady Queen of Angels (Nuestra Señora Reina de Los Angeles), across from Olvera Street, right where the city first began.

I am a native son, though many still see me as foreign, in a land and city where the people have spoken Spanish for hundreds of years. But these days some people would have you believe that English is the "official" language.

I call myself Chicano (or Latino) because I was born on this side of the border, though as a young boy I was simply Mexican. And in a real sense I understand that I remain still simply Mexican to the rest of the nation, which has a hard time seeing beyond the notion that only black and white people are born in this country.

So I am Chicano, or Latino, or Mexican, but I am rarely American.

Not surprisingly, California, the most populous state in the Union, has the largest Chicano/Latino population, with more than 3 million in the Los Angeles–Long Beach metropolitan area alone, according to 1990 Census figures, and at least twice that many throughout the state. Texas has the second-largest population, and New York, where most of the Latinos are Puerto Rican, is third. Significant numbers of Latinos of all varieties are also present in Arizona (where my father and a grandfather were born early in this century), Colorado, Connecticut, Florida, Illinois (where census figures record close to 800,000 in Chicago), Massachusetts, Michigan, Nevada, New Jersey, New Mexico, Pennsylvania, and Washington.[1]

I try to tell this to people at times: Latinos are nothing new, nor foreign, to this land; where I come from, that is all there are (just about). The world I have lived in has never looked merely black and white. For me, the United States has always been made up of many more than two peoples and cultures.

I am fortunate that my parents sacrificed to send me to small Catholic schools in Los Angeles, in order that I get the best education possible. The grammar school and high school I attended both had predominantly Mexican student populations, at least 90 percent, I would say, given the stray African American, Anglo, or Asian. On the other hand, the public schools in the district where I lived, as well as the district itself, were predominantly African American at that time during the 1960s and 1970s.

Once, when I was eight or nine years old, my brother and his friend and I were "jumped" by a large group of black boys our age. We were outnumbered three to one and caught off guard (so we could not run) near the railroad tracks. Three of them stood before me, glaring. The middle one asked me if I had a dime for him, a seemingly reasonable request. Another spoke more plainly: "Give me your money." I knew my brother and his friend had their own trios to contend with, so I just told the group that I did not have any money.

Surprisingly, nothing happened to me after I said that. The group just walked away from me. Today, I like to think that they believed what I had said to them; I like to think that the group of them realized at that moment that their Mexican counterparts on those streets were no better off than themselves in that city, just other poor and dark-skinned little boys.

Almost exclusively, "authority" was white: nuns, priests, teachers, police, judges, doctors, and dentists (at the county clinic); granted there was the occasional black policeman, Mexican nun, or Filipino teacher, but believe me they were rare.

In California, there has always been a strong "majority" bias. To remedy this, Hollywood has given the world the "fun-loving beach boy" and "90210 rich kid" to represent the "native" Californian. As a result, too many people on the East Coast—and I am afraid all across the country—wrongly believe that everyone in California enjoys the same lifestyle of privilege, opportunity, and luxury, no matter the color of their skin, their ethnic background, or where they were born.

At the same time this industry has tried its hardest, and with great success, to remain rife with caricatures and stereotypes of Latinos, Native Americans, Asian Americans, and African Americans from its very beginnings, that is, when they bother to include a person of color at all. Television and the movies are still loaded with these Hollywood images of "superiority" and "inferiority," "majority" and "minority."

I sat among those "native" Californians for the first time when I went to college. I was alone (almost literally, considering how few Chicano students there were in the early 1980s) in among the thousands of them. They were alien to me and I to them all. They were as different from me in their "California" or "L.A." experience as different could be. I was a ghetto youth, admittedly, something off the six o'clock news.

However, I ran into the real-world model in college, not the made-for-television variety. When I lived on campus (for the short time that I did), there was no doubt that I was in their world. I had three different roommates the first week of my dormitory contract.

Perhaps it was me, living among the sons and daughters of architects, doctors, judges, lawyers, police, politicians, and professors, and unwilling to cooperate. I was unwilling to assimilate any further than I had already.

One night in college, three friends and I were "jumped" by a large group of white fraternity boys outside of the Beta Theta Pi house. They had asked to see our green cards. We were insulted, then assaulted. I can still remember them, beach boys and rich kids, leaping off their front deck and onto my friends and me. The numbers were no better than they had been ten years earlier near the railroad tracks. In the end, I was lucky to have made it out of college alive, let alone with a degree.

And, of course, the discrimination against Latinos (specifically, those of Mexican descent) continues in the Southwest and California, whether this means a group of suspected "illegals" getting the crap beaten out of them by law enforcement officials on national television; or my sixty-eight-year-old aunt Lala waiting with a broken hip for twelve hours in a hospital emergency room (while they made sure she was legal); or a child who only wants to learn but is denied the chance to attend public schools.

This is true in Los Angeles, where a small number of "majority representatives" have wielded their terrible power for years, effectively pitting people of color against each other, fighting over limited opportunity, in a city founded by Mexicans, although it seems very few are willing to acknowledge or remember this piece of history.

In Los Angeles, the number of people of Mexican descent has always been considerable, even in the face of overwhelming Anglo-American migration in the years since the city came under the jurisdiction of the United States. For years already the Mexican population has been in the millions, second only in the world to Mexico City. However, political power for Mexicans (or Chicanos or Latinos) in that city has remained elusive.

Growing up Chicano in Los Angeles, I learned early that "majority" and "minority" in the United States mean more about power than actual numbers. And we will all see this in the next few years when Anglos become a minority in California, and then next in the United States. Already the U.S. Supreme Court has taken the first step in shoring up "majority" power with their recent (June 1985) decision (*Miller* v. *Johnson*) on the redrawing of voter district lines in Georgia, where it was discovered that too many African Americans were electing too many African Americans to public office.[2]

Again, California did not begin as an Anglo country. Perhaps this is the reason for the prejudice and hatred that has been directed toward Latinos, both historically and today. One recent event makes it all too clear that the situation is not getting better but worse: Proposition 187.

Immigrant-bashing in California is nothing new; Proposition 187 is only the latest incarnation. Those who support the proposition claim that it would help the state's economy by saving money currently being spent on caring for and educating illegal immigrants. But the truth is that the state's economy is suffering for other reasons. In addition, even if some money is saved, the cost will be high. The proposition would unfairly affect, first and foremost, those who are weakest among us: the sick and poor and elderly, denying them care; and children, who have no control over where their parents live, throwing them out of public schools and into the streets.

And after all, how can a person tell illegal from legal without first taking away my civil rights?

In order to save money, should we choose a racist and xenophobic path?

Should we support fascism because it costs less?

Those who supported Proposition 187 hoped to make this latest anti-immigrant (specifically, Asian and Latino) hysteria "nice and legal."

And I am, once again, "foreign" in my native land.

Within a few days after Proposition 187 passed in California, a letter to the editor of the *Philadelphia Inquirer* called for similar legislation in Pennsylvania. This disappointed me, but it did not surprise me.

It was unusual to read anything in the newspaper about Latinos, even a letter to the editor. In California, they remain an invisible population, neither on mainstream television nor in the newspapers, unless the authorities are looking for a "crime" or "welfare" story (or a nanny, housekeeper, gardener, or farmhand). The same appears to be true on the East Coast. This is despite a population of almost 2 million Latinos in the New York metropolitan area, almost 1 million in the Miami-Hialeah metropolitan area, nearly a quarter of a million in the Washington, D.C., metropolitan area, and almost 200,000 each in the Newark, New Jersey, Boston-Lawrence-Salem-Brockton, Massachusetts, and Jersey City, New Jersey, metropolitan areas (again according to 1990 Census figures from Temple University Electronic Library).

In addition, Latinos are projected to surpass African Americans in numbers in the not so distant future. Already Chicanos are the largest "minority" group in the Southwest and make up 60 percent of the Latino population nationwide.[3] On the East Coast, from what I can tell, most of the Latinos are Puerto Ricans. This is not surprising, given the relatively short distance to the island.

In Philadelphia, there are nearly 100,000 Puerto Ricans, according to the 1990 Census of Population and Housing. However, I sometimes wonder where they are, since I do not see many of them downtown near where I live, shop, and work. My conclusion is that they never leave the barrio, or so it seems. I understand the feeling; I know what it is like to live outside of the Anglo world.

In Chicano communities, similarly, there are people who never venture beyond the comfort of the barrio, if they can help it. For the barrio is a place where you can speak Spanish freely, if you choose to do so, and both be understood and accepted. In the barrio you can be Chicano, or Mexican, or Puerto Rican (and more recently, Salvadoran, Guatamalan, or Dominican). The barrio is a place where, for the most part, you are safe from your person being wrongly judged just because of your ethnicity, your accent, or your taste in clothes, food, or music. Although the great majority of Latinos in this country work and pay taxes, politicians and the media still wrongly characterize us as all on public assistance or criminals, ignorant and lazy. And, unfortunately, our communities are still policed by racist and brutal law enforcement agencies, supported and protected by a social, political, and judicial system too often biased in favor of "majority" people and against "minority" peoples of color, all across the nation.

Unlike Mexicans, Puerto Ricans are citizens by birth. However, this latest campaign of anti-immigrant (Latino and Asian, primarily) hatred, which includes English-as-"official"-language legislation and the proposed national ID card system, is not really about citizenship. It's about "majority" power dictating who is and who is not a "good" American, and what one can and cannot do. Being American still means, first and foremost, "majority" white and "minority" African American (as long as they do not vote for too many African American candidates for public office). Everyone else, they would rather not include.

The truth is that American history has been none too kind to people of color. And this has not been because they were absent, only locked out. From Native Americans and African Americans to Asian Americans and Latinos, in far too many instances, America has offered them something too close to second-class citizenship. American history has proven itself to hate not only Native Americans and African Americans, but Asian Americans and Latinos as well, especially the educated ones.

American history. Philadelphia history.

One hot and sticky afternoon last summer, I stood outside Independence Hall, staring at the line waiting to go inside and contemplating whether I needed to take the tour once more. I wondered if I could stand among the tourists—Anglos, Asians, and blacks—foreign or domestic, illegal or legal (who can tell the difference?), as they took in the majesty and awe of it all.

I have always held dear those ideals of equality and freedom expressed in such documents as the Declaration of Independence, the Constitution, and the Bill of Rights. The problem has been the hypocrisy of those slaveowners who meant the words only to be applied to the white "majority" (the wealthier the better), a hypocrisy that cannot be so easily discounted, explained away, or rationalized since remnants of it, however little, still linger today.

I have lived my life in a country still biased in favor of one group of people (what they call the "majority") and against people of color (what they call the "minority"). And this bias has nothing to do with ability or intelligence, citizenship or numbers.

At the same time, "majority" representatives still espouse those ideals of equality and freedom, pointing to their mere utterance as proof of their existence (as long as you do not complain about, criticize, or question their "authority").

On the other hand, those same "majority" representatives have sought through their actions, laws, and policies to limit equality and freedom for Latinos and other people of color every chance they get, still shouting the words "equality" and "freedom" ever louder to drown out the thud and crack of "majority" justice against people of color—too often treated first as guilty, then forced to prove their innocence.

"Majority" power comes at the expense of "minority" people of color, who must be seen as "inferior" as a consequence of the supposed "superiority" of the "majority." As a nation, we are left with the demagoguery we see today that views "majority" power as always right, even when it promotes and perpetuates racism and xenophobia, then sends representatives in suits and ties and with million-dollar bank accounts to be mayor, judge, district attorney, police chief, congressman, attorney general, senator, governor.

To a large extent, the future of this country is first played out in Los Angeles, then California. Not far off in the distance, I see a glow in the western sky, heading east. From crosses burning on lawns? Gobbling up civil liberties along the way?

Mine only?

Or yours too?

■ ■ ■

NOTES

1. Scholar's Information Center at Temple University Libraries. Temple University Network: Saber Software Corporation. Government Information and Statistics, *1990 Census of Population and Housing*. Summary Tape File 3C: U.S. Summary, March 29, 1996.
2. Aaron Epstein, "High Court Strikes at Race-Based Districting," *Philadelphia Inquirer*, June 30, 1995, p. A1.
3. See Victoria Van Son, *CQ's State Fact Finder: Rankings Across America* (Washington, DC: Congressional Quarterly, Inc., 1993), and Marlita S. Reddy, ed., *Statistical Record of Hispanic Americans*. 2nd ed. (Detroit: Gale Research Inc., 1995).

A Chicano in Spain

■ ■ ■

RUDOLFO ANAYA

My wife and I first traveled to Spain in the fall of 1980. We took an overnight train from Paris to Barcelona, journeyed through Andalucia and then on to Madrid. We returned home with wonderful memories of the Alhambra, Toledo, Madrid, El Escorial, and many other places we had wanted to experience. At the famous El Prado museum I fell under the spell of the genius of Goya, and the images of his prophetic vision are with me today. In 1988 when we returned to Spain, my trip was in part a pilgrimage to meditate again in the presence of Goya's work and to visit and contemplate the genius of Gaudí's inspiring church, La Sagrada Familia, in Barcelona.

That return was made possible by my invitation to Barcelona to discuss my work at the Third International Conference on Hispanic Cultures of the United States; after that conference I attended a small gathering of Spanish scholars, and professors from the University of New Mexico at La Fundación Xavier de Salas in Trujillo. Again I had the opportunity to discuss my work as a Hispanic writer from New Mexico.

Spain was preparing for the celebration of its quincentennial explorations in the Americas, and the conferences were the beginning of a series intended to rekindle the relationship of Spain with Hispanic America. We, the *Hispano Nuevo Mexicanos,* share in that history, and so my thoughts turned to those historic events and their implications in the life and history of the Hispanic population of our Southwest.

The great majority of the *Mexicanos* of the Southwest are *Idohispanos,* part of *La Raza* of the New World, the fruit of the Spanish father and the Indian mother. We have taken pride in our Hispanic heritage, that is, we know the history of the Spanish father, his language, and his character. We know that in this country it has been more seductive to identify with one's white, European ancestry. But the focus of that identification with that which is Spanish has, until recently, caused us to neglect our indigenous native American roots, and thus we have not known and honored the heritage of our mother, the Indian mothers of Mexico and the Southwest.

In world mythology there are few archetypal searches for the mother, perhaps because the mother is always in evidence, she is always there; in early religions she was the goddess of the earth, the provider. We forget that it is the mother who cultivates and in many ways creates our nature, both in an individual and communal sense. For the *Mexicanos* of the Southwest the mother is Malinche, the Mexican woman who was the first Indian woman of Mexico to bear children fathered by a Spaniard. But the mother is more real than the symbolic Malinche; in our mothers is embodied the archeytpe of the indigenous Indian mother of the Americas, and it is her nature we must know. Why have we neglected her? In other words, why have we neglected that part of our history which was shaped by indigenous America?

I was born and raised in *Nuevo México,* heir to the land of my *Hispano* ancestors, son of these Spanish and Mexican colonists who settled the fertile Rio Grande Valley of New Mexico. My ancestors settled in the Atrisco land grant, across the river from present-day Albuquerque. I trace my family back a few generations because the land grant has created a sense of communal belonging for the Anayas. As I think of the quincentennial of Columbus's crossing, I ask myself how I relate to that Hispanic legacy which left the peninsula in 1492 to implant itself in the New World. How do I relate to the peninsular consciousness of the people who crossed the Atlantic five hundred years ago to deposit their seed on the earth of the New World?

Located at the heart of what is now the Southwest United States, the people of *Nuevo México* have retained the essence of what it means to be Hispanic, having preserved the Spanish language, the Catholic religion, and the folktales and folkways which came to us from Spain. But our nature was also formed by intermarriage with the Pueblo Indians of the Rio Grande. Our Spanish heritage and character are evident; it is a legacy left by those who came from Spain to settle in *Nuevo México*.

Those ancestors imbued the history of *Nuevo México* with their particular worldview. For more than four centuries those ancestors lived in the isolated frontier of northernmost New Spain. But they did not survive and multiply in a vacuum; they survived and evolved because they adopted many of the ways of the Pueblos. The Spanish character underwent change as it encountered the Native Americans of the Southwest, and from that interaction and intermarriage a unique American person and perspective were born.

We need to describe the totality of that worldview which was formed in what we now call the Southwest, understanding that we are heirs not only of our Spanish character but of our Native American nature as well. The Spanish character is the aggressive, conquest-oriented part of our identity; the Native American nature is the more harmonious, earth-oriented side. I believe we must give attention to the characteristics of both sides of our identity in order to be more spiritually and psychologically centered when relating to the world. To pay attention only to one side of our sensibility is to be less self-actualizing, therefore less knowledgeable of self. If we are to understand our potential, it is important that we know the indigenous side of our history, not just the European.

As I review my writings, I understand that it is the indigenous American perspective, or New World view, which is at the core of my values. I have paid attention to the nature of my mother, not only the symbolic Indian mother, but the real Indian mothers of the Americas. The blood that whispers the essence of the earth and people of the Americas is the nature of my mother; it reveals the symbols and mythology of the New World, and that comprises the substratum of my writings.

During the Columbus quincentennial festivities, a discourse was to take place between Spain and its former colonies in the Americas. I wish to add a definition of my New World view to that discourse, hoping not only to share some of the findings of my personal literary quest but also to encourage my community of *raza* to pay more attention to our multicultural and multiethnic history. The journey is always toward illumination of the self, toward that which is called the authentic self. We must know more of the synthesis of our Spanish character and Indian nature, and in that way know ourselves better.

The Americas represent a wonderful experiment in the synthesis of divergent worldviews, and each one of us is a representative of that process. The illuminations of self that are revealed as we explore and understand our true natures can be one of the most rewarding experiences of our lives, for so much of the sensitive part of life is a search and understanding of the inner self. To define ourselves as we really are and not as others wish us to be allows us to become authentic, and that definition carries with it the potential of our humanism.

Our Hispanic ancestors in the mid-sixteenth century settled along the Rio Grande of *Nuevo México,* bringing to the land their language. They gave names to the land and its features. It is in the naming that one engages in the sacred, that is, by naming one creates a *sacred sense of time,* a historic sense of time. By engaging in naming, our ancestors imposed themselves on history and gave definition to history. The language used in that naming ceremony is our birthright.

I live in Albuquerque, a name that invokes some of the history of the Iberian peninsula. In Spain I spoke my *Nuevo Mexicano* Spanish, a dialect that was preserved by my ancestors and which evolved in the mountains and valleys of New Mexico. But language changes with the passage of time and the vicissitudes of survival, and so I returned to Spain more proficient in English than in Spanish. All my novels and stories are written in English. While my parents' generation still communicated only in Spanish, my generation converses almost completely in English, a function of our professional lives. Still we struggle to retain our Spanish language, not only because it relates us to that part of our heritage, but also because it connects us to our brethren in Mexico and Latin America.

I returned to Spain to share with Spaniards the nature of my New World consciousness. At times I felt uncomfortable in believing I had to conform to the Spanish character, but the truth is that I now realize we who return to Spain no longer need to feel constrained to conform to the Spanish character. My generation of *Hispanos* liberated ourselves from that constraint by naming ourselves Chicanos. For us, using the word "Chicano" was our declaration of independence, the first step toward our true identity and the institution of a process by which we rediscovered our history.

By naming ourselves Chicanos we stamped an era with our communal identity, we reaffirmed our humanity by exploring and understanding the nature of our mothers, the indigenous American women. Those of us of Mexican heritage took the word "Chicano" from *Mexicano,* dropping the first syllable and keeping the *Xicano.* We are proud of that heritage even though we are not Mexican citizens, and although we are citizens of the United States we are not Anglo-Americans. The word "Chicano" defined the *space in time* as we struggled to define our contemporary history, and therefore Chicano came closer to embracing our Native American heritage.

Our first declaration of independence was from Anglo-America; that is, we insisted on the right to our *Indohispano* heritage. Now I believe the declaration has to go further. We have to insist on being the *señores of our own time,* to borrow a phrase from Miguel León Portilla. To be the *señores and señoras of our time* is to continue to create our definition and sense of destiny in time; for me it means a bonding of the character of our Spanish heritage with our Indian American heritage.

Enough of the search after the father, let us turn now and know our mothers. And so this essay is a declaration of independence from a narrow view which has defined us as *Hispanos* with only a Spanish heritage. The definition of our identity must be a New World definition. Such a definition should encompass the multiple roots and histories of the Americas; it should encompass the nature of the mothers whose soul provides the unique aesthetic and humanistic sensibility that defines us.

Language is at the essence of a culture, and so we must remember that in *Nuevo México,* as in the rest of the New World, there existed pre-Columbian languages. The indigenous Indians had named their tribes, the rivers, the mountains, and the flora and fauna. They were the *señores of their own time.* The New World did not live in silence, awaiting the sound of European languages; it had its languages and it had participated in the sacred ceremony of naming long before 1492. This is a fact which we *Hispanos* from the southwest United States must accept when we discuss our ethnicity, for not only was the Mexico of our indigenous ancestors peopled with Indians; the Rio Grande Valley, which became the home of our Hispanic ancestors, also was thriving with many great Indian pueblos.

Language follows the urge of the blood, it moves with the adventurer to take root and be nourished by the colonist who tills the new soil. Languages mix, as does the blood, and so the gene proof of this *Hispano* from *Nuevo México* is both Indian and peninsular. Knowing this allows me to honor my mothers as much as my fathers. My journey has been that of a writer, and in my first novel it was the *curandera* Ultima, the indigenous woman who came to speak to me and share her secrets. She reflects the nature of *La Virgen de Guadalupe,* the indigenous mother born of the synthesis of Spanish virgin and Indian goddess. It is through Ultima that I began to discover myself. In my writings I have sought the true nature of the New World man, that person who is authentic to the New World view. The truth is that I had only myself to encounter in the journey, and so I am the New World man I have sought. I am an indigenous man taking his essence and perspective from the earth and people of the New World, from the earth which is my mother.

But for me the question of celebration is much more than a return to Hispanic roots; it is a philosophical question which speaks to the character of my nature.

How did you begin this journey of self-knowledge, people ask me. I listened to the *cuentos* of the old people, the stories of their history, and in retelling those stories and starting my own odyssey, I had to turn within. I had to know myself. Everyone does. The spiritual beliefs and mysticism of the Catholic Church and the love of the earth were elements of my childhood, so I turned to those sources in my stories. The folkways of my community became the web of the fictions I create, for the elements of drama exist within the stories of the folk. Even today, when I feel I have outgrown some of the themes I explored as a young writer, I know my best writing still comes when I return to the essence of my culture.

But in all writing the depth of the universal element is that which allows us to communicate across national or ethnic boundaries, and so for me the most meaningful and revealing area to enter in search of the New World person was mythology. It is in myth that we find the truth in the heart, the truth of "our place in time." It is possible for anyone to enter and explore his or her memory, and to discover there the symbols which speak to the personal and collective history. It is in this search that I found the legend of the Golden Carp and the other mythological symbols which permeate *Bless Me Ultima* and my later work. I found universal archetypal symbols, but these symbols were colored with a Native American hue. The earth, the elements, the sacred directions, the tree, the owl of the old *curandera* Ultima, the golden carp, the shaman as mentor or guide—all of these elements spoke to me of my New World nature. And it was Ultima, my Native American mother, who led the way and taught me to see.

My search continued. In *Heart of Aztlán* I worked with the myth of Aztlón, a legend which describes the place of origin of the Aztecs. I attempted to make that legend meaningful in a contemporary context by exploring its possibilities as a Chicano homeland. In *Tortuga* I continued the search into the earth and totem animals, the search into the healing process of water and earth as well as the art of writing itself. The writer may well be the new shaman for the old, displaced tribes of the Americas. In the novel *Tortuga* I returned to the important revelations available to us in the nature of the mother, whether the mother was viewed as earth goddess or the feminine presence of the young girl who loves Tortuga.

My search has allowed me to understand that we often praise our Hispanic identity and its roots in the same breath as we shun the indigenous roots which have also nurtured our history. If I declare my independence of consciousness from the Iberian peninsula, it is because I have found that the symbolic content which best describes my nature comes from the people and earth of the Americas. So I declare, as an important step in the process of knowing myself, my independence. I see myself as a New World man, and I feel that definition is liberating and full of potential.

During this time of the Columbus quincentennial, it is important to look at the evolution of the consciousness of the Americas and to discern the unique world views which that evolution created. It is important for us and for Spain to look at the Americas and find, not an image of the Spanish character, but an image of our unique New World nature.

When I first traveled in Spain in 1980 I went into Andalucia. There in those wide expanses and mountains which reminded me of New Mexico, I felt at home. But a person needs more than the landscape to feel connected; we need the deeper connection to the communal body, we need to feel connected to our community.

The broad, political history of the independence of the Spanish colonies in the Americas is well known; now we must turn to an exploration of our personal and communal identity. That is what Chicano writers and artists have been doing since the cultural movement of the 1960s. The definition of Chicano culture must come from a multicultural perspective. Many streams of history define us and will continue to define us, for we are the synthesis which is the Americas.

Christ and Quetzalcóatl are not opposing spiritual figures; they fulfill the humanistic yearning toward harmonious resolution. Harmony within, harmony with neighbors, harmony with the cosmos. The Virgin of Spanish Catholicism and the Aztec Tonantzin culminate in the powerful and all-loving *Virgen de Guadelupe*. And *los santos* of the Catholic Church and those more personal saints of my mother's altar merge with and share the sacred space of the *Kachinas* of the Indian pueblos.

This metaphor, *Los santos are the kachinas,* has become a guiding metaphor of synthesis for me. The Old World and the New World have become one in me. Perhaps it is this syncretic sensibility of harmony which is the ideal of New World character. The New World cultures accepted the spiritual manifestations of Catholicism; Christ and the saints entered the religious cosmology of Indian America. A new age of cultural and spiritual blending came to unite humanity's course in the Americas. It was an age born in suffering, but the very act of birth created the children who were heirs to a new worldview.

The New World view is syncretic and encompassing. It is one of the most humanistic views in the world, and yet it is a view not well known in the world. The pressure of political realities and negative views of the mestizo populations of the Americas have constrained the flowering of our nature. Still, that view of self-knowledge and harmony is carried in the heart of the New World person.

What is important to me as a writer is to find the words by which to describe myself and my relationship to others. I now have the insight that allows me to speak of my history, and to posit myself at the center of that history. There I stand poised at the center of power, the knowing of myself, the heart and soul of the New World man alive in me.

This is a time of reflection for those of us who are the mestizos of the New World, and I believe the reflections in my writings and my attention to the myths and legends of Mesoamerica and the Rio Grande help expand the definition of our *Indohispano* heritage.

My trip to Spain was beneficial for me. I brought back memories of the Alhambra where I felt my soul stir to Moorish rhythm, and in the paintings of Goya's dark period I saw his apocryphal vision of an era ending. At La Sagrada Familia of Gaudí I bowed to genius, in the Valle de los Caídos I reflected on the Civil War . . . and on the wide expanses of Andalucía I thought of home. In all these places my memory stirred, and still I yearned for my home in *Nuevo México,* the mountains I know, the sacred places of my way of life. In that yearning the message whispered its secret, it was time for me to state my declaration of independence, time to center myself in the consciousness of the New World.

I was the New World man I had sought, with one foot in the glorious *mestisaje* of *México* and the other in the earth of the *Indohispanos of Nuevo México;* my dreams are woven of New World earth and history. I could walk anywhere in the world and feel attached, but it was *Nuevo México* that centered me, it was the indigenous soul of the Americas that held my secret.

It is important to know that the search for identity is not an esoteric search and not a divisive process. It is a way to reaffirm our humanity. We are all on this search, we all advocate justice, basic human rights, and the right of all to declare their independence of consciousness. We hope the spirit generated in Spain during the 1992 celebration addresses and encourages these basic rights.

History and the collective memory are vast. One delves into these powerful forces and finds that one is part of every other human being. I am extremely proud of my New World heritage, but I know the tree of mankind is one, and I share my roots with every other person. It seems appropriate to end on this archetype of the tree. The tree, or the tree of life, is also a dominant symbol of the Americas, and its syncretic image combines the tree of Quetzalcóatl and the cross of Christ. My ancestors nourished the tree of life; now it is up to me to care for all it symbolizes.

The Colored Trickster and the Frida Painter

On the Utterance of Multiculturalism in Our Own Land

■ ■ ■

JUAN FELIPE HERRERA

In my journeys south to the Indian communities of Mexico during the last three decades, I have been faced with the possibility of following many paths, especially those inherited from New World Spanish invaders and Anglo-European anthropologists and archeologists. No matter what my motives have been, I have had to displace myself from the well-traveled grooves of Anglo-European representation and interpretation in the Americas. It is an odd maneuver to be a Chicano, a person of color, en route to a "native" topography; the most formidable folly has to do with swallowing the Master's Conquest language in order to liberate one-self, that is, to initiate the process of resolving one's cultural disenfran-chisement in the United States. In short, I have had to become a trickster, a language saboteur, an akimbo, cross-eyed seeker of self. The path of the colored trickster requires fracture; we must disrupt the terms, figures, and images of colonialism, first, if we dare go looking for the way back home.

From a Chicana and Chicano metaphysical angle, Frida Kahlo has become our psychic and ethnopoetic metaphor. We are all condemned to be Fridas. We know that the central column of our cultural vertebrae has been shattered, we have no unified and authentic discourse of what we are; all we know is that we have been tightened into a cast—our re-aligned body. And yet, from the inside, we know that we inhabit a radically difference space. Because of the cast and the terrible accidents to our historical self, we go about immersed in the enterprise of self-portraiture; at every juncture, we seek our shape, our face. And again, paradox overwhelms us: what we paint is seen as minute and gracious in comparison to the full-bodied enterprise of the Master painter, who seems to walk about freely, scale walls, and launch his mediums and letters with such public gaiety and open-air affection.

The notions of the colored trickster and that of the Frida painter as starting points for culture critics of color are uncanny maneuvers, in themselves limited and collapsible. Yet they make sense in our search of and for ourselves, since they conjure a spirit of rebellion and resistance in the task of applying received frames of Native history and community. Since language, at the outset, is one of the key mediums of our searches, we are faced with the choice of refashioning various terms, and most of all the interpretive space of colony and conquest. To begin any historical investigation, I must ask myself, as a colored trickster, can I incorporate, utilize, give credence to the term "multiculturalism"?

The term "multiculturalism" bothers me; somehow, it encourages a white-bearded God to wake up, rise, and prowl the pyramids and the basalt shrines in search of tropical converts. It gives permission to friars and clerics in new body wraps to scurry late at night poring over what they have gathered from their devoted Indian informants. How does this term speak of a fettered Indian Latin America barely breathing within the inherited boundaries and systems of servitude, finca and hacienda, labor-credit-debt relations, female sexual credit payment (*derecho de pernada*), and military occupation and trusteeship? How does the language of multiculturalism frame the recent Chiapas revolt? If the Mexican PRI monolith pays homage to multiculturalism, perhaps there is cause to shudder and truly run toward the Ejercito Zapatista. There is little left for us to do other than become tricksters of color and Frida painters.

To repeat, language is at the center of the trickster's enterprise. In the past, in order to begin my journeys into Huichol, Totonac, and Mayan country, I have had to understand that as I speak of Mexico, Indians, and indigenous cultures, I wade into a dangerous pool of representations. Where is Mexico, what is Mexico? How far does America really stretch—what is an Indian?

The verbiage of "multiculturalism" has made me highly skeptical; terms are cloaked with senses of amelioration and defense. When I consider the economic and cultural plight of Indian Mexico, I become aware that horror is best propped with the tone and wordplay of honor. The way a nation speaks about itself gives me clues, especially the talk of a superpower; officially sanctioned violent actions and systems continue in motion because in many ways we make them culturally palatable. We may move out of the barrio, we may even say that in the ghetto, life is more "authentic," or that "back home" in the mountains and deserts of the United States, life is more "real" and experiences are "more vital" and "deeper." Yet, as we speak in these terms, we condone the squalor, deprivation of resources, and the corruption of federal and state agencies that are responsible to our home communities. Atrocities become acts of national fortitude, usurpations become salvations, much in the same fashion as in the early episodes of the conquest of the Americas. Throughout the last five hundred years, the vicious campaigns launched against Indian Mexico have been filtered and assuaged by language, and legitimized by our most respected social institutions, where rhetoric plays a major role, as in the case with the trinity of religion, law, and literature.

The position as colored trickster and Frida painter is a challenging one, since it not only involves displacing "honored" systems of knowledge and interpretation but also motivates us to tackle their institutional bases. We know that one of the most powerful wedges for the maintenance of rigid class, gender stratification, and caste systems is that of religious fervor; the Church as well as the state remain our key targets. Religious agency gives us the possibility to transform, to suffer with the Other, and to expatiate and save ourselves, most of all. At the level of our collective experience, religious rhetoric makes room for national celebrations, holidays, festivals, rallies, and other significant social occasions where we "paste in" the alien object into our daily life while keeping the subject at bay—distant, demolished, and powerless. In a sense, being a colored trickster or a Frida painter requires that we attack the pillars of society, as framed by stolid religious systems and other social institutions, especially those whose rhetoric supports the idea of cultural celebration severed from the facts of cultural genocide. Can we paste up a poster of Cancun pyramid-shaped hotels paying tribute to the indigenous ancestors of Yucatan as the PRI purchases millions of dollars' worth of riot gear in anticipation of an intensified Tzotzil-Tzeltal, Tojolabal, and Lacandon Maya rebellion?

What language do we need to watch for when we speak "multi-culturalism"? Here is a sample from the Colored Trickster and Frida Painter Personal Dictionary:

Mexico: Nonexistent; only at margins of continent where Mexicans still live.

Indian: Identity label given to those outside of the Center; also used for auto-definition at the edge (see *Mexico*).

Tourism: Interventions into Mexican territory, highly dependent on consumer relationships, as in NAFTA.

Visit: Personal encounter during or after the "tour" (see *Tourism*); however, here ideas and behaviors are purchased.

Indian Art: Nonexistent; a superimposed European category that objectifies life flow as art for economic benefit and public display.

Golden Skin: Refers to skin color, with underlying orientations of group hate, collective racism, and guilt for personal and "accidental" whiteness.

Customs: Nonexistent; a superimposed term used to catalogue culture traits and activities in order to justify abuse and usurpation of same group.

Indian town: (see *Tourism, Golden Skin,* and all of the above).

The Colored Trickster asks the following questions in as many ways as possible: *Who* is recognizing the worth of "distinctive cultural traditions"? What tension is under consideration—one shaped by religion, by ethnicity, race, sexuality? How do these quandaries reinforce conquest in our homelands? The Colored Trickster and the Frida Painter keep journals, for themselves and their friends for the most part. They veer off into other directions, at times. We must remember, they are cross-eyed. They attempt to look upon themselves in a fashion much different from that of the Master, with a familiar yet distinct stranger-gaze. Here is a journal entry, titled "Red Rebozos," taken from a larger manuscript, *Mayan Drifter,* on a recent experience in San Cristobal de Las Casas, a year before the Mayan uprisings:

> *This is a multitrack of unknown numbers,*
> *realities, red rebozos, and violence*
> *in a raging semi-feudal continuum.*

> *The women from Ch'enalo lean forward in the protest march around the city square. Their dark foreheads lead them to el planton de la catedral. Scarves flurry in the late afternoon winds.*
> *They multiply. Their bodies and arms spread and disperse into each one of our souls and memories. They are Rigoberta Menchú with*

crossed arms and staunch hearts. Young and barefoot, combed and stern, full of compassion and terrible pictures held tight in their braided hair. They are the braided spirits of Doña Petrona Chona, whose body was cut into twenty-five pieces by the machete bodyguard of a finca landowner in Guatemala; pieces that Rigoberta Menchú's father placed in a basket;

> *Petrona Chona,*
> *shredded*
> *into small pieces*
> *congealed*
>
> *flesh*

because she didn't permit Carlos Garcia, the landowner's son, to rape her. Petrona, in pieces, comes back to us this afternoon. Her head, her arms and hands. Her legs and thighs, her belly and her breasts. She is woven back, through stone, through national borders and border guard time; she has come back through the valley of machetes, broken galeras and fincas, and is present in this sudden multitude, calling out for justice. Petrona Chona leads the march with her Mayan sisters and brothers; this is why people stare. This is why we have stopped breathing. The Indian women here know Petrona Chona did not die in vain. They know the women of Ch'enalo were not raped and wounded in vain.

What about us,

the onlookers, the note takers, the accountants, the bookkeepers and anthropological shadows? What do we know? What taste burns in our mouth, who is hidden inside the tufts and bright locks of our hair? What pictures fall from our heads onto the public square in such a loud and loving fashion?

The Indian women and men gather at the open square facing the entrance of the church. I stand at the back, sit and smoke. A few of the men sit by me; young men burned by the sun, looking ahead at the archaic and sealed doors of the cathedral where the leaders raise los estandartes of La Virgen de Guadalupe, the Mexican flag, and their own red and gilded cloth on sticks.

In front, the rest stand at attention, in silence, about a hundred or so. Around us another two hundred; children run about, the mothers pull out foodstuffs from their satchels and hand them out. A voice in Tzotzil comes through the speakers. Ahead, I can see the speaker: a young Tzotzil man kneeling at the foot of La Virgen de Guadalupe.

His voice carries a cavernous tenderness; slow, then quick. He sings, almost, but he is beseeching the pueblos of Mayan Indians before him. He names the raped, the innocent, he cries out and his voice shakes. Cries out with one arm holding the estandarte of la Virgen and the other arm, down, still, close to his chest. I don't know the words but I can feel the pain.

Walk up closer. A woman with a child to my right and a tall man wearing white to my left. Everyone's head is bowed down as they listen, crying out for their families, stricken once again. The other two estandartes are held up by women who lift their rebozos to their face with their free arms so they can cry into themselves. The whole plaza is mourning the dead; all the men and women, all the children—in tears. I let my crying take me to their crying and envelop me in their weeping; this is one thing I can do. It comes up without question or analysis, without notes or reflections; I am singing with my Indian sisters and brothers, singing for the dead and wounded and for their transformation into fullness and freedom.

One of the Indian women takes the microphone after the man's voice falters. Her voice is determined, clear. In Spanish, she says that later there will be a gathering for the Indian pueblos inside the church quarters. She speaks with her head up and her shoulders bright.

The thick doors of the church never open. Where is the bishop? It is as if the Indian has come to seek solace at the foot of an ancient shrine. It is not the church itself. All I see are Indians standing at the gate of the church, crying, singing up and holding up their own faith and community. There is something that has been buried under the church, under San Cristobal de Las Casas, that lays there, with its eyes awake and its heart ready to fly. They gather their strength here. They know, I know, that the onlookers will go home with a different taste in their mouths, with something that they have kept hidden from themselves in their mercado baskets.

Sit down again and offer a cigarette to the Tzotzil Tzeltal men next to me. They are surprised and thank me. Smoke again and listen to the demands in Tzotzil, to the names of the lost and the names of the determined.

A tight group of tourists swivels behind us. Questions. I can hear them speaking in English. It is Mercedes, the Chamula Indian woman with a degree from the university, and her tour. I recognize her from the folded cloth on her head, a Indian woman's attire mixed in with her Ladino dress.

Night comes to the cathedral. The streets empty and a few people linger. In San Cristobal there are no visible party palaces as in Veracruz, Mexico City, or the big cities. Here, the night wraps the streets and leaves a few idle wanderers smoking cigarettes or listening to a small box radio inside a hole-in-the-wall abarrotes storefront, where they sell stacked kilos of tortillas, pan dulce, bollillos, *tall Coke bottles, eggs, dry chorizo on a wire vine, and Raleighs and Mexican Winstons.*

I make another round through the kiosko so as not to appear awkward. I am the only Ladino man out in the plaza next to the church. The Tzotziles huddle inside the back quarters of the Bishop's rectory. They have nailed two effigies on the wooden beams that hold up the veranda. The phosphor light from a small light bulb spills on the ragged and ashen figures.

Murmurings, night words and unknown languages of ascensions. They gather in the back, some form a line against the wall. It is about rape distilled from a larger vat of venom—genocide.

I step inside:

I receive you like the Chamula cloth dolls at birth, this draped night, this second half of the sky dome, I clutch you without language, without a text for my transformation. You are changing before my eyes and my skin; you with the same bent as my mother, with the same crooked elbow as my father; I receive you as I received those that gave me birth, I take you with your severities and assassinations, with your meager landscapes of torture, cornslush, incense, and woven faces. I receive you with your night-stringed innocence, with your oppressors nailed, knifed in wooden slats, as effigies, as practices to sweep the evils from your soul, from your village of blue navels, from the iris of your mountainous village waters. You are transforming before my walking, before me. In my absence and in my presence you have transformed; I would have stayed and remained alone, inside the city bank, inside the fashion fair prowls of my metropolitan euphorias, in my escape ladder suits worn with melancholy and ice intelligence. I would have stayed in that balsa, that crumbled American pocket of losses and tiny furies at the feet of the beggar-boy; I would have stayed back there, in my comfort and in my high-rise grape-picking valley, in California, or in my open desert floodwater volcanic Midwest stone, in the land of Lincoln, next door to Dorothy's flight to Oz; I would have kept all my fine flared writing pens, my self-made quills and tall proud notebooks, and have looked elsewhere for my rain. I would have looked elsewhere, somewhere between fanciful Americanness and brown-skinned oblivion. Instead, I took a tiny

step, for a few seconds back, then forward, through persistence and
memory, through timelessness and ripped out sidewalk trails, rock 'n'
roll moss, city steam and Indian town fungi taxis; I took a second or
two and ran into you, by mistake; I was looking for a tour and an
interpreter but my suit had grown too thin and I was freezing. I
needed your smoke, your boiled woolyness, your fawn-colored
warmth, your eternal half smoke ferocity face, and your warrior prayer
hands pointing to the effigy on the Bishop's veranda. I receive you
without any words; I am still unformed, I am changing with you as
you go to your uncombed triumph, gilded with your names up in the
sky flares, held up by the women of the villages, to continue to
remember that you continue; I go on through this street of a thousand
flayed hearts asking for your name, but all I hear in the distance, on
this cobbled ribbon of Calle Diego Dugelay, is music.

Much has been said of culture, that old word rooted in fourteenth-
century European conceptions of husbandry, cult, and later, in the nineteenth century, civilization and the arts. Now we speak of a cultural
plenum, an open-ended field of relative values, actions, events, and orientations. "Multiculturalism," we say. We cough up a hydra-headed lexi-
axe that has the potential of slashing our own necks. Better that it slash
our tongues. The figures of the Colored Trickster and the Frida Painter
are starting points as we traverse on the fracture-body of new territories
and peoples in search of floating homelands, in search of an Anti-
America, a lower-case, lowland america, shaped and determined by its
own peoples.

3

■ ■ ■

TO PASS OR NOT TO PASS

Being Mixed in America

■ ■ ■

TENNESSEE REED

I am quite privileged for someone my age. I travel by airplanes a lot. I've been to Europe, Alaska, Hawaii, the Caribbean, Japan, Mexico, and around most of the continental United States. I get to go to private schools. My parents always make sure I have a lot of clothes, books, art supplies, and other stuff that will help me feel good about myself and learn to think and create. I'm a very healthy and active person. I hardly ever get sick. But I have one problem: My race.

People on the street, at school, or places like camps ask me, "What's your nationality?", a question I truly hate with a passion. I hesitate and say, "I have too many to list." I am one-half Russian/Jewish/Tartar. My other half is one-eighth Cherokee, one-eighth white (Danish, French, and Irish), and one-quarter Nigerian.

My name, Tennessee, is Cherokee for "Bend in the River." My last name, Reed, is Scots-Irish. It was the surname of my father's stepfather. Ironically, it was one of the four famous last names of the Pulaski, Tennessee, Ku Klux Klan. Pulaski is where the Klan originated. Since I was in kindergarten, people have made racist comments about my heritage.

Some white people hate me because I'm black and Jewish, and some black people hate me because I'm light-skinned.

I feel like I don't fit anywhere. I don't think I would have survived the civil rights movement and segregation in the schools. Which bathroom or water fountain, "white" or "colored," would I have been required to use? Sometimes I think that some white people in America are more racist than the white people in Germany, or anywhere in Europe for that matter, even though in October I was scared to go on the subway in Berlin because of my Jewish heritage and my black heritage. The week before I traveled to Berlin from Bonn, some skinheads had beaten up thirty-six people on the train. Not only foreigners, but Germans too.

One day at school I read a story called "Of the Meaning of Progress," by W. E. B. Du Bois. It was about racism and how black children were not allowed to learn to read and write before the Civil War and how after the Civil War the schools began the practice of segregation. I loved this story, but I felt cheated. I was in such a rage about not reading that many black authors and American Indian authors in school that when I came home, I burst into tears and poured out my troubles about being mixed in America. Whereupon my dad told me to read three essays in a book he's editing called *Multi-America,* about whether people of different colors can get along in the United States. One essay was by Allison Francis, a graduate student at the University of Washington in St. Louis who has two black parents, and a second was by Karla Brundage, a poet and graduate of Vassar College who has a black mother and a white father. Both young women have had the same problem as I: being light-skinned. The third essay was by a dark-skinned woman, a writer and film maker who graduated from Harvard University, named Ngozi Ola, whose father is Yoruba and whose mother is African American. She writes about her experiences in Berlin, some of it pleasant and some not so pleasant. She said that despite German racism, no whites fled a neighborhood when she moved in.

After reading these essays, I didn't feel so alone. I calmed down and wrote this. I read somewhere that mixed kids are the fastest-growing group of children in the United States. Many people think it will be us who mediate the problems between blacks and whites, but I don't think we can. The problems of race in this country are too big for us mixed-race people to solve alone. It's going to take everybody in the country to change the way we are.

I have a lot of friends of many racial backgrounds. I have friends in other countries. That's why I can't understand why people can't accept people for who they are. When I was thirteen, I had trouble finding out who I was, and I still do at seventeen. I think I will for the rest of my life. The next time someone asks, "What's my nationality?" though, I'll say, "Who cares?" Because it's more important who I am inside than outside. Besides, many scientists say that there is no such thing as separate races. Everybody's mixed up.

Passing

■ ■ ■

KARLA BRUNDAGE

It happens all the time . . . I am walking down the street and a complete stranger stops me, maybe even interrupting my conversation, and urgently asks, "What are you?"

Or I am minding my own business, living on my street, when I notice that the Black woman who lives next door to me, who has a child the same age as my child, blatantly ignores my "hellos" and my "we should have tea sometimes." Then one day I find that we have a friend in common. From this friend I learn the reason for her standoffishness. My neighbor does not know I am Black, but I live with a very Black man. She finds such a relationship repulsive. I make her sick.

What about my other neighbor, a Black woman of forty-plus with a grown child, who speaks only to my partner, and won't even wave to me from the car?

Or what about my sister-in-law who warned me, serious and superstitious, "Don't cut that hair, girl. You know your man won't like it; you got good hair."

I can't forget my partner's teacher and spiritual leader, who said off-hand to him after meeting me, "Shit, man, you already got yourself a white girl."

"White girl! White girl! How dare he," came my response.

My partner looked at me almost innocently and said, "Karla, he didn't mean what you think he meant. What he meant was . . ."

"Don't even try to explain. I know what he meant . . ."

"But . . ."

"I said, I know what he meant. I certainly don't need you to try and explain it. End of conversation."

He was talking about passing. He was talking about all of those instances I just listed. He was trying to explain my life to me. Do I think I am white? Many people want to know. Do I think I can pass as Black? I cannot give a definitive answer. That is the problem. People are always trying to define me, while at the same time limiting my answer. I have had people ask me what I am, and then refuse to believe me. Others never ask; they just hate me for not fitting into their little box. Meanwhile, I have been teaching myself all my life to define myself in uncertainties, in abstractions, in illusions. I am not who you think I am. Even you, reader, may have a fixed opinion from generalizations that are easy to make. My vital statistics make stereotyping even easier.

I was born in Berkeley in 1967. My parents were flower children. According to my father, they thought they could save the world through love. The story is shaky. I think they really got married for two totally different reasons. My mother, who was born and raised in Tuskegee, Alabama, had gone to all-white boarding schools much of her life. I don't think she planned to marry white, but it happened. My father, who was from Pleasantville, New York, came from a dysfunctional alcoholic family. He was being educated at a liberal arts college, and he really felt that there was no better way to live out his newfound beliefs than by marrying this Black woman he met on a college exchange and with whom he fell head over heels in love. He believed—and still believes—that by having an interracial child, along with others in their generation, they would be one step closer to ending racism.

So I was born with a cross to carry, so to speak. I say this because I have always known of my father's expectations as well as his bitterness that the sexual revolution did not save the world, and especially at the failure of his marriage, which could not overcome racism. But that's another story.

This is who I am and where I came from: conservative, middle class, educated, on both sides, Black and white. My parents were the rebels.

They were married until I was three. During this time, my mother's first cousin, who was involved with SNCC, was killed for using a white bathroom. It is my opinion that my mother could never really love my father in the same way after that incident. After all, his family is very racist. I have some relatives who still refuse to meet me. After her cousin Sammy's death, my mother became involved with the Black Panthers, and my father became resentful that she could exclude him from her life when, in his mind, he had sacrificed his, having been disowned as a result of the marriage. So they moved to Hawaii to try to escape the racism that they had once been willing to fight. This is the beginning of my memory.

I lived with my mother. I had a happy childhood, most of which was spent outdoors, playing. However, although my mother is a professor in African American studies at the University of Hawaii, she could not provide for me what did not exist. I knew of racism, I knew I was Black, but I did not grow up knowing what it is to be Black. I had no Black culture or community. In Hawaii, there are many brown people. I was brown, so I fit right in. I basically grew up as a local girl. If people asked, I would tell them I was Black, but people rarely asked. In a weird way, I have been passing for something or another all my life.

I remember at seven and eight wishing to be Hawaiian. I wanted nothing more than to really be what people thought I was. I wanted to go to Kamehameha School, which is a school for people who have traceable Hawaiian blood in them. I can remember using my spare time, when I wasn't swimming in the ocean or running relay races in our huge yard, trying to think up ways to get into that school. In the bathtub was one of my favorite places to dream. I would stand in front of the mirror wet and with a towel on, pretending it was native Hawaiian garb, and that I was really Hawaiian. I don't remember when I accepted the fact that it would not happen.

In seventh grade, my mother told me that we were going to move to the mainland for a couple of years. My fantasy changed, although not so abruptly. I remember now at age twelve lying in bed and praying to God: "God, please let California be fun. Let me have a boyfriend, and God, if there is any way, can you please take the time to look at my eyes? See God, they are brown. And God, my dad has blue eyes. I know that people in California have blue eyes and light skin. I mean, they are white. I don't have to be white, but maybe while I am there I will be a little lighter, and then I'll be tan, and if my eyes were blue . . . It would be perfect, not to mention my hair, which if it were just a little lighter. My dad has blond hair; if only I could just look more like my dad. I am not asking for much, just to look more like my dad than my mom. Please, God, just let me be more beautiful."

This is not a lie or even an exaggeration. I prayed this prayer all the way up until the night we left. Many years later when I read Toni Morrison's *The Bluest Eye,* I broke down crying from relief. My secret was out, and it wasn't just me. *The Bluest Eye* connected me to other Black women in a way I had never been able to connect, in that I am always told that, because of my near-white attributes, I somehow think I am better than others. That story is one of the truest tales I know.

So I moved, but not to California. Instead, I moved with my father to upstate New York; Hope, to be exact. I lived in Hope for one year. I hoped that no one would find out that I was black. I often wonder what it was that made me think I needed to pass in order to survive up there in the land where my father was raised and the KKK thrives. Was it my mother, who cried every day before I left, telling me that people are racist, especially when they see a brown girl with a white man? Or was it my father, who did not give me the strength to stand up for who I was. I remember telling him that I told my new friends I was Hawaiian, but I don't remember him giving me any helpful advice. I didn't even have to lie; it was easier than that. When they asked where I was from, I said, "Hawaii." And they said, "Oh, so you're Hawaiian, then." And I just smiled, my killer Hawaiian smile. All the people in Hope were thrilled, because they had a real Hawaiian living in their town. My wish had come true.

The only problem was my mother. She ruined my plan. She called almost every other night from California, and cried. "Karla, don't deny me," she would say, "please, don't deny me. Don't lie about who you are." But I was thirteen, I had never been Black before, and I wanted to have friends. I was in a new place completely foreign to me. It was too hard. I chose to tell only one person who I really was. She was my best friend, her name was Squeaker. And Squeak she did. It wound up that eventually everybody found out that I was really Black. Some people resented that. Some were just bummed that I was not a "real" Hawaiian. But I really think that misleading them to think I was Hawaiian first softened the blow. I mean, I was already a cheerleader by the time the word got out. This was what I think was the beginning of a long series of events in which I learned how to objectify myself in order to survive. I was making myself more and more invisible, in order to escape the lasso of definition.

In ninth grade, I finally did move to Oakland, California. In Oakland,

I was for the first time immersed in Black culture. And for the first time, I had a boyfriend who told me I was beautiful for who I was, a Black girl with a white father. Of course, this was my first love, and he was also mixed. What I did not know about was the deadly lines drawn between dark and light within the Black community itself. Since I did not know, I existed happily. Loving myself for perhaps the first time. I had Black and white friends. I declared myself a rebel from the traditional cliques of high school, the "stoners," who were white; the Chicanos; and the soul or disco lovers, who were Black. I declared myself a peacemaker between the three sides, neutral by virtue of my skin. After all, I looked more Chicano than anything. For a time it was my father's dream of racelessness come true.

When I finally went to college, passing became an issue again. Once again I found myself on a plane bound for upstate New York—Poughkeepsie, to be exact. Vassar College was like no place I had been before. Looking back on it, I see that I spent most of my college career in culture shock. I was not only adapting to race but to class differences. I entered Vassar with the same attitude that I had when I left Oakland. I was Black and white, and therefore part of both groups.

What I found at Vassar was that I could never be a part of the elite white world, and worse, the Blacks there resented me for even trying. I remember walking into the cafeteria on the first day of school with my new roommate, who happened to be white. I walked past a table where all ten of the Black freshmen were eating dinner and said hello. They barely looked at me, and when I walked away I heard someone comment that I must think I am white. From the first day, I was never accepted by the African Americans at Vassar; it was a very small, very tight group. Those who were mixed were forced to choose sides, and most of us chose white. The animosity between lighter- and darker-skinned Blacks, especially women, was a part of Black culture that I did not yet understand. I did not get why they would hate me or why they would think I thought I was white.

I was so hurt. I figured if they did not like me, then I would just hang out with the whites. This was a big mistake. During my entire college career, I was never invited to anyone's house for Thanksgiving, I was never asked to a ball. What I could not see was that with the whites, I was accepted as an object, an exotic. I existed on the periphery.

To lessen the pain, I drank excessively and found myself sinking deeper and deeper into a hole of self-hatred. Yet I refused to see my rejection as racially motivated, until one night when I was at the school bar, drunk as usual. A man I had slept with grabbed me and locked me in a phone booth. While in the phone booth, we began to argue about what had happened between us. I accused him and many of his friends of using me. To this he replied, "Don't you see, Karla, it's your fault! You are beautiful, so beautiful and exotic, and don't you know what that does to men?"

That night I cut off all my hair. That night I also began to see that I had been trying to be white most of the time I was at college, and that in reality, I did not know who I was. By the time I graduated, I was an alcoholic, and I knew that I had to go back to Oakland to be around Black people.

I don't know if I thought it would be better to be in the Black community, but I knew that I was missing something. I have lived in Oakland for five years now, and one thing I have learned is that as a people, we as Blacks have been truly indoctrinated into racist ways. When I first arrived, I obtained a position as a teacher's aide at a home for emotionally disturbed teens, many of whom were Black. These youths had nothing to hide in their evaluations of me. I began to notice by their reactions to me the confusion we feel as a people about our skin. Most did not believe I was Black. I found myself in a position again where I felt forced to disguise my real identity. Instead of answering that I was part Black, mixed, *hapa,* half, or mulatto—all terms that I had used my entire life—I found myself saying I was Black. I wanted so desperately to be accepted as Black, but still no one would believe me. Whenever I said, "Black," in response to the question, "What are you?", the person attacking me would say, "Black and what . . . ?"

So, I began to denounce my whiteness. I was angry at my father for cursing me. I was angry at all white people for being racists and for promoting racism everywhere. Once again I looked for acceptance of my new identify in men. I chose Black men who were "revolutionary" in their beliefs, men who had forsaken the system completely. Over and over I found myself in the same predicament. I was not Black enough for them. Yet to this day almost all the men in that group are living with (off) white women. Naturally, I began to hate white women. All the anger I had felt at Vassar surfaced and I was able to bond with Black women for the first time, as well as justify my hypocrisy, until I began to realize that many Black women hated me, too, for the same reasons. They thought I was white.

This was my latest disillusion. It was really all too much for me. I opened my eyes and began to look at my life. Many of my friends are mixed. Not deliberately, but maybe out of some common pool of experience. I realized that it was not only hypocritical but impossible to hate my father, a part of myself. At the age of twenty-five, I finally realized that I am mixed. Not definable, not in any box, and probably not all that new a phenomenon. But certainly an enigma.

Still, people are constantly trying to define me—all people, white and Black. For a while I wanted to wear a sign around my neck that said, "I am Black." But slowly I began to realize, I am not just Black. I certainly am not white. I am mixed. What does it mean to be a mixed-race, Black/white woman in America in the nineties? Recently, my mother told me that we are actually one-eighth Cherokee. This is another part of me that I never even explored, let alone identified with. I am still trying to figure it all out, but I think right now it's about defining myself, taking that step to say, Hey, I am mixed. I am not going to pretend anymore. I am not going to go to Castlemont, a predominantly Black high school in East Oakland, and argue with teenagers about my race. I am not going to drive myself to the point of suicide trying to be white, either. I am just going to be me.

Why Am I Still Onstage at the Cotton Club?

■ ■ ■

ALLISON FRANCIS

What are you? *Mulatto creole exotic.* What color are you? *High yalla bunana red.* Are you black or white? *Light skinned Black wommin.*

Every time a stranger on the street accosts me about my skin color (and it happens frequently), the old frustration and anger begin to creep up my spine. Once, while I was sitting in front of the post office, a man I didn't know walked up to me and before he even bothered to introduce himself, he asked me whether I was black or white: *Hey, is you a sister? I never did like me no high yulla woman, but you do all right.* Suddenly I'm back with the black girls in my elementary school bathroom who threatened to cut off my hair because I thought I was too cute. Or I see the white girls in high school who ran up to me after summer vacation and compared their tanned arms to mine, squealing with delight if their skin was darker. Or I'm rushing up the stairs to catch an El train in Chicago, Illinois, while a black woman warns everyone to make way for the *white devil.* Or I'm walking down a fashionable street in St. Louis, Missouri, with a dark-skinned brother, when a couple passes us and observes out loud that *vanilla always has to be with chocolate.*

My "yellowness" makes me either subject to jokes and threats or an object for comparison and contrast. My light skin may signify beauty, may signify ugliness, may signify bourgeois aspirations, but it never signifies me. As a light-skinned woman, I am sometimes forced to occupy a nether space, a third race, that mediates between the color politics of black and white communities. I become an abstraction, rather than an actual person, through which other people confront their color. Many times in the past, I have despised the color of my skin because the negative responses I frequently receive label me as something other than black and have made me feel disconnected from my ethnicity. However, why should I undermine my self-worth because of the percentage of melanin in my body? Am I any less Black because the surface of my skin is not dark brown?

My status as an African American woman is constantly questioned. Not only must I contend with my subordinate position as female in a male-dominated society, but I must also consider how others perceive my association within the black community. The fact that I know who I am should be enough, but I'm continually required to define and defend my "blackness" just in case I forget where I came from, on account of my lightness.

Someone says, "But you don't look black," or, "You talk too proper," or, "Is your momma white?" Is there a certain way I should act, I should talk, so I can be identifiably black when my skin tone alone is not enough evidence? Unfortunately, my ethnicity is predicated on my skin color, and if my pigment is lacking, so is my cultural affinity, unless I can manifest my blackness through certain "ethnic markers" such as language ("Black English") or musical taste (gospel, soul, R & B, gangsta rap) or food (black-eyed peas, collard greens, ham hocks).

I once asked two brothers on a street corner in Oakland, California, if they had change for a dollar so that I could feed my parking meter. One man began to pull coins from his pocket and then stopped and carefully looked at me.

"What are you, black or white? 'Cause if you white, I won't give you my money."

I immediately asked him what he would do if I were mixed, a mulatto if you will. He responded, "If you mixed, then you cool, you my girlfriend. If not," he shrugged, "well, I just don't like white people."

I stood there with my mouth gaping while he exchanged my dollar for four quarters, wondering how many other people have refused to help me because they could not see beyond my skin color. And conversely, how many times has my light skin color proven advantageous?

Lena Horne once said in one of her interviews, "I was unique in that I was a kind of black that white people could accept. . . . I had the worst kind of acceptance because it was never for how great I was or what I contributed. It was because of the way I looked." Similar to Horne, my light skin color supposedly functions as a passport into the white world that I would be foolish not to exploit; however, if I make use of this so-called advantage, I'm guilty of selling out or passing for white. When people assess my actions based on my surface appearance, they ignore who I really am.

But I ain't a contemporary house nigga and my personality and behavioral patterns should not be predetermined by the color of my skin.

Frequently, I see high-fashion magazine ads in *Essence* and *Vogue,* television shows like *Martin,* and films like *School Daze* and *Strictly Business,* that tend to reduce light-skinned black women to static symbols of desire. Or I'll read works of fiction like Harriet Beecher Stowe's *Uncle Tom's Cabin,* which romanticizes the "tragic mulatto," and Gwendolyn Brooks's *Maud Martha,* which represents light-skinned women as seductive but voiceless commodities. Unfortunately, these images perpetuate stereotypes that rely on unchallenged codes of behavior (*she think she too good for us; she too uppity!*) and perception (*she think she too cute with that long hair; must be a weave!*) which are recognizable to both the white and black communities.

It's no wonder (but inexcusable) that people I don't know, and people I do, question my identity since popular culture and social myths compare shades of black and assume that being lighter is better because light skin supposedly is akin to white skin. Therefore, if a black man wants to "git with" a light-skinned black woman, people may accuse him of expressing a mimetic desire for the white female he traditionally cannot have. Light skin is either admired, despised, or both, depending on the viewer's point of reference (i.e., skin color).

Either reaction, or their combination, is humiliating for me because it relies on a one-dimensional concept of my color, not individuality. Needless to say, dark-skinned black women also must contend with demoralizing and degrading stereotypes that represent them as undesirable and unattractive. However, where and how do women colored like myself respond to the negative renderings of light-skinned females that pervade our media, our literature, and our society?

I believe that these colorist (mis)conceptions must be challenged and that intra-racial color lines should be dissolved. African Americans are a diverse people with diverse skin tones—from buttercream to dark amber to the deepest ebony. When we subscribe to one means of identifying ourselves for others, be it through class, gender, geographical location, or skin color, we risk reifying racist stereotypes and denying our cultural diversity.

My intent is not to belittle dark skin tones or even disregard my own light skin color, but I am tired of dancing with feathers at the Cotton

Club, and I will no longer shoulder the burden of these negative societal expectations inherent in my being perceived as a "light-skinned black wommin."

Just because I talk too proper; just because I sometimes hang out with white people; just because I'm high yalla honey-coated dipped in tea-colored soda water almost white with back too tight, don't make me not Black!

The African Heritage of Italian and Other European Americans—and All Peoples of the Earth

■ ■ ■

LUCIA CHIAVOLA BIRNBAUM

Recently I wrote a book on black madonnas of Italy, suggesting that they are a metaphor for a memory of the time when the dark earth was venerated as the body of a woman, a memory visible in Italy in the folklore, in historic cultural and political resistance, and today in Italian transformative movements for justice and equality.[1]

Since the book was published, I have come to realize that black madonnas may be more than a metaphor. The memory of a dark woman divinity may, as contemporary geneticists say, be "encoded in our genes"—a memory of the first human migrations out of Africa into Europe, Asia, and every continent of the earth.

Today, the trick mirror of white racism against dark-skinned peoples, which reached a nadir of violence in the United States, has been cracked by anthropologists and geneticists who agree that "the earliest human, *Homo erectus*, walked out of Africa, into parts of Europe, and all the way to eastern China and Indonesia . . . more than two million years [ago]."[2] One million years ago, *Homo erectus* populations lived in three continents:

in Africa; in the region that became Europe thirty thousand years ago; and in Asia.

Whether *Homo erectus* evolved differently, in different regions, into *Homo sapiens* (modern man) is a subject of controversy. The view with the most support from anthropologists and geneticists is the "Noah's ark" theory: *Homo sapiens* derived from a single source, Africa. As Stephen Jay Gould says, "For various reasons, including the presence of the best and oldest remains of fully modern humans (100,000 to 125,000 years old) in Africa and the discovery of the greatest genetic diversity among contemporary African peoples," indicating that modern humans have lived longer in Africa than anywhere else, "Africa seems the strongest candidate for our pinpoint source under the Noah's ark theory."[3]

An Italian geneticist from Genoa, L. Luca Cavalli-Sforza, emeritus professor of Stanford University, has verified the "out of Africa" thesis with research tracking early human migrations in the DNA of our genes. In the Cavalli-Sforza and a world team of demographers conclude that the genetic inheritance of "white" Europeans is 65 percent Asian and 35 percent African.[4] The ratio reflects Asian westward migrations after the first human migrations out of Africa into Europe, Asia, and every continent of the globe.

DNA research also supports Marija Gimbutas's theory, based on archeological evidence, of the Kurgan invasion into Europe and India between 6000 and 3000 BCE, which subordinated earlier peaceful, matrilineal, earth-bonded cultures, and imposed the violent cultures of sky gods, war, and slavery that have dominated world history up to the present.[5] Yet the deep memory of the peaceful, egalitarian age associated with the goddess persists in vernacular cultures of Third World peoples, and in the tangles of matristic as well as patriarchal threads in the genetic histories of all peoples of the earth.

Tracking my own genetic inheritance in the histories of the Sicilian birthplaces of my paternal and maternal ancestors, my primordial ancestors were Africans. In the Neolithic era, my ancestors were Sicani—from Africa, Asia, then Spain and Liguria, who came down the Italian Peninsula into Sicily.

After 1100 BCE Hebrew Canaanites enter my genetic spiral, Canaanite Jews from Asia Minor who when defeated by Israeli Jews established a base in Carthage in North Africa, and carried Astarte and other goddesses from Africa and Asia Minor wherever they sailed. Or settled, as Hebrew Canaanites did in my paternal grandparents' and father's towns in southeastern Sicily.

After 1000 BCE, the violent sky gods of the Indo-Europeans enter my genetic inheritance with the Siculi, who came down peninsular Italy in 1000 BCE and joined Indo-European Greeks who colonized South Italy and Sicily as Magna Graecia in 750 BCE, succeeded by Indo-European Romans after 350 BCE.

In my case, the African and Semitic inheritance is renewed again from 265 to 146 BCE with Carthaginians (Phoenicians/Africans), against whom Greeks and Romans waged the Punic Wars in Sicily and Africa. Following 70 C.E., Israelite Jews came to Sicily and Italy after the destruction of the Temple. Subsequently my genetic and cultural history is knotted with invaders from Northern Europe (Germanic tribes after 238 C.E.) and made vibrant with spirals from Asia Minor: the Byzantine branch of Christianity with whom Sicilians identified after 330 C.E., and Arab/Muslims after 700 C.E., with whom Sicilians were compatible but whom the Pope considered "infidel."

After the Norman invasion of Sicily in 1060 (six years before they took England), Sicilians endured one long line of invaders from the north, a roll call in which peasants included the Pope: Lombards, German Swabians, French Angevins, Spanish Aragonese, Spanish and Austrian Bourbons, and Northern Italians—all of them, like Sicilians, of African, Asian, and European heritage; all floating sets and subsets of different genetic inheritance. "All races or ethnic groups," states Cavalli-Sforza, "now seem to be a bewildering array of overlapping sets and subsets that are in a constant state of flux in fairly short periods of evolutionary time."[6]

From genetics we learn that all peoples of the earth are ultimately of African origin and all ethnic groups are an array of genes so bewildering that an African American may have fewer genes connecting her or him to the continent of Africa than may a European American.

Which presents us with the importance of differing historical experience, and with choice. African Americans experienced slavery, economic and social servitude, and lynchings in a racist experience that may have been unique in human history for its violence. At the crest of U.S. racism against African Americans, Native Americans, Latin Americans, Asian Americans, and so on, Italians came to the United States and were categorized with other "people of color." Although all were targets of racism, the historic experiences of "people of color" varied.

The violence of the racism of Europeans who invaded a continent already inhabited by Native Americans, and who justified the "extermination of Native Americans and enslavement of Africans," was undoubtedly connected to concurrent developments in capitalism, the formation of the modern nation state, and the Protestant Reformation and Catholic Counter-Reformation.[7] Yet U.S. racism of the seventeenth, eighteenth, and nineteenth centuries by dominant groups toward dark-skinned peoples remains glaring in its uniqueness, and mitigated very little by Christian beliefs. Racist beliefs were part of the Protestant Christianity of English Puritans, as much as the Catholic Christianity of the Spanish in their early invasions, rape and plunder, settlements, and missions in North America.

Dominant white Anglo-Saxon Protestants inflicted varying degrees of humiliating racism on all peoples who came to North America after their invasion of the seventeenth century—Irish and Germans before the Civil War, Jews after that war—but WASP racism against dark-skinned "others," including Asians after the Civil War, was cruel and violent. In the twentieth century, the United States, having swept across the continent, looked outward to imperial conquest of dark-skinned peoples of the Philippines, Cuba, et al., and to "social control" of dark others at home.[8]

WASPs perceived Italian immigrants as dark. Although they had applauded Garibaldi and the Risorgimento, were fond of traveling to Italy, studied the Roman classics, and admired the Renaissance, when they saw Italians in their own cities, they were vaguely troubled. Italians prayed to the Madonna, not to the austere Calvinist father God. WASPs perceived Italian women as sensual, Italian men as surly, and all Italians as "unsuitable American citizens." Southern Italians were seen as "swarthy" and "usually dark-mooded, sad-faced men," different from Northern Italians, who were "part of Western civilization," and whose "Germanic blood" and "artistic achievements" distinguished them from the "ignorant peasants of Southern Italy," who appeared to be "a yet half-civilized stock."[9]

The similarity of Italians and African Americans threw William Dean Howells, Boston brahmin man of letters, off balance. He loved high Italian culture so much he learned the language, but in Boston he was unsettled by African Americans, whom he described as having "supple cunning" and "abundant amiability," while Italian Americans were "wily and amiable." As more African Americans came north and more Italian immigrants came to stay, late nineteenth-century WASP novels referred to the "explosive" implications of dark-skinned people.

Explosive implications became palpable in the 1890s and early twentieth century as the movement for populist reform threw poor whites and blacks together, and as South Italians, who had participated in socialist uprisings (suppressed) in their own country, immigrated to the United

States in the period when socialists attained their highest numbers in U.S. history.

The movement for "social control" of others after 1900 by WASP social scientists, who traced their heritage to the first Puritan settlements, sought the authority of science to subordinate other people. They found this "scientific" justification in the new science of intelligence testing and the conditioned-reflex methods of behaviorist psychology.

In intelligence tests after 1900, African, Native American, and Asian Americans were placed at the bottom of the IQ pyramid. Southern and Eastern Europeans were placed slightly above the bottom—in tests that reflected (and continue to reflect today) racist attitudes and the economic/political/social pyramid of U.S. capitalism.[10]

Until intelligence tests are devised by Pygmies of Africa, or other ancient peoples of the earth whose societies since prehistoric times have been cooperative, peaceful, egalitarian, and nurturant—societies that care for the weak, and consider the earth their divinity—we are not likely to value the kind of intelligence that human beings need in order to survive.[11]

Racism was part of the high culture of Europe and of the United States in the early twentieth century even before the "science" of intelligence testing institutionalized it.[12] Educated classes read the European ideologist of racism, Gobineau, who was later quoted by Hitler. As Martin Bernal has documented, a racist Hellenomania in nineteenth- and twentieth-century Europe and the United States elevated Greek culture (thought to be Aryan), and denigrated Egyptians and Phoenicians as Africans and Semites, thereby justifying racism against dark-skinned peoples and a racial anti-Semitism. Gobineau affirmed the Anglo-Saxon sense of superiority over African, Native, and Asian Americans, and described the "new immigration" (Jews, Italians, Slavs) as a modern-day case of a Carthage that would corrupt white civilization.[13]

First-generation Italian (and other new immigrants) made the external obeisances to "Americanization" that were necessary for survival (they had lots of experience in this, having survived invaders and the Inquisition) but kept, for the most part, their "pagan" earth-bonded beliefs. Their children, however, were to be severed from their ancestral culture by "Americanization" campaigns that became the ground of U.S education after World War I. During that war, WASP leaders—including those who hoped for socialism, like John Dewey—were impressed by the efficacy of wartime government propaganda and the results of intelligence tests given to army recruits that flattered dominant WASPs and reduced the intelligence of soldiers of other ethnic groups to the age of thirteen.[14]

As African American slavery had done earlier, and the enforced removal of Native American children to boarding schools would do later, education for "Americanization" from the 1920s up to the 1960s divested subordinated ethnic groups of their history, language, and culture.

The larger meaning of this education for Americanization has been a political legacy of conservative conformity in the United States. The dominant WASP fear that "people of color" and "hyphenates" at the bottom would come together behind the hope for socialism escalated during World War I, turned into violent suppression of Italian American and other radicals in 1919, and influenced the restrictive immigration legislation of 1924, aimed at Italian and other peoples of Southern and southeastern Europe. Intelligence testing, which took away the self-esteem of those placed at the bottom, in addition to conditioning techniques in education have subsequently served the dominant class well in banishing socialism as "un-American."

In the 1960s in the United States, the possibility of a new and just civilization was envisioned by Malcolm X and Martin Luther King, Jr., but also by people of other ethnic groups; for this essay, the Italian American student leader Mario Savio is relevant. Racism may be the most important variable in preventing this new vision of a just society from coming true.

Today, an unprecedented convergence of scholarship is overturning arguments that have historically shored up violent racist notions. Multicultural, interdisciplinary, and feminist scholars are pointing out that the source of violence, from the beginnings of Western civilization, has been the attitude that defines "ourselves" and "others." Early "others" were Canaanite Jews, "pagans," Israelite Jews, "barbarians," Muslims, and by the early modern era, not only lepers and Jews but women. Major "others," after the European invasion of North America, were, first, dark-skinned Native Americans and African Americans; later, Latin and Asian Americans.[15] For dominant WASPs in the twentieth century, Italians, Jews, and Slavs were also "others."

Studying their history comparatively in Italy as well as in the United States, Italian Americans have learned that the racist dichotomy of "ourselves" and "others" was evident in Italy after unification in the last quarter of the nineteenth century. A racist ideologist, Cesare Lombroso, supported Northern Italian views of Southern Italians as dark, backward, lazy, superstitious, and ignorant. This Northern Italian racism could be found, as Antonio Gramsci pointed out, even among socialists of the early twentieth century. The racism persists today in the Northern Leagues, who with Fascist allies swept to right-wing national victory in 1994. In this contemporary Italian racism, industrialized North Italians regard themselves as superior to economically underdeveloped and darker South Italians—a racism that is aligned today with the persecution of African immigrant workers in Italy.

Genetics may determine our lives, but the complexity of each of our sets and subsets of genes makes it very unclear how the determinism works. So the political choices that human beings make are critical to the way history turns. Choice is implicit in the contemporary non-violence movement of millions of Italians in volunteer organizations, who disregard political boundaries in their opposition to the Mafia and the implicit fascism of the Berlusconi regime; in their commitment to change the political economy non-violently; in their work to make their communities livable; in their belief that saving the environment is "saving creation"; and in their identification with the dark peoples of the South of the planet.[16]

A new civilization can also be glimpsed in the United States today, even in what sometimes appears to be the morass of "identity politics." Among Italian Americans, for example, scholars study the vernacular values of justice, equality, and transformation in the peasant culture of their grandparents. Italian American women, who are often poets (such as Diane Di Prima and Rose Romano), identify Italian Americans not with white culture and the political economy of capitalism but with the poor and dark peoples of the earth and the hope for a just planet. A new organization, Italian Americans for a Multicultural United States (IAMUS), regards Italian Americans, like the rest of the peoples of the earth, as "peoples of colors."

U.S. multicultural and feminist scholars are converging with contemporary African and other scholars, notably Cheikh Anta Diop and Martin Bernal, who point to the centrality of Africa in world history.[17] Diop earlier, and Bernal later, deconstructed the racism that credited white Aryans with Greek high civilization. Contemporary feminists, from another perspective, point out that Greek civilization was scarcely a model to which anyone should look since it was violent, cruel, splintered the primordial goddess into female figures contoured to the male imagination, subordinated women, and enslaved others.[18]

Diop demonstrated that Egyptians are Africans, and Martin Bernal found that the notion that Egypt was "not African" was part of European racism supporting nineteenth-century imperialism. Diop documented the Southern African origins of Egyptians and tracked the presence of

Grimaldi man (skeletons with African characteristics) in the area that came to be known as Europe.[19]

Stating early on what archeologists, anthropologists, and geneticists are today verifying, Diop found that the "first inhabitant of Europe was a migrating Black: the Grimaldi Man."[20] Grimaldi skeletons have been found all over Europe and Asia, from the Iberian Peninsula to Lake Baikal in Siberia, to France, Austria, the Crimea, Russia, and Italy. Bernal has rescued the Hebrew Canaanites of West Asia from denigration and analyzed their pivotal role in carrying African and Asian cultures everywhere in the known world during the pre-Grecian era.

A wise historian, Diop states that history cannot be restricted by ethnic group, nation, or culture: "Roman history is Greek, as well as Roman, and both Greek and Roman history are Egyptian because the entire Mediterranean was civilized by Egypt; Egypt in turn borrowed from other parts of Africa, especially Ethiopia." For Diop, Africa is the "birthplace of humanity," a continent where "the historic kinship of Islam, Christianity, and Judaism with Egyptian religious thought" was lived out.[21]

In my own research of the connection between the pre-Christian woman divinity and black madonnas in Italy, I have verified the African connection in artefacts found near my ancestral paternal site in Sicily. The statue of the goddess of Grammichele has an enigmatic smile, her hair ordered in African corn rows. The statue of the seated goddess who suckles two children was found, along with a skeleton identified with the "Negro race," in the city of Megara Hyblaea, in the sixth century BCE before the Greeks arrived. The statues, and other artefacts of Megara Hyblaea, are of African and West Asian provenance.[22]

The civilization of the goddess documented by Marija Gimbutas for Old Europe—a matristic, egalitarian, and peaceful society clearly evident from 6500 to 3500 BCE, a civilization that never knew war or slavery—was, according to Diop, a society very similar to "the sedentary, agrarian and matrilineal African societies." From Diop's perspective, the cult of black madonnas of Europe derives "directly from the cult of Isis," which preceded Christianity in the Mediterranean.[23]

The statue of Isis holding Horus is, indeed, very similar to icons of Madonna and Child in Christian culture. I have found a good deal of evidence of the persistence of the image and values of Isis in the vernacular and contemporary political beliefs of Sicilians. Contemporary Italians find significance for a new society in the African values of the civilization of Isis, as the poem at the end of this essay shows.

My research for *Black Madonnas: Feminism, Religion, and Politics in Italy,*[24] and for my *Godmothers and Others of Colors: Le Comari, a Sicilian*

Story, converges with Diop's findings and with those of Bernal on the significance of African and West Asia for world history.

The immediate antecedents of black madonnas of Italy were the three major woman divinities of the late Roman Empire, dark, and from Africa and Asia Minor: Isis of Africa; Diana of Ephesus; and Cybele of Anatolia. Roman legions, drawn from the lower classes of three continents, carried dark goddesses of Africa and Asia Minor all over the known world in Europe, as well as Asia and Africa, where early statues of the goddess and later black madonnas may still be seen.

The memory of a dark woman divinity of a thousand names persisted into the Christian era in black madonnas. Culling evidence from archeology, myths, legends, rituals, pilgrimages, heresies, fables, and the values of the age of the goddess, I have found that this memory of a dark mother remains alive in Italy today. Elsewhere the memory is deeply submerged in dominant patriarchal cultures, but it can still be glimpsed in earth-bonded vernacular cultures, notably cultures of the Third World.

For dominant patriarchal cultures, it will take more excavating. But a dark woman divinity and her values of justice, equality, and transformation can probably be found everywhere early Africans migrated—which means every continent on earth.

The surfacing of this deep memory of a dark mother may be critical for the transformation of violence and injustice into a green and just world.

> *Struggle for happiness*
> *like people with little struggle for bread*
> *and remember that love is the seed and the*
> *fruit of joy*
>
> *Love one another and love yourselves*
> *Be born without fear*
> *because she who gives you life gives you*
> *a fertile earth*
>
> *Do not be fearful of hunger, or of the years,*
> *or of growing old*
> *because at each season of life you will find*
> *new wisdom.*
>
> —*Civilization of Isis,* 1996 years BCE[25]

■ ■ ■

NOTES

1. Lucia Chiavola Birnbaum, *Black Madonnas: Feminism, Religion, and Politics in Italy* (Boston: Northeastern University Press, 1993).

2. Stephen Jay Gould, "So Near and Yet So Far," *The New York Review*, October 20, 1994.

3. Luca and Francesco Cavalli-Sforza, *Chi Siamo: La storia della diversita' umana* (Milano: Arnoldo Mondadori Editore, 1993).

4. Ibid.

5. See Marija Gimbutas, *The Civilization of the Goddess* (San Francisco: Harper, 1991).

6. Cavalli-Sforza quoted in Louise Levathes, "A Geneticist Maps Ancient Migrations," *New York Times*, Science Times, July 27, 1993.

7. See Martin Bernal, *Black Athena*, Vol. I: *The Fabrication of Ancient Greece 1785–1985* (New Brunswick, NJ: Rutgers University Press, 1987; 1991).

8. I can attest to anxiety causing whites to perceive people as dark. In 1968 when I was a professor (shortly to be fired) at San Francisco State in the student/professor strike against racism and imperialism, a non-striking white colleague came up to me and said, "I didn't realize you were so dark."

9. All quotations here are from John Paul Russo's excellent paper, "From Italophilia to Italophobia: Representations of Italian Americans in the Early Gilded Age," presented to the conference of the American Italian Historical Association, Philadelphia, November 1991.

10. This is a convoluted story, analyzed in depth in my doctoral dissertation, *John Broadus Watson's Behaviorist Psychology and American Social Theory, 1913–1933*, University of California, Berkeley, 1964.

11. See "What Is Intelligence and Who Has It?", *New York Times Book Review*, October 15, 1994. The books reviewed are Charles Murray and Richard J. Herrnstein, *The Bell Curve: Intelligence and Class Structure in American Life* (New York: The Free Press, 1994); J. Philippe Rushton, *Race, Evolution, and Behavior: A Life History Perspective* (New Brunswick, NJ: Transaction Publishers, 1994); and Seymour W. Itzkoff, *The Decline of Intelligence in America: A Strategy for National Renewal* (Westport, CT: Praeger, 1994). Referring to IQ scores, these authors speak of an "emerging underclass" that is "black." Correlating intelligence test scores and ethnic groups, the racist assumptions of these contemporary testers, like their early twentieth-century antecedents, are evident, although they have had to adjust their statistics for earlier bottom groups who perform well on tests— Asians who generally score a few points higher than whites, and Ashkenazi Jews of European origins "who test higher than any other ethnic groups."

For Pygmies and other still-existing ancient peoples, see Cavalli-Sforza, *Chi Siamo*.

12. See Birnbaum, *John Broadus Watson*, particularly the chapters on philosophers, psychologists, sociologists, and educators.

13. See Bernal, *Black Athena*, chapter 8.

14. See Birnbaum, *John Broadus Watson*, loc. cit.

15. See Ronald Takaki, *Strangers from a Different Shore: A History of Asian Americans* (Boston: Little, Brown, 1989).

16. See Lucia Chiavola Birnbaum, "The Social Ecology of Nonviolence," in *The Ecological Imagination in Italy*, edited by Renate Holub and Itala Rutter (unpublished work).

17. See Cheikh Anta Diop, *Civilization or Barbarism: An Authentic Anthropology* (Brooklyn, NY: Lawrence Hill Books, 1991; first published Paris: Présence Africaine, 1981).

18. See Charlene Spretnak, *Lost Goddesses of Early Greece: A Collection of Pre-Hellenic Myths* (Boston: Beacon Press, 1984).

19. A good exhibit of Grimaldi Man may be found in Musée de l'Homme, Paris.

20. Diop, *Civilization or Barbarism*, p. 13.

21. Ibid., pp. xviii, 5–6.

22. My research for *Black Madonnas: Feminism, Religion, and Politics in Italy* and for my completed manuscript, *Godmothers and Others of Colors* (1996), documents the case for African origins, converging with Diop's findings and with Bernal's case for the significance of Africa and West Asia for world history. I differ from Bernal in that I consider high Greek civilization to reflect aryan invasions and to have replaced earlier matristic, harmonious, and egalitarian civilizations of Africa and West Asia with "western civilization" grounded on violence.

23. Diop, *Civilization or Barbarism*, p. 13.

24. Isis, melded with west Asian dark mothers—Astarte and Cybele—as the origin of black madonnas of Europe, has been extensively documented in my *Godmothers and Others of Colors* (completed manuscript, 1996). See my *Black Madonnas*, the chapter on carnival in particular.

25. See Carlo Consiglio, *Una societa' a misura di natura* (Catania, Sicily: Alfa Grafica Sgroi, 1981). Also, Birnbaum, *Black Madonnas*, pp. 73–74.

Black and Jewish Like
Jesus and Me

■ ■ ■

ROBIN WASHINGTON

> *"Some of the greatest men in the world were
> epileptics," country hick Virgil Roseboro
> explains to the protagonist in Mordecai
> Richler's* The Apprenticeship of Duddy Kravitz.
>
> *"No kidding?" replied Kravitz.*
>
> *"Julius Caesar . . . Jesus Christ, even. Dostoevski.
> Charlie Chaplin."*
>
> *"Charlie Chaplin is a Jew."*
>
> *"A guy can be both, you know."*

For all the carloads of ink fueling the presses on the conflicts between blacks and Jews, it is amazing that none of the great minds expending so much gray matter on the subject has ever stopped to consider the Roseboro Axiom: When speaking of two non-mutually-exclusive groups, remember, a guy can be both.

In fact, Roseboro offers the single best example. Epilepsy aside, everyone knows Jesus was also a Jew. And no self-respecting Afrocentric this side of J. A. Rogers is about to let go of the one-drop rule for Christ's sake. So the next time you let go a "funny-he-doesn't-look-Jewish" guffaw to a rerun of *In Living Color*'s "Menachem! I've just met a boy named Menachem!" skit, remember: the Saviour of the Christian world suggests otherwise.

Yet does Jesus say anything about the Judaic complexion of the United States today? Sure, there was Sammy Davis, Jr., but who can name another? Although most Jews would at first say they cannot, they stumble at the postulation that in almost every Reform or Conservative synagogue, there is at least one Black Jew.

"Not at my shul," asserts one matronly congregant. "We do have one interracial couple, but the husband didn't convert."

"Do they have children?" I ask.

"They have a boy and a girl. But what does that mean?"

"It means your congregation has two Black Jews."

Those two are among some 200,000 in the United States, who make up 3 percent of all American Jews. Sources for this estimate include a 1990 Council of Jewish Federations survey which suggests there may be more than 250,000 self-described Black Jews in a broad definition of "who is a Jew" and 120,000 Black Jews in a stricter analysis.

And so defines me. Black Jew, Jewish African American, African American Jew, American Jew of African descent; put the adjective where you wish, it still comes out the same. No, I'm not from Ethiopia, I'm not in a cult, and I didn't convert. But what difference would it make if I had?

Although most of us find it insulting to be asked how we became Jewish—our lighter-skinned brothers and sisters rarely face such an inquisition—we are happy to share our heritage as we belatedly join as a community celebrating the Black Jewish experience in America.

That experience includes, like myself, the children of black and Jewish parents, the legacy of the oft-referred-to better times between the groups. We are also the living testament of a 1970s survey that found blacks as the likely spouses of Jews who married interreligiously and Jews the usual choices of blacks who married interracially.

Then there are black converts to Judaism, who despite quiet disclaimers that "they aren't real Jews" are indeed so according to *halacha,* Jewish law.

There are also several thousand members of the Ethiopian Hebrew Congregations, who despite their name are not East Africans but very American and a very religiously observant group that originated half a century before the Black Muslims in the United States.

There are other black groups further removed from mainstream halachic Judaism, including the Hebrew Israelites, the Black Hebrews and the followers of Yahweh ben Yahweh, and others too numerous to name. Some, formed just decades after slavery, still worship Jesus or include his name in their official titles.

Mainstream Judaism has been less than keen on accepting the latter groups as true Jews, but that's beside the point; not all have asked for that acceptance or even have a use for it. And not all call themselves "Jews," either, drawing distinctions between Jews, Israelites, Hebrews, and other lost tribes. The old adage of Judaism in general clearly applies to those who are black: Put two on a desert island and you get three congregations.

As the child of a black and Jewish couple of the 1950s, who's going to question my identity? Because my father was black I am, by every law of race in this country, definitely black. And because my mother is Jewish I am, like Jesus, Fiorella LaGuardia, and Karl and Groucho Marx, halachicly Jewish. Belonging to a conservative shul, keeping kosher, and knowing prayers by memory rather than writ doesn't make me any more or less so than anyone.

As a Black Jew, even a halachic one, I probably have as much in common with the Yahweh ben Yahweh folk as I do with my Lubavitch brothers and sisters. Basically, I'm down with both and not interested in anyone who would dis either of them.

Which brings up the question of what Black Jews think about black/Jewish relations. Some time ago I conducted an informal survey of light-skinned American Jews of various European backgrounds and African Americans who were not Jewish. To the Jewish respondents, I asked, "Do you consider yourself white?" and, "Do you believe there is such a thing as black anti-Semitism?"

Most Jews who considered themselves white said there was no widespread problem of black anti-Semitism because blacks who hated them did so because they hated all white people. Jews who thought of themselves as something other than white, however, concluded if blacks hated them it was precisely because they are Jews.

Yet the few blacks who made a distinction of Jews as a separate group showed an admiration, at least begrudgingly, for them, as in "We should do like the Jews do." Most made little distinction and echoed James Baldwin's assessment of black attitudes toward Jews as "a different type of white person who goes to church on Saturday instead of Sunday."

As a Jew of color, however, I've often wondered where Jews who think of themselves as white ever came up with that notion. Although they are correct in their assessment of Black America's perception of them, they surely cannot believe for a minute that white America thinks of them as members of their club. Go ask any bellboy.

With no end of hype to the "Black/Jewish Relations" question, I suspect these attitudes have changed. Yet for most blacks today, Jews are not an issue, and even less of an issue than they were thirty years ago when black and Jewish neighborhoods were concentric or abutted each other. Taking far more prominence in black life today are keeping our children alive and finding some kind of job without being backlashed by an angry white male, not necessarily Jewish. For most blacks, Jews simply don't enter into the picture as much as they once did.

So too are Jews in suburban enclaves isolated from the reality and concerns of blacks in the inner city. Given the great misperceptions among blacks and Jews about each other and even themselves, it is hardly surprising to find that they don't see the Reverend Louis Farrakhan through the same lens.

I am at once amused and annoyed to find that what has been obvious to me since the age of childhood color consciousness is suddenly enlightening the high-powered intellectuals of both sides of my heritage. "How white are Jews of European descent in America?" asks Cornel West on a book tour with Michael Lerner. "And if they don't perceive themselves as white, how do they engage in a dialogue with black brothers and sisters, who often have been seeing you as white all along?"

Jews who have a more realistic and, I suggest, healthier self-identity as something other than white must recognize that blacks don't necessarily see it that way. Yet the recognition by both groups that blacks may sometimes be Jews and Jews may be blacks may do wonders for the self-image of each group.

Celebrate Jewry, my people, and know that you are celebrating the shtetl as well as the slave shack; that you are Europe and Asia and you are Africa and South America; that you are white, yellow, red, brown, black in every corner of the world.

Be proud in blackness, my brothers and sisters, and know that you are beautiful as Christians and Muslims, as Jews and Hebrews and Israelites, Rastafarians, Buddhists, and Animists of a powerful, powerfully believing people.

All this is not to suggest that Black Jews are at once the magic bullet to return to the land of kumbaya and we shall overcome, someday, someday. Or the hopeful phone calls received ad infinitum in my office at Boston's black newspaper, such as:

"I'm looking for Robin Washington?"

"This is he."

"He—? I thought you were a woman. I'm sorry."

"Not as sorry as I am."

"Well, Mr. Washington, I'm calling from the Black-Jewish Improved Relations Society. And we're sponsoring an event that we think will greatly affect our community."

"Really? Which community is that?"

"Um, aren't you the newspaper for—African Americans?"

"Yep."

"Oh, good. Well, what we're doing is really exciting. We're bringing an Ethiopian Jew here to serve as a bridge between the black and the Jewish communities in Boston!"

"Uh, good. Does he speak Boston English?"

"Oh I don't know ... I don't think so. Do you think that's important?"

The lesson of Black Jews in America is that we are a part of both worlds and full members of each. We are not the internally torn souls of so many tragic mulatto movie characters, forever at conflict with ourselves, but we do feel the joy and pain, the love and hurt that defines blackness and Jewishness in America. And though we do not have the answers to "Can't we get along here?"—who does?—as Jews, as African Americans, we certainly understand the question.

4

■ ■ ■

IS EUROPEAN AMERICA

DEAD?

Breaking the Silence

■ ■ ■

LOIS MÄTT-FÄSSBINDER

A trip from Placid to Guttenberg was only forty miles, but even at a very young age, I realized that these two worlds were very different: we lived in the first, but never belonged, but in the second there was always a sense of familiarity and "home." Guttenberg was where all my mother's and father's family lived. Whenever we visited, the drive was a geography lesson about where all these successful farmers came from: Austria, Luxembourg, Germany, Switzerland, Liechtenstein. My father always seemed more at ease, open and talkative, as he neared his boyhood home. When I walked through town with my mother or father, everyone seemed to know me. I understood that who my mother and father were was very important. The recitation of lineage was always part of the conversation.

It wasn't until much later in my life that I came to understand that the real story of the family was in the silences: those who were not included in the family story, and why there was so little interest in going back to the country of origin.

By the time I was in high school I no longer took the trips. All my grandparents were dead. As family gatherings were to bury my parents' generation, the silences deepened and lengthened. I had my own life.

Times were different. There would be time to fill in the many blanks later. Someday, when I had time, I would make my family history a focus of my research. The stories were interesting, that I realized very early, but trying to get past the silence would take time and effort I did not have.

When I consider my own journey of cultural awareness, it had less to do with the books I read, the classes I took, the courses I taught, or the articles I wrote than with being raised as a culturally German Catholic; joining a Franciscan community of nuns who had fled Bismarck's Germany in the 1870s. These same women had taught my mother and father and knew my family for generations. My teaching assignments took me from the racial and religious homogeneity of Iowa to St. Louis at the beginning of the 1960s.

St. Louis. History of two-hundred-year-old diversity. French outpost, site of the *Dred Scott* decision, battles of reconstruction and post-reconstruction still alive in the social, political, and economic climate of the city. I stood and watched Martin Luther King, Jr.'s, "I Have a Dream" speech on television in between community meetings and realized that the moral and political consciousness in America were merging. The mirror that was America reflected back to me untold diversity, and King's message to the millions watching rested on challenge of New Testament faith principles and constitutional promises. Each person had a story of how they saw themselves in this political union we call the United States.

1968: An incredible year. The University of St. Louis was typical of campuses across the United States. The impact of the assassinations of Martin Luther King, Jr., and Robert F. Kennedy fed the confrontation of student unrest over civil rights and America's involvement in Vietnam. Ethnic and racial identity lived at the heart of most discussions: social, economic, or political.

After five years at the center of the storm, I needed a vacation: One month of travel to all the places my father had pointed out on the map. Germany was now divided, but most of the places associated with my family were in West Germany. Even Berlin was accessible to the tourist.

I landed in Germany the day the Chicago Democratic Convention blew up. Headlines and pictures of police beating up political dissidents greeted me in city after city. Each time I visited with German students, the same question arose: What was happening to the "melting pot"; was "one from many" breaking apart?

The world had changed with the end of the war. The changes were gathering momentum both in this country and in Europe. All the questions left me with a profound understanding of my superficial historical perspective.

1969: The climate of controversy reached a fever pitch. No time for academic distance. My own understanding of what role the perceptions of race, ethnicity, nationality, and religion played in shaping my personal notions of social dynamics became very obvious.

As a director of field research in St. Louis University's School of Social Work, I realized the danger of academic distortions used in preparing students to work in diverse communities. The traditional literature and textbooks were of little use. I was confronted with developing my own materials and methods of training.

I saw before me students who came from the same limited experience as myself having little occasion to correct the deficiency before they began to make important professional decisions about clients.

This was the beginning of a profound shift at every level of cultural consciousness, with its complex mix of ethic, national, religious, and racial diversity. The pressure of the times revealed the fear, ignorance, prejudice, and bigotry of the process of change. Time and time again I was brought back to answering the question: What do you know about your own immigration story? I knew my family was one of millions of families who had immigrated to the United States for reasons unknown to me. I had many strong feelings and impressions, but little factual documentation.

For the first time I knew that understanding the social, political, and economic dynamic of American society had to start with what it meant to me to grow up German Catholic in an Irish Catholic rural community during the era of World War II. The minute I opened the lid of the family box of history, like Pandora, there was no turning back.

I had to begin at the very beginning, with the sound of my father's voice as he told me about the story of my birth: late afternoon, January 5, 1937, during the middle of a very bad winter storm. The doctor couldn't get to the farm, so my great-aunt Minnie delivered me. My mother was Lucile Frances Matt and my father was Hubert William Fässbinder.

Five days later, on January 10, my father's birthday, I was bundled up and taken by my godparents, my father's brother and his wife, to St. Joseph's Church in Guttenberg, Iowa, to be baptized.

Names were important. Lois Lucile Frances Fässbinder. Each had a special meaning in the family. Lois was the only part that was not a family name. My mother had insisted that she didn't want a Lucile Junior.

Infant deaths were common, but the fear of my soul spending eternity in limbo without the benefit of baptism was greater than the fear of taking a tiny baby out in bad winter weather to a cold church. My father made it clear that the obligations of the Catholic Church started in infancy.

1941: We no longer lived in the place of my birth, but for reasons that were never made clear to me, we moved to Placid, Iowa, where we were one of two German-heritage families in a totally Irish farming community. None of that made any difference to me until one Sunday afternoon: December 7, 1941. All the adults around me registered the seriousness of the occasion. When President Roosevelt spoke of the declaration of war against Japan and Germany, the conversations between my mother and father were of the anti-German sentiment during World War I. From the way they were speaking, I knew the point was important, but I didn't connect any negative outcomes to my family.

Catholicism was the dominant force in my life outside the family, and Sister Lillian at St. John's Parochial School taught religion as a deadly serious business. Only Catholics would go to Heaven, and any parent who did not send their child to parochial school was condemned to Hell. I knew that some of my relatives were German Lutheran, but the family never talked about that.

Sister made it very clear that all the trouble in the Catholic Church had started in Germany. At school my family name made me the butt of ridicule. Germany was the enemy, and I was left in total confusion.

At home my father read and recited from the works of Goethe, Heine, and Schiller. He would read the passages in German and then translate them, showing me how much more beautiful they were in the original language. I knew I couldn't talk to anyone about the books my father had in German. Without anyone's telling me, I began to understand what fear does to people. I didn't know the word "scapegoat," but I felt the reality.

Even in the face of that fear of community reaction, my father never stopped longing for the freedom to use the language and teach it to his children. We all learned basic prayers in German, and at Christmas followed the German traditions with traditional carols in German.

It was in that tension that I tried to protect myself from the embarrassment I felt when the movie newsreels, radio, and newspapers reported on Adolf Hitler and his Aryan philosophy of the Third Reich. My father's response only added to my confusion as he showed his own confusion and prejudice: "Adolf Hitler was not German, he was Austrian." There was no discussion.

Public sentiment prevailed. The stories about German culture stopped. The message was clear. Families who refused to give up any sign of connection to the "fatherland" were targets of suspicion. My parents spoke

English without any hint of a German accent, although German had been their primary language through the years in high school. They prided themselves on blending in.

My parents were proud of being culturally German, but I never sensed any desire to return to Germany to visit or to discover any personal connect to the part of the family that had remained in Germany and Liechtenstein.

My father's German history books were filled with pictures of Köln Cathedral and its century of building. This was where his family came from, and they were craftsmen. The name was a trade name: *Fässbinder*—"barrel binder," translated "cooper." The spelling of the name had not been changed, and as long as we knew the correct German spelling and pronunciation, it would be safe.

Young as I was at the time, and much as I wanted to be English or Irish, with a name like Cooper or McDermott, I listened to my father's grief over the destruction of the Germany that he knew from his history books. War was the overriding reality. Cousin after cousin was reported as killed or missing in action. My father was drafted into a defense plant.

In the spring of 1944 my brother was drafted and my sister enlisted in the Army Corps of Nurses. Rationing covered every aspect of life. No more non-essential travel. Food and clothing could only be purchased with ration stamps.

The forces of good were battling the forces of evil, and my family, paying the price as we all did, still feared the suspicion of their patriotism. The last casualty in the family was a cousin. James Matt was a Thunderbolt fighter pilot, shot down and killed just days before the end of the war in Europe. Later his parents found out that his body had been discovered by some farmers and he was buried in the American military cemetery in Italy. He was my mother's godson and she kept his aviator flight school picture with the family pictures.

As soon as the war was over, the images of Hitler's Germany were filled with the horrors of the concentration camps throughout Europe. Newsreels and newspapers spoke of incomprehensible inhumanity in the name of ancient prejudices and ethnic hatreds. By 1947 and the Nuremberg Trials, the world was confronted with the lengths hatred can reach if left unchecked at an early stage. From that point on, my father and mother fell silent about any cultural connection.

For the next twenty years I had little or no contact with the family history. My father died in 1960, just as I started teaching. I had decided that being American in the twentieth century was about breaking the hyphenated cultural connection. But that resolution never rang true.

I learned enough German to pass the graduate school language requirement. As I read philosophy and literature in German and was called upon to read aloud, the professors would comment on my perfect pronunciation and my lack of conversational vocabulary. I never explained.

The delicate balance of knowing your personal family history without getting trapped in it. Discovery and understanding do not guarantee change for the better, but history denied or distorted takes on a power that poisons and eventually becomes the cancer at the heart of personal, family, and group survival.

Growing up in America is a tricky business, with our attitude about "manifest destiny" running like a thread through our collective consciousness. At every level we leave out those pieces of history that make us struggle to define who we are as a diverse society. I saw that same reality in my family, with their silence about the pain they felt in denying the bridges to the past.

My mother realized that shortly before her last illness made it impossible to do anything about it. She had submitted an application for a passport. We were to go to Liechtenstein—she wanted to go back.

1992: A period of poor health gave me the time to review what I had about my family history. By this time computerized data made research more available without extensive travel. Through a series of inquiries, I came upon the Liechtenstein Historical Society twenty-year research project, which has traced the immigration histories of all the families who left that tiny country with its population of less than sixty thousand.

I received information from one Julius Buehler of my mother's family and their history. The documentation was amazing. In addition to a copy of my great-grandfather's passport, it included a copy of a letter to the headmaster of the school in Mauren describing in detail the first year in America and all the differences experienced in this strange new land.

Also in the packet was a picture of the family house, purchased in 1816 by my great-great-grandfather, Franz Joseph Mätt. Although the building was torn down in 1975, the land remains with the family who stayed. Julius Buehler sent me the family chart, pointing out that he is the great-grandson of Katharina Mätt, the only sister of Mathias Mätt, my great-grandfather. The family history is charted back to 1635 from the records in Liechtenstein.

1995: Cousins communicating across the bridge of 143 years of history. More than anything else I have done, my parents would have enjoyed this. But the real demons lay ahead. Everyone in Liechtenstein hastened to assure me that they are *not German*. The people in Germany seem more guarded about my investigation, although I have come to understand that the name holds weight. I have even come to understand why the picture of my father connected me immediately to the controversial Rainer Werner Fässbinder. The clerk in the hotel in Köln had told me that almost thirty years ago.

At the end of the twentieth century, my family history represents one variation on the millions of themes of immigration history. The German-speaking people from Colonial times through two world wars were a powerful force that assimilated into the dominant English-speaking culture with little obvious trace. When the children of this final decade of the century ask their parents and grandparents about the paradoxes of the past, the record will be a bit more complete. The rest of the record is up to them.

The Case of the Missing Italian American Writers

■ ■ ■

HELEN BAROLINI

It was a bizarre moment during a New York University conference on the Italian presence in America: at a four-person panel, whose topic was Italian American literature, three reported on what had been written and what was being written. The fourth panelist, Gay Talese, got up to say there was no Italian American writing worth talking about because there were no Italian American novelists. Modestly he gave himself as a case in point: as a writer, successful, yes; famous, yes; honored, courted, and interviewed, yes; rich, quite; but oh, so unhappy with his Italian American background which, he said, was precisely what kept him from being a novelist.

Gay Talese turned to journalism to barricade himself in facts and to distance himself from his feelings. And all the time he envied those American writers who could freely let all their emotions, passions, resentments, and family wars into their fiction. He attributed his becoming a reporter of other people's lives, rather than a narrator of his own in novels, to the dread inspired by his family should he reveal in autobiographical fiction any of their secrets. Talese started a novel on his father and then put it away, unfinished, into a drawer. It was eventually transformed into *Unto the Sons*, a huge, unrelenting documentation of his father's Calabrian background and a tedious rehash of Italian immigration history. It does not, as fiction might have done, transform facts and characters into art.

Talese later elaborated his theme into a piece that appeared on the front page of the Book Review section of the *New York Times* on March 14, 1993, headed: "Where Are the Italian-American Novelists?" Talese's position that there aren't any proves only that he's never bothered to look for them.★

Still, he had inadvertently disclosed something that, sooner or later, hits every Italian American: that is, that what's missing is the perception among readers, critics, teachers, and the public in general of the contribution by writers of Italian background to the body of American literature. Why is there almost no recognition of an Italian American novel beyond *The Godfather*? Why is there silence?

One answer is that there are very real prejudices and presumptions operating in the publishing world which effectively block writers of this group from recognition. It is not so much that we are missing as that we've hardly been included. Yet rather than examine the causes of exclusion, Talese accepts it as an indictment of Italian American culture. Failing to recognize a subtle and pernicious form of bigotry, he manages only to extend it.

Any group can be widely distorted through the media. Norman Podhoretz disclosed in *Making It* that in the American scheme of things, an individual's progress can be limited or enhanced by the status of his/her larger ethnic group—a status that is determined by the supposedly "neutral territory" of mass media. The *New York Times* is the nearest thing we have to a national paper, and its influence is powerful. In light of this, individual Italian Americans have much to ponder in the way their whole group is perceived and portrayed by the paper of record which gave such prominence to Talese's piece.

★Some of the overlooked: Richard Russo, Marie Chay, Frances Winwar, Jerre Mangione, Guido D'Agostino, John Fante, Mari Tomasi, Marion Benasutti, Michael DeCapite, Raymond DeCapite, Robert Canzonieri, Diana Cavallo, Octavio Capuzzi Locke, Rocco Fumento, Jo Pagano, Giosi Rimanelli, Dorothy Calvetti Bryan, Julia Savarese, Kenny Marotta, Tony Ardizzone, Daniela Gioseffi, Anna Monardo, Nancy Maniscalco, Tina DeRosa, Joseph Papaleo, Salvator La Puma, Lucinda LaBella Mays, Eugene Mirabelli, Carolyn Balducci, Denise Giardina, Rachel Guido deVries, Anthony Valerio, Josephine Gattuso Hendin, Jeanne Schinto, Chris Mazza, Carole Maso, Mary Caponegro, Mary Bush, Mary-Ann Tirone Smith, Ralph Lombreglia, George Cuomo, and Edward Bonetti.

That Talese may have been blocked from being a novelist is one thing, but for him to project his own lack of psychic fortitude onto others of his background and claim that all Italian American writers are subject to the same dread is an astounding fabrication. It goes against all the evidence of how Italian American novelists have, in fact, used family as prime material in their work.

It happens that Gay Talese and I are descendants of immigrants from the same Calabrian hills that he described in his article as drenched in superstition and warped by misrule into a region of cowering people united only "in the fear of being found out." Supposedly, as Italian Americans we still figuratively cower. But not only do I not find my two sets of Italian grandparents in Talese's description of a benighted people, neither was I blocked from relating their story. On the contrary, I found their background a rich mine that I used fully in my first novel, *Umbertina*, without a quiver of anxiety.

Indeed, imagining and narrating my forebears' story seemed a right and worthy thing to do; it gave them a history, and from the letters I received, I know it gave readers positive insight into the Italian American experience as lived over four generations.

While Talese sees family as inhibiting, I found that though traditional Italian family mores *do* create tension, the tension itself becomes both prime motivator and subject of Italian American writing. In fact, a century of work by Italian American novelists belies Talese's argument that family code has rendered us mute as novelists of our own material. Liberated by the very act of writing, many of us have translated our family-based dilemmas into fiction.

There have always been taboos against writing about one's tribe; we have only to remember the fracas that ensued when Philip Roth put Mrs. Portnoy on the map as *the* Jewish mother. He was accused of calumniating his people and making public things about Jewish families that were not for wider knowledge. And the Dubliners of his time never forgave James Joyce his portraits of them. Defying them, Joyce has Stephen Dedalus declaim: "When the soul of a man is born in this country, there are nets flung at it to hold it back from flight . . . nationality, language, religion. I shall try to fly by those nets."

Talese, on the other hand, has fear of flying. If writing for Talese means playing it safe on the way to fame and fortune, just as surely safety becomes an exercise in self-censorship, a dodging of inner truth.

Writing does risk everything. Being an artist, a writer of novels, means wrestling down family or national loyalty or whatever net in order to overcome restraints on the truth. If not, novelists would be no more than studio photographers air-brushing away the flaws and blemishes, valuing flattery (and lucrative commissions) above art. It's truth novelists must go for, not safety, and, yes, it takes nerve.

That Talese suffers a failure of nerve about private revelation and carries within him the emptiness of being an unrealized novelist is his business. But his extending that failure to all Italian American writers immediately makes it ours.

Worse yet, Talese has internalized the contempt he's absorbed from media and publishing circles toward Italian Americans rather than question it. His ethnic pride is hurt by being a member of a group that has produced, he asserted, few writers of eminence (Pietro Di Donato wrote just one book; Don DeLillo doesn't touch Italian American material; and there are no women novelists to mention). Equal to him in fame there is, in his estimate, only Mario Puzo. Where, he wondered, are the "Italian American Arthur Millers and Saul Bellows, James Baldwins and Toni Morrisons, Mary McCarthys and Mary Gordons, writing about their ethnic experiences"? What Talese's outcry established was his astounding lack of familiarity with what Italian Americans have produced. Had he made the effort to look and learn, he would have found that Italian American fiction goes back to 1886, with Luigi Ventura's collection of stories, *Misfits and Remnants*, published by the respected Boston firm of Ticknor & Company. He would have found the outpouring of works in the 1930s and 1940s, among them the fine novels and stories of John Fante, now back in print; of more recent date he would have found the plays of Albert Innaurato, the poetry of Diane Di Prima—all dealing with family and transformation, with the push and pull of dual cultures.

A proven investigative reporter, an able researcher and versatile writer for his past books on the *New York Times*, on massage parlors and adultery, and on the father-son relationship in a Mafia family, Talese nowhere questions the negative stereotyping put on Italian Americans which he quotes from newspaper editors and those in trade book publishing. Talese accepts and repeats the stereotypes. Is this not strange for a reporter of his talents who should be able to smell a story? His position, in fact, sounds a pathological note: it is something that Amiri Baraka long ago recognized (but got past) when he said: "I am inside someone who hates me."

Out of Talese's psyche endlessly roiling come the charges: Italian Americans don't read, aren't interested in education, don't buy books; Italian Americans really can't be writers because they're still Old World villagers who haven't evolved beyond family dependency and thus are incapable of the solitary stamina that writing requires.

It is a burning matter with Gay Talese that Italian Americans are not, in his estimate, better than they are, do not come up to his own celebrity status. Taking on the persona of his feared father (the very thought of whose displeasure kept him from novel writing), Gay Talese himself, with his litany of negatives, becomes the terrible chastizing *paterfamilias* whose progeny, far from enhancing him, offend him in their lowliness.

Worth, in an era of hype and fifteen-minute fame, is debased to whether one is notorious enough to be interviewed on television. It was (and, repeated by Talese, still is) a dispiriting display of lack of independent critical judgment and historical understanding. It is the attitude of the rejecting parent culture of the past that asked testily of its migrant descendants (the runaways from home), why aren't you better than you are?

The why is in our history. And the literature reveals it.

What Gay Talese showed himself oblivious to is that the residue of having been marginalized from the dominant culture, the internal feeling of being outsiders, the estrangement from both Old and New worlds, the clash of generations as the children of immigrants remade themselves from outside the traditions—all this has been the very stuff of literature for Italian Americans, as it was and is for writers of other backgrounds.

Whereas Gay Talese describes himself with a sense of loss as a "hybrid" or "fractional" American, many others of us who have also experienced the energy of contrasting cultures have become enriched by such duality in our lives and in our writing. Not only Americans of Italian origin, but all other Americans grapple with this central theme of the national literature: the quest to meld the connection between a specific identity and being American.

All evidence is that we Italian American novelists have been peculiarly tied in our material to the fathers, to family—that we are only now beginning to range far from home; most of the tensions of ambivalence and inner qualms we have experienced in the struggle to emerge from Fortress Family have already been expressed in writing, and the newest authors are exploring other material. The Italian story in America has been told. Today's fiction writers—Richard Russo, Jeanne Schinto, Agnes Rossi, Ralph Lombreglia, Tony Ardizzone, Mary Capogrosso—have turned their sights elsewhere, have become stylistically freer and more imaginative. Though they have won literary awards, none is a best-seller, so Talese takes no notice.

His measure of a writer's worth is tied to newspaper best-seller lists; he mistakes current prominence for permanence and gives himself over to the Literary Fallacy—believing that a list of ad hoc winners is not only the measure of a culture but unimpugnable, and not subject to the winnowing of time, which sorts things out.

"It is a fact," Talese wrote in the *Times*, "that there is no widely recognized body of work in American literature that deals with this profound experience," of Italians in America. The operative words are "widely recognized." The fact that Talese might better address is why the existing body of work which *does* reflect the Italian American experience has received so little attention. What he has not considered is how the books that do reflect that experience are buried by not being reviewed by people like himself with name recognition.

What are the preconceptions within the national literature that marginalize the experience of a people? Who makes the rules about who will be "widely recognized" and who will not, and how is this translated into which authors were reviewed, interviewed on television, perpetuated in anthologies? Why has Gay Talese looked only at best-seller lists and overlooked college reading lists on which books by Italian American authors do appear?

Why does Gay Talese assert that Italian Americans do not support education—the proof being, he says, that no academic chairs are underwritten by rich Italian Americans? But I can counter by naming the palatial Casa Italiana in New York City, which was built with donations from the Italian American community and given to Columbia University; I think of being invited to the Humanities Institute at Brooklyn College to give the Sal Cannavo Lecture in Italian Studies, an endowed series; I think of the Cesare Barbieri Center at Trinity College, long distinguished by the eminent Italian artists and writers it brings to the Hartford campus. Peter Sammartino founded Fairleigh Dickinson University. These names came immediately to mind; I could find others. Why can't Gay Talese?

Another fallacy Talese repeats about Italian Americans is that they don't read and buy books. Publishers use this cliché to justify not publishing more Italian American authors. But there is no such thing as a single market for books. Italian Americans are not writing to be read only by Italian Americans any more than African Americans write only for African Americans, or West Indian Americans only for West Indian Americans. We all write as Americans for everyone who will read us, including Gay Talese, who is invited to become acquainted.

A publishing house, however, is like a convenience store with most editors as compliant clerks, willing to pigeonhole product (as books are now called) for the publisher's bottom line and for the presumed convenience of consumers. And so books and authors are ethnically labeled, stereotypes adhered to. Italian American novelists are part of American literature and should by now have been more welcomed by American publishers who have, instead, preferred to focus on the stick-figure, one-dimensional Italian American stereotypes available in Richard Condon's Prizzi books, the plays of John Patrick Shanley, or such exploitive, ghosted non-books as *Mafia Princess*.

It's regrettable that Gay Talese, with all the attention he engenders, did not bother to track down the "missing" writers, read them, present them. His pose is that he is truly hurt by the lack of attention given to Italian American writers. If that is so, why does he not review or discuss our books? Because they are not best-sellers like Puzo's?

Talese's ambivalence is monumental—he talks of literature, but thinks in terms of market notoriety. *Kirkus* reviewer Thomas De Pietro offers a suggestion: Why not bring back the neglected, forgotten Italian American novels—"properly marketed with Introductions by writers like Talese these books could find the audience that didn't exist on publication."

What a shame Talese hasn't used his talent for other than repeating tired bromides such as Italian Americans being more given to art and film than writing because they're a visual people—much as Blacks are rhythmic and inclined to be jazz or basketball players but not scientists? (This view is also offered, Talese tells us solemnly, by none other than self-proclaimed genius Camille Paglia, lest we grow restless with his non-sense.) Upon what other group of American writers would they dare use such stereotyping?

There are, a friend reminds me, those pusillanimous beings who accommodate the damaging stereotypes of their ethnic group in "profoundly bad faith," sure that they are the exception, and in order to be in step with prevailing cultural modes and reap the rewards of celebritydom by feeding the appetites for such views. That seems to be Talese's case.

American literature is an ocean, says the novelist Ishmael Reed, and it's large enough for all the currents that run through it, a body of literature reflecting all facets of what America is—a many-cultured society. And in that ocean are the writers: each caught in the paradox of striving for personal identity, while claiming not the fixed sameness that leads to stereotyping, but complexity.

There is no perfect osmosis—one lives both at large and in one's skin. Individuation is a balancing act. It is a future direction for fully matured Italian American writers. In the meantime, Gay Talese's indictment notwithstanding, novelists of the Italian American experience are here present. In a twist on Pirandello's characters, we are authors in search of an audience.

Misery, it's said, seeks company. Gay Talese would like to inveigle us all into his personal crisis by declaring that "we reluctant Italian American writers are extending the reticence of our forebears, evading scrutiny as they had for centuries . . . lying low."

But it's just not so.

Is There a Renaissance in Italian American Literature?

Si, si, and we're all in it together!

■ ■ ■

DANIELA GIOSEFFI

Most Americans are still unaware that the largest mass lynching in U.S. history was of a group of innocent Italian immigrant laborers in New Orleans at the end of the nineteenth century. There were blue laws on the books of many localities which forbade intermarriage with Italians and home sales to them, just as to Blacks and Jews. Discrimination against Italo-Ams. was rampant throughout the USA. Stereotypical Mafia films still abound from Hollywood and television, so that writing about ordinary Italian American people continues to be absent from the American consciousness. Most Americans are not ready to see our group as sufferers from prejudice who might require some measure of sympathy. We're thought of as hardened criminals who can take care of our own, rather than ordinary people—with the added problem of being unrecognized as an offended minority. This phenomenon has been exacerbated by many Italian Americans, themselves assimilated and interbred, who prefer to identify with American WASPishness rather than ethnic culture. By the end of the 1970s, many Italian American writers had seen the light and knew that the multicultural movement was where they belonged if they were going to gain a foothold in American letters. Despite the growing use of "PC" as a pejorative in a *reactionary* attempt to stop the dialogue that's begun in recent years regarding racism, sexism, prejudice, and the *opening* of the American mind and literary canon, most of our writers have joined the revolutionary movement founded by African American scholars. There's clearly a reawakening, or birth, happening in Italian American writing, as evidenced by several magazines and books recently published which bear a definitive and self-proclaimed ethnic pride.

By the 1990s we "ethnic writers"—of many kinds—have swum up to the surface of U.S. literature, to find ourselves Americans of every kind. We've begun to listen to each other's poetry, relish each other's food for stomach and thought, glad to have survived the oppression of the WASP mystique, which up to now has plagued even the white Anglo-Saxon Protestant with an uptight stereotype. As Richard Robertiello, the Harvard-trained psychiatrist and author of *The WASP Mystique* (1987), explained in his book:

> Although a nation of ethnics, our established ethic is WASPishness, the standard by which assimilation is judged, while WASP conduct, for its part, was early on patterned on the model of the British upper class. Altogether, this has proved to be a very bad thing, making Americans WASP-worshipers, with an attendant devaluation and dilution of ethnic pride.

Robertiello wrote his book with a graduate student author and a WASP, Diana Hoquet, who had herself come to resent the WASP biases she was raised with. Jews who went into professional jobs tended to emulate the WASP mystique as they presented their case histories to Dr. Robertiello in his Manhattan practice, but Blacks and Italians, too, and other folk, made themselves miserable in their pursuit of WASPishness. The inferences of Dr. Robertiello's study were a cause for alarm, as so pervasive and pernicious was the mystique that "even WASPs wanted to be more like WASPs," and made themselves unhappy in their attempt to be so. But this was just before the dawning of the "multicultural" movement, and the American Book Awards given by the Before Columbus Foundation, and we are all wiser today. Or are we?

There's no doubt that the very act of writing remains a fight for cultural identity, as Ishmael Reed explained in his book *Writin' Is Fightin'*, but Italian American writers—partly because of a fierce independence, somewhat because of the desire to assimilate, and mostly out of a fear of being dubbed Mafiosi if they tried to congregate—have had trouble organizing against the stereotypes that plague and pigeonhole them as spaghetti-sucking Mafiosi or "Guidos" who don't read or buy books. But through the late eighties and early nineties, not only was *Italian Americana,* a journal founded by Dr. Richard Gambino and Dr. Ernesto Falbo in the early 1970s, refurbished, but a vital new literary and cultural review entitled *Voices in Italian Americana,* known as *VIA,* was born. Edited by Anthony J. Tamburri at Purdue University in West Lafayette, Indiana, Paolo A. Giordano at Loyola University, and Fred L. Gardaphe at Columbia College in Chicago, it has quickly blossomed into a periodical read throughout the country. Just prior to founding *VIA,* the trio had compiled a compendium, *From the Margin: Writings in Italian Americana* (1991), which contained the work of many writers of note. It quickly sold out and is now in a second edition. And there are many other journals, such as *Differentia,* a review of Italian thought located at Queens College in New York, or *Fra Noi* of Chicago, to name just two. The publication of *Blood of My Blood,* (1974), a widely read sociological commentary by Richard Gambino of Queens College, pioneered the current flurry of publication in the nineties. Dr. Gambino was able, early in the seventies, to establish the first Italian American Studies program in the country.

Recently, the John D. Calandra Institute, located in the Graduate Center of the City University of New York, won a court decision that charged discrimination against Italian American professors. The Calandra Institute had studied the problems of urban youth and discovered that Italian American teens had one of the highest rates of high school dropouts, statistically in the upper ranges with Black and Puerto Rican youth. Noting this fact, the Institute proceeded, under the leadership of Dr. Joseph V. Scelsa, to demonstrate that despite a large population of Italian American students, CUNY grossly shortchanged Italian American professors when it came to faculty recruitment and promotions. In November 1992, Judge Constance Baker Motley, an African American woman, granted a preliminary injunction against the university, ending in a settlement which in effect concluded that *civil rights are everyone's rights,* and that federal statutes apply to Italian Americans as well as to traditionally defined minorities.

This was one of the recent instances when Italian Americans were able to cooperate to defend themselves against discrimination. One might say that the spirit of labor organizers Sacco and Vanzetti, executed in 1927—by the influence of Judge Thayer, a bigot who dubbed them "dirty dagos" and "filthy guineas"—was at last vindicated by Judge Motley's decision. Edna St. Vincent Millay and Edmund Wilson were part of a progressive movement among American writers to save the labor organizers, who'd called themselves "anarchists" against an unjust system. Millay wrote a poem, "Justice Denied in Massachusetts," about the incident. But not until recently has there been any sort of successful movement among Italian American intellectuals to undo ruthless or subtler forms of discrimination against them. The Calandra Institute sponsors a cable television show, *Italics,* which interviews Italian American literary figures and posts a rich calendar of varied cultural events throughout the Northeast.

Dr. Robert Viscusi, director of the Wolfe Institute for the Humanities at Brooklyn College, in 1991 organized the Italian American Writers Association (IAWA), which has established a literary salon and readings throughout New York City and in Greenwich Village where IAWA meets of a Saturday evening at the Cornelia Street Café. Luciana Polney, playwright and poet, inspired the group to read at the progressive Nuyorican Café in the East Village, and interculturalism was encouraged. Activities began to connect more and more with the multicultural movement. In 1993, with Peter Caravetta, Robert Viscusi managed to institute a graduate course in Italian American literature at CUNY's Graduate Center in midtown Manhattan as well. Another first! Similar activities are blossoming in the Chicago area under the leadership of Fred Gardaphe and Paolo Giordano; for example, a series of readings sponsored by the journal *VIA* at the Caffe Trevi on North Lincoln Avenue in the windy city. Of course, Lawrence Ferlinghetti, the man who made publication of the Beat Generation poets possible with his City Lights Book Store and Press, was a pioneer of the current flurry of Italian American names in poetry, as was Diane Di Prima, who moved to the West Coast many years ago, after her work in the sixties in New York as founder of the Poets Press with Amiri Baraka. Ferlinghetti and Di Prima, like the well-known poet John Ciardi, made inroads for the current Renaissance, if only by virtue of their surnames, as they were very much a part of the "mainstream" progressive movement in literature.

Today, there's a press—Guernica Editions—in the important literary center of Toronto, Canada, founded and run by editor and author Antonio D'Alfonso, which has put out an entire line of Italian American poetry and fiction, including a recent compendium of Italian American women's fiction entitled *The Voices We Carry* (1993). Edited by Professor Mary Jo Bona of Gonzaga University in Washington State, it brings together twelve authors of note from around the country. Earlier, in 1986, Helen Barolini edited *The Dream Book: Writings of Italian American Women,* showing how that group had been neglected even as they were producing a wealth of literature peculiar to their ethnic background. In her introduction, she cited forgotten role models like the Nobel Prize winner and prolific novelist Grazia Deledda, who had been neglected not only by the male establishment but by the feminist canon as well. Barolini reminded us, too, of Frances Winwar, who was forced to change her name from Vinciguerra, in order to publish in America, and who was one of the most prolific American biographers of the century. In 1945, Winwar wrote the applauded bastion of feminism *George Sand and Her Times: A Life of the Heart*, still in print; but she has managed to be forgotten as an Italian American by American feminists, to say nothing of the male establishment.

So when, in 1991, a book of Italian American writings by both men and women appeared from the University of Purdue Press, the afore-mentioned *From the Margin: Writings in Italian Americana*, it spurred a storm of readings, reviews, and networking sessions among Italian American poets and writers of fiction and criticism. For the first time in the history of the Academy of American Poets, Dana Gioia was able to publish a piece on "Italian American Poetry" questioning if such a thing existed. Though Gioia's short article, featured on the front page of the academy newsletter, wounded many by its omissions—particularly of prominent women poets—it was a first. And it created a controversy that led to a heated debate among Italian American writers by the time a front-page piece on the cover of the *New York Times Book Review* written by Gay Talese appeared. One of the few big Italian American names on the New York and PEN American Center scene, Talese questioned whether there were any Italian American novelists beside himself—despite the fabulous plaudits, National Book Awards, and American Book Awards, received by many. Because Talese's article implied that Italians are illiterate non-readers, it drew angry reaction from our community of writers, and lists began to appear naming our accomplishments. The *Times* received a myriad of letters but printed none by the accomplished authors who named their ethnic brothers and sisters.

A bibliography of fiction writers appeared in *Italian Americana*'s Fall–Winter 1993 issue, along with answers to Talese's assumptive head-line: "Where Are the Italian-American Novelists?" Some of the finest and most well reviewed among them are Carole Maso, known for *Ava, the Art Lover, Ghost Dance*, and *The American Woman in the Chinese Hat*; Don DeLillo, National Book Award-winning author of *Libra or the White Noise*; Chris Mazza, winner of PEN's Nelson Algren Award, and author of *How to Leave a Country*; Philip Caputo's much-praised *Means of Escape* and *DelCorso's Gallery*. The list goes on with names like Jerre Mangione and Ben Morreale, who aside from their fiction had just written *La Storia*:

Five Centuries of the Italian in America, a large history from HarperCollins that had two lengthy chapters on writers of Italian American background. Another book by Rose Basile Green, *The Italian American Novel: A Document of the Interaction of Two Cultures*, had in some measure answered the question of twenty years earlier. And Barbara Grizzuti Harrison's travel memoir *Italian Days* had been well received a few years earlier. New York and other cities began to blossom with Italian "pasta" salad and fashion boutiques, almost outnumbering the spaghetti and pizza parlors. Middle-class Italian chic was born across America. Italian American writers began to wonder and hotly debate—more than ever—why the few writers in the mainstream seemed to downgrade their own community of writers and its obvious audience. It seemed not to occur to some that if they kept denying the existence of fellow authors and audience, they were helping to perpetuate a syndrome of invisibility, broadcasting to publishers to refuse them further entry into the mainstream of American letters.

Of course, the issue is not merely one of surname, but cultural validation. As Fred Gardaphe wrote in *Italian Signs, American Streets: Cultural Representation in Italian/American Narrative Literature*, "The study of ethnic literature is more than reading and responding to the literary products created by minority cultures; it is a process that, for its advocate, necessarily involves a self-politicization that requires moving a personal item onto a public agenda." Even with the current "Renaissance," we have yet to see the portrayal of "ordinary" Italian Americans, with their simple human struggles like everyone else's, enter the mainstream consciousness, as it seemed to for one brief shining moment in the 1930s during the labor movement, when *Christ in Concrete* by Pietro Di Donato deeply wounded America's social conscience. Guernica Editions of Toronto is still the only North American Italian American press, even if it does sport a long list of fiction and poetry. And even if authors, including yours truly, have begun to win recognition by the American Book Awards and the progressive arm of the multicultural movement.

Today, *VIA* has become a magazine secure enough among its own to allow me to institute an intercultural "Guest Feature," which welcomes writers of other backgrounds. A signal that many Italian Americans understand that they belong within the multicultural movement, proving "we're all in this together." Still, there are those few who feel threatened by the fight against "Eurocentrism," thinking that it means to dispel the glories of the Italian Renaissance or the Etruscan legacy, along with the demise of the old "literary canon," which greatly excluded "ethnic" and "women's" literature except for a few tokens, like Langston Hughes or

Emily Dickinson—and which doomed many fine writers and artists to obscurity behind less worthy figures aptly dubbed "ole dull mouths" by Amiri Baraka—Henry James, T. S. Eliot, Ezra Pound, etc. And though snobbery is more subtle than bigotry, it can have the same effect on the literary canon.

Perhaps we need to recognize that Italian Americans, in upholding the multicultural movement's ever-growing and changing "canon," are in a somewhat difficult position—different from other groups. After all, the Before Columbus Foundation, which gives the now coveted and respected American Book Awards, does belie Columbus, for years the central symbol of Italian American ghetto pride. Many Italian American poets have begun to portray the irony in that problem. *VIA* has published its first chapbook, by Robert Viscusi, *An Oration Upon the Most Recent Death of Christopher Columbus*, a fabulously sardonic tour de force on the problem. Viscusi pictures Columbus—who after all died in prison having sailed under Hapsburg Teutons for Spain, not Italy—as sitting in an ashtray, looking dejected. Viscusi then begins a dialogue with him which mounts irony upon irony for the Italian American, still stereotyped by the mass media as a "thug" or "Guido"—just as one-dimensional as any "Black Sambo" or "Aunt Jemima"—only with the added difficulty of being seen as the source of all underground evil in the world, as though CIA drug dealing, Pentagon germ warfare, S&L scandals à la John Keating, or the robber barons of old (Astor, J. P. Morgan, Rockefeller, Mellon, et al.) never existed. To say nothing of the massive crimes of Exxon, Bechtel, Union Carbide, or G.E. . . . Viscusi's epic satire declares: "I look forward to the rise of a columbian theology/Columbus, it will teach, lived five hundred years/in the character of a god/once he died/ he acquired a new nature as a limit/we study the theology of columbus to learn/what are the boundaries of enterprise./. . . Columbus will inspire a cult of the carefully considered future and re-examined past. . . ."

Meantime, ghetto Italian Americans have had their only institutionalized celebration for ethnic pride, the Columbus Day Parade, downgraded, and this has caused some to react against the anti-Eurocentric movement, which seemed to say that Italians alone had invented Eurocentrism. Yet, in October 1994, Maria Mazziotti Gillan, a poet who took back her Italian name only a few years ago, managed to found a center for multicultural activity on the campus of Paterson, New Jersey's Passaic County Community College. She brought ethnic poets from all over the country to debate the issues of a curriculum of diversity in a three-day conference which celebrated a multiethnic anthology entitled *Unsettling*

America, edited with her daughter, Jennifer Gillan, who teaches at Bentley College in the Boston area.

Times have greatly changed since 1979 when, as a young poet, I was invited to give a reading at the State University of New York at Buffalo, and was approached by an elderly language professor of Italian, who said: "Do you realize that you are one of only two or three Italian American women to make any name for yourself at all in American literature? You are a pioneer!" For the first time in my budding career, I was forced to contemplate that my "Italian" surname might have anything to do with my struggle to make headway in American letters. Suddenly I searched for role models and found only one name, Diane Di Prima's, to look up to in contemporary letters. Hers and mine were the sole Italian female names included in any of the feminist poetry anthologies of the 1970s. Since then, a bevy of names has surfaced among our women writers, greatly due to the help of Helen Barolini's pioneering efforts. The professor who spoke to me after my poetry reading in Buffalo was Ernesto Falbo, who would soon pass away, a few years after he'd founded *Italian Americana* at SUNY with Richard Gambino of CUNY, Queens, author of the seminal book, *Blood of My Blood* (1974).

The current Renaissance in our literature, pioneered by that book, includes too many names to mention here, but one which shouldn't be omitted is Grace Cavalieri. Poet, host, and commentator of a syndicated radio show from Washington, D.C.'s, Pacifica station, *The Poet and the Poem*, Cavalieri has hosted most of the accomplished poets of *every* canon and built one of the largest audiences for contemporary literature in the country. She has published many books and is among the long list of Italian names now known in American letters. Names like Ferlinghetti, Sorrentino, Stephanile, Carnevale, Capello, Cavallo, Galassi, Romano, Stortoni, Ciavollo, Maso, Mazza, Di Pasquale, DiPalma, Citano, or De-Lillo, which are not associated with the stereotypical Hollywood Mafia story fostered by Gay Talese, Mario Puzo, or Frank Pileggi. A few of our talented men made a fortune by giving Hollywood what it thirsted for to the eternal detriment of the rest of us. Ever since Edward G. Robinson in 1931 portrayed "Little Caesar" in a gangster film neither written, acted in, nor produced by Italian Americans, Hollywood hungered for Italian criminals, as though Dillinger, Boss Tweed, Louie Lepke of Murder Inc., or Legs Diamond were worth little box office compared to the exploits of an Al Capone. Still, to be fair, Mario Puzo starved writing his best and earlier book, *The Fortunate Pilgrim*, relatively unknown to American readers to this day, as it portrays hardworking Italian immigrants in their ghetto lives rather than sexy thugs in dark suits driving black limos with blond beauties as their gun molls. Thus Puzo learned to give Hollywood the image it wanted from Italian American culture with *The Godfather* and the rest unfortunately is history—a Hollywood image that plagues all peoples with Italian surnames and probably will unto eternity, regardless of how many Toscaninis take their beatings from Fascist thugs in protest against bigotry and oppression. Regardless of how many Viola Liuzzos die for demonstrating with Martin Luther King against the Ku Klux Klan of white supremacy. There's the rub. Despite the flurry of activity among Italian American authors, despite their journals and prizes and modicum of fame, our culture has yet to experience the "ordinary people" of our immigrant struggle toward the American Dream. Maybe because that dream died, just as the second and more educated generation began to write about and explore our immigrant ancestors.

The closest we've come to being *charming* in Hollywood is to being *Moonstruck* bakers or bigoted pizza vendors. And no writer does a better job of explaining this phenomenon than Michael Parenti, the Italian American Ishmael Reed. Though not a poet like Reed, Parenti is an astute social commentator, particularly in his *Make-Believe Media*, which should be one of the bibles of the multicultural movement, as it proves beyond a doubt that we ethnics are indeed "all in this together." Even if the shoe doesn't yet exactly fit, we're hobbling around in it—waiting for that big novel or screenplay in the sky that will set us free from stereotyping. Meantime our fiction writers and poets are churning out stories. And as for me, at fifty-four years, I've begun to appear in textbooks used in the schools, like *Kaleidescope: Stories of the American Experience*, along with Zora Neale Hurston, Maya Angelou, Amy Tan, William Saroyan, N. Scott Momaday, Leslie Mormom Silko, Saul Bellow, Maxine Hong Kingston, *and* Nathaniel Hawthorne! So I know that I'm in this together with all writers of every burgeoning subculture. Still, beware, *sorelle e figli* (sisters and brothers). "Divide and conquer" is still the tactic of the day. As for we Italians in 1996, even as Joseph Ceravalo, years dead, in a cover story in *American Poetry Review* is praised for his forgotten innovations in poetic style by Kenneth Koch, Ecco Press has published a new translation of Dante's *Inferno* by twenty writers, not one single Italian American or Italian among them. According to Dana Gioia—known for his translations from the Italian, as is Jonathan Galassi, like John Ciardi before him—not one single contributor to the Ecco publication has had a lifelong connection to Dante's language. Omission persists—even where the Italian culture is valued. But the Italian American Renaissance is palpable, even as the internal debate grows as to what exactly characterizes Italian American literature.

How World War II Iced Italian American Culture

■ ■ ■

LAWRENCE DI STASI

In 1940, fifty years after their mass migration to the New World, Americans of Italian descent numbered over 5 million people. This made them the largest foreign-born group in the United States, and a force to contend with nationwide: they had mayors in New York City (LaGuardia) and San Francisco (Rossi), a lieutenant governor in New York State, and congressmen and representatives in various legislatures. Joe DiMaggio, with his assault on the consecutive game-hitting record, would soon be revered as a true American hero. In the arts, Italian Americans from the time of Jefferson had been recognized as seminal forces in music, painting, and sculpture. Now they were beginning to establish a presence in literature as well. Pietro Di Donato was being lionized for his best-selling novel, *Christ in Concrete*. John Fante was being critically acclaimed for his *Wait Until Spring, Bandini*, and *Dago Red*. Jerre Mangione would soon find his *Mount Allegro* on best-seller lists. Other writers focusing on the Italian experience in America were already published or waiting in the wings.

When all this is added to the fact that the immigrant generation was steadily improving its economic prospects, while its own sons were joining the U.S. Armed Forces in record numbers—with half a million in uniform, they would be the largest ethnic presence in the service—it becomes reasonable to posit that the Italian moment in America was at hand. The population was large, growing, and concentrated in Little Italys in all the major cities. The culture had the kind of unity of experience and vision that occurs only when its best and brightest are alive, together, and in possession of a healthy sense of entitlement. With Benito Mussolini apparently proving that Italy was now a world power to be reckoned with, strength was added to the growing feeling among Italian Americans that their time as a potent presence in the American institutions heretofore closed to them was at hand.

All this collapsed with World War II. The man whom President Roosevelt had once characterized as "that admirable gentleman," Mussolini, with his attack on France in June 1940, became a "backstabber." The friendly nation to which FDR sent his cabinet officials (Social Security, the WPA, and other New Deal innovations were copies of Mussolini's programs), Italy after Pearl Harbor became an enemy of the United States, the target of its propaganda and its bombs. As a result, anyone associated with Italy became likewise targeted—particularly those in the United States who, for various reasons, had failed to complete the process of citizenship. Whether they were Italian-language teachers who taught from books provided by the Fascist government, or aging mothers who, without English, wanted to avoid the humiliating citizenship process of the time, all were branded "enemy aliens."

With this designation came a series of blows in 1941 and early 1942 that frightened, fractured, dispersed, and silenced most Italian Americans for a generation. For some, the silence still prevails—a silence that until the 1990s included the story of the very events that did the job.

What happened was this. On the night of December 7, 1941, only hours after the attack on Pearl Harbor, the FBI went into action. It activated the list of "dangerous" aliens it had been preparing, and took into custody much of the Italian American leadership throughout the country. Hundreds like Pietro De Luca, president of a small New York social club called the Tito Minitti Club, were interned on Ellis Island. On the West Coast, several hundred others were picked up and, after perfunctory hearings, sent to the internment camp at Fort Missoula, Montana. Filippo Molinari of San Jose described how he was taken in his slippers, with no chance to put on shoes or other clothing suitable for the 17-degree Montana weather.

This roundup of "dangerous" aliens continued into late February 1942. Though it left most of the six hundred thousand Italian Americans designated "enemy aliens" at liberty, it and the measures that followed accomplished their aim: to keep Italian Americans in a state of fear and apprehension that any or all of them could be rounded up next.

The events of January 1941 underlined the threat. Despite the fact that they had just registered in 1940, all six hundred thousand Italian aliens nationwide had to re-register now—get newly photographed and finger-printed, and carry their pink-covered ID booklets at all times. Along with registration came restrictions—no travel of more than five miles without a permit, no move without notifying authorities, and no possession of so-called contraband (shortwave radios, weapons of any kind, cameras, and even flashlights) with which they might commit sabotage. Those suspected of retaining such materials were subject to search, seizure, and summary detention.

In California, more extreme measures followed. First came a curfew: "enemy aliens" were confined to their homes between the hours of 8:00 P.M. and 6:00 A.M. This hit hard at those who worked odd hours—the scavengers, fishermen, restaurant workers, truck farmers. Within days it hardly mattered, for the next blow was evacuation: almost the entire coast was declared a prohibited zone. After February 24, "enemy aliens" could not live, work, or even be within five miles of the waterfront. This meant mass evacuation. Anyone without citizenship had to leave the prohibited areas. Though no one knows the exact figures, it is estimated that more than ten thousand Italian Americans had to leave their homes. In the little fishing village of Pittsburg, the whole of which was a prohibited zone, mothers with several sons in the service, grandfathers who had lived in Pittsburg for fifty years, children under the age of fourteen, were all forced to find housing, jobs, lives elsewhere. A few were so undone by the prospect of pulling up stakes that they committed suicide. Others simply bent their heads and left, to endure the next months as best they could. The lucky ones found refuge with relatives; others, tired of the humiliation of being turned down by landlords who refused to rent to "enemies," crammed into migrant-worker bungalows; Bettina Troia could only find shelter in a chicken coop.

Most of the restrictions against Italian aliens were lifted the following October, but ironically, this was the time when perhaps the most flagrant abuses occurred. As evacuees were rejoicing in their return home, the recommendations made by state Senator Jack Tenney's committee were going into effect. At those hearings in May 1942, some few dozen Italian Americans had been accused of being the leaders of San Francisco's Fascist movement. Notwithstanding the fact that they were all U.S. citizens, or that no illegal action had been alleged, much less proved against them, they were ordered to leave the state for the duration of the war.[1] They could return, with the internees, only in 1943, when Italy surrendered.

It doesn't take much familiarity with civil rights law to conclude that the rights of Italian Americans were violated during World War II. What is under discussion here, however, is not so much the individual acts of injustice as their long-range effects. It is these longer-term and subtler ripples—some of which still endure—which constitute the real, the enduring injustice that was perpetrated.

Consider what happened to the leadership in Italian communities. Almost overnight, hundreds of teachers, editors, and club leaders disappeared. Even their wives were not told where they were going or what their eventual fate would be. The Italian-language schools staffed by many of those interned were closed. Many Italian-language newspapers they ran stopped publication. Anyone associated with them was automatically suspect.[2] Those trying to correspond with relatives in Italy found that letters from Italy were opened, thus reinforcing the message that anything to do with that country or that language had become suspect. Within the community, such suspicions grew and magnified. No one knew who might be informing on whom, or how an old rivalry might now bring one down.

The worst of it was, most of those affected were isolated. To this day, even those who were arrested or evacuated have only vague ideas about why they were targeted or how many were affected. Mary Lou Harris of San Mateo, for example, reasoned that her uncle had been picked up and detained at Tanforan for several months because he was a single Italian male, and thereby suspect. Such lack of information can only magnify feelings of guilt and shame.

How much the government intended its actions to remain arbitrary, and thereby more intimidating, is not clear. What is obvious is that it intended to frighten people as efficiently as it could. Its poster of the time conveys this quite well: over cartoon figures of Hitler, Tojo, and Mussolini, speaking in their "traitor's language" such lines as "It's necessary to destroy democracy," there runs the upper-case admonishment: DON'T SPEAK THE ENEMY'S LANGUAGE. The double entendre here is clear, but the effect on Italian Americans over a wide range was singular; many parents warned their children to stop speaking Italian. Italian stores and clubs put up signs that declared: *No Italian Spoken for the Duration of the War.*

The upshot is clear. People who do not know what is happening to them, or why it is happening, end up feeling guilty. The syllogism infiltrates the soul. Italians were arrested; in America no one gets arrested without cause; the arrestees *must* have been guilty. We *all* must have been guilty. But of what? Nothing was done. It must be what we are. Therefore, to the extent that it is possible, stop being that. Stop being Italian, stop using Italian, and as for one's name—necessarily a word in that "enemy" language—stop that too. Drop it: from "Ardente," drop the e to make it Ardent, American. Which is precisely what William Ardente, and many others, did.

Studs Terkel's book *The Good War* has a variation on this same theme. In the interview he gave Terkel, the Italian American architect Paul Pisicano, with no apparent knowledge of the wartime restrictions, describes the change in his Bronx neighborhood after the war:

> Since the war, Italo-Americans have undergone this amazing transformation. . . . We stopped being Italo and started becoming Americans.
>
> We had all lived in one big apartment house my father built. He built a wine cellar. The guys, after they'd worked hard all day—not in offices, in factories—they'd have their dinner, there was no TV, they'd go downstairs, during the grape season, and they would crush. *It was a communal effort.* Everybody in the apartment house worked on the harvest. . . . My father would provide the machinery. Big vats of wine. Everybody would have his own grapes. The whole cellar was a vineyard.
>
> After the war, nobody used the wine cellars. The whole sense of community disappeared. You lost your Italian-ness. . . . Suddenly we looked up, we owned property. Italians could buy. The GI Bill, the American Dream. Guys my age had really become Americanized. They moved to the suburbs.
>
> Oh, God, I see the war as that transition piece that pulled us out of the wine cellar. It obliterated our culture and made us Americans. That's no fun.

Pisicano's testimony has been repeated in countless variations by others. World War II marked a watershed for Italian American culture. Large numbers moved out of the old colonies and into neighborhoods that were new, trim, American. How many did this consciously in response to the wartime stigma is not clear. What *is* clear is that the U.S. government has implemented just such a dispersal program for others, particularly Native Americans, whom it began to disperse after the war. It even had a name for this: "mainstreaming." If you can induce a population to scatter, its coherence and strength as a unified force responding to and exerting pressure is vitiated. Though this movement for Italian Americans was not forced or complete, it happened to enough of them to make a difference.

The difference can be gauged by what happened to the very wartime experiences under discussion. The story has been suppressed and repressed. Like victims of abuse, Italian Americans took the blame on themselves and handled it as they had handled all else—with silence. For fifty years, few would talk about what had happened. Even now, many Italian Americans would prefer to keep the story buried. It seems that the U.S. government, and those who write the histories, agree. Routinely, it is stated that for Italian Americans, such wartime restrictions *never happened*.

> The spirit of a community or collective can be wiped out, tradition can be destroyed. We tend to think of genocide as the physical destruction of a race or group, but the term may be aptly expanded to include the obliteration of the *genius* of a group, the killing of its creative spirit through the destruction, debasement, or silencing of its art. Those parts of our being that extend beyond the individual ego (i.e., that pertain to community) cannot survive unless they can be constantly articulated.
>
> And there are individuals—all of us, I would say, but men and women of spiritual and artistic temperament in particular—who cannot survive, either, unless the symbols of zoë [transcendent] life circulate among us as a common wealth.

The quote is from Lewis Hyde's remarkable book *The Gift*. It raises the issue I have been aiming at all along: *the silencing of a community's spirit*. Where they are even mentioned, most discussions of Italian Americans during World War II focus on the loss of physical community, agreeing that, to one degree or another, such communities in America lost coherence and power as a result of the war. Italians "Americanized," and not the least of that Americanization was their tendency to lose their sense of place, their sense of culture, and with these the sense of self they once had.

These are serious losses, but in some ways they have been reversed—not physically so much as organizationally—through the revitalization of some of the old clubs and the blossoming of new organizations in the late sixties. Though there was a hiatus of twenty-five years, Italian Americans in many areas have renewed their affiliations with the Italian language, and with their ancestral *Italianità* in general.

Here, however, I am concerned with what Hyde refers to: the loss of spiritual community. This is a more subtle, but to my mind more permanent, loss. Earlier, I referred to the Italian moment that appeared to be peaking just prior to the war. Its artists and writers were expressing themselves with a vitality that bespoke confidence and entitlement. Di Donato, Fante, and others knew they had something to say, knew it was challenging, and sensed that American audiences wanted to hear it.

The war brought "Don't." It brought silence, and not just to those who were targeted. It silenced their spokesmen, too—their children, their teachers, and those ultimate community spokesmen, their writers. It diverted them into other areas. Who knows how many potential novelists became lawyers or ad writers? How many poets became teachers or social workers? We shall never know. All we can do is look at some we do know and gauge the overall result.

After the war, Pietro Di Donato wrote little. Using the same material from *Christ in Concrete*, he reprised it in 1960 in *Three Circles of Light*, a little-read novel. Then a book about *Mother Cabrini*. Then silence. John Fante followed a different but no less discouraging trajectory. He went to Hollywood and wrote screenplays. Like Faulkner, it was death to him, but unlike Faulkner he lacked the confidence (or was it the cultural sanction?) to go home. To his credit, he continued to write novels in his spare time, but had it not been for a comment about him by Charles Bukowski, he'd still be totally unknown, rather than almost unknown. Jerre Mangione, it is true, published *Mount Allegro* in 1943, but it was really a memoir, not a novel, and its determined optimism fed into the climate expected of Italian America after the war: Though we're exotic, we're American, we're loyal, we're happy to be, and happy to be here.

Michael de Capite wrote two novels, *Maria* and *No Bright Banner*, in the 1940s, and Mari Tomasi wrote her best work, *Like Lesser Gods*, in 1949, yet the climate for their work, and the work of the few others writing truly about Italian America, can be gauged by counting the handful who even know it exists. The case of Salvatore Lombino suggests why. He is the most widely published Italian American we know; his first book was a runaway best-seller; besides movies, TV scripts, and plays, his detective novels are considered classics of that genre. Never heard of him? Perhaps that's because he has never written under his Italian name, and only late in life about his Italian roots. Instead, he concluded early that the name "Evan Hunter" (*The Blackboard Jungle, The Birds*) or Ed McBain (the pseudonym the already pseudonymous Hunter uses for his 87th Precinct crime novels) would serve an American writer better. It's an old story among Italian Americans, allowing authors as disparate as Frances Winwar (Francesca Vinciguerra), Hamilton Basso, and Don DeLillo to "pass."[3]

Mario Puzo confirms the pattern. He wrote a fine novel, *The Fortunate Pilgrim*, in 1964, but he saw the writing on the wall: America was massively uninterested in novels about Italian America. Conversely, it was massively obsessed by Italian American criminals. So Puzo decided to Americanize. In his case, that meant, "give 'em what they want." His *Godfather* became a best-seller, and the rest is history.

The irony at this point is heavy, even grim, for in my opinion even this pandering to criminality has roots in the wartime. That is, at the same time that Italian Americans were being restricted and interned for their suspected loyalty to Mussolini, U.S. Naval Intelligence was embarking on one of the darkest ventures of the war. It was choosing to court the Mafia—specifically, the imprisoned Lucky Luciano—in a deal that would get underworld help to secure the New York waterfront in exchange for the gangster's freedom after the war. The deal was proposed, and concluded. The waterfront became secure; Luciano was pardoned by Governor Dewey in 1946, and deported to Italy. This was only part one, however. The second part of the deal concerned the invasion of Sicily. Mussolini had been the first (and the last) Italian head of state to succeed in controlling the Mafia: he simply jailed all suspected Mafia figures, many on remote islands. Their hatred for him knew no bounds—so they had no hesitation in agreeing to the Allied proposal, brokered by the American Mafia and Luciano, to give all possible aid to the Sicilian invasion in return for freedom. Thus was forged a second devil's pact; but the real devil was in the details. Not only were Sicily's Mafia leaders released; not only were they made mayors of the towns they had formerly terrorized. They were also given carte blanche to carry on the heroin trade, which thenceforth moved from Marseilles to the cities of southern Sicily. It was a trade that would supply them with far more money than they had ever amassed before—enough money, indeed, to gain them virtual control of the postwar Italian government right up to the most recent scandals over such Mafia/government collusion in 1992 Italy.

These machinations reverberated through Italian America from 1941 on. They signified that the U.S. government, through its eagerness to deal with organized crime, was thereby elevating those criminals to abnormal, even heroic status. In other words, the U.S. government during World War II didn't just neutralize the traditional leadership in the Italian community. It also helped, by example, to replace it with the criminals it apparently preferred to deal with.

No wonder Italian American writers have been rejected for treating what is close to their hearts. No wonder they have been induced to write about crime. The majority culture, aided and abetted by the federal government, has concluded that criminals *do* in fact constitute the community's leadership. And this has contributed to the spiritual genocide Hyde refers to—not so thoroughly as to destroy Italian American culture, but sufficient to debase, divert, and silence it for a generation, and more.

Has this, in fact, happened? A recent article in the *New York Times Sunday Book Review* is indicative. There, Gay Talese posed the question: *"Where Are All the Italian-American Novelists?"* Where indeed. Though many Italian American scholars and writers took him to task for his ignorance, the question hangs over the community still. Where are they? Where have they been hiding?

That is the question. And the answer, in my opinion, is that they, along with their audience, were silenced during the war. Since then, their art and their spirit have been debased by the continuing, repetitive message that then arose: "Give us gangsters. Give us crime. Or give us 'most happy fellas.' That's what Italian America is about. That's what we—the publishers, the editors, the arbiters of American culture—will listen to."[4]

It has been a spiritually crippling message. In the last two decades, to be sure, Italian American novelists have arisen who are trying to counter all this; Italian American scholars have arisen who are trying to resuscitate a tradition. But it is by no means certain that their work will amount to much more than the faint reflection of a fire whose flame has already gone out.

That is the real tragedy of the wartime. A community's moment may come but once. Miss that moment, and a community's vital spirit may be gone forever.

■ ■ ▪

NOTES

1. It is worth noting that even before war's end, the government recognized that it had erred in acting against civilians it suspected of being "dangerous." In a May 1942 memo, the Justice Department admitted that "persons are at times interned where there is considerable doubt as to whether they are guilty of conduct endangering the nation." Another memo from July 1943 goes even further. It admits that the government's method of classifying aliens as to "dangerousness" was neither authorized nor justified, and that "the notion that it is possible to make a valid determination as to how dangerous a person is in the abstract and without refer-

ence to time, environment, and other relevant circumstances, is impractical, unwise, and dangerous." Memo from Attorney General Francis Biddle to Hugh B.
Cox and J. Edgar Hoover, July 16, 1943, found in the file of Nino Guttadauro,
one of those excluded from San Francisco as "dangerous" in 1943.

2. Harold Ferrari attended one such Italian-language school in Berkeley. When he
   volunteered for the armed forces in 1943, he was detained for a week and interro-
   gated about his loyalty to the United States and his ability to shoot at Italian soldiers if necessary.

3. "Passing" here means more than just changing one's name to sound American. It
   also means studiously avoiding anything that might get one tagged as an "ethnic"
   writer; or, as Lombino has his alter ego say in *Streets of Gold* (his one "ethnic"
   book), "I changed my name because I no longer wished to belong to that great
   brotherhood of *compaesani* whose sole occupation seemed to be searching out
   names ending in vowels."

4. To read about this repressive literary climate in detail, see Helen Barolini's introduction to her anthology of writings by Italian American women, *The Dream Book*
   (New York: Schocken Books, 1985). There she points out the almost total absence
   of Italian American writers and their works from the accepted literary canon.

"Living in America": Politics and the Irish Immigrant

■ ▪ ▫

DAVID LLOYD

In the United States of late, the notion of "diaspora" has become more and more frequently invoked by ethnic groups to describe the global dispersion of their populations. The word derives of course from the Greek word for the scattering of the Jews after the destruction of the Temple by the Romans in the first century A.D. But the term "diaspora" has lately been extended to cover the experiences not only of African Americans, North, South, and Caribbean, but also of Asian Americans, most particularly the Chinese in their connections to Chinese cultures throughout the world, and South Asians living in the Americas, Europe, the Caribbean, and Africa. There is also an Arab diaspora, particularly the Palestinian version, which quite deliberately inverts the notion of the Jewish diaspora by highlighting how the establishment of a Jewish homeland meant the displacement of the Palestinian population in turn. Of late, there has even begun to be talk of the Irish diaspora: we are, after all, a population scattered by transportation, exile, and emigration throughout the world, though mostly throughout the "English-speaking world" of the formerly British settler colonies.

The term is powerfully affective. For the Jews, it was and continues to be one that encapsulates not simply scattering, but the survival of a culture, a religion, and an ethos through the many and various forms and disguises that exile historically demanded. The survival of the culture principally turned on two things, the "book" (or Talmud), and the hope of an eventual return to the promised land, though the idea of return was often allegorical rather than actual.

As the notion of diaspora has been taken up by other communities here, the emphasis has mostly been on the cultural meaning rather than return. This has been especially true of the African and Chinese adoptions of the term: there are few African or Chinese Americans now for whom the notion of a return to the homeland is a powerful or even viable one. But insofar as "diaspora" refers to the survival of cultural forms and values through all the vicissitudes of exile, it has a vital emotional and, more importantly, political significance. The long tradition of African American scholarship, which has only recently begun to gain some of the respect it deserves, has constantly sought to demonstrate how African cultural and religious practices, languages, and social forms survived, even if in disguised or hybridized ways, throughout slavery and the dispersal and mixing of African peoples in the "New World." Though often caricatured in mainstream publications, the understanding of the continuity as well as the breaking and destruction of African cultures has been an invaluable means to affirming black political identity in a racist society.

Yet I hesitate to welcome the extension of the term to the Irish community in the United States. It's not just that conditions for Irish Americans are entirely different from those for other ethnic groups. Though they are: for all the long struggle Irish immigrants had to gain acceptance in the United States against deep religious and racial prejudice, Irish Americans are now a fully integrated element of white and mainstream American society. Irish "illegals," immigrants without the green card, are rarely picked up in random sweeps of the Mission District of San Francisco or south-central Los Angeles, unlike their Latin American and even Chicano counterparts, many of whom turn out to be citizens after all. Return is no longer a powerful emotional idea for Irish Americans, except in the mostly sentimental and fetishizing desire to establish their genealogy in the old country. That desire has been augmented recently by the successes of liberal "multiculturalism," which has left many white Americans, whose roots are by now twisted and entangled in the soil of several European lands, seeking the cultural distinctiveness that they have learned to see as the "privilege" of ethnic minorities.

It is this very sentimental and thoroughly depoliticized desire that threatens to be confirmed in the notion of an Irish diaspora. Writing recently in *The Irish Reporter*, an Irish broad-left quarterly, Mary Corcoran quoted one American Irish immigrant leader as saying that "there is an Irish nation, but it is a diaspora. We are like the Jews. Ireland is a home base—like Israel, the promised land. We cannot all live on one small island, we have too much to offer the world." The invocation of an "Irish diaspora" has the effect of naturalizing the continuing massive outflow of skilled and unskilled labor from Ireland, as if there were some given population level for the island that we have already exceeded. But as the historian Joseph Lee has recently been emphasizing, reasonable demographic projections from the moment of independence would have estimated the probable population of the Republic for 1990 as around 14 rather than 4 million. Only the constant hemorrhage of emigration has kept the population so low, and, as Declan Kiberd and others suggested in the same issue of the *Reporter*, so conservative.

In the often sentimental memorialization of the Famine and of the continuing mass emigration that followed it, little mention has, until recently, been made of the massive restructuring of Irish society that followed. Yet of the millions who left in the second half of the nineteenth century and since, the vast majority were the landless and largely disenfranchised working classes. Their departure consolidated the political and economic power of the large and middling farmers who have been described as the "nation-building class." And of course the nation they built, for numerous reasons, has conformed to their interests and ideology: conservative, principally agricultural, and dominated by the most conservative kind of Catholicism imaginable. The classes among which opposition to such a polity thrived, and who throughout the war of independence stood for quite radical transformation of the society, created soviets, and maintained if not an anti-clerical at least an anti-episcopal stance, were decimated by emigration.

The term "emigration" has accordingly its own resonances both in Ireland and abroad, resonances not simply echoing from ballads like "The Leaving of Liverpool" or "Carrickfergus," but with both folk and historical recollections of famine, of eviction, of dispossession, and of economic depression and failure. The word itself bears for us the reminder of the political and economic legacies of colonialism, and particularly where Irish emigrants meet those from other nations, the shock of recognition of our alignment with the postcolonial world that so many would have us forget. Emigration is not the spontaneous overflow of surplus population from a land without contraception, but part of a pattern of movements of labor linked to systemic underdevelopment as surely as transnational capital flows are linked to the global disequilibria of wealth, exploitation, and consumption. To give but one striking instance, it is with the Philippines that Ireland is paired as the world's greatest exporters of female nursing and domestic service workers.

Emigration is a slow and individualized national trauma, often sentimentalized and dressed up by the very cultural forms—most importantly music—that have helped the emigrant to survive. Its very slowness, and the fact that it is apprehended by individuals and families in ways that statistics fail to touch, prevent that trauma from being sufficiently engaged at the political level. We grow up anticipating departure in ways that deeply affect the culture. But that experience is not unique to Ireland: multicultural America is built on immigration from countries marked by imperial wars and conquests, anti-colonial and decolonizing struggles, economic exploitation, and the massive migration of peoples. The schools of Los Angeles, San Francisco, and New York are alive with the children of workers from the Philippines, Mexico, Korea, Laos, Vietnam, Cambodia, El Salvador, Puerto Rico, Haiti, not to mention those whose families have gradually become, often painfully, Americanized.

Whereas the invocation of "diaspora" tends to emphasize, and even to celebrate, the mostly *cultural* by-products of nearly two centuries of Irish migrations, that of "emigration" keeps in mind both the economic and political reasons for our leaving, and helps to affirm the vital relationship between our historical experience and that of other decolonizing societies. Constantly to recall this is the political work of the emigrant communities. One aspect of the accidental political effects of emigration is said to be that many from the Republic become aware for the first time of the issues underlying the Northern conflict, simply because they for the first time meet people from Belfast or Derry. But there is also the effect of English racism on Irish people coming to Birmingham or London, which helps them understand the perspective of British blacks. Or the encounter in San Francisco with Chicanos and Latinos, which helps us situate our experience in terms of the larger global history of the New World Order.

In 1847, hundreds of Irish soldiers in the Anglo-American army fighting against Mexico deserted to form the San Patricio Corps, identifying with the Mexican people. Mostly Irish-speaking, they had undergone the racism of their Anglo officers and watched the burning of Catholic churches and the rape and slaughter of Mexicans. Their understanding of the links between English domination of Ireland and Yankee domination of Mexico was immediate. Many died in the war and many more were executed by the United States for desertion, but the descendants of the survivors, Spanish-speaking Mexicans, still meet to commemorate the brigade in Mexico City. In 1993, Luis Camnitzer, an

Argentinian Jewish artist based in the United States, held an exhibition in Mexico City commemorating the San Patricios.

These intersections between Irish and Latin American experiences continue, though they are less well known than the stories of Irish presi- dents and film stars. Catriona Ruane wrote eloquently in *The Irish Reporter* of how her own experiences in Nicaragua prepared her to under- stand the situation in Belfast on her return to Ireland. These are not the "typical" experiences of the Irish diaspora in popular media and myth, but they are crucial examples of the ways in which experiences in emigration can be politicizing in affecting not only our understanding of "abroad" but also what we want to bring back home. These are the ways in which we can make a new sense of our dispersion, historically and in the pres- ent. Music is the most famous, but not the only scene that can be trans- formed by the encounters emigrants make with others, from Ireland or elsewhere. But, as the current conservative resistance to a campaign led by the Labour Party in Ireland to grant an emigrant vote indicates, we do need to find ways to bring our experience home and make it count.

But we also need to find ways to make it active here in the United States. The longer history of the Irish American experience has tended to be more about the separation of the Irish immigrants from the people of color here, at least insofar as it has been a matter of official historical record. That history is in some senses the familiar one of dividing and ruling. The Cromwellian depopulation of Ireland in the seventeenth cen- tury sent thousands of Irish to the Caribbean as slaves and indentured ser- vants alongside Africans, giving rise to the "redshanks" of the West Indies. Records of plantation owners reveal the anxieties created among slave-owners by the apparent solidarity between Irish and Black slaves. By the mid-nineteenth century, a different era of Irish immigration resulted at first in those savage mainstream caricatures of both the Irish and the Black as equivalently degenerate races that L. P. Curtis has so well docu- mented. For Anglo-Saxons, both "Celt" and "Negro" were a comparable threat to their society.

But things changed with the increasing political and labor power of the Irish, which Joseph Lee has recently suggested came about through a combination of their superior competence in English over other Euro- pean groups and the practice in political mass organization that they brought with them from the many anti-colonial struggles in Ireland. Rather than the shared experience of discrimination leading to solidarity with Black or Chinese workers, the Irish adhered to the new racial cate- gory of "whiteness," by and large becoming—through the police force, the labor unions, and the city political machines—the agents of the dominant racial formation of the United States. E. L. Doctorow's *Ragtime* is probably the best known portrait of this tendency in ethnic relations earlier in the century.

Given such a history, it is surely impossible now for Irish Americans to evoke the memory of their experience of discrimination as some kind of ethical hedge against their access to what is still the privilege of whiteness. Of course one hears, all too frequently, the retort in debates around affirmative action or ethnic relations that "we had to struggle, too," and this simplified history of the struggle for integration into dominant American culture has given shape in a more scholarly version to the formulations of Nathan Glazer and Daniel Patrick Moynihan. For them, exactly those trials of European, and especially Irish, immigrants provide the ideal model for American narratives of successful immigration and assimilation. This makes it all the more important for us to open up the other histories that are less often invoked, difficult as that may be.

The task is not to comfort Irish Americans for now occupying the ethically unenviable position of being identified as white, whether by reminding them of their own history of oppression in this country or by cultivating a re-ethnicizing obsession with roots. The task is rather to begin to trace alternative histories, histories which may not spell success in terms of the dominant paradigm, and may even, like the San Patricios, spell failure. Alongside the well-documented history of the gradual assimilation of Irish immigrants into American culture, there must be many, less well documented memories of other decisions and other affiliations which Irish laborers and peasants made on the basis of their own experiences of racism and colonialism. We need to retrieve these stories, not so that they can become another dominant history, displacing the former, but so that they can form a repertoire for what I would call the history of possibilities, thinking, after Walter Benjamin, of the ways in which even the defeated struggles and gestures of the oppressed remain in memory as images that flash up in moments of emergency. These stories serve to remind us that the history of the integration of Ireland and the Irish into Western modernity is not only not the sole story but also not the sole possibility. Our history is full of reasons to seek out both international and inter-ethnic connections, because of what we know and because of what we *could* know better of ourselves and of others. And because the struggle against injustice is not ended simply by becoming legal.

I write as an Irish citizen living in America and speaking therefore with a double consciousness and a dual interest. The recent intensification of racialized politics in the United States, by which recent Irish immigrants, whether documented or undocumented, are directly and acutely addressed, demands our response. It is a moment in which Irish migrants must either choose solidarity with people of color or once more hide under the veil of our whiteness. But that choice has repercussions in Ireland and for Irish political directions also. Perhaps more than for any generation of emigrants, the current generation can be alert to the geopolitical meaning of mass emigration.

Though many of us are professionals, able easily to integrate into the middle classes of our host societies, the vast majority of emigrants continue to be working class, displaced by the conditions of postcolonial dependency or continuing colonial occupation. Even among those who have been privileged and qualified by class and education, many come away politically and culturally disaffected from the longstanding conservatism of the official Irish nation, leaving Ireland as much in disgust as by necessity. In addition, almost thirty years of anti-colonial political struggle in the North of Ireland, a struggle which more fully than at any previous moment in Irish republicanism has affirmed its links with other insurgencies globally, has had profound effects on our sense of possible affiliation.

More than ever, this is a moment in which it is possible for Irish emigrants to both identify with and learn from the issues of Third World and minority peoples, and to direct some of the lessons learned homewards. As the Irish elites rush toward integration into the new, racialized "Fortress Europe," we emigrants need to reinvoke our colonized past, not only in an America that continues to play out the gambits of colonialism internally and externally, but also in Ireland, bringing back home the knowledge that integration with the dominant order has never been the only or the most liberating possibility.

5

■ ■ ■

FRICTION: INTER-ETHNIC, INTERNECINE, FRATRICIDAL

Black and Latino Relations: Context, Challenge, and Possibilities

■ ■ ■

MAULANA KARENGA

It is now common consensus that U.S. society is passing through a critical period in its tragic and problematic history of race and ethnic relations. The biracial Black-White paradigm of race and ethnic relations has given way to multi-ethnic patterns defined by increased complexity, fluidity, cooperation, and conflict.[1] How these relations work out will determine both the quality of life in these various communities and our capacity to realize the collective quest for a just and good society. Certainly, none of these patterns of relations is more critical to our understanding of this new reality than Black-Brown relations. Much has been written in the popular press about relations between African Americans and Latino Americans, but there is little in the scholarly literature that reflects serious and sustained thought about this critical issue. Approaches in the popular press range from liberal angst and alarmism[2] to deconstructionist diversions,[3] and often simply portray conflict rather than the numerous instances of cooperation or the possibilities inherent in the relations between the two communities. Nevertheless, the focus on relations between African Americans and Latino Americans is both timely and urgent.

African Americans, currently the largest racial ethnic group (30 million plus), have historically played a vanguard role in expanding the realm of freedom in this country, compelling it to deal seriously with issues of social justice, and opening up social space and opportunities for other ethnic groups and other marginalized groups such as women, seniors, the disabled, and even immigrants. Given this history and the role they have played as the most devalued "other" in the white racist paradigm, race and ethnic relations were understood to a great extent in terms of Black victimization by and resistance to racism, oppression, inequality, and injustice. As other ethnic groups rise to prominence, however, legitimate claims on society by Blacks are balanced off by similar claims from others, or even overridden by other claims, and this has caused both injury and apprehension among Blacks.

Latinos are currently the second largest racial ethnic group (22.3 million plus) and, according to U.S. Census Bureau projections, will exceed the numbers of African Americans in the first decade of the twenty-first century, with a third of the increase coming from immigration. This new numerical reality has had a profound effect on social policy and social relations, for it brings with it an expanded set of social claims and social discourse. As a result of these changes, the two groups now find themselves in competitive and conflictual situations which, depending upon how they are handled, could lead either to increased hostility and repeated and destructive clashes, or to cooperative efforts for common good. This is especially true of Africans and Mexicans, who have the largest numbers, the longest history of interaction, the most extensive relations with allies, and the most varied and widespread institutional base from which to engage each other and society.

Thus, given their size, history of impact, and current contacts in the public square, and the possibilities of both cooperation and conflict, a critical examination of the current issues that shape Black–Brown relations is of major significance. In fact, although much has been written about the importance of Black–Jewish relations,[4] it is clear that Black–Brown relations have become and will continue to be most determinative of ethnic relations in this country. For, given the factors cited above, these two communities, if directed correctly, will not only play decisive roles in the reconception and reconstruction of American society but will also pose a paradigm of ethnic and human relations essential to the building of a truly multicultural, just, and good society.

The challenge, then, is first to discuss and grasp critically the meaning of the social dynamics which often divide them on one hand and yet call urgently for their mutual respect, collaboration, and common struggle on the other. Second, the challenge is to take this critical understanding and translate it into a policy of mutual respect and cooperation among the communities and into specific action programs in order to shape a mutually beneficial framework directed toward the historical and ongoing quest for a just and good society.

The Issues: Context and Dimensions

To examine the question of relations between Black and Brown people in the United States, one must begin by putting the question in context. First, the development of relationship between these two largest American racial-ethnic groups is marked by both cooperation and conflict. Whether it is called "fusion and friction" in Dallas or "cross-cultural alliances in the midst of racial strife" in Los Angeles,[5] there are always everywhere those who seek to build and sustain common ground and cooperation in the midst of conflict and tension.[6] Second, it is also important to note that the conflict, although real, is too often poorly addressed by leaders, and seemingly always badly and exaggeratedly reported by the media. Therefore, one is generally instructed by selective interviews of those with grievances, sensational reports of the media, excessive claims of ethnic chauvinists, weak refrains by liberals, and the bewildered silence of the left. In such a context, clarity is scarce, and solutions of substance and duration are even more difficult to achieve. But the reality is that like all critical junctures in history, this juncture represents both *danger* and *possibility, risks* and *promise,* and it is the ongoing tension between these that can bring out the worst or best in people. The task is to create and institute a public philosophy and program, which will cultivate and lead to success.

Third, the evolution of Black-Brown relations takes place in the changing context of the rise of multi-ethnic patterns of relationships and exchanges, and the unraveling of the traditional biracial alliance and assumptions of Blacks and liberal whites. Thus, although Black-Brown relations are a key concern, they must and can only be developed in a positive way in the context of the careful crafting of social strategies and social policy for multiethnic collaboration and cooperation. Black-Asian, and especially Black-Korean, relations stand out as a central concern in this effort, and their impact in both the academy and society should not be minimized.[7] Within this multiethnic context, a host of issues exist around which cooperative efforts can be made—especially in education, economics, environmental concerns, police misconduct and abuse, political representation, and in immigration, particularly for Haitians and Continental Africans.

Fourth, the development of these relations is also defined by a series of fundamental social changes and processes, including: (1) major demographic shifts; (2) the progressive deindustrialization of U.S. society; (3) a turn toward social policies marked by diminishing resources; (4) worsening economic conditions for the working and middle classes; and (5) the convergence of these conditions with an increasing rise of nativist and racist sentiment and actions against immigrant and native-born people of color.

Clearly, the demographic shift in which Latinos have increased in number in the United States and begun to seek housing in formerly all-Black or predominantly Black neighborhoods; to acquire jobs in previously all-Black or predominantly Black areas of employment; and to demand appropriate representation in public employment and administrative and political spaces yields the defining factors in the development of relations between African Americans and Latinos. Even many native-born Latinos have reacted negatively to this increase in population brought about by the liberalization of the 1965 Immigration and Naturalization Act, and by the Amnesty Act of 1986, which legalized the residency status of many Mexicans and Central Americans.[8] The Latinos' sense is that immigrant populations put strains on limited resources, create added tensions, and in the case of the Central Americans, have proven politically more assertive than the rather demure politics of a segment of the established Mexican middle-class *condones*. But clearly many Blacks feel they are most directly and negatively affected by this new shift in population.[9] And it is this sense of being negatively impacted that informs much of Black discourse about Latinos, as well as Latino responses to them and to the new realities. Nowhere do these factors combine more clearly than in the city of Compton on one hand and in Los Angeles on the other.[10] And how these tensions are confronted and worked out will most likely set a model for Black-Brown relations in the rest of the country.

The process of progressive deindustrialization and restructuring of regional economics during the last few decades adds to both sources of tension and possibilities.[11] The central dynamic of capitalism is the perpetual pursuit of profit; thus, the corporate world seeks to maximize profit by "downsizing" and relocation in contexts of cheap labor and minimum or no health, safety, and environmental constraints. This has destroyed many of the industrial jobs that were once the center of a strong Black urban working class. Moreover, as the move toward privatization has occurred, Blacks find that the economic and racial preference of new employers excludes them and seeks Latinos. For Latinos are seen by these employers as vulnerable, less contentious, and more tolerant of low pay and low standards of health and safety on the job. Finally, economic restructuring, which makes a sharp division between highly skilled, information industry jobs and low-paying, unskilled service jobs, also proves problematic for many Blacks. Lacking the skills for the high-tech jobs, they find themselves unable to get even old and new service jobs; also, they are blocked from low-skilled contractor and garment industry jobs. Instead of perceiving this as the result of employer preference—racial and economic—their common-sense conclusion is that it is caused by Latinos who "took" their jobs.

In the context of worsening economic conditions, federal, state, and local governments are adopting social policies of diminishing resources. This leaves Blacks and Browns and other people of color, the poor, and other needy groups to struggle over a reduced set of resources. Moreover, a significant segment of a threatened white middle class finds itself unable even to pretend to a sense of security and confidence in the future in this context of deteriorating economic conditions. They therefore become even more prone toward racist and nativistic sentiment, mean-spirited attitudes toward the poor, and dangerously vulnerable to right-wing political manipulation. Latinos and Blacks, facing each other across the table of diminished resources, contested space, and limited power, often fail to appreciate the fact that in the eyes of the established order, both groups are problematic, devalued and unworthy of shared wealth and power in this country. They often fail to see and act on the fact that they have it in their hands to demand and achieve through struggle, along with other progressive allies, a just society in which there is a more egalitarian distribution of wealth and power, and in which they will not have to contend over crumbs. The task—indeed, the challenge—then is to focus both the separate and combined communities on a mutually beneficial set of possibilities, and then to organize and engage in practice collectively to bring these into being.

Toward Collective Engagement

In order to build on the cooperative possibilities of Black-Brown relations, avoid mutually destructive conflicts, and collectively pursue the quest for a just and good society, several factors are necessary.

THE CHALLENGE OF NEW DISCOURSE

The first of these is the development of a new discourse of ethnic relations. This will move from the simple Black-white discourse forged especially in the sixties and on to a more inclusive discourse, which recognizes the presence and essential relevance of each ethnic group in the project of reconceiving and reconstructing U.S. society. Moreover, this new and *inclusive* discourse will not exclude or minimize the importance of Blacks as active subjects, nor speak of Latinos exclusively or along with Asians as the sole groups of central importance in the political and economic processes of the future. This is clearly one of the biggest mistakes made both by scholars and by policy makers in their assumption that the growing numbers of Latinos and Asians will render almost insignificant the political power, presence, and claims on society of African Americans. Such reasoning not only aggravates the problem of Black-Brown cooperation, but hides the fact that the decisive elements in struggle are not numbers but the political consciousness, the level of organization, the compelling and legitimate aspirations and claims of the people, and their willingness to sacrifice for the greater good.

Whites have outnumbered Blacks for years and yet Blacks have launched, fought, and won with their allies key battles against white domination. And this ongoing struggle has expanded the realm of freedom in this country, changed its original character and course, and benefited all marginalized groups. Thus, other groups and peoples on the national and international level have borrowed from and built on the moral vocabulary and moral vision of our struggle, and posed it as a model to emulate. This represents an ongoing tradition of social justice that is of profound importance to both the history and the future of this country.

Moreover, even though Latinos and Asians are the fastest-growing ethnic groups, an inclusive and effective multicultural discourse will not emphasize numbers, but rather the building of a just and good society in which all have a meaningful role. Appeal to numbers without social justice considerations has historically proved both immoral and oppressive. In fact, the history of ethnic relations in the United States has essentially been a continuous struggle against the tyranny of the majority.[12] Furthermore, even when Latinos become the most numerous ethnic group, they will still not outnumber whites, and thus the majority projected in 2076 is a majority of people of color, not Latinos alone.

In the final analysis, to challenge the established order effectively and create a just and good society requires a cooperative effort by all progressive forces in the country. The factor of critical importance, then, is not the large numbers of a single group but the *cooperative engagement* of all progressive people in the struggle, and a collaborative concept in the context of maximum human flourishing. The new discourse will be a deracialized discourse, one that informs a social policy respectful of common economic and political concerns while remaining sensitive to ethnic and cultural community identities and interests.

It is important to note here that the category "Latino," or its official version, "Hispanic," hides an extensive diversity which translates into internal conflict as well as cooperation. In fact, one of the lessons from the Los Angeles 1992 revolt was that segments of the established Mexican middle class found no common ground with the newly arrived Central American participants and were quick to distinguish themselves from this "politically problematic" group. In addition, native-born Latinos and new immigrants often do not easily find common ground for political, economic, and even cultural reasons. The category "Latino" also includes Black Latinos and thus complicates a strictly racialized discourse. Likewise, there are clearly differences between the right-wing and Republican politics of the Cuban American community, the Democratic politics of the Mexican and Puerto Rican communities, and the commitment to grass-root and radical politics of many of the Central Americans. And certainly the Black tourism boycott of Miami and its Cuban-controlled government around the Mandela controversy, and the subsequent agreement worked out with business, civil, and political leaders, represent different kinds of economic and political issues than those pursued with less economically and politically powerful Latinos in other parts of the country. Moreover, it is a well-known fact that Latino numbers, with the exception of Miami Cubans, do not usually translate into registered voters or widespread political participation. What one has is an organized segment of the middle class in the various Latino communities who speak for this diversity called "Latino" and thus bear a heavy burden not only to represent them correctly, but also to provide them with a vision of possibility that lies not in problematic discourse on numbers, but in the cooperative project of the quest for a just and good society.

THE CHALLENGE OF MORAL LEADERSHIP

A second fundamental requirement for a cooperative spirit and practice between Blacks and Browns is to meet the challenge of developing a moral leadership committed to providing a moral vision of our just and good society, and mobilizing the energies of the various communities to engage in the cooperative effort to build such a society. The pressing need for such leadership was revealed in a poll commissioned a year after the

1992 Los Angeles revolt by the Spanish-language media, KVEA-TV, and the newspaper *La Opinión*.[13] In a survey of 305 Blacks and 301 Latinos in the south-central and Pico Union districts, 82 percent of those surveyed thought their political leadership cared little or nothing about neighborhood problems, and 85 percent said that the leadership had done little to ease inter-ethnic conflict.

Thus, there is an urgent need for a politically capable leadership, which is normally sensitive to the need of the two communities to put an end to inter-ethnic conflict and increase the effort to achieve the conditions and means to live good and meaningful lives. Such a leadership will respect cultural differences and sensitivities, but will not cater to racial and ethnic animosities, fear, or stereotypes. It will pose projects that bring out the best in persons and peoples, not pander to the worst and most destructive. It will be a leadership committed to a vigorous and vital multiculturalism, which embraces and builds on diversity. This leadership will stress the value of principled challenging of ourselves and others in both critical thought and corrective practice. It will challenge us to think in new ways about old problems, and to discover new ways of being human and living in a multicultural society. It will challenge us, finally, to confront the established order of things and extract the hidden possibilities of human community.

THE CHALLENGE OF MULTICULTURALISM

Any solution to this awesome and critical challenge for Blacks, Latinos, and the country must include at its center a genuine appreciation and practice of multiculturalism, which will express itself in a new public philosophy and ongoing social policy. Certainly, what is proposed here is not a multiculturalism of days devoted to ethnic food and clothing, pro forma mention of diversity on special occasions, or recognition on calendars and workdays of holidays of various ethnicities. "Multiculturalism" here means thought and practice informed by a profound appreciation for diversity, which expresses itself in four fundamental ways.

First, serious multiculturalism, of necessity, begins with mutual respect for each people and each culture. This means always engaging the peoples and their cultures as equally valuable expressions of humanity in all its rich and instructive diversity. And this in turn translates as adequate representation and dignity-affirming treatment of the major five population groups (Native American, African American, Latino American, and Asian American, as well as Euro-American) in all areas of social life.

Second, a substantive multiculturalism requires mutual respect for each people's right and responsibility to speak their own special cultural truth and make their own unique contribution to how this society is *reconceived* and *reconstructed*. This, of course, recognizes the fact that U.S. society has been historically molded in a Eurocentric form in spite of its multicultural composition; thus, it must be conceptually reimagined and structurally recast to accommodate the just demands and legitimate aspirations of people of color. This process of reconception and reconstruction, which has as its central thrust the quest for a just and good society, will of necessity include dialogue and common struggle with other oppressed and marginalized groups to achieve their common goal.

Third, a real and vital multiculturalism requires a mutual commitment to the constant search for common ground in the midst of our diversity.[14] Indeed, it is the successful balancing of our respect for diversity and the demands of continually discovering and cultivating common ground in the midst of our diversity that will determine our capacity to build a just and good society. For without genuine and substantive respect for diversity, there can be only continuing oppression. But without the capacity to establish and build on common ground, there can be only vitiating conflict and consuming chaos. Thus, it is important to find common ground with other progressive forces in the larger American context.

U.S. society is not a white finished product, but a multicultural, ongoing unfinished project. Given this, the multicultural character and promise of the project requires that the reconstruction of social policy be a multicultural process. This does not mean that African Americans should play a less important role in reconstruction. On the contrary, it means that if they are to play their historical vanguard role effectively, they must be, more than ever, sensitive and attentive to the multicultural concerns and evolving character of society. This requires that they take the lead in insisting that race, class, and gender—as well as culture—be recognized not simply as issues but as fundamental aspects of social reality, and that they pose paradigms of possibilities available in the context of a truly multicultural society.[15]

Therefore, they must struggle to ensure that attention be paid to giving voice and power to the many peoples who make up this multicultural society, especially the marginalized groups: people of color, women, the poor and vulnerable, the disadvantaged and disabled. This, of course, is a necessary reaffirmation of the best values of our social justice tradition. The *Million Man March/Day of Absence Mission Statement* asserts that this will require "respect for the dignity and rights of the human person, economic justice, meaningful political participation, shared power, cultural integrity, mutual respect for all peoples and uncompromising resistance to social forces and structures which deny or limit these."[16] It is in the pursuit of this inclusiveness that social policy becomes a process of conceiving and achieving the common good. For this common good is created out of the common aspirations of the many peoples, the many cultures who share this society and want the best context for human freedom and flourishing, and thus are willing to cooperate in order to achieve it.

Finally, a multiculturalism which both reflects and reinforces the quest for a just and good society unavoidably requires a mutual commitment among the various peoples to a *social ethics of sharing*. This includes at a minimum a mutual commitment to shared space, shared wealth, shared power, and shared responsibility in defining and bringing into being the society, and indeed the world, we all want to live in. This social ethics of sharing is, of necessity, informed by and grounded in the mutual respect of persons, cultures, and rights, and the mutual commitment to common ground discussed above. It expresses itself, first, as respectful recognition that we are members of various communities and a single society in which we share common space and, in a real sense, a common future; and second, that this is to be seen not as an unwanted imposition, but as a ground of possibility for collectively conceiving and pursuing the common good.

Africans, in honoring the best of their social justice tradition, must realize that some of the reactions they have to Latino entrance in their communities and the resultant transformation too often resemble the reactions of the whites who watched with horror and loathing as we moved into neighborhoods to which they once claimed exclusive rights. Our oppressor cannot be our teacher. On the contrary, our tradition of social justice must always instruct and inspire us. Thus, we must realize that Latino immigrants come to our neighborhoods because of the existence of inexpensive and available housing; that they, like us, have a right to housing anywhere in the United States, but they also, like many of us, can only afford it in certain places.

On the other hand, Latino leaders must be sensitive to the concerns of Blacks about the coming of large numbers of immigrants and the resultant transformations of neighborhoods. Conversations about this being Mexican country are not helpful, not only because they gloss over Native American original claims, but also because they show an insensitivity to people who actually and legitimately live in and care about these neighborhoods, and are concerned about changes they don't initiate and seem to have no power over. What is required here is a series of planned encounters, forums, exchanges, and cooperative projects to bring old and new residents together: they need to talk about common and differing concerns, and to work together to build and shape the communities they now share.

An ethics of sharing also requires commitment to shared wealth. It speaks to the challenge of the democratization and moral grounding not only of political but also of economic life. For economic democracy is the indispensable complement to political democracy. On a larger level, this means the need for collaborative and cooperative projects encompassing all people of color and progressive people. This, in turn, requires democratic initiatives to control and halt: (1) local and state governments, and the transfer of social wealth into the hands of private capital; (2) corporate relocation "downsizing," and the exploitation of vulnerable, non-unionized workers; (3) race, gender, and age discrimination; (4) disinvestment in the social structure; and (5) the practice of environmental racism, which leads to placing the majority of toxic waste in neighborhoods of color and giving us the choice of degrading the environment of working.

But the ethics of sharing also requires an honest dialogue about the pressing problems of Black displacement through employer preference. In many cases the ethnic chauvinist exaggerates the problem, but the liberal often avoids or minimizes it; in both cases, the result is that the problem is aggravated rather than solved. We need to state the problem clearly and honestly, and to conduct our dialogue in a context of civility, mutual respect, and equality. Equally important is to present the problem in a deracialized language of common ground.

For example, there is no need to deny that in significant instances, immigrants are displacing Blacks in jobs that require relatively low skills and education. Nor should we deny that this is due in great part to the general willingness of these immigrants to work for lower wages and to tolerate substandard working conditions.[17] But even more important here is the factor of *employer preference*. The reality is that for both racist and capitalist reasons, employers prefer a Brown worker over a Black worker, and a capitalist clearly prefers a vulnerable, undocumented, non-union worker to a documented and unionized worker.

Here is a clear example where a limited language that places this problem exclusively in Black and Brown terms hides the key role of the capitalist or petty-bourgeois employer in choosing Brown over Black and vulnerable over organized worker. Moreover, it hides the fact that this concern about manipulation and exploitation of vulnerable Latino workers has historically posed a problem for the United Farm Workers, a Mexican-led union, and that this union has also opposed the hiring and exploitation of undocumented workers. It also is important to recognize the problem of vulnerable and non-union workers for the labor movement in general, and the need to collaborate collectively to solve it in a just way.

But again, the key focus in the solution must be on employer's preference and exploitation. For once the key role of employers in displacement of Black workers is established, it becomes easier to move Blacks and others from a common-sense anti-Latino posture to one that makes labor and political alliance for the common good more plausible and possible. Furthermore, one can begin to see that even as there are grounds for conflict, there are also grounds for cooperation, not only in resisting common problems of dislocation by both Blacks and Latinos[18] and the attacks of Affirmative Action,[19] but in planning and prefiguring the kind of society we want to bring into being.

An ethics of shared power means realizing both the problems and the possibilities inherent in achieving a truly democratic political life. It cannot mean a process in which people of color argue and fight with each other over marginal and limited space while white power stays intact. Again, it calls for ethical sensitivity and ethical political practice by both Africans and Latinos. The legitimate claims of Latinos of the right to participate in a meaningful and proportionate way in the politics of Black-controlled cities must be respected. They cannot be rebuffed with claims that they want now to take what we alone won. This denies the collective character of the struggle for justice in this country in spite of the vanguard role of Blacks, and it does not give adequate weight to the fact that we all have fought separately and together at various times to end white domination and improve the quality of life. We do not deny the clear vanguard role that Blacks have played in challenging and changing the established order, but we must give necessary recognition and credit to other peoples of color in this ongoing and unfinished struggle to create a just and good society. Such rebuff to legitimate claims also contradicts our social justice tradition, which stresses the right of everyone to political participation and shared power, and the right of each people to participate in every decision that significantly affects their destiny and daily life.

For their part, Latino leaders must recognize the central role Blacks have played in expanding the realm of freedom in this country for everyone, including them; must be sensitive to Blacks' concern for displacement in still another area; and must balance their pursuit of positions held by Blacks with pursuit of real power held by whites. In addition, they cannot suggest that Blacks are responsible for their lack of representation in society when Blacks don't control society and are themselves still struggling for adequate representation and power. In other words, in the context of mutuality and building common ground, Latinos cannot justly stake a claim to proportional or equal representation only on Black-controlled municipalities and institutions. They must stake it on white-controlled structures of power also, and more often. For these structures are clearly more numerous and more central to the inequity of both power and wealth in this country from which all people of color suffer. The two communities must realize, further, that it is an old and dishonorable tradition of the oppressor to pit two oppressed groups against each other by taking from one to give to another while keeping his own large portion of wealth and power intact, untouched. What is required, then, is that both communities stop focusing on each other as the main source of their problems, begin to discuss seriously the structure of wealth and power in this country, and together develop cooperative projects to challenge and change the situation.

Serious and difficult discussions also must begin on the difference between the rights and claims of citizens and the rights and claims of immigrants who are not citizens; on the priority of resource allocation to citizens versus a moral sensitivity and responsibility to the needy regardless of status, and how to balance the two justly. These discussions will be some of the most taxing, requiring the best values of each of our traditions and the most instructive lessons of our history for a just and morally sensitive solution to the issues.

Finally, an ethics of sharing of necessity involves shared responsibility in defining and bringing into being the society we all want to live in. This is a reaffirmation of the right and responsibility of each people to speak its own special cultural truth and to make its own unique contribution to how that society is reconceived and reconstructed. Especially key to the formulation of strategies of cooperation is to learn the lessons of past and current cooperation between the two communities. Certainly, the early cooperative efforts in fighting against segregation in the South by the National Association for the Advancement of Colored People (NAACP) and the United League of Latin American Citizens (LULAC) should be studied and emulated, as well as the current cooperative work of the NAACP and the Mexican American Legal Defense and Education Fund (MALDEF). Another instructive example of cooperative exchange is the work that my own organization, US, did in the sixties in training Black and Brown community organizers within the Social Action Training Center (SATC), and our cooperative projects and relations with the Brown Berets, the Alianza Federal de Pueblos Libres led by Reies Tijerina, and La Cruzada para la Justicia led by Corky Gonzales, as well as other Chicano groups. Moreover, we participated in numerous rallies of support for Chicano issues and for the United Farm Workers and continue to observe the boycotts it calls. Continuing this tradition of cooperation and alliance, US has exchanges with campus and community Latinos to establish mutually beneficial dialogue and work together for common interests. These include: Casa Nicaragua; the Committee in Solidarity with the People of El Salvador; the Farabundi Marti Solidarity Committee; the Guatemalan Information Center; and the Coalition in Solidarity with Cuba, as well as personal and professional exchanges with leaders, scholars, and creative artists from Cuba and Brazil, Colombia and Peru.

Other excellent examples of multicultural cooperative efforts would include organizations like the South Central Organizing Committee, an African American group that sponsors cooperative projects around housing and employment; the Los Angeles Partnership, a coalition of contractors of color working to rebuild L.A.; Concerned Citizens of South Central, an African American group that formed an alliance with the Central American Refugee Center (CARECEN), provided it with space, and aided it in obtaining economic development and in creating a Latino block club; and the Los Angeles Multicultural Collaborative and the Rainbow Coalition, led by the Reverend Jesse Jackson, both of whose programs are crafted to include multicultural leaders and participants as well as issues of common ground. All of these models are key, for they pose historical and current paradigms of achievement and possibilities. And the younger generation urgently needs to be aware of this historical and current reality and to be involved in such a cooperative tradition and process.

Finally, it is equally important to ensure that the centrality of Black-Brown relations does not obscure or minimize the need to involve all other groups in this project. Certainly, Native Americans have a special and compelling claim on this country and must be included. Asians, too, must be given due consideration, and be included in local projects as well as in the national project of reconceiving and reconstructing society. Clearly, there are critical issues still to be resolved between Koreans and the Black and Brown communities arising out of the tremendous losses and injuries suffered by the Koreans during the 1992 L.A. revolt.[20] This inclusiveness will show a necessary commitment to the ethics of sharing and also ensure that no one is left out and alienated, and that every people and culture contributes to defining the kind of society we want to live in. The challenge posed here is admittedly a great one, but so are the demands of our history and the promise of a truly just multicultural society. For the struggle we must wage is one that unavoidably points toward an even greater goal: a human future free from want, toil, and domination, and supporting the context for mutually beneficial human exchange and flourishing.

■ ▨ ▨

NOTES

1. See Thomas E. Gail, *U.S. Race Relations in the 1980's and 1990's: Challenges and Alternatives* (New York: Hemisphere Publishing, 1990); Wallace E. Lambert, *Coping with Cultural and Racial Diversity in Urban America* (New York: Praeger, 1990); and U.S. Commission on Civil Rights, *Racial and Ethnic Tensions in American Communities*, Washington, D.C., 1995.

2. Jack Miles, "Immigration and the New American Dilemma," *The Atlantic* 270, 4 (1992), pp. 41–68.

3. Jorge Klor De Alva, Earl Storris, and Cornel West, "Our Next Race Questions: The Uneasiness Between Blacks and Latinos: A Colloquy," *Harper's* (April 1996), pp. 55–63.

4. Michael Lerner and Cornel West, *Jews and Blacks: Let the Healing Begin* (New York: G. P. Putnam's Sons, 1995), and Paul Berman, ed., *Blacks and Jews: Alliances and Arguments* (New York: Delacorte Press, 1994).

5. See Catalina Camia, Selwyn Crawford, and Enrique Rangel, "Fusion and Friction: Dallas Hispanics, Blacks Often at Odds in Quest for Parity," *Dallas Morning News*, October 18, 1992, p. 1A, and Lynell George, "The Real Westside Story: Racial Strife and Murders in Venice Make Headlines, but Beneath the Surface Studies of Gangs and Drugs, Cross-Cultural Alliances Bloom There . . . and Everywhere," *Los Angeles Times*, July 22, 1994, Part E, pp. 1ff.

6. Joe R. Hicks, Stewart Kwoh, and Frank Acosta, "Where's the Leadership on Race Relations?" *Los Angeles Times*, March 29, 1996, p. B9.

7. See Chancellor Chang-Lin Tien, "A View from Berkeley," *New York Times Education Life*, March 31, 1996, p. 30, and Norimitsu Onishi, "Affirmative Action: Choosing Sides," ibid., pp. 26–29, 32–35.

8. Lynne Barnes, Kenneth Weiss, and Sonia Nazario, "Natives, Newcomers at Odds in East L.A.," *Los Angeles Times*, March 4, 1996, p. A1.

9. Charisse Jones, "Arrival of Latinos Spurs Black Self-Examination," *Los Angeles Times,* February 18, 1992, p. A1.

10. See Mike Davis, "The Sky Falls on Compton," *The Nation* 259 (Sept. 19, 1994), pp. 268–271; Emily Adams, "Compton Mayor Offers Plans to Ease Tensions," *Los Angeles Times*, September 8, 1994, p. B3; D.E. Bautista and G. Rodriguez, "In South Central Se Habla Español," *The Nation* 260 (Feb. 13, 1995), pp. 202–204; and Gary Lee and Roberto Suro, "Latino-Black Rivalry Grows: Los Angeles Reflects Tensions Between Minorities," *The Washington Post*, October 13, 1993, p. A1.

11. Victor Valle and Rodolfo D. Torres, "Latinos in a 'Post-Industrial' Disorder: Politics in a Changing City," *Socialist Review* 23, 4 (1994), pp. 1–28; see also Mike Davis, *Quartz City* (London & New York: Verso, 1990).

12. See Lani Guinier, *The Tyranny of the Majority: Fundamental Fairness in Representative Democracy* (New York: The Free Press, 1994).

13. Eric Malnic, "Blacks, Latinos Express Sense of Isolation," *Los Angeles Times*, May 13, 1993, p. B3.

14. Maulana Karenga, "African Americans and the Reconstruction of Social Policy," *Harvard Journal of African American Public Policy* 1, 1 (1992), pp. 55–74.

15. See Maulana Karenga, "Afrocentricity and Multicultural Education: Concept, Challenge and Contribution," in Benjamin Bowser, Terry Jones, and Gale Auletta Young, eds., *Toward the Multicultural University* (Westport, CT: Praeger, 1995).

16. Maulana Karenga, *The Million Man March/Day of Absence Mission Statement* (Los Angeles: University of Sankore Press, 1995), p. 00.

17. James Daniel, "Are Immigrants Replacing Black Workers?" *Population and Environment* 17, 1 (September 1995), pp. 59–62.

18. Paul M. Ong and Janette R. Lawrence, "Race and Employment Dislocation in California's Aerospace Industry," *Review of Black Political Economy* 23, 3 (Winter 1995), pp. 91–101.

19. Roberto Santiago, "Hey! Where's That Affirmative Action?" *Hispanic* 8, 10 (November 1995), p. 116.

20. See Haki R. Madhubuti, *Why L.A. Happened: Implications of the '92 Los Angeles Rebellion* (Chicago: Third World Press, 1993), and Robert Gooding-Williams, *Reading Rodney King: Reading Urban Uprising* (New York: Routledge, 1993).

Asian Americans: Decorative Gatekeepers?

■ ■ ■

ELAINE H. KIM

It looks as though Asian Americans might have more opportunities in the future than ever before to contribute to the shaping of American ideas, attitudes, and identities. There was a time within recent memory when it was difficult for educated Asians in the United States to enter careers outside science or engineering. Today, Asian American artists are making history with new novels, poetry, films and videos, sculpture, painting, installation, and performance art. We are already familiar with the Asian American female television news anchors. Now we are beginning to see more and more Asian American bylines at many daily newspapers across the country—not just in Honolulu and Los Angeles, but also in New York and Philadelphia. They write news stories of all kinds, as well as book and film reviews. One of President Clinton's speechwriters was a young Chinese American Yale graduate. Record numbers of Asian Americans are entering the professions, including law, public policy, and public administration. If present trends continue, the twenty-first century should be a century when Asian Americans will speak and write as well as listen and read, when they will be taken seriously as readers, viewers, voters, and constituents.

But unless all Americans are able to more effectively address deep-rooted social problems, Asian Americans may find ourselves stuck in twenty-first-century versions of today's "model minority" identity. Whenever I have a chance, I tell Asian American students to be vigilant lest they find themselves one day schooled, credentialed, and trapped in the old "buffer zone" or middleman "model minority" position, mediating between those who have the power to make the rules and those who are oppressed by them. Whether as newscasters, attorneys, or middle managers, they could be positioned to serve as apologists for and explicators, upholders, and functionaries of the status quo. We seem to be hurdling toward the bifurcation of U.S. society into two major economic classes—the very rich and the poor—and young Asian Americans could find themselves in an increasingly untenable position.

In my view, one of the challenges for Asian Americans in the twenty-first century will be resisting the "gatekeeper function," with a strong and focused commitment to place first priority, in whatever arenas they occupy, on the needs and well-being of the disenfranchised. This may be done with one foot in the margins and the other in the mainstream much of the time. But most important, it will require working in coalition with, rather than in opposition to, other Americans of color.

It goes almost without saying that working in coalition is not possible without discovering common issues of concern, whether these be in issues of drug abuse, jobs, housing, or education, rather than too vaguely general an issue, like "oppression." But of course work around a narrow problem must emerge from a collective vision and ideological basis. Even so, the specific issues can be key sites of conflict for different groups at different points in time; coalition work among oppressed people of color is made even more difficult because alliances built around very specific issues are necessarily shifting and temporary. And of course in a society held together by hierarchical arrangements of power and the privileging of competitive individualism, it is extremely difficult for groups of color to deal with each other on an equal basis, without falling into competition, ranking, and scrambling around hierarchies of oppression. All this despite the indisputable fact that people of color in the United States wear at different moments and often at the same moment the face of both victim and victimizer.

In my view, among groups of color at this time an overreliance on bi-racial theorizing persists, not only in terms of black-white paradigms of race relations, but also in terms of white–non-white binaries. One of the issues we need to address in Ethnic Studies at Berkeley is how to move away from always speaking to the dominant and rarely speaking to each other. Historically, for example, much of our teaching and research has emerged from the impulse to educate ourselves and challenge exploitation in our communities by accusing, protesting to, trying to convince, and even beseeching the dominant about our histories, needs, and interests. This approach might have made sense when students of color were few. We have not addressed each other enough. We have only lately begun to think systematically about what it means to teach, say, about Native American history and literature to a group of mostly Chicano, Latino, and Asian American students.

Within groups of color, such as among Asian Americans, hierarchies also operate. The concerns of smaller and less politically powerful groups—such as Filipinos, Koreans, Pacific Islanders, and South Asians in the past and Southeast Asians and Pacific Islanders in the present—have historically been sidelined and subsumed by those of the larger and more established groups, such as Chinese and Japanese. When Asian Americans came to fuller voice with the African American–led civil rights movement of the 1960s, that voice, which has been the loudest ever since, was male, English-speaking, Chinese or Japanese, and heterosexual.

Given this picture, for Asian Americans to work together across nationalities, languages, generations, genders, and sometimes social classes is in itself rather miraculous. A few years ago, when the question arose whether Berkeley was experiencing cultural diversification or racial "balkanization," I remember thinking that experiences of cultural diversity were being defined exclusively from a dominant culture standpoint. For many students of color who come from communities where their group is very much in the minority and who have been overwhelmed with growing up brown, yellow, red, or black in a culture defined by whiteness, being with other students of color is experiencing cultural diversity. And even though all Asians may look alike to others, it is quite a step for some Korean Americans to make friends with Filipino Americans or for some Vietnamese Americans to take classes with South Asian American students. Perhaps we need to redefine what we mean by "coalition."

Racial meaning extends into social relations and social practices. What indeed *is* a person of color? I remember hearing that on some West Coast college campuses, Asian Americans are sometimes regarded as "inauthentic people of color." But different people of color experience racism and racialization differently. As our patriarchal comrade Frank Chin noted years ago, there is racist hate and there is racist love. After World War II, he has written, Asian Americans have been pretty uniquely the recipients of racist love—the pat on the head, the label of "model minority"—

"kissass" rather than "badass." Still, racism against Asian Americans takes other unique forms, such as resentment and fear of yellow peril takeover, and characterization as unassimilable foreigners who excel at copying but cannot originate, or as robotic automatons and nerdy buffoons with no human or animal feelings. Asian American men have often pointed to the feminization of Asian Americans, who whether male or female, gay or straight, are only good for the "bottom" position.

Since their information comes primarily from the dominant culture, people of color are almost as susceptible to racist stereotyping as anyone else. Thus it should not be surprising that what Cornel West has called xenophobia is so prevalent among African Americans, that many Asian Americans stereotype African Americans as unreliable or crime-prone, that many Latinos can routinely call an Asian of whatever background *el chino,* or that many Korean immigrants in Los Angeles refer to all Latinos as "Mexican."

Some Asian American activists feel that other people of color do not respect and trust Asians in coalition work and that other people of color have a hard time accepting the idea of Asian American leadership. Asian members of the Oakland East Bay African Asian Roundtable have conjectured that this may be because they accept the Fu Manchu notions of Asians as untrustworthy aliens. I recall the National Conference poll, according to which more than four blacks and Latinos in ten and 27 percent of whites agreed with the stereotype of Asian Americans as "unscrupulous, crafty, and devious in business" (*San Francisco Chronicle,* March 3, 1994). Perhaps it is difficult for most people to imagine Asian American leadership in coalitions because except for a few spectacular examples, mostly in agricultural labor organizing during the first half of this century, there has been little history of Asian Americans undertaking such leadership. This is hardly surprising, given the fact that the majority of Asian Americans are pretty much newcomers, who have been in this country less than twenty-five years.

It has been suggested that other people of color have good reason not to trust Asian Americans, who have not been widely known for risking our own hides or sticking out our own necks. On the contrary, African American skulls were cracked in protests over employment discrimination, but Asians stepped in to take up the consent decree jobs. Recently, Ling Chi Wang was fêted by the National Association for Bilingual Education for his role in *Lau* v. *Nichols,* which had far-reaching effects on the language and education rights of both Asians and Latinos. The organization boasts a membership of ten thousand Latinos and Chicanos, yet very few Asians actively participate. Some suggest that Asians are fewer and far less politically and linguistically powerful than Latinos, especially because there are so many different Asian languages, including multiple Chinese and Filipino languages. Whereas El Paso and Miami are virtually bilingual cities, there is nowhere in this country where a Chinese or Korean can survive, let alone thrive, without English; thus it is easy to understand why Asians are not as unequivocally supportive of bilingual education as Latinos.

At times, to be sure, issues that unite Asian Americans separate us from other people of color. That Los Angeles' Black-Korean Alliance folded after the uprisings can be understood in light of the fact that Korean shopowners needed it much more than people from the African American community. It is often said that most Asian American concerns have just not been particularly high on a long list of urgent priorities for black and brown people working on human rights issues. But we all know that there are many shared concerns in the overall battle against racism and social injustice.

In my view, what has most dramatically separated Asian Americans from other people of color has been manifested in terms of attitudes toward what we call "America." For many Native Americans, America means stolen land. For many Chicanos, it means occupied territory conquered and taken from Mexico 150 years ago. For many African Americans, it means the country built on slave labor brought here by force. For a large number of Asian Americans, especially of the recent and immigrant generation, America means "promised land" or "dream country." Having immigrated or come as refugees from colonized countries, often escaping from Socialist and Communist governments, many Asian Americans still feel like guests in the house or as daughters-in-law in her mother-in-law's house. Like a guest or a new bride living with her mother-in-law, she needs to be grateful, obedient, and uncomplaining. She needs to be mindful of the rules and of her host's or mother-in-law's generosity, without which where would she be?

Thus it is easy to see why the Japanese American internment fifty years ago and the Los Angeles uprisings in 1992 are signal moments, because they demonstrate what can happen to the guest or daughter-in-law who clings to her American Dream and call into question how "America" and "American" are defined.

That Asian Americans have difficulty working in coalition with other people of color is not to say that coalition work is easy for anyone. And coalition is not right for everything we do. Perhaps it might help for us to view coalition not as a site of comfort and refuge but as a site of struggle. The fact is that the ever-increasing visibility of Asian Americans means we can no longer be dismissed as honorary whites, honorary blacks, or a wedge between the two. We need to end "biracial theorizing" and zero-sum thinking. We need to call for coalition work that is more inclusive of cultural positionings and differences while centering on certain clearly defined common interests, whether immigration reform, domestic violence, fair employment, or educational equity.

Further, Asian Americans need to envision political activism farther beyond non-profit organization work, which may be seen as siphoning off the energy of progressive Asian Americans into funding-driven social service work and away from a wider vision and advocacy. For Asian American progressives to devote themselves solely to non-profit organization work may be keeping the lid on the communities. Strangely, too, in some ways social service work can perpetuate a kind of narrow cultural nationalism, not only because non-profits are often organized around ethnicities (frequently in competition with each other for funding) but also because social services for the communities can be viewed as an extension of working for the family and not necessarily in the interests of a larger collectivity or the society as a whole.

From what I know of it, Oakland's Asian Immigrant Women Advocates (AIWA) is a model for organizing. For one thing, AIWA has been able to deal successfully with internal diversities by uniting women of different ethnic and language groups—Chinese sewing factory workers, Filipino hotel maids, Vietnamese and Korean electronics assembly workers—around very specific shared interests, which include their identity as women, as immigrants, as people of color, and as workers, but focus on employment rights and empowerment. Refusing to focus on social services alone, AIWA articulates as its goal the development of worker leadership, a goal that sets the organization off from almost all other successful Asian American non-profits. But most interesting is AIWA's outreach to Asian American women college students, who might have middle-class characteristics and aspirations but who might also know someone or have a relative who is an immigrant seamstress, maid, or food service worker. AIWA organizers have claimed a space at the nexus of the women's movement, the civil rights and ethnic-consciousness movements, the consumer movement, and the labor movement to build a boycott against dress manufacturer Jessica McClintock on behalf of unpaid Asian immigrant garment workers. This boycott juxtaposes one aspect of the woman's experience—the romantic fantasy that accompanies a $200 lace party dress—with another, the harsh reality of the woman who made it for $5. Young Asian American consumers, having learned about the issue, have joined forces with the seamstresses, refusing to buy the dresses and writing letters of protest to the manufacturer. Recognizing the permeability of social class boundaries in America in the 1990s, AIWA has transformed the old United Farm Workers' tactic of appealing to the middle-class produce consumer. When Asian American high school or college students across the country refuse to buy Gunne Sax dresses, they may be helping bring McClintock to her knees, with profound implications for every garment manufacturer in the country and perhaps to the industry worldwide.

Asian Americans need to question the superordinate voice of the middle class, but without romanticizing the working class, all the while recognizing that like race, social class in the United States in the nineties is slippery and sometimes paradoxical. The old categories of nineteenth-century Europe cannot be transferred here. Marx could not have imagined a Los Angeles swapmeet in 1994. If he had been able to, would he have classified the immigrant swapmeet vendor as a bourgeois in relation to a native-born, skilled factory worker? Several years ago, I interviewed a Filipino hotel room cleaner who also owned two duplexes in San Francisco. To which class or classes does she belong?

Further, old paradigms of immigrant assimilation, which never applied much to immigrants of color anyway, are of no use at all to us in a day when we don't really know *who* is being assimilated into *what*. I am thinking of a Minnesota teacher I encountered a couple of years ago who was clinging steadfastly to his notion of Hmong refugees needing help in making the move from their alien and preindustrial, read "primitive," past into the American, read "civilized," future. He told me that his teenaged student was suffering from culture class and language barriers, and that her parents were pitifully backward and still poorly adjusted even though they had been in this country for ten years. The Hmong teenager that I met loves rap and has a Latino boyfriend. Although she is not becoming assimilated according to the great "American plan," she bore no resemblance to the hapless heathen image that the teacher was so invested in. Asian American is marked by continually shifting internal diversities.

In the face of these diversities and these continual shifts, it is clearer and clearer that Asian America needs new visions and new leadership. In recent decades, Asian Americans have been pressured by white Americans to be just like them. To counter this "racist love," Asian American progressive leadership has often urged us not to try to be "just like whites" by trying instead to be "just like blacks."

It is difficult to sustain coalition on supportive work alone. I am thinking of the attempt to unite Asian Americans around the common denominator of anti-Asian violence, which in my view was greatly weakened because it was rooted in acceptance of a black-white paradigm of race relations. This approach made it impossible to explain non-white violence against Asians specifically or violence among people of color against each other in general except as divide-and-conquer conspiracy.

To resist the buffer-zone position and the gatekeeper function, then, Asian Americans need to claim our own space, from which we can work in coalition with others as equals, as legitimate subjects in our own right, with all our continually shifting specificities. From our quite different exclusions, from our specific sites of contradiction, from our heterogeneous communities of resistance, perhaps we can reach across our pain and differences to build bridges to one another so that we can mobilize a courageous, collective effort toward the peace and justice that will benefit us all.

Blacks, Browns, and Yellows at Odds

■ ■ ■

BRENDA PAYTON

"If we were the majority, if we were in power, we wouldn't treat other people the way we've been treated. We wouldn't exclude them and discriminate against them because of their color."

As African Americans, we have often dreamed of a world where we were in charge. In our dreams, the justice and equality for which we've struggled would not require an organized movement; in our world, racial discrimination would not exist. Unfortunately, the dream quickly falls to a less egalitarian reality when the concrete issues of inclusion and power sharing come into play. As indicated by events that have pitted African Americans against Latinos and Asian Americans in racially diverse California, it's a lot stickier to create a fair and diverse society than it is to imagine one. The challenge is replete with ironies, many of them less than flattering about people who have themselves struggled against discrimination and inequality.

In November 1994, Californians passed Proposition 187 by a comfortable margin. The initiative would deny public education and non-emergency health care, along with other social services, to illegal immigrants, including children. The courts have blocked its enforcement, calling the proposition itself illegal. The measure was a mean-spirited and racist expression (the ads supporting it depicted Mexicans coming across the border) of an anti-immigrant sentiment fanned by Governor Pete Wilson. Wilson, who had the lowest rating of any governor in the history of poll taking, was able to reverse the slide and win reelection by blaming illegal immigrants for the state's multiple and complex economic problems. Sadly, African Americans voted with the majority; 55 percent of the African American voters approved the measure. Fifty-five percent of Asian American voters also approved it; 23 percent of Latino voters and 63 percent of white voters voted for Proposition 187.

Though there was little else in Wilson's campaign rhetoric that African Americans could embrace, the immigrant-bashing struck a chord. Like most people who find immigrants a threat, African Americans who ascribe to that thinking are motivated by economic concerns. You hear older African Americans bemoan the fact that entry-level menial jobs once held by African Americans are now held by immigrants. But people who blame immigrants for their economic woes ignore the complexity of our economic system that in fact relies on cheap illegal labor. (Both candidates for the U.S. Senate from California, Dianne Feinstein and Michael Huffington, were embarrassed by revelations that they had hired undocumented workers). They overlook the reality that African Americans would not work for the pay or under the conditions most undocumented workers are forced to accept.

The vote for Proposition 187 was cruel and discriminatory. The proposition targeted the workers, not the employers, for punishment. If employers were not providing jobs for undocumented workers, they wouldn't come to the United States. But more to the point, it was un-African American. Given the history of African Americans in this country, how could we have supported a measure that would deny children education and health care? We have suffered ignorance, illiteracy, ill health, and death because we were denied those basic human rights. How could we ever turn around and support similar discrimination, particularly when it denies other people of color? *"We wouldn't treat other people the way we've been treated."*

During that same election, residents of Oakland were choosing a mayor. The population of Oakland is majority African American, with a quickly growing Latino population and a significant Asian American one. The candidates were incumbent Elihu Harris, the city's second African American mayor, and newcomer Ted Dang. Dang is Chinese American and a fiscal conservative, with no previous government experience. Dang sounded the conservative themes that resonated across the country—less government, more police. While Oakland tends toward a more liberal approach to government, it wasn't so much Dang's political ideology or even his lack of experience that African American voters faulted. Early in the campaign, African Americans across the spectrum began to support Harris's reelection—again, not so much because of his successes, but because they viewed Dang's victory as a threat to black political clout. "We worked too hard to get power in this city," people said. "We can't let them take it back now."

For starters, Chinese Americans have never controlled the political power of the city. African Americans struggled to wrest power from the conservative white, monied establishment. But the statement lumps Asian Americans, whites, and probably anyone who isn't black, into a huge threatening category of "other." Asian American politicians were understandably disturbed by the sentiment which suggested that the African American political structure in Oakland was unwilling to share power with other racial minorities.

To be sure, some African American political leaders stepped out in support of Dang, saying it was time for more aggressive leadership. But the majority apparently felt that an Asian American mayor would not represent the interests of African American communities. In Oakland, as in most cities with black political leadership, there is a question as to whether African American politicians have truly represented the interests of the overall African American community, or, as most politicians, just the interests of a small group of their friends. It would have been one thing to support the African American candidate because of his accomplishments or oppose the Asian American because of his inexperience. However, it was unacceptable to oppose Dang because of a perception that he would usurp African American political power. If African American politicians are not willing to share power, there is no basis for meaningful coalition. Why should Asian American voters support African American candidates if African American voters won't reciprocate? In the end Dang lost the election, in part because of his own inexperienced bungling as a candidate. But the undercurrent of racial politics cannot be discounted. *"If we were the majority, we wouldn't exclude other people."*

Farther south in the state, another conflict has pitted one group of racial minorities against another. A Compton police officer beat a non-white suspect. With eerie parallels to the infamous Rodney King case, the beating was captured on videotape by a witness. But there was an unusual twist to the familiar story of police brutality. This time the police officer was an African American and the victim was a Latino. The incident outraged the Latino community and sparked a protest against the city administration—the mayor and police chief are both African Americans. Latino community leaders began questioning the underrepresentation of Latinos in city government and on the police force. Compton, which was a predominantly black city, now has a population that is majority Latino. They make the same points African Americans have made over the years: more Latino police officers and city workers would reduce the incidence of police brutality.

The African American leadership finds itself in the uncomfortable position of answering questions that were leveled at all-white city administrations when African Americans began pushing for inclusion and representation. Why doesn't the city work force reflect the Latino population? Why are Latinos frozen out of City Hall? The former protesters are now the target of the protest. I suspect the African American city officials never imagined they would be accused of racial exclusion and discrimination. *"If we were in power, we wouldn't discriminate against people because of their color."*

The fruits of the African American battle for civil rights are the positions of power held by African Americans in the public and private sectors. And now we find ourselves in the position of defending that power against other people pushing for inclusion. Though we pride ourselves on our leadership role in civil rights, paradoxically, we guard the success jealously. "We're the ones who marched in the streets and got our heads busted. Where were they? But now they want to get in on the benefits." Yet the tension has more to do with the present than the past. And it's not significantly different from the tension between the white establishment and the African American or other groups that have challenged the imbalance of power. The issue is power and the unwillingness to concede it; color and gender are only the convenient excuses to exclude competitors. It's not so much that white males don't want black or brown people or women to go to college or get promoted, it's that they don't want to give up what they view as their slots in college or on the management team. The black administration of Compton isn't against Latinos holding city jobs, it is against losing its power base of African American workers.

Of course, those political calculations accept the divisions and definitions along racial lines. They enforce the divide and conquer strategy—let the minorities fight over one slice of the pie. There is no reason that Compton officials couldn't hire more Latino workers who would be just as beholden to them as are the African American workers. There is no reason that Oakland political leaders could not cut deals with an Asian American mayoral candidate just as they do with an African American candidate.

Diversifying the basis of power makes it broader and that much stronger. The only hope for groups who have been excluded from the economic and political structure, all groups, is coalition. As long as we fight among ourselves or take on the posture of the white establishment defending its turf from an outside threat, we will continue to be disadvantaged. Of course, as the above examples indicate, coalition is a lot easier to discuss than to accomplish. We must get over our distrust and suspicion of other groups. As African Americans, we have to let go of our possessiveness about the civil rights movement and its benefits. We don't own it. We simply were the catalyst that set in motion the realization of the U.S. Constitution's promise—for everyone.

I'm hoping that some of the conflict and tension we've seen are just growing pains. That as we evolve politically and economically, we will be better equipped to act on a more sophisticated, inclusive, and constructive level. We don't have much choice. Because it won't be long before we will be appealing to the largest minority group—Latinos—for inclusion and fairness. And then it won't be a matter of the unrealized hope of a dream world where the previously excluded would be fair and inclusive. Then it will come down to the all too familiar adage: What goes around comes around.

The Possibilities of a Radical Consciousness: African Americans and New Immigrants

■ ■ ■

AMRITJIT SINGH

I

People of South Asian origin in the United States number nearly 2 million now and may be regarded as an "imagined community" within the broad framework of Benedict Anderson's definitions.[1] Although American conceptions of "race" play a significant role in how all immigrants of color are perceived (more on this later), their assimilation into American life parallels in many ways what earlier European immigrant groups have undergone. The replication in North America of homeland attitudes and hierarchies or even of subcontinental conflicts is not unique to our ethnic group, nor is the feeling of despair at the fragmented sense of community we frequently experience. Yet, in some ways, we are privileged today to have many significant new models of assimilation and hybridization beyond the "melting pot" metaphor that dominated the scene until the 1960s. These radically new approaches to immigration and ethnic diversity—suggested by the frequent use of such phrases as "mosaic," "descent" and "consent," "kaleidoscope," "salad bowl," "double consciousness," and "multiculturalism"—have opened new spaces for self-definition for most new Americans.[2] Now that these approaches have become part of the public discourse in North America, it is no longer possible to insist on treating immigrants and the cultures they bring with them as inevitable sacrificial lambs on the altar of a real or illusory American Dream.

Ironically, these recent attempts to acknowledge or celebrate long-standing multicultural American realities have also inspired many prophets of doom—such as Patrick Buchanan, Allan Bloom, and our very own Dinesh D'Souza—to invoke the dangers of "balkanization." The real perils of balkanization lie most probably not in these new conceptions of immigration or multiculturalism but in the giant-size failure of all Americans—white, black, or brown—to make a difference in the way racism and poverty, unemployment and underemployment, drugs and crime, continue to plague the lives of our largest community of color: African Americans. There are more South Asians in this country now than the combined populations of Rhode Island, Wyoming, and Alaska. African Americans, however, outnumber the total population of Canada, and form a large and diverse "nation within a nation."

South Asians have much to learn from African American history about being acculturated in North America, because of the myriad ways "race" complicates our real-life experiences, including inter-ethnic behavior. Recent demographic shifts such as the emergence of Asians as a visible large minority in some California locations (including, for example, the University of California, Berkeley, campus)—and white responses to such developments—are already persuading South Asian students and professionals to become more fully aware of their own history on this continent. I first came to the United States in 1968, and a major debate in the 1970s (evidenced in the early issues of *India Abroad*) was whether or not South Asians should seek or accept a minority status and give up the emotional and psychological advantages of being considered "Caucasians," as they were then classified by the U.S. Census Bureau. Today, some twenty-five years later, most of us would find the idea of our empowering ourselves as caucasoid not only laughable, but even sinister. The ironies are further compounded when we learn the history of this concept in the struggle of South Asians to get acceptance as migrants or naturalized citizens in the early years of this century. The Naturalization Act of 1790 passed by the Congress employed explicitly racial criteria limiting citizenship to "free white persons." When this act was successfully challenged after the Civil War on behalf of African Americans (notwithstanding the complicated history of black citizenship between the notorious compromise of 1877 and the Civil Rights/Voting Rights Acts of 1964 and 1965), Asian Americans of all backgrounds became the most significant group excluded from citizenship.

In 1922, in a case that denied naturalization to a person of Japanese birth, the Supreme Court circumvented the question of color by defining "white" as "Caucasian." In 1923, when a South Asian immigrant, Bhagat Singh Thind, tried to gain citizenship by arguing that he was a "Caucasian," the Court brushed aside anthropological and historical issues and invoked the popular meaning of the term "white." In turning down Thind's request, the Court applied the criterion of assimilability to separate undesirable from the desirable immigrants: Asian Indians were distinguished from the European immigrants, who were deemed *"readily assimilated"* (italics in original) with the immigrants "already here." In 1924, the Johnson-Reed Act established immigration quotas based on the existing ethnic population of the United States, effectively excluding most Italians, Slavs, and Jews.[3] For South Asians, other similar painful lessons about "race" in North America are likely to emerge from a closer examination of the details surrounding the 1914 *Komagata Maru* incident in Vancouver, British Columbia.[4]

The assumption for ourselves of the label "South Asian" is a major challenge under any circumstances, but would be even more difficult without adequate attention to the constantly shifting labels for other groups, including African Americans, Latino Americans, and Asian Americans in general. An attempt to forge a South Asian identity is sure to recall a history of similar attempts in the 1960s to reject the exoticizing label "Oriental" in favor of the term "Asian American," which, as Sauling Cynthia Wong has noted, "expresses a political conviction and agenda," a recognition that (a) all Americans of Asian American descent "have been subjected to certain collective experiences that must be acknowledged and resisted"; and that (b) if "Asian American subgroups are too small to effect changes in isolation, together they create a louder voice and greater political leverage." Further, this "larger pan-Asian identity has to be voluntarily adopted and highly context-sensitive in order to work."

The process of realizing such political choices might also permit an understanding of the "legal contortions," outlined above, that have been used to achieve Asian Americans' exclusion from mainstream life, resulting in their historically functioning "as a peculiar kind of Other (among other Others) in the symbolic economy of America." Although as much voluntary immigrants as the Europeans, Wong continues, Asians "are alleged to be self-disqualified from full American membership by materialistic motives, questionable allegiance, and above all, outlandish, overripe, 'Oriental' cultures." And yet that does not exclude the possibility that they would occasionally be seen as adding "the spice of variety to American life," or "being held up as a 'model minority' to prove the viability of American egalitarian ideals."[5]

On lower frequencies, the label "South Asian" offers some of the same potential for valuable coalitions and political leverage as the term "Asian American." "South Asian" is based on an implicit recognition that new Americans of various national backgrounds in South Asia (India, Bangladesh, Pakistan, Sri Lanka, Nepal, Bhutan, and the Maldive Islands) and possibly others of South Asian ancestry from elsewhere in the diaspora (e.g., Fiji, East Africa, Guyana, Surinam, or Trinidad) have a common stake in how they come to terms with significant elements of homeland cultures as they grapple with their new situations in the United States. The adoption of a South Asian identity clearly calls for an acceptance of our shared culture (food, clothes, language, customs, languages, cultural attitudes, and so on), despite subcontinental divides of religion, politics, and nationality, requiring a deliberate effort on our part to come to terms with experiences, needs, or agendas that bind us together as participants in American politics, culture, and economics. But any effort in that direction is retarded by our strong sense of marginalization and isolation in the United States, pushing us toward some kind of homeland activism. There is a tendency to see our lack of status in American society as a direct result of mainstream indifference or lack of respect toward a given national background, be it Indian or Pakistan or Bangladesh.

Contributing to this fragmented consciousness are our own nostalgia for homeland and our genuine concerns about public issues affecting the lives of family and friends still living there. The diasporic South Asians have been heavily invested in projects that serve the needs of homeland nationalisms of one kind or another—political, religious, ethnic, or regional. The net effect of these tendencies is to reinforce "national" or religious identities and impede any progress toward global citizenship or alert participation in American life, leaving us vulnerable to manipulation by several constituencies: self-styled leaders representing one cause or another on our behalf; our centers of worship: Hindu temples, Sikh *gurdwaras,* Muslim mosques, and Christian churches; homeland embassies and consulates; and "pro-India" or "pro-Pakistan" members of the U.S. Congress.

Most South Asian student organizations on U.S. campuses, like our community organizations in general, project the image of being predominantly "Indian" or "Hindu" or "North Indian" or "Punjabi" or "Gujarati," which discourages free and full participation by South Asians of other backgrounds. At one level, many young South Asians have imbibed the attitudes and biases of their parents' generation—for the most part immigrants who have arrived here since 1965 from the subcontinent or other diasporic communities. But the new generation also faces challenges as new Americans that the older generation has been able to avoid by means of a "sojourner" stance, or through the classical immigrant psychology of "paving the way for our children," or by seeking shelter in emotional ghettoes made up entirely of food and videos shared with South Asian friends. Caught in their own confusions and struggles, South Asian immigrants of my generation, now in their forties and fifties, have not been very helpful in preparing their children for the cultural conflicts they face in their American lives. If anything, many of us have imposed our own ideas of pure identity upon them. For most of us, our idea of homeland is frozen in the moment we left our town or village or state or region. It is difficult for us to recognize that the "nation" we represent in North America is large and complex and constantly shifting, and that we are ourselves being challenged by the evolving new constructions of gender and family. Most of us continue to hoard real or imagined fond memories of homeland life, hoping they will serve as a bulwark for our children against the seductive and subliminal messages from the American media.[6]

Having made an uneasy truce with "glass ceilings," but functioning otherwise in an officially egalitarian and open setting, we are often aware of serious difficulties with certain homeland values such as caste and other assumptions about life and duty we call *samskaras*. But we keep our thoughts to ourselves, either because of our own ambivalence, or because we are afraid of turning our children away from homeland cultures and pushing them further into the lures of North American values and lifestyles. All this is complicated by the undue pressure we place upon our children to become doctors or engineers, and our general lack of respect for humanities and social sciences—disciplines that might allow us and our children to create spaces of understanding all of us desperately need to negotiate our immigrant, diasporic lives. Few of us are ready to acknowledge that after two decades or more in the United States, we are neither purely Indian (or Pakistani) nor American. We have also failed to notice that despite the claims of some reactionary pundits, there has never been a fixed definition of being either Indian (or Sri Lankan) or American; for diasporic South Asians, these ideas are constantly shifting. Yet our dialogic existence represents a rich potential for perspective and action instead of the powerlessness we so often identify with. Once we become aware of other ethnic histories in North America, not only can we learn from their sense of their past, we can also form mutually supportive coalitions with other ethnic or racial groups caught in the same whirlwind of change and resistance.

II

Not long ago, my wife, my teenaged daughter, and I were in Maryland, near the Beltway, to attend the wedding of a friend's daughter. My friend, who migrated from India in 1985 at the age of fifty-six, lives in a town house with his wife and four adult children—two sons and two daughters, one of them the bride-to-be and the other the single mother of a lively nine-year-old daughter, Asha. We admire the way my friend and his wife have found it possible to play supportive roles in the new lives of their four children. The wedding takes place at a local hotel which, I am told, caters ethnic foods of many varieties, something unheard of only ten years ago. Money, it seems, is persuasive; local businesses adjust quickly to accommodate new shades of population. Indian food is served at this wedding, which has gone very well indeed—with help from friends and neighbors. The "exotic" wedding ceremonies are explained in English for the non-Indian guests, who appear to enjoy this multicultural setting.

After the wedding, we stay on at our friend's house. It is late afternoon. Several videotapes of the affair are now available for viewing and everyone is eager to experience this instant transformation of the event into magnetic memory. Besides the three of us, there are two other visiting families in the living room: a scientist and his wife from upstate New York, and a real estate agent from Queens, New York, with his wife and two children, an eight-year-old girl named Roshni and a baby boy whose arrival three months earlier, we learn, had occasioned an extravaganza in honor of his maleness. My wife and I have feasted all day on rich, oily food and Indian sweets. We are ready for fresh air. My friend's granddaughter, Asha, and her young friend, Roshni, accompany us for a short walk around the neighborhood. The girls are eager to talk and show off. Asha, whose name means "Hope" in Hindi, has promised to show us her school and the park she visits daily. As we walk away from the street my friend lives on, we leave his quiet suburban neighborhood behind. Several rows of well-kept town houses give way to a busy metropolitan road.

Like the unexpected encounter with a stranger, this major road that runs through an otherwise sheltered neighborhood triggers in me other thoughts and memories. I think of a recent incident in Bellingham, Massachusetts, near us. A five-year-old Southeast Asian girl walking by herself on a busy road near her home was apparently lured by a driver into his car and then raped and murdered. All of a sudden I become protective of these two little girls who exude so much openness and trust. I ask them if they would walk all by themselves along a road such as the one we are now on. They assure me they would not, that they have had strict instructions never to do so. But at this point, Roshni, whose name means "Light" in Hindi, bursts out, "But, Uncle, I have this friend in New York—she is twelve—and she goes all over, even to those streets where black people live. Her parents have told her many times that blacks would rob her and kill her but she does not listen. She is a bad girl, very bad."

I am shocked more at the tenor than the content of her statement, as I have often heard similar sentiments mouthed by Asian Indian and Pakistani adults at social gatherings. In this very American view, broadly prevalent in Asian American communities, "black" or "Negro" is almost a synonym for violent crime and drugs. But at some of the same gatherings, I find one or two younger people protesting the view. Unlike their parents, they have African American friends and have developed a better understanding of how racism and poverty operate in American society. Although their responses may not fit some sophisticated intellectual view of race and ethnicity, these young Asians appear to know at some level that the alienation they sometimes feel at work or school is experienced even more intensely by their black peers. They are also often in tune with rap and reggae. Maybe the deep sense of alienation expressed in contemporary Afro music resonates with their own sense of rebellion against their parents' double standards: an insistence on seeing African Americans harshly through the prism of caste even as they cloak themselves in highest American ideals of fairness and equal opportunity. Occasionally, young people have also read Richard Wright's *Black Boy* (1945), or *The Autobiography of Malcolm X* (1966), or Toni Morrison's *The Bluest Eve* (1970), or seen a film such as *Do the Right Thing* or *Boyz 'N the Hood*. And while they may criticize the film *Mississippi Masala* for one representational flaw or another, most of them do not share their parents' discomfort at the love scenes between an Indian woman and a black American man.

But in Maryland that evening, when I think about Roshni's tender age, I am filled not with hope and light but with despair. So when we return from our walk, I decide to talk with her father. At first, he appears a bit embarrassed: he even acknowledges his role in encouraging or shaping young Roshni's views. My daughter has perked up at this discussion; I know she likes political arguments, especially when she smells "racism" in the corner. When she makes the point—with the righteous idealism of youth—that we are all human, that we all have the same blood, and that a black person's blood might save his life in a hospital emergency, Roshni's father, joined soon by his wife, releases in mindless fury some of the worst stereotypes of African American life.

I ask him if he has any black friends; he pleads not guilty. But he asserts with confidence that Michael Jordan will soon go the way of Mike Tyson (rape conviction?) or Magic Johnson (HIV-positive: AIDS?); that if middle-class people like us are paying unusually high taxes, it is only because of "all those blacks on welfare"; that blacks do not want to work or work hard; that blacks have contributed "brawn" but no "brain" to the development of this country. When I remind him about the need to understand the history of slavery and Jim Crowism, he informs us that he is not interested "in the past, only in the future." My daughter and I express our concerns about Roshni's future if she grows up with such negative attitudes toward any one group, but realize soon that we are not getting anywhere.

III

As Thomas Powell and others reminded us in the wake of the 1992 Los Angeles riots, many middle-class whites use their "feel-good" racism to try to rationalize the decline or stalemate in black American lives in terms of the "good choices," based on their character and determination, that they make, but which blacks do not.[7] But it is equally important for us to examine the process by which the new immigrants have for over a century (mis)translated the black American presence into their often perplexed lives. In his 1929 essay, "Our Greatest Gift to America," the black novelist and journalist George S. Schuyler suggested, rather impishly, that the greatest contribution of American Negroes to the United States was not buildings and bridges, King Cotton, or Duke Ellington, but the sense of superiority over blacks which new European immigrants were able to maintain in adjusting to the painful realities of their American existence. It was this false superiority, Schuyler tells us, which inspired the "hope and pride" of European immigrants, and spurred them on to "great heights of achievement.[8] Half a century later, in his 1981 introduction to *Invisible Man* (first published in 1952), Ralph Ellison noted how the African American's "darkness . . . glowed . . . within the American conscience with such intensity that most whites feigned moral blindness toward his predicament."

Ellison went on to point out that this "moral blindness" has been shared by "the waves of late arrivals who refused to recognize the vast extent to which they too benefited from [the African American's] second-class status while placing all of the blame on white Southerners." Cornel West and others have rightly directed attention to the need for the American discourse on "race" to move away from the "us-them" binarism in which the desire to blame seems to take precedence over finding ways of changing foundational structures that sustain racism; but we cannot move forward without grasping how the powerful mythology of "whiteness," a pervasive ethnocentrism, came into existence in the first place, and how millions of poor and rich whites continue to benefit from it psychologically and materially.[9]

I do not think new Asian immigrants have disengaged themselves entirely from this pattern by which the old immigrants empowered themselves as "whites" instead of remaining ethnic Italian, or Irish, or what have you. The new Asian immigrants cannot become "white," so they seek overcompensation in real estate and material goods. Like Roshni's father, many Asian Americans make up for their lack of whiteness by acquiring a consciousness that is often as "white" and assimilationist and "mainstream" as that of most whites. Although it is understandable why most new immigrants would want to stay away from the underdog and identify aggressively with WASP culture instead, their continued failure to recognize the palimpsest richness of a multiethnic America only contributes to the terrible human consequences of racism, sexism, and ethnocentrism.

For instance, while Asian parents are quite concerned about the power of peer pressure in their children's lives, they are unable to see the extremity of that pressure in, say, the life of little Pecola in Toni Morrison's The Bluest Eye. Pauline, Pecola's mother, has internalized mainstream images of "romantic love" and "physical beauty," which are described by Morrison's implied narrator as "probably the most destructive ideas in the history of human thought." Pauline "collected self-contempt by the heap," in having "equated physical beauty with virtue." Now, through the depth of generational self-hatred and parental abuse, Pecola has convinced herself that she remain "ugly" unless she can acquire blue eyes.

In an evocative brief scene, Morrison's protagonist walks into the neighborhood grocery store to buy Mary Jane penny candies whose wrappers picture "smiling white face. Blond hair in gentle disarray, blue eyes." Although Mr. Yacobowski, the immigrant storeowner, could not be held responsible for Pecola's feeling closer to dandelions and cracks in the pavement than to human beings, "nothing in his life" suggested that he might acknowledge Pecola's humanity. In a devastating critique of the "whiteness" mythology, Morrison's narrator raises the question, "How can a fifty-two-year-old white immigrant storekeeper with the taste of potatoes and beer in his mouth, his mind honed on the doe-eyed Virgin Mary, his sensibilities blunted by a permanent awareness of loss, *see* a little black girl?"[10] Can our Roshnis and Ashas really flourish as Americans until all of us can come together to break the cycle whereby countless Pecolas end up on heaps of rubbish every year?

Like Claudia and Frieda, the young narrators in Morrison's novel, many immigrant readers might feel beautiful beside Pecola's ugliness, eloquent beside her inarticulateness. In real life, most new immigrants are jolted into a shock of recognition only through their own first experience of subtle or open discrimination. The Jewish immigrants have in some ways represented the insoluble aspects of this eternal dilemma. As a group of predominantly European stock, American Jews have had the real possibility of going the way most European ethnics have gone in acquiring a white American identity; but as a group with a resonant "rememory" of their own past persecution—in Toni Morrison's sense of experiencing the affirmative possibilities of the past—they have had a tradition of resisting that temptation. Despite the widening black-Jewish rift in recent years, many Jewish Americans would acknowledge that there is no effective way of fighting anti-Semitism without making a similar commitment to oppose white racism and ethnocentrism.

In the 1960s and 1970s, many Asian American writers, intellectuals, and artists were inspired by the civil rights movement and black consciousness. Ronald Takaki, for example, had written several books and articles on Black Studies before publishing his major book on Asian American history, *Strangers from a Different Shore* (1989). Elaine Kim learned from African Americans "to reject the false choice between being treated as a perpetual foreigner and relinquishing my own identity for someone else's Anglo-American one." For Kim, "African-Americans permanently defined the meaning of 'American.' "[11] The protest writings of Frank Chin and others were inspired by African American models, and some of their characters reflected an unusual awareness of black culture. For instance, the walls of the Japanese American artist Kenji's apartment in Frank Chin's *The Chickencoop Chinaman* (1974) are covered with posters of "black country, blues and jazz musicians which clash with the few Japanese prints and art objects."[12]

Today, as a community with a growing population and fragmented consciousness, Asian Americans are painfully aware of the variety of obstacles they face in their own pursuit of the American Dream, but seem to have little direction or resolve to examine their new lives. Community newspapers and TV programs continue to inject homeland concerns and tensions into the lives of new Asian immigrants in unfocused and abortive attempts to create meaning. As mirrored in the multiplicity of regional, ethnic, and religious topics discussed on South Asia newsgroups on the Internet, these trends continue to grow unchecked. Even though a sizable number of new Asian immigrants have arrived here better informed about American realities than were their counterparts earlier in the century, their participation in American society is held back by intricate patterns of nostalgia and parochial conflicts. Some had been alert observers of the American scene long before they became landed immigrants. Many have probably migrated less out of economic desperation than for purely professional reasons, or possibly because of a deeply felt attraction to the American ideology of "Life, Liberty, and the pursuit of Happiness" for all. Their awareness of choices and limits in this "nation of nations" has been much sharper than anything experienced by any earlier generation of immigrants. (Notice how some of this applies also to European immigrants arriving now, but not to Southeast Asian refugees since the 1970s, who reflect the more classical pattern of immigration.) The expectations these new immigrants have of America are higher, and so are their disappointments when confronted with "glass ceilings" in corporate life, or discriminatory quotas in university admissions.[13]

Perceptions based in "race" complicate the lives of all Asian ethnics, not just new immigrants. As David Mura has noted, the Sansei, third-generation Japanese Americans, find themselves visible targets in recurrent rituals of Japan-bashing, even though they haven't fully recovered yet from what the second-generation Nisei experienced during World War II.[14] Many fourth-generation Japanese Americans, over 90 percent of whom do not know the Japanese language, have also observed how a young new immigrant with a thick German or East European accent finds immediate and wide acceptance as an "American," whereas they are constantly asked to explain "where they learned to speak English."[15] It is frustrating also to deal with the "racial" biases of juries that have not returned strong convictions for the perpetrators of hate crimes directed at Asian American citizens in Michigan, New Jersey, and elsewhere.[16]

In the 1980s, however, the Reagan and Bush administrations and the media focused not on these problems but on presenting Asian Americans as a "model minority"—a burden in itself, which has in turn laid the groundwork for self-serving politicians of both parties to continue their divisive tactics on family values, deflecting attention from the urgent need

for systemic change and collective responsibility.[17] Instead of addressing
the root cause of the many problems all Americans of color face in some
measure, the government agencies and the media have attempted to use
the same stick to scratch the backs of Asian Americans that they have used
to beat African Americans with. Many educators have escaped their own
responsibility by asking the simplistic question, If Asian Americans can
make it, why can't blacks? It has become a common habit to assign individual responsibility without reference to the effects of harsh circumstance
or long-term systemic exclusion.

Our urban public schools—unable to meet the challenges of de facto
segregation and the surrounding social chaos—have come to mirror the
unfulfilled promises of a democracy. An expensive neighborhood in
Nassau County, Long Island, where my cousin, a new immigrant, bought
a house in 1965, is still forbidden territory for upwardly mobile black
families. Such neighborhoods and their real estate agents have mastered
the art of accommodating new immigrants as a way of deferring their
struggle with their deep-seated racism against blacks. Frequent attempts to
treat "black" as just another color in the American rainbow are indicative
of the widespread patterns of denial in American life with reference to its
racial obsessions. No wonder Gloria Naylor observed wryly in 1994 that
Americans have learned new ways of talking about "racism," but not new
ways of *thinking* about this painful reality. Even as we approach the
twenty-first century, blacks are twice as likely to have a mortgage application turned down as others. Danny Glover and Bill Cosby still cannot
successfully hail a cab in Manhattan without assistance from white
bystanders. Meanwhile, Affirmative Action continues to deliver on its
promises repeatedly to the same class of black individuals and families,
even as it gropes in the dark for its truly intended targets amid the ever-
widening underclass.[18]

The heterogeneity of Asian American communities has compounded
their general indifference to political participation and a marked absence
of strong leadership. Many Asian American intellectuals and writers also
seem to have bought into the divisive strategies which have dominated
the political discourse in recent years. Possibilities of connection and
coalition with other Americans of color are lost, for instance, in the vesti-
gial colonial ventriloquism of Dinesh D'Souza and the celebratory assimi-
lationism of Bharati Mukherjee. In a novel like *Jasmine* and writerly
statements such as "Immigrant Writing: Give Us Your Maximalists!"
Mukherjee's cheerful, forward-looking attitude toward the possibilities of
assimilation is achieved through a reductive and stereotypical representation of South Asian realities, a fantastic view of human psychology and

individual consciousness, and debatable generalizations about immigrant and expatriate writing. While one may make valid distinctions between expatriate and immigrant writers, some of Mukherjee's own work illustrates that the immigrant experience in literature could be as "dead and 'charming,' " or as exoticized as the recreated experience of an ancestral land.[19]

There is little desire among Asian Americans today to learn from the long experience of Native Americans, Latino Americans, and African Americans in fighting discrimination. This indifference to other group experiences and to public life in general preempts the possibility of linking the politics of national origin and ethnicity to the politics of shared goals and issues, and of placing conscience and global citizenship above identity politics, when necessary. The new Asian Americans, who often display a "raw nerve"—a combination of naïveté and boldness—in attempting to sprint their way to a color-blind America, may have much to learn from African Americans, who have been marathon runners against racism. There is much for all "racialized" Americans to ponder in the extended lyrical meditations W. E. B. Du Bois offers in his classic, *The Souls of Black Folk* (1903)—from his responses to the failure of Booker T. Washington's ideology and practice as a "race" leader, to his own journey toward self-definition as African American through his first encounters with southern racial realities in Tennessee and Georgia.

Among the challenging lessons all new Americans of color could absorb is the coded message offered on his deathbed by the narrator's grandfather to his immediate family in Ellison's *Invisible Man*: "Live with your head in the lion's mouth. I want you to overcome 'em with yeses, undermine 'em with grins, agree 'em to death and destruction, let 'em swoller you till they vomit or bust wide open." In facing such challenges of strategy and identity—as Ellison's young protagonist does—we will open up the possibility of keeping our souls intact, of coming to terms as individuals with our own backgrounds and situations without surrendering easily to goals or labels supplied by others. The words of Woodridge, the protagonist's English teacher, are likely to ring in our ears too, as we puzzle through the meanings of Ellison's textured novel in the context of our new lives. "Stephen's problem, like ours," exclaims Woodridge with reference to James Joyce's young protagonist, Stephen Dedalus, "was not actually of creating the uncreated conscience of his race, but of creating the *uncreated features of his face*. Our task is that of making ourselves individuals. The conscience of a race is the gift of its individuals who see, evaluate, record." In the process, asserts Woodridge, we would create both a "race" and a "culture."[20]

Maybe Asian Americans bear no direct responsibility for what happened to the blacks in the past, but can we afford to ignore what gets done *now,* if we are to ensure a better tomorrow for all our Roshnis and Ashas? Asian Americans cannot expect to escape the effects of racial neglect, benign or otherwise, and, as many of us know now from firsthand experience, the solution certainly does not lie in focusing our energies on moving from one colorless suburb to another. As self-conscious citizens of the world, we are implicated not only in the continuing patterns of violence and human rights violations in our ancestral lands but also in the complicated national histories of our adoptive homelands. Asian American denial of responsibility for the consequences of Native American, Latino American, and African American histories in the present American moment is no less problematic than the self-professed innocence of many young Euro-Americans—including some of my students at Rhode Island College—who prefer to think of racism against blacks either as something that happened in the past, or as something that happens elsewhere (generally in the South), or both.

Unlike earlier European immigrants, some Asian Americans who have been here since 1965, when U.S. immigration laws were liberalized for Asians, have been able to move quickly into two-income suburbs without experiencing their Americanization in the crucible of the city. But most new immigrants still tend to hover around the metropolis, where they find a generous measure of acceptance and opportunity. In a 1992 speech, Governor Mario Cuomo noted that 370,000 native-born residents left New York City between 1980 and 1987, but were replaced by 575,000 immigrants, preventing a massive decline in population. Our cities provide the most significant arena for action if we want our precious diversity and "difference" to become assets for all of us instead of remaining disadvantages for some of us. The economic future of the United States is dependent upon how we educate, train, and integrate our growing underclass into the political mainstream. Although it would be a mistake to diagnose the despair of our cities purely in terms of existing patterns of misunderstanding between blacks and Asian Americans (because surely the sources of African American despair lie much deeper in United States history), the situation does call for a much wider role for organizations such as the National Urban League, the NAACP, and the Black-Korean Alliance in California.

According to the historians Arnold Shankman and David J. Hellwig, though black Americans do have a history of economic envy and ethnocentric contempt for immigrants, they have not generally shared the white nativist's need to scapegoat immigrants in times of recession. When questioned about this, blacks "often indirectly acknowledged that the source of their bitterness was American racism rather than the lowly immigrant." Also, "with near unanimity and consistency Afro-Americans rejected schemes to limit or exclude Asian immigrants while the much larger flow from Europe continued virtually unchecked. . . . As with the Jews, blacks found comfort in the successes of Asians, especially the Japanese, in the United States. If other visible minority groups could overcome racial barriers, so could they, many reasoned."[21]

At the same time, 1990 studies done by the Alexis de Tocqueville Institution, the American Immigration Institute, and the Hudson Institute show that new immigrants have always made strong contributions to the U.S. economy and to the revitalization of cherished American values, without taking jobs away from other Americans. Most new immigrants, European or Asian, choose to have minimal interaction with black individuals or communities. Koreans are the only ones in recent years to bring new capital and energy into "unsafe" black neighborhoods. As Korean Americans find ways of connecting more meaningfully with black youth and church groups around them, blacks might learn from the models of thrift and small business success that some of their Korean neighbors represent. Today, many in poor, disenfranchised African American communities find satisfaction in scapegoating Asian Americans for the continued lack of opportunities that black youth faces. For example, many blacks believe that Koreans have received favored treatment from U.S. banks. They blame the absence of capital in black communities upon the modest success of Asian Americans (even though we know from researchers that the reasons for the absence of capital and savings among African Americans are historically complicated and systemic).[22] Most Koreans and Hong Kong Chinese, however, deny such allegations, asserting that they have often invested in their new businesses the life savings they brought with them into the United States. We need to fight not one another, but the redlining and other discriminatory practices that have hindered minorities, especially African Americans, in the first place.[23] To extend the words of warning issued by Elaine H. Kim after the Los Angeles riots of May 1992, "without an understanding of our histories," blacks and Latinos in one city, Asians and Latinos in another town, blacks and Asians in yet another neighborhood, would all be "ready to engage in a zero-sum game over the crumbs of a broken society, a war in which the advancement of one group means deterioration for the other."[24]

As a result of major changes at home and around the world in recent years, the American identity is under immense new pressures today—

pressures comparable to those of the 1940s and the 1950s, when American Studies as we know them now first came into being. There is a significant difference, however. Challenges to old and familiar definitions of America have come this time primarily from new immigrants of color and the continuing need to address the levels of discomfort that African Americans still experience about their Americanness. White ethnocentrism informs the many pessimistic predictions about the cracking up of the American identity under an "incredible" pace of change and accommodation demanded by a growing acknowledgment of our multicultural realities. But surely the phoenix of a new American identity will rise out of the ashes of the old one, with constitutional structures serving once again as the wings.

The visible tensions within and between American ethnic groups often mirror homeland realities or cultural differences, but they are more often symptoms of their shared economic powerlessness. Our lives in these United States as well as the futures of our Ashas and Roshnis are surely intertwined in the ways in which all of us, as Americans, learn to address issues of race and caste, gender and class, and to find new solutions rooted firmly in our ideals of equal opportunity and equality, fairness and harmony.

■ ■ ■

NOTES

A short version of this essay appeared as an Op-Ed piece in the *Chicago Tribune* on November 4, 1992. I am grateful to several friends and other readers for their feedback toward the preparation of this revised version.

1. Following Benedict Anderson's *Imagined Communities* (New York: Verso, 1991), p. 6, one might view "South Asians" in North America as an "imagined political community [a kind of nation] . . . both inherently limited and sovereign. It is imagined because the members of even the smallest nation will never know most of their fellow-members, meet them, or even hear of them, yet in the minds of each lives the image of their communion."

2. The metaphor of "descent and consent" is derived from Werner Sollors, *Beyond Ethnicity* (New York: Oxford University Press, 1986). Suggesting that an emphasis on ethnic identity is not always helpful in understanding many key aspects of American culture, Sollors sees "the conflict between contractual and hereditary, self-made and ancestral, definitions of American identity—between *consent* and *descent*—as the central drama in American culture." He posits that "descent" is traced back to a non-American culture, while "consent" implies an embracing of all that is American. In viewing American diversity as "kaleidoscopic," Lawrence H. Fuchs in *The American Kaleidoscope: Race, Ethnicity, and the Civic Culture* (Hanover, NH: University Press of New England, 1990) asserts that the shared identity of Americans can no longer have exclusivity in the Judeo-

Christian tradition and observes how the United States is now home to a growing number of Hindus, Muslims, Buddhists, and Sikhs. The concept of "double consciousness" was formulated by W. E. B. Du Bois in 1897 and is enshrined in the opening chapter of *The Souls of Black Folk* (1903); for the origins of this concept in nineteenth-century thought and its continuing influence, see Dickson H. Bruce, Jr., "W. E. B. Du Bois and the Idea of Double Consciousness," *American Literature* 64, 2 (June 1992), pp. 299–309; Bernard W. Bell, *The Afro-American Novel and Its Tradition* (Amherst, MA: University of Massachusetts Press, 1987); and Gerald Early, ed., *Lure and Loathing: Essays on Race, Identity and the Ambivalence of Assimilation* (New York: Allen Lane, the Penguin Press, 1993).

3. The information in this paragraph and the one that follows is based on Sau-ling Cynthia Wong, *Reading Asian American Literature* (Princeton, NJ: Princeton University Press, 1993), pp. 1–17. Wong's discussion of these matters is based in turn on Sucheng Chan, *Asian Americans: An Interpretive History* (Boston: Twayne, 1991); Michael Omi and Howard Winant, *Racial Formation in the United States from the 1960s to the 1980s* (New York: Routledge, 1986; Jeff H. Lesser, "Always 'Outsiders': Asians, Naturalization, and the Supreme Court," *Amerasia Journal* 12.1 (1985–86), pp. 83–100; Elaine Kim, *Asian American Literature: An Introduction to the Writings and Their Social Context* (Philadelphia: Temple University Press, 1982); and William Peterson, ed., *Concepts of Ethnicity* (Cambridge, MA: Harvard University Press, 1982).

4. In May 1914, a group of 376 South Asians—340 Sikhs, 24 Muslims, and 12 Hindus, mostly men, all of them from the Punjab—led by Gurdit Singh, chartered the Japanese freighter *Komagata Maru* (renamed *Guru Nanak Jahaj*) for $66,000 to test the Canadian immigration laws as "British citizens." For two months, the ship was anchored in Vancouver Harbor and the passengers were not permitted to disembark. After a series of complicated maneuvers that involved the local South Asians, undercover agent William Hopkinson, and the legal system in British Columbia, the ship was forced to leave Vancouver on July 23, 1914, arriving on September 26 in Calcutta, where a confrontation with the colonial police left twenty-six of the surviving passengers dead and most others in jail. For further details, see Joan Jensen, *Passage from India: Asian-Indian Immigrants in North America* (New Haven: Yale University Press, 1988); Hugh Johnston, *The Voyage of Komagata Maru: The Sikh Challenge to Canada's Colour Bar* (Delhi: Oxford University Press, 1979; Vancouver: University of British Columbia Press, 1988); Sohan Singh Josh, *Tragedy of Komagata Maru* (New Delhi: People's Publishing, 1975); and Ted Ferguson, *A White Man's Country: An Exercise in Canadian Prejudice* (Toronto: Doubleday, 1975). The incident has inspired dozens of poems and at least two full-length plays: *The Komagata Maru Incident* (1976) by Sharon Pollock; and *Komagata Maru* (1984), in Punjabi, by the Vancouver-based writer Ajmer Rode. In 1989, the Canadian government supported several events in Vancouver and elsewhere to commemorate the seventh-fifth anniversary of the tragedy as part of its official diversity goals.

5. Wong, *Reading Asian American Literature*, pp. 5–6.

6. For an extended discussion of the complicated ways in which race, ethnicity, and immigration affect issues of American identity, see the introductions to Amritjit Singh, Joseph T. Skerrett, Jr., and Robert E. Hogan, eds., *Memory, Narrative, and*

Identity: New Essays in Ethnic American Literatures (Boston: Northeastern University Press, 1994), and Amritjit Singh, et al., eds., *Memory and Cultural Politics* (Boston: Northeastern University Press, 1996). For other views of generational styles and tensions within immigrant Asian communities, see R. Radhakrishnan, "Is the Ethnic 'Authentic' in the Diaspora?" (pp. 71–100) and Elaine Kim, "Between Black and White: An Interview with Bong Hwan Kim" (pp. 219–234), both in Karin Aguilar-San Juan, ed., *The State of Asian America: Activism and Resistance in the 1990s* (Boston: South End Press, 1994). Bong Hwan Kim talks eloquently about the pain and possibilities of his American upbringing, but even more significant are his reflections as a community activist on the challenges of forging an alliance between Korean Americans and African Americans in Oakland and Los Angeles.

7. Thomas Powell, "Feel-Good Racism," Op-Ed page, *New York Times,* May 24, 1992.

8. George S. Schuyler, "Our Greatest Gift to America," in V. F. Calverton, ed., *Anthology of American Negro Literature* (New York: Random House, 1929), pp. 405–412.

9. Cornel West has made this point most forcefully in *Race Matters* (Boston: Beacon, 1993) and elsewhere. In her keynote address, "The African-American Image in American Literature," at the Mark Twain House Symposium on "The Power of Language" in Hartford, Connecticut, on October 1, 1994, Gloria Naylor discussed how the relationship between power and language might be illumined by our understanding of the process by which the American mythology of "whiteness" was created in the first place, and how it continues to influence all Americans, including new immigrants. Naylor makes some of the same points in her introduction to *Children of the Night: The Best Short Stories by Black Writers, 1967 to the Present* (Boston: Little, Brown, 1995). See also Noel Ignatiev's "'Whiteness and American Culture: An Essay," *Konch* 1.1 (Winter 1990), 36–39; he argues that by "becoming whites, immigrants renounced the possibility of becoming truly American" (36). Studs Terkel, *Race: How Blacks and Whites Think and Feel About the American Obsession* (New York: New Press, 1992), corroborates the worst fears and realities about "the American obsession," and many of his respondents expose their guilt or ambivalence in having abetted or benefited from racist traditions and practices.

10. Toni Morrison, *The Bluest Eye* (1970; New York: Penguin, 1994), pp. 122, 50, 48. Although some elements that shape Pecola's self-loathing are peculiar to her family situation, there are, as Morrison notes in her November 1993 afterword, other "aspects of [Pecola's] woundability [that are] lodged in all young girls." In narrating the story of how Pecola is destroyed by "the damaging internalization of assumptions of immutable inferiority originating in an outside gaze," Morrison says she tried hard to "avoid complicity in the demonization process Pecola was subjected to" by social rejections throughout her short life: "I did not want to dehumanize the characters who trashed Pecola and contributed to her collapse" (pp. 211–212).

11. Ronald Takaki, *Strangers from a Different Shore: A History of Asian Americans* (Boston: Little, Brown, 1989); Elaine Kim, "They Armed in Self-Defense," *Newsweek,* May 18, 1992, p. 10.

12. Frank Chin, "Act I of *The Chickencoop Chinaman*," in Chin, et al., eds., *Aiiieeeee!: An Anthology of Asian-American Writers* (1974; Washington, DC: Howard University Press, 1983), p. 55.

13. For a discussion of "glass ceilings" in corporate life and informal quotas imposed by many Ivy League universities on the admission of Asian American students and the response of University of California to similar complaints on the Berkeley campus, see Chan, *Asian Americans*, pp. 179–181, and Takaki, *Strangers from a Different Shore*, pp. 479–480.

14. David Mura, "Bashed in the U.S.A.," Op-Ed page, *New York Times*, April 29, 1992.

15. Takaki, *Strangers from a Different Shore*, p. 30.

16. In June 1982, Vincent Chin, a twenty-seven-year-old Chinese American, was chased and beaten to death with a baseball bat in Detroit by two white men, who were apparently expressing their resentment over growing unemployment in the automobile industry because of stiff competition from Japan, and mistook Chin for a Japanese. Asian Americans were outraged when Wayne County Circuit Judge Charles Kaufman sentenced both men to three years' probation and a fine of $3,000 each plus $780 in fees. Despite appeals and retrials, neither man spent a single night in jail. Sucheng Chen (*Asian Americans*, p. 178) notes that the lesson learned in the Vincent Chin case was not lost and Asian Americans immediately mobilized to monitor developments after Ming Hai Loo, another Chinese American, was killed in Raleigh, North Carolina, in July 1989. See also Takaki, *Strangers from a Different Shore*, pp. 481–484. The South Asian community in Jersey City was geared into action in autumn 1987 by the racist threats and assaults against them by "Dotbusters" (a youth gang named after the ritualistic dot, *bindi*, worn on their foreheads by many Hindu woman), and the heinous murder of Navroz Mody, a thirty-year-old Citicorp executive, by a gang of Latino youths who did not touch Mody's white companion.

17. See Chan, *Asian Americans*, pp. 167–171, and Wong, *Reading Asian American Literature*, pp. 37–39, 160–163, for the complex and conflicting ways in which the "model minority" idea is used in Americans' discussions of race, class, and culture. Charles P. Henry, "Understanding the Underclass: The Role of Culture and Economic Progress," pp. 67–86, in James Jennings, ed., *Race, Politics and Economic Development: Community Perspectives* (New York: Verso, 1992), notes that in presenting Asian Americans as a model of economic success to blacks, neo-conservative scholars such as Thomas Sowell ignore the difficulties faced by many Asian communities (such as Filipino Americans) and the growing class cleavage within each Asian American community.

18. Naylor, "African American Images." "The black underclass" is generally defined as "a growing number of black persons who are uneducated, unemployed and often unemployable . . . living in unrelieved poverty, and immersed in a culture conditioned by such abject circumstances, with only limited chances or no hope for upward mobility" (p. 54). This definition is provided by Mack Jones in "The Black Underclass as a Systemic Phenomenon" (pp. 53–65) in Jennings, ed., *Race, Politics and Economic Development*. See also Henry Louis Gates, Jr., "Two Nations, Both Black," *Forbes*, September 14, 1992, pp. 132–138, and William Julius Wilson, *The Truly Disadvantaged: The Inner City, the Underclass, and Public Policy* (Chicago: University of Chicago Press, 1987).

19. Bharati Mukherjee, *Jasmine* (New York: Fawcett, 1989); "Immigrant Writing: Give Us Your Maximalists!" *New York Times Book Review*, August 28, 1988, pp. 1, 28–29.

20. Ralph Ellison, *Invisible Man* (1952; New York: Random House, 1981), pp. 16, 345–346.

21. David J. Hellwig, "Strangers in Their Own Land: Patterns of Black Nativism," in Amritjit Singh, et al., eds., *American Studies Today: An Introduction to Methods and Perspectives* (New Delhi: Creative Books; Providence, RI: Off Campus Books, 1995), pp. 329–330, see also Hellwig, "Afro-American Reactions to the Japanese and the Anti-Japanese Movement, 1906–1924," *Phylon* 38 (March 1977), 93–104. Arnold Shankman, "Black on Yellow: Afro-Americans View Chinese Americans, 1850–1935," *Phylon* 39 (March 1979), 1–17; and Shankman, *Ambivalent Friends: Afro-Americans View the Immigrant* (Westport, CT: Greenwood Press, 1982).

22. Extensive commentary (including several essays in Jennings, ed., *Race, Politics, and Economic Development*) on the problems of capital formation and the relative absence of savings in the black community highlights long-term poverty, unemployment, and exclusion; the lack of resources to transfer savings and assets from one generation to another; and the consequent low net worth of black families in comparison to white families with similar income. In 1984, according to the U.S. Census Bureau, black families with incomes between $24,000 and $47,000 had a net worth of $19,068, while the net worth of white families in the same income group was $60,304. Parallel figures for families with incomes over $48,000 were $70,125 for blacks and $150,045 for whites. Jacqueline Jones, *The Dispossessed: America's Underclass from the Civil War to the Present* (New York: Basic Books, 1992), establishes that "in their commitment to formal education, to family, and to hard work, African Americans have adhered to values shared by other Americans regardless of race, class, or regional identification." But by "emphasizing patterns of resourcefulness common to blacks and whites of a similarly low material condition," Jones also seeks to "illuminate the historic forces of marginalization that [have] engulfed the poor of both races" (pp. ix–x).

23. There is considerable documentation of continuing discrimination against blacks in both housing and mortgages. A Boston Federal Bank study of 1991 mortgage applications found that blacks of all income levels are rejected for mortgages at twice the rate of whites. "Eye of the Beholder," *National Review* 45, 18 (July 1993), p. 18.

24. Elaine H. Kim, "They Armed in Self-Defense," *Newsweek*, May 18, 1992, p. 10.

The Interaction of the Black Mainstream Leadership and the Farrakhan Extremists

■ ■ ■

MARTIN KILSON

I will hold the world in my hand
as if God and the Weather could be blamed
for all the wrong

no. Gods and rain fall forever.

and you can fall in the well of life
forever
and never touch the sides

Gods and rain fall forever.

as if miracles could be explained
by a change in the weather

no.
Gods and rain fall forever.

There was something more to the attempt to fashion a formal nexus between Black mainstream leadership and Reverend Louis T. Farrakhan's Nation of Islam in the fall of 1993 than an assault on the sensibilities of Jewish Americans, an interpretation that was common in the American press at the time. This interpretation is mistaken. The bid to link up the mainstream Black leadership with the Farrakhan extremists was a genuine attempt toward taming Farrakhan's anti-White and anti-Semitic extremism. The following analysis of the linkup will support this claim.

Faced with an influential competitor in the form of xenophobic Afrocentrists, a new leader of the National Association for the Advancement of Colored People (NAACP), Ben Chavis (who was appointed executive secretary in 1992), initiated the idea of the mainstream Black political class forging cross-cutting ties with Afrocentrist leaders. Such cross-cutting ties among ideologically fissured leadership groups would involve fashioning alternative interest options within the rigid or homogeneous political persona of a given leadership or interest group, thereby reining in or attenuating the more rigid (ideologic, xenophobic, etc.) features of the group's persona. These ties are commonplace in a pluralistic and highly competitive democratic polity like the United States, of course, and cross-cutting ties typically involve odd-bedfellow alliances.

The focal issue in this case was the vicious cycle of crime and violence that has plagued Black inner-city communities for two decades. So, in the fall of 1993, the NAACP, under Chavis's leadership, hosted a conference of Black groups which fashioned plans—a "covenant"—for mobilizing broad categories of Black organizations in an attempt to reverse the tenacious cycle of crime and violence in Black communities.

Inevitably, perhaps, the inclusion of the Nation of Islam in a new cross-cutting-type coalition (other groups were the Congressional Black Caucus and Jesse Jackson's Rainbow Coalition) sparked divisions within the mainstream Black leadership (some Black congresspersons did not participate, for example). But in general Black organizations lent their moral support, taking a wait-and-see position. On the other hand, Jewish organizations and leading Jewish figures vehemently criticized this bid to interact with Afrocentrist groups. Conservative Jewish intellectuals were also involved in this criticism.

Following a viciously anti-Semitic speech by Khalid Muhammad of the Nation of Islam at Kean College, New Jersey, in December 1993, several prominent Jewish intellectuals published major articles that chastised the African American intelligentsia generally, and the leadership groups associated with the cross-cutting coalition in particular, for what they viewed as softness toward anti-Semitism among Blacks. Columns by A. M. Rosenthal in the *New York Times* and Richard Cohen in *The Washington Post*, and syndicated articles by Nat Hentoff of *The Village Voice*, were the most prominent. These were reinforced, so to speak, by full-page advertisements by the Anti-Defamation League in major daily newspapers with national circulations. That leading Jewish intellectuals and organizations should mount an attack against anti-Semitic outbursts by Nation of Islam leaders was as expected as Black mainstream leaders mounting an attack against anti-Black outbursts by David Duke. But the attack by Jewish leaders extended far beyond the anti-Semitic Black Muslims, to the African American intelligentsia generally, and also to the nascent bid for cross-cutting ties between mainstream and Afrocentrist Black leaders. Given the long-running task of overcoming Black/Jewish discord, the attack that was sparked by Khalid Muhammad's outbursts lacked balance and was often analytically shallow.

For one thing, the charge that the African American intelligentsia in general has been soft on Black anti-Semitic extremists is just factually wrong. Anyone close to the Black intelligentsia cannot be unaware of its vigilance against extremists. Although the White media have virtually never recognized it, this vigilance has prevented or at least helped to prevent the export from the African American community of demented extremists to crisis areas such as South Africa, where during the period of intense Black/White conflict they could wreak terrorist havoc. Such leading figures among the African American intelligentsia as Reverend Leon Sullivan, Reverend Jesse Jackson, Andrew Young, Congressman John Conyers, Congressman John Lewis, Judge Leon Higginbotham, Attorney William Coleman, Julian Bond, Toni Morrison, Cornel West, and Alice Walker (to name just a few) have exerted serious intellectual, moral, and organizational pressure through their everyday and institutional interactions against extremist discourse among Black Americans. Neither A. M. Rosenthal, Richard Cohen, Martin Peretz, Nat Hentoff, nor any other Jewish intellectual who has charged the Black intelligentsia with coddling anti-White and anti-Semitic extremists can produce evidence to the contrary.

Further, it is ironic that the kind of dangerous and intellectually shameful coddling of ethnocentric extremists charged to the African American intelligentsia is far more prominent among certain White ethnic groups. Indeed, it was a Jewish American organization, the late Rabbi Kahane's Kach movement, that in the spring of 1994 organized the irresponsible shuttling abroad of extremist American citizens—along with the financial resources to support them. One of its members—a medical doctor—massacred some thirty Palestinians who were at prayer in a West Bank mosque. Until this terrorist event, many Jewish American leaders virtually ignored terrorist-tinged extremists like those in the Kach movement.[1] In this matter of reining in extremists, the African American intelligentsia has a much better track record than its Jewish American counterpart. And also a much better track record than the Irish American intelligentsia, which until bold moves recently by some Irish intellectuals for peace in Northern Ireland did little to checkmate the contribution by Irish Americans of organizational and financial support to the IRA. Only a few Irish American intellectuals were vigilant in checkmating such ties with extremists in Ireland—intellectuals like Senator Edward Kennedy and Senator Daniel Patrick Moynihan.

The soft-on-Black-extremists rhetoric leveled against Black leadership by Jewish intellectuals is not just factually wrong, it also lacks elemental fairness.

While the Irish Americans, WASP, and Italian American intelligentsia are typically lauded for their devotion to upholding America's pluralist and anti-extremist values, the African American intelligentsia's efforts have been criticized. Further, the soft-on-Black-extremists rhetoric sets an absurdly pristine leadership standard for African Americans that is never expected of other ethnic-bloc intelligentsias or of leadership groups generally. This pristine standard would have us believe that every bigoted utterance by, say, the zealot right-wing sector among WASPs is challenged immediately by mainstream WASP intellectuals; that every extremist utterance by the zealot wing among feminists is always challenged by mainstream feminist intellectuals; and that every extremist utterance by zealot disciples of the late Rabbi Kahane is challenged by mainstream Jewish intelligentsia. This kind of unrealistic standard is thrust at African Americans but not at any other ethnic group. Such double-standard behavior by conservative Jewish intellectuals unnecessarily inflames Black/Jewish discord.

Some Jewish intellectuals have claimed that the odd-bedfellow linkage associated with the bid for ties between mainstream and Afrocentrist Black leaders would inevitably favor the Afrocentrists. While this issue might presently be moot in view of Chavis's dismissal (in August 1994) as secretary of the NAACP, it is important to recognize that the Black political class possesses a serious carrot-and-stick capability in relation to Farrakhan and the Nation of Islam. It happens that today's Nation of Islam is heavily dependent on public resources for much of its operating revenue. This revenue is derived in large measure from sizable contracts with federal housing projects in inner-city neighborhoods that involve the NOI Security Agency—a subsidiary of the nation of Islam that performs policing duties in drug-infested and crime-riddled housing projects and neighborhoods. The Security Agency employs large numbers of Nation of Islam members through these contracts. In cities like Pittsburgh, Chicago, Philadelphia, Los Angeles, and Baltimore, such contracts amounted to over \$2 million in 1993, and more recently the NOI Security Agency was negotiating a \$5 million contract with the Chicago Housing Authority.[2] The Black political class—through the legislative influence of its own congresspersons, housing administrators, and mayors—exercises an important leverage over contracts of this sort.

Finally, even the overall developmental history of the Black political class suggests that it is not naive about the odd-bedfellow ties it forged in the fall of 1993 with Afrocentrist leaders. Indeed, the Black political class has demonstrated, at different stages of its bedeviled evolution, much sophistication in regard to the need for a tough-minded, pragmatic outlook toward coalitions in American politics, however disconcerting in moral terms any given arrangement might be. For example, President Franklin Delano Roosevelt's New Deal policy advances, which benefited broad sections of the American poor and working class (the middle class too), were realized in a sea of odd-fellow-type coalitions—coalitions riddled with Ku Klux Klan–supporting politicians and groups. Though infuriated and bitter about these racist-tinged relationships, the mainstream African American leadership of the NAACP, the National Urban League, and Black church leaders in the 1930s to 1950s did not choose to fracture the political and voting basis of the New Deal itself. Jewish critics of today's Black political class' efforts as part of a broader strategy for combating the cycle of crime and violence in Black communities (and other social anarchic patterns as well) could learn from such precedents.

A key element in the process of taming and reversing the xenophobic dimensions of Afrocentrist elements will be some kind of interplay between these Afrocentrists and mainstream Black leadership. In the short run, both Black and Jewish mainstream leadership groups should give high priority to limiting the Afrocentrists' cynical tendency to weaken the ability of the mainstream Black political class to ally with White interest groups, including of course Jewish groups. The long-standing legitimacy of the mainstream Black leadership depends upon the expansion of its electoral and legislative capability. Liberal, moderate, and even proactive-oriented conservative White politicians and interest groups generally (and Jews in particular) carry a special responsibility in this regard. Such militant conservative White interest groups as the Christian Coalition and such ideologically rigid politicians as Newt Gingrich, Phil Gramm, and so on, are still prone toward exploiting neoracist and phobic electoral and legislative strategies. They cannot be expected to facilitate the hopes of the mainstream Black leadership. Quite the contrary, in fact.

It is very important, therefore, to fashion steps—even small steps—among Black and Jewish intelligentsia that pave the way to a steady reduction of discord. Small beginnings were apparent in the off-year elections in the fall of 1994, especially in the pattern of Black/Jewish voting on the candidacy of Carl McCall for Comptroller of New York—a candidacy that pitted a Black leader against a Jewish candidate who cynically exploited the Black/Jewish discord but failed to gain enough votes from Jews themselves, who wisely endeavored to move in another direction. The result was the election of the first African American ever to an executive office in New York State.

It should also be noted that next to the 92%–95% Black voter support for Democratic candidates in the elections in Fall of 1994 was the second largest constituency vote for Democratic candidates—namely, the Jewish vote, at 79% for Democratic candidates nationally, followed by the Latino vote at 70%.

These voting patterns suggest that it is indeed now possible for Blacks and Jews to put their twenty-year discord behind them. The emerging neoracist and militant ideological tenor of the national Republican Party demands that this be done swiftly.

It is important, in concluding this essay, to mention the most recent endeavor by key elements in the pragmatic-activist sector of mainline African-American leadership to undertake what I call an odd-bedfellow coalition interaction with the extremist sector of Black leadership represented by Rev. Louis Farrakhan. That event was the Million Man March, which occurred on September 6, 1995, and was, I believe, a crucial event toward the ultimate goal of odd-bedfellow coalitional interactions among Black leadership groups—namely, to tame and purge the anti-White, anti-Semitic, anti-Feminist, and homophobic style associated with certain militant Black nationalist, or what I also call Black ethnoradical, groups. Following upon his quite inept tenure as executive director of the NAACP—a tenure that resulted in Chavis's dismissal by the National Board of the NAACP—Chavis joined forces with Farrakhan in late 1994 to launch the idea of the Million Man March. What was politically unique about the march was that, despite the initiating role played by an extremist figure like Louis Farrakhan (counterbalanced, of course, by a mainstream leadership figure like Ben Chavis), the everyday elements throughout the nationwide African-American middle-class population seized upon the idea of the Million Man March. The mainstream Black middle-class sector gained full local organizational control over the march in most communities nationwide, and it was therefore overwhelmingly responsible for the bulk of the organizational activity required to bring 800,000 African-American males to Washington, D.C. Thus a survey after the Million Man March by Howard University's political science department found that some 41 percent of the participants had family incomes upward of $50,000, and nearly 40 percent completed four or more years of college, a proportion three times the college-going population among Black males generally. Also, some 71 percent of the participants had family incomes ranging upward of $25,000.

Thus, in organizational terms, it was the overwhelming prominence in the march of new grassroots Black middle-class associations and networks that should be emphasized: networks among Black lawyers, engineers, computer scientists, accountants, money managers, businessmen, corporate managers, scholars, schoolteachers, etc. In Philadelphia, for example, my nephew Thomas Kilson Queenan, who is an architect and holds an MBA from the Wharton School of Business, participated in the massive middle-class groundswell around the march in the greater Philadelphia area. As deputy treasurer of the city, he helped persuade Mayor Rendell and other city officials to support the idea of the Million Man March. The result was a 60,000-man delegation to the march from the Philadelphia area—the largest single-city delegation present at the march. Also keep in mind that leading personalities among the Black leadership personally endorsed the Million Man March even though they did not participate in the event. Among these march-endorsing personalities were women like Dorothy Height, head of the National Coucil of Negro Women, Dolores Tucker of the National Political Congress of Black Women, and leading male personalities such as Congressman Kweisi Mfume.

In short, the Million Man March represented the first nationwide event among African-American leadership groups that fused in one event the two main approaches among Black American leadership:[3] the community uplift approach that Farrakhan's group is a representative of (an approach going back to Booker T. Washington in the 1890s and Marcus Garvey's movement in 1920s), and the egalitarianization or civil rights approach that organizations like the National Political Congress of Black Women, the National Council of Negro Women, and most of the Black-elected political class (some 8,500 officials nationwide) represent. Of course, Congressman Kweisi Mfume was a crucial figure among the Black-elected political class back in 1993, so his endorsement of the Million Man March helped to reinforce the fact that it was the new Black middle-class networks nationwide that organizationally prevailed at the march.

And when the National Board of the NAACP announced in January

1996 that the new executive officer of the NAACP would be former congressman Mfume, it was apparent without a doubt that the ideological ambience of the Million Man March was understood throughout African-American leadership groups to have been controlled by the pragmatic sector of middle-class Blacks and their organizations. Even though the extremist personality of Louis Farrakhan was prominent in the march and that personality gained some benefits through the march, the event was not simply "a Farrakhan affair," as many conservative White commentators and pundits remarked. I believe, along with a broad sector of Black American mainline intellectuals, that the Million Man March was a progressive event precisely because of its odd-bedfellow coalitional attributes: It organizationally brought together pragmatic-activist mainstream Black leadership figures and xenophobic militant Black leadership figures. It brought them together in a coalitional event with the goal of eventually taming and purging the extremist, xenophobic approaches of Farrakhan and his followers. It was this—a crucial goal and a feasible goal—that impelled mainline African-American intellectuals like Professor Cornel West (Harvard University), Professor Michael Dyson (University of North Carolina), Professor Manning Marable (Columbia University), Professor Michael Hanchard (Northwestern University), and myself, among many others, to endorse the Million Man March. We who endorsed the march—challenged in this sometimes by our intellectual and political allies among some Jewish intellectuals—must now make sure that the goal of taming and purging xenophobic and extremist patterns among groups like Farrakhan's Nation of Islam organization does in fact take place.

■ ■ ▨

NOTES

1. On the Jewish American elements that support the Kach movement, see Steve Fainaru, "Jewish Extremists Rely on Funds from U.S. Sympathizers," *Boston Globe*, March 14, 1994.
2. See the *New York Times*, March 4, 1994.
3. On the possible implications of the Million Man March for Black politics in general, see Martin Kilson, "Colin Powell: A Flight from Power," *Dissent* (Spring 1996).

Black/Brown Relations: An Unnecessary Conflict

■ ■ ■

ROBERTO RODRÍGUEZ AND
PATRISIA GONZALES

In writing about Black/Brown relations in 1963, the *Los Angeles Times* journalist Ruben Salazar pointed out that the city of Los Angeles was founded not by Spanish dons but rather by a mix of Black and Brown settlers. Despite that common heritage, Salazar noted the beginnings of tensions between the two communities. The Mexican American community felt that while the needs of African Americans were beginning to be addressed, the plight of Mexican Americans was being ignored.

Salazar, a highly respected journalist, was felled seven years later by an armor-piercing nine-inch tear-gas projectile, fired by a Los Angeles County Sheriff's deputy, at a rally against the Vietnam War. He was considered a pioneer because he was the first Mexican American to work for the *L.A. Times* and because he wrote about issues that today are considered cutting edge—identity, the border, police brutality, and race and race relations.

During the 1960s, he documented the attitudes of both communities. Mexican Americans felt left out of our nation's discussion over civil rights and many felt that only African Americans were benefiting from this revolution. African Americans, on the other hand, felt that Mexican

Americans were largely absent during the struggle for civil rights and were now attempting to benefit from the blood, sweat, and tears of the African American community. Some members of both communities simply saw the rising tensions as "fighting over the white man's crumbs."

Despite the fact that these competitive perspectives were generally rooted in myths, they persist to this day. And as the demographics of our nation continue to change, that conflict threatens to widen. Demographers predict that shortly after the turn of the century, Latinos will become the largest "minority" group in the country. Sociologists suggest that as a result, African Americans and Latinos will be continually butting heads over scant resources. In fact, some say the conflict is already here—on the streets, in prison, in schools, on college campuses, and even in Congress. However, this prescription for disaster need not be. That's not to say that relations are good or that they are smooth everywhere. They're not. But just as there is conflict, there are innumerable instances of cooperation that point toward better relations for the future. One of those examples is the fight to preserve Affirmative Action.

Mike Davis, the author of *Los Angeles on the Edge of Ethnic Cleansing* (1996), which documents the escalating and deadly violence between the two groups, says he is somewhat surprised, given the fact that both groups coexist in the poorest neighborhoods, that the conflict hasn't arisen sooner. "It's the case of a glass being half-empty or half-full. The real story is how well they've gotten along," says Davis, speculating that there would be much more conflict if it were Italians and Irish living side by side.

The violence over the past few years between the two groups in Los Angeles—particularly in Compton, the mid-city area, and Venice—has been deadly. It has ranged from random drive-by shootings to full-scale gang wars. There have also been dozens of racial brawls at area middle and senior high schools, and hundreds of violent incidents in one jail facility alone, including upward of one hundred full-scale racial riots between the two groups.

"The real motor for the conflict is the jails and the prisons," says Davis. Law enforcement officials maintain that the violence is a war started by a Mexican prison gang to wrest control of the drug trade from black gangs. In reality, the cause of the conflicts is even more ominous. He believes that the tensions are purposely kept alive and fanned by penal authorities. The way jails are administered does more to poison relations than any other factor, Davis says. Every time there is a racial confrontation in a facility, there are repercussions, both inside other jails and prisons, and out on the streets; and, he adds, the authorities "stand back and let it happen."

The only way to reduce the tension on the streets is to alleviate conditions in the jails and prisons, including the severe overcrowding. Even cases of police brutality and police misconduct—which have nothing to do with that violence—have inflamed racial tensions, particularly in Compton. In 1994, an African American Compton police officer was captured on video viciously and repeatedly clubbing an unarmed Latino youth. Compton, like the rest of south-central Los Angeles, which was formerly a Black community, is now predominantly Latino and has experienced a bloody Black/Brown gang war over the past few years. An even deadlier gang war took place in Venice during the same time period. Both wars have left dozens of intended and unintended casualties. A yearlong struggle in 1993–94 in Venice claimed approximately twenty lives. The violence was so brazen that many of the killings took place in the daylight and the retaliations came within hours.

Almost unnoticed was the fact that during this same time frame, hundreds of Latino gang members were killing each other. And hundreds of Black gang members were warring on each other, with scores of casualties. All of these outbreaks occurred during the same time as the well-publicized truce among the Black gangs of Los Angeles and a truce among Latino gangs.

Law enforcement officials say that although gang killings were down by approximately 15 percent in 1994, the truces were but a cover for consolidation of forces along racial lines, orchestrated by prison gangs. But gang workers disagreed, maintaining that the truces were genuine efforts to halt the violence. Incidentally, the unofficial slogan for the Watts Gang Truce was "Crips plus Bloods plus Mexicans—Unite!" The slogan appeared prominently on city walls during the uprising in 1992, when Black and Latino residents caused approximately $1 billion in damage in response to the Rodney King beating verdict.

Relations between the two groups in Los Angeles are not all strained. A multi-racial coalition of groups, spearheaded by Service Employees International Union 660, has worked to improve Black/Brown relations. They also denounced Proposition 187, commonly known as the SOS or Save Our State initiative, as being divisive and anti-immigrant. The 1994 initiative, which passed, would require doctors, nurses, teachers, and other public servants to cooperate with the Immigration and Naturalization Service (INS). The primarily Latino and Black union, along with the coalition, also denounced the new three-strikes-and-you're-out law, which disproportionately affects African Americans and Latinos. And in the face of severe budget cuts in Los Angeles County, they have fought hard to preserve their jobs.

Many African Americans complain that Latino immigrants displace African American workers and siphon off resources. Many Latinos say that African Americans prey on immigrants. Both complain that each group has emulated white or bigoted attitudes and behavior toward the other. While the media plays up these fears and accusations, organizing against the SOS initiative in some parts of the state showed an unprecedented alliance between both groups, along with Asians, unions, and many other sectors.

Exit polls showed that while African Americans voted in higher numbers for Proposition 187 than did Latinos, it was not a majority. Recently, the Mexican American Legal Defense and Educational Fund (MALDEF) established a leadership project in 1995 in south-central Los Angeles. Its objective is both to empower the Latino community and to create better relations between the African American and Latino communities. MALDEF and the NAACP organized a summit in Compton in 1994 to address such common problems as gang violence, unemployment, and racial tensions. Along with these efforts, twelve Los Angeles community organizations have banded together to create the Multicultural Collaborative, which seeks to mediate inter-ethnic disputes, especially those that take place in high schools.

Lindsey Haley, of the Social and Public Art Resource Center (SPARC) in Venice, says her center has been instrumental in giving a voice to the Latino and African American communities. "A piece of artwork will tell you a lot about a community," she says. SPARC, known for creating "The Great Wall of Los Angeles," purportedly the largest mural in the world, painted by youth of all races, sponsored a mural in 1994 at the Young People of Watts Youth Center. The mural depicted Malcolm X, Cesar Chavez, and other cultural symbols of both communities. "There's quite a bit of intermarriage in Watts," says Haley. During the mural dedication, Latinos and African Americans came to celebrate. "That's an example of how a community was getting along—African Americans and Latinos coming together."

In 1994, SPARC, through its *Great Wall Unlimited—Neighborhood Pride Mural Program*, also attempted to do a mural of the Black Panthers in south-central Los Angeles, but it met with some resistance. Opponents believed it would provoke violence, Haley says. SPARC would like to paint a mural in the Oakwood section of Venice—the site of the on-and-off gang war—but again the time is not right. "Both sides have lost a lot of people," says Haley. "There's still a lot of anger."

Lindsey Haley points out that there is a relationship between open green spaces, resources, and violence. The more open space and the more economic resources a community has, the less violence. The open spaces, she says, happen to be where the white community lives. Relations between African Americans and Latinos around the country have not deteriorated as badly as they have in Los Angeles. Down the Santa Ana Freeway in nearby Orange County, "there is a civil rights alliance," Haley says. There, in the past few years, the League of United Latin American Citizens (LULAC) and 100 Black Men of Orange County, along with other groups, have come together to denounce a series of beatings and killings of African Americans and Latinos by white supremacist groups and the pervasive discrimination against non-whites. "There are more hate groups in Orange County than there are in Alabama," says Arturo Montez, president of the Santa Ana chapter of LULAC. "In Los Angeles, everyone is fighting. In Orange County, ignorance, bigotry, and racism on the part of whites has united Blacks, Latinos, and Asians."

In one case, a Black athlete, Robert Vaughn, was severely beaten and stabbed by thirty to fifty white youths. The district attorney failed to prosecute this as a hate crime, nor did he charge the mob with acting as a gang. On the other hand, six Latinos—who were not a gang—were charged with murder as gang members for the killing of a white youth. Montez says he believes they were acting in self-defense—in the face of a white mob at a beach. Prosecuted as gang members, they faced stiffer penalties. This, he says, shows a clear double standard of justice.

Police harassment in Orange County includes photographing and harassing minority youth who are dressed in "gang attire," adds Montez. "If a Black, Latino, or Asian kid wears baggy pants, it's gang dress. If white kids wear baggy pants, it's fashion." Orange County has always been known as anti-Mexican, but it is anti-Black as well, says Eugene Wheeler, president of the Orange County chapter of 100 Black Men. "It's anti-anything that isn't white." Latinos and Blacks have worked closely to combat the racism, says Wheeler, adding that a big challenge is intervening in the Orange County Jail, the site of a 1994 racial brawl between both groups. He lays responsibility squarely on the jail authorities: "They get a kick out of the conflict." Wheeler thinks that it's typical divide and conquer: "We share a common struggle," he says. "None of us have much. What is there to fight about? It is a threat to the county fathers to see a coalition between Mexicans and Blacks. Can you imagine what would happen if the two groups united [nationally]?"

The truth is, more Blacks kill Blacks and more Latinos kill Latinos, but now they're starting to kill each other. "It's not an accident. Unless we understand the causes, we'll destroy ourselves and each other," says Wheeler. Latinos, Blacks, Asians, Native Americans, and the Jewish community also united in Orange County to denounce the racism and the SOS initiative, adds Wheeler, who grew up in South Carolina. "That was a different kind of hate," he says of the South. "Even during the height of segregation, the relationship between the races was one of white paternalism. They treated us as though they owned us. It was a love-hate relationship on the part of whites. Here, [the anti-immigrant sentiment] is very vicious."

David Amin, president of the Los Amigos organization in Orange County, believes that "too many of our Black and Brown brothers are swayed by scapegoating. There's a great percentage of Latinos who fall into the trap. They don't see that it [SOS] would create a subservient culture." Amin says of Black/Brown relations in Orange County, "We firmly believe that what they do to a Black, they do to us."

Around the country, there are other examples of Black/Brown conflict, as well as cooperation. Three days of disturbances erupted in Washington, D.C., after a Black police officer arrested a Salvadoran man in 1991. In Dallas, roving bands of Black youths attacked Latinos in 1992 at a Dallas Super Bowl victory parade, causing tensions to rise in the city. And in Detroit, the Latino community was inflamed over the disparate handling of police abuse cases there in 1994–95. Officers in the shooting of an African American were promptly put on trial, but Black officers who shot an unarmed Cuban immigrant were not prosecuted. In Miami, relations between Cubans and African Americans have rarely been good. The biggest strain came a few years ago when Cuban Americans boycotted the presence of Nelson Mandela in Florida. The 1994 Mariel boatlift again strained relations, with some African American leaders denouncing the displacement of African Americans by Cuban newcomers.

In the nation's capital, a Latino Civil Rights Task Force was created in the wake of riots. Racial tensions flared up again in 1994, due to inflammatory comments by a radio personality and efforts to close down Bell Multicultural High School, a school designed to help immigrants, says Pedro Aviles, head of the task force. He points out that Latinos are still short-changed in terms of services and resources. The African American community feels it fought hard for what it has and is unwilling to share the resources, says Aviles. "No money is coming our way."

Not all these communities are still embroiled in tension. In fact, in Detroit, a change in City Hall has resulted in markedly better relations, says Jose Cuello, director of Chicano/Boricua Studies at Wayne State University. Juan Jose Martinez, a counselor at the same center, ran for a position on the Detroit School Board with the support of the African

American community. "The community has stopped fighting along racial lines," Cuello says.

The higher education community has not been untouched by Black/Brown conflicts. In the recent past, members of Historically Black Colleges and Universities have expressed concern that the creation of the Hispanic Association of Colleges and Universities (HACU) potentially threatens to divert scarce resources away from their organization. HACU officials deny that their existence comes at the expense of Black colleges. Acknowledging the importance of the subject, for the past several years HACU has held workshops on African American/Latino relations during their annual conference.

In 1994, Black/Brown conflict exploded on the campus of the University of Nebraska-Lincoln when Latino students instituted a boycott of the Multicultural academic support services office, claiming their needs were being ignored. That boycott was triggered by the hiring of an African American, as opposed to a Latina. Teresita Aguilar, associate professor at Teacher's College there, says conflict exists because Latinos feel completely unwelcome on campus, including in the only office that's supposed to be the most diverse. But Aguilar faults the administration, pointing out that Latinos and all students of color should be welcome on the entire campus. Part of the problem, beyond resources, stems from the fact that African Americans don't know the history of discrimination against Latinos nor their civil rights struggles, says Aguilar. For instance, it is not widely known that many Latinos fought the early court battles to dismantle segregation—some of which were the basis for *Brown* v. *Topeka*.

In 1946, a young Mexican American and Puerto Rican couple in Southern California tried to enroll their son in an all-white school. The school district refused. That action resulted in *Mendez* v. *Westminister*, a desegregation lawsuit which led to the closing of so-called Mexican schools throughout the state. The earliest desegregation lawsuit filed by Mexican Americans was *Romo* v. *Laird* (Tempe, Arizona) in 1925. However, the victorious plaintiffs did not challenge the legality of segregation per se. They charged—and the court agreed—that segregation against Mexicans was illegal because the schools were separate but not equal. Of the hundreds of Mexican American desegregation battles waged prior to *Topeka* v. *Brown,* some of those that made it to and succeeded in court were: *Independent School District* v. *Salvatierra* (1930, Del Rio, Texas); *Alvarez* v. *Lemon Grove School Board of Education* (1930, Lemon Grove, California); *Delgado* v. *Bastrop Independent School District* (1948, Bastrop County, Texas); *Hernandez* v. *The State of Texas* (1948); and *Gonzales* v. *Sheely* (1951, Tolleson, Arizona)

Among the hundreds of other desegregation struggles, one little known but significant battle occurred immediately after World War II. In many parts of the country until the 1950s, Mexicans generally weren't allowed to speak Spanish in school, and were not allowed into public swimming pools, barbershops, restaurants, hotels, or other public accommodations, says Pete Sandoval, who immigrated to Garden City, Kansas, from Mexico in 1927. Signs that read, "No Niggers, Mexicans or Dogs Allowed," were common in Garden City and many parts of the Southwest and Midwest, he says. Sandoval attributes the disillusionment of African American and Mexican American World War II veterans—who had fought for democracy abroad, only to return to segregation and discrimination at home—as the catalyst for the civil rights movement. In Garden City, a group of Mexican American veterans, including Sandoval, created the Latin American Club, which brought an end to the segregation of Mexican Americans and African Americans in their hometown in 1948. This organization predated the American GI Forum—the national veterans organization that was formed in 1948 after a Chicano veteran was refused burial in an all-white cemetery.

"When they opened up the swimming pools, I was the first one in," says Sandoval. "My wife and I were also the first ones in the theater."

Lacking knowledge of that history, many African Americans treat Latinos as though they're riding on the coattails of the Black civil rights movement. "Many Blacks believe that gains for Latinos are at the expense of Blacks—that for Latinos to want more means Blacks will have less," says Aguilar. Many Latinos feel that "minority" mostly means Black, she says, adding that institutions still operate as though we lived in a black and white world.

Some Latinos also feel that African Americans want Latinos to wait for their turn. "We ought to bring our forces together, but there is a divide," says Aguilar. One of the main stumbling blocks to unity is nationalism. Many times, Blacks or Latinos protect their own, even when all are being served poorly. One example took place when she was at Arizona State University. When a Chicano faculty member was accused of wrongdoing, Chicano faculty members wanted to send a letter of support. But she and other Chicano faculty members objected, arguing that they shouldn't be supporting that type of behavior, "regardless if he's a brother." Mediocrity serves no one, says Aguilar. When all things are equal in a hiring situation, the position should go to the individual from the group which is the least represented. Latinos not only need role models but can also serve all populations, she says.

Jimmie Smith, director of the Multicultural Office at the University of

Nebraska–Lincoln, says the real problem is that his office doesn't have enough resources to make a dent by bringing in a sufficient number of students of color on campus. More importantly, the university does not provide sufficient support or resources to meet the needs of students of color. To do so, it must create a comprehensive plan, says Smith.

Latino students had similar concerns two years ago at the University of Kansas, but the dispute was satisfactorily resolved, says Sherwood Thompson, director of the Office of Minority Affairs there. In fact, African American students were also dissatisfied with the performance of the minority office on campus. Once students understood the source of power on campus, they united in their efforts. "We did have a turbulent time," says Thompson, pointing out that the key to resolving the problem was in not denying there was a problem. It took a special effort to unite the efforts of all minorities. "We [the office] didn't want to be seen as promoting revolution or being a roadblock to minority concerns." As a result of discussions, Latino, Native American, and African American task forces were established. The three groups joined in a partnership to put forth recommendations to promote diversity campuswide. The way his office handled the situation should be considered a model, Thompson says.

Many student activists argue that schools such as Nebraska are the exception, citing nationwide protests the past few years by Latinos at hundreds of campuses nationwide to create Chicano and ethnic studies departments; to protect Proposition 187; and against the efforts to dismantle Affirmative Action programs. The protests generally had the full support of African Americans. Latinos and African Americans along with Asians and Native Americans fighting together has been the norm for almost thirty years. Conflicts at the campus level are normally fights between bureaucrats.

What divides Blacks and Latinos on college campuses are superficial things, especially when compared to what is happening out on the streets, says Gil Gonzalez, a professor at University of California at Irvine. "The deeper issues are not being touched," he says. "It's time to drop the nationalism. It keeps people's perspectives narrow and keeps them from acting politically."

Gonzalez, who has studied the history of discrimination of Mexican Americans, says a graduate student of his recently completed his thesis on the Black and Chicano civil rights movements of the 1960s and found them to be strikingly similar—from demands to tactics. There was a whole series of similarities, from demanding ethnic studies to sit-ins and boycotts, he says. And it makes a lot of sense, he says, adding that "it is absolutely necessary to have an alliance [between Blacks and Latinos] if there's ever going to be change."

Unknown to most people is that those alliances have existed in the past. But most people are not historians, and are thus not aware of the shared struggles in the Americas. For example, few people know that Vicente Guerrero, one of Mexico's greatest Independence heroes, was part Black. It is also generally unknown that there were more Blacks in Mexico during the Colonial era than there were Spaniards. And they didn't disappear, but mixed with the Indian Mestizo population. Mexico and Indian territory in the United States was sanctuary for runaway slaves. Incidentally, a statue of Dr. Martin Luther King, Jr., stands opposite Abraham Lincoln in Mexico City—two figures in American history highly respected by the people of Mexico.

The Unity '94 journalism conference in Atlanta may be the model of cooperation for the future. The conference, which was attended by Black, Latino, Asian, and Native American media professionals, drew more than six thousand participants. Another Unity conference is planned for Seattle in 1999. "The key to surviving and thriving in a diverse society such as ours is to emphasize what we all have in common, not what divides us," says *Washington Post* columnist Dorothy Butler Gilliam, president of the National Association of Black Journalists. "What it takes is the will."

A better model may already exist in the state of Washington. At the end of August 1994, a cross-burning in Lynden, Washington, occurred in front of a migrant labor camp located near the U.S.-Canadian border. There, the flaming ten-foot wooden cross sent terror throughout the camp, populated mostly by Mexican workers. A few days after the incident, 350 people, including members of the Puget Sound chapter of the NAACP, LULAC, and the Lummi and Nooksack Indian nations, staged a march and rally in support of the workers. "It didn't matter that it was aimed against Mexican farmworkers," says Christina Castoreña, president of the local LULAC. The community would have united regardless of what group had been targeted. "When you burn a cross, you stir the meaning of the history of its use . . . of fear and violence."

Renee Collins, president of the Puget Sound NAACP, agrees: "We all know the meaning of the cross. We know what it symbolizes, what it represents, and what is has meant to people."

As a result of the cross-burning, a multiracial committee formed to fight against further acts of racial terror, but they already have a unique history of organizing and organizations. On the local board of the NAACP are African Americans, Latinos, Native Americans, and whites.

"There's strength in numbers," says Collins. "We deal with the same issues. It's just a matter of time before it's your group." And they didn't create such a board and organization in response to the cross-burning. Although some other chapters of the NAACP disapprove of their structure, which they formed in 1991, "we believe we represent the new direction Ben Chavis was talking about" (before he was ousted as head of the NAACP).

The battle against the anti-affirmative action California Civil Rights Initiative generally has helped solidify Black/Brown relations, though not without its hitches. Many Latinos are still smarting over Proposition 187—angry at everyone who supported it, but particularly at African Americans, feeling that in a time of need, a natural ally abandoned them. Despite those feelings, the attacks against affirmative action have proved to be a common cause for both communities.

Manning Marable, director of the Institute for Research in African American Studies at Colombia University in New York, says that Blacks and Latinos do indeed have many parallels. "Latinos did experience systemic and legal discrimination. Any historian knows it's true." Marable suggests that alliances between both groups and between Asians and Native Americans should be based on the principle of respect. "Shared oppression is the basis for unity," he says. Relationships between Blacks and Latinos shouldn't have to be antagonistic. The key to unity is moral authority. Having lost such moral giants as Martin Luther King, Jr., Malcolm X, and Cesar Chavez, both communities don't necessarily need to replace their leaders but to look for the moral leadership within everyone. Doing so isolates the oppressors and usurps the ground they stand on.

White Fright Over Oakland Redistricting

■ ■ ■

WILLIAM WONG

One of life's clichés is that change is never easy. That well-worn aphorism is especially evident in the world of politics and how new population groups are seeking some power while established groups don't want to relinquish any.

A telling example was the political redistricting that took place in Oakland, California, in 1993.

The most striking population shift in the 1980s in Oakland, a city of almost 400,000 people, was the doubling of Asians and a near doubling of Latinos, a reflection of immigration and refugee trends over the past thirty years. Consequently, the percentages of the white and African American groups decreased.

Oakland has used district voting in recent elections to elect city council and school board members to increase the chances of non-white residents winning places on the city's two top governing bodies. A bigger factor in Oakland's political changes, however, has been suburbanization. Just before World War II, Oakland was largely a white city, with small African American, Asian, and Mexican communities. Military industrialization in Oakland and the San Francisco Bay Area lured thousands of

African Americans from Texas, Louisiana, and other southern states. These workers stayed on after the war. But many in the white middle class didn't. New freeways, cutting deep into the heart of Oakland, carried white middle-class families to the burgeoning suburbs. Industrial jobs began to shrivel up. Once vibrant with many department stores, Oakland's downtown, like that of other American cities, became a virtual ghost town.

A small group of conservative white Republican men used to control Oakland politically and economically. But as they too passed from the scene and as the American economy transmogrified, political and economic vacuums developed.

In Oakland, the mid-1970s were a turning point. Black Panther Party leader Bobby Seale ran for mayor in 1973. He didn't win, but he paved the way for a moderate African American, Lionel Wilson, to become Oakland's first black mayor, in 1977. That marked the first significant political transition in the post–World War II era—the rise of African American political power in a city that was now more than 40 percent black. The disputed 1993 redistricting struggle was the second wave of the city's political evolution.

Lionel Wilson's mayoral victory in 1977 and subsequent reelections (until a defeat in 1990) ushered in an era in which other African Americans won seats on the city council and school board. Their ascendancy was helped by district, rather than citywide, elections. Ironically for the smaller Asian American population, individual Asian Americans were able to win election to the city council, starting in the late 1960s with Raymond Eng and Frank Ogawa. Eng served less than ten years, but Ogawa stayed on until his death in 1995. Though both men had support from Oakland's Asian Americans, neither relied on the Asian vote to win, because the Asian vote was minuscule. When Wilma Chan and Jean Quan both won seats on the school board in 1990, more Asians voted than was the case in the 1960s, but their numbers still weren't dominant.

As the Asian population keeps growing, Asian leaders dream of greater collective power. They're pleased that individual Asians have been able to win electoral office, but they wish to have more group influence on city policies.

Oakland's Chinatown, the base of the Asian community, was in District 3 during the 1980s redistricting, but two nearby neighborhoods with growing Asian populations were in two other districts. Seizing an opportunity that comes along once a decade, Asian political activists aggressively promoted the idea of consolidating Chinatown with the two other neighborhoods—popularly called China Hill and New Chinatown—into a newly drawn District 2, which would have an Asian population of about 35 percent, more than double the percentage of Asians in the three separate districts. In doing so, they ran into the established political powers of the old District 2, city council member Mary Moore and some of her white supporters.

Moore took a seat on the council at the same time Lionel Wilson became mayor, a white liberal supporting the rise of African American political power. Over the years, she gained a reputation as an environmentalist and neighborhood advocate. Her most devoted neighborhood supporters tended to be white residents in middle- to upper-middle-class areas. Even though the China Hill neighborhood, with significant numbers of Asian residents, was also a part of her old District 2, Moore paid little attention to those residents, except for electioneering appearances. But when Asian activists put forth redistricting plans for a new District 2, Moore recoiled because she would lose some of her strongest white neighborhoods. She even told an Oakland Asian leader in private that white people have power in this society and will allow Asians to get only so far. She denied saying that, but at least one other person in Oakland had heard her make similar remarks.

During the months of meetings and hearings, Moore's white supporters said Asians were "overrepresented" in city electoral positions. One even introduced the inflammatory terms "nuke" and "napalm" into the discussion. "The proposed map [favored by Asian activists] *nukes* District 2 and *napalms* District 3," this Moore supporter said.

Perhaps the Moore forces didn't mean to conjure up the imagery of a nuclear bomb and incendiary napalm in connection with people of Asian descent, but the linkage was undeniable. After all, it doesn't take too long a memory to recall that the only atomic bombs ever used in war were dropped on two Japanese cities, and that napalm was a destructive weapon used to wipe out Southeast Asian villages. This openly white racist rhetoric was shocking in a city that for all its faults has at least developed a reasonable level of interracial relationships.

A generous interpretation of the reactionary attitudes of Moore and her followers is that they simply didn't want to give up their power base to an emerging non-white group. As it turned out, Moore, beset by a contentious divorce, decided not to run for the council seat representing the new District 2 in 1994. The Asian activists, successful in getting the city council to redraw the city's district lines so that the three Asian neighborhoods were consolidated, decided to put forth an Asian American candidate, Lily Hu.

Hu's chief opponent was a white man, John Russo, an attorney who had run unsuccessfully against Moore in 1990 under the old District 2 lines. Russo, a liberal Democrat, easily defeated Hu, who had never run for political office before. Even though the new District 2 has an Asian population of 35 percent, the percentage of Asian voters is much lower. White voters still have a disproportionate influence in District 2. In fairness to Russo, he didn't run a racial campaign. Rather, his message was one of inclusion. His greater political and civic knowledge led to his easy victory.

In another odd twist in this local political saga, Hu got Moore's endorsement—yet another example proving the old adage that politics makes strange bedfellows. Indeed, few people seemed to mind that the Asian race-baiting Moore had somehow conveniently forgotten her hateful words in order now to back an Asian candidate.

The Asian activists have learned a lesson from the heated political battlefields of 1993 and 1994. The defeated Hu remains active in Chinatown and city politics and even hosted a fund-raiser for Russo to help him reduce his campaign debt. And Russo has gotten off to a fast start on the council, as he has assiduously courted residents in the Asian neighborhoods and other diverse areas he represents.

In a larger context, however, the 1993 redistricting wars were a benchmark in Oakland's continuing transition from a city once ruled by a cadre of white Republican men to one groping with concepts of shared power among different racial and ethnic groups.

A Countryless Woman:
The Early Feminista

■ ■ ■

ANA CASTILLO

I would have spoken these words as a feminist who "happened" to be a white United States citizen, conscious of my government's proven capacity for violence and arrogance of power, but as self-separated from that government, quoting without second thought Virginia Woolf's statement in *The Three Guineas* that "as a woman I have no country. As a woman I want no country. As a woman my country is the whole world." This is not what I come [here] to say in 1984. I come here with notes but without absolute conclusions. This is not a sign of loss of faith or hope. These notes are the marks of a struggle to keep moving, a struggle for accountability.
—*Adrienne Rich, "Notes Toward a Politics of Location,"*
Blood, Bread, and Poetry

I cannot say I am a citizen of the world as Virginia Woolf, speaking as an Anglo woman born to economic means, declared herself; nor can I make the same claim to U.S. citizenship as Adrienne Rich does, despite her universal feeling for humanity. As a mestiza born to the lower strata, I am treated at best as a second-class citizen, at worst, as a nonentity. I am commonly perceived as a foreigner everywhere I go, including in the United States and in Mexico. This international perception is based on my color and features. I am neither black nor white. I am not light-skinned and cannot be mistaken for "white"; because my hair is so straight I cannot be mistaken for "black." And by U.S. standards and according to some North American Native Americans, I cannot make official claims to being Indian.

Socioeconomic status, genetic makeup, and ongoing debates on mestisaje aside, if in search of refuge from the United States I took up residence on any other continent, the core of my being would long for a return to the lands of my ancestors. My ethereal spirit and my collective memory with other indigenas and mestizo/as yearn to *claim* these territories as homeland. In the following pages, I would like to review our socioeconomic status, our early activism and feminismo, and to begin the overall discussion that moves toward a Xicanista vision.

In the 1980s, leftists and liberals recognized the atrocities of U.S. intervention in Central America, as similar sympathizers did with Vietnam in the 1960s. Their sympathy is reminiscent of North American leftists and liberals who in the 1930s struggled against fascism during the Spanish Civil War. In each instance, there is the implication that these liberal individuals are not in any way responsible for the persecution, and that it is all their government's fault. These same humanists have vaguely and apologetically acknowledged the injustice done to the descendants of their country's former slaves and to the Native Americans who have been all but obliterated through genocide and dispossession.

Yet, mestizo/as, those who are Mexican citizens as well as those who are U.S. born, are viewed less sympathetically. We are advised to assimilate into white dominant society or opt for invisibility—an invisibility that we are blamed for because of our own lack of ability to take advantage of the supposedly endless opportunities available through acculturation.

Racism has been generally polarized into a black-white issue. U.S. mestizo/as of Mexican background, therefore, are viewed by many white people, by many African Americans and, yes, by some Native Americans as having the potential to "pass" for white, in theory, at will. This general view is based on the assumptions, lack of information, and misinformation that accompanies policies, media control, and distorted historical documentation disseminated to the general populace by the white male–dominated power system that has traditionally governed this country. The United States cannot deny its early history of importing Africans as slaves, which explains the presence of African Americans throughout the Americas. However, censorship continues regarding the extent of genocide of Native Americans. As for mestizo/as, we were identified as a mongrel race, a mixture of the dispensable Amerindian race and the lowly Spaniard. Little is known by the general public of how these attitudes caused ongoing persecution of Mexic Amerindians and mestizo/as in what was once Mexico and later became U.S. territory. For example, while it is well known that in the South there were lynchings and hangings of African Americans, it isn't common knowledge that Mexicans were also lynched and hung in Texas and throughout the Southwest.

Most people in the United States have little awareness of this government's ongoing dominant-subordinate relationship with Mexico since, of course, this is not taught in schools as part of U.S. history. The general public assumes that all Mexicans are immigrants and therefore *obligated* to assimilate, just as European immigrants did and do.

Most members of a dominant society have very little understanding of the numerous ways that a country, especially one supposedly based on the free enterprise system and democracy, systematically and quite effectively disenfranchises much of its population. While some white members of society have an understanding of this from an economic and historical standpoint, they do not or will not recognize that there are, to this day, economic inequities based on racism. Many more do not understand or refuse to accept that today all women suffer, in one way or another, as a result of the prevalent misogyny legislated and expounded in this society.

For the last twenty years the leaders of the U.S. government have tried to convince its population that the civil rights movement succeeded in creating a true democracy and that increasing poverty and unemployment are primarily a question of world economics. If indications of the growing frustration on the part of women and people of color who cannot overcome job and educational inequities based on race, gender, and limited economic resources were not evident enough to the federal government, the national riots after the Rodney King verdict serve as the final argument.

While I have more in common with a Mexican man than with a white woman, I have much more in common with an Algerian woman than I do with a Mexican man. This opinion, I'm sure, chagrins women who sincerely believe our female physiology unequivocally binds all women throughout the world, despite the compounded social prejudices that daily affect us all in different ways. Although women everywhere experience life differently from men everywhere, white women are members of a race that has proclaimed itself globally superior for hundreds of years. We live in a polarized world of contrived dualisms, dichotomies, and paradoxes: light versus dark and good versus evil. We as Mexic Amerindians/mestizas are the dark. We are the evil . . . or at least, the questionable.

Ours is a world imbued with nationalism, real for some, yet tenuous as paper for others. A world in which from the day of our births, we are either granted citizenship or relegated to the netherstate of serving as mass production drones. Non-white women—Mexicans/Chicanas, Filipinas, Malaysians, and others—who comprise 80 percent of the global factory work force are the greatest dispensable resource that multinational interests own. The women are, in effect, represented by no country.

Feminists of color in the United States (and around the world) are currently arduously reexamining the very particular ways our non-Western cultures use us and how they view us. We have been considered opinionless and the invariable targets of every kind of abusive manipulation and experimentation. As a mestiza, a resident of a declining world power, a countryless woman, I have the same hope as Rich, who on behalf of her country aims to be accountable, flexible, and learn new ways to gather together earnest peoples of the world without the defenses of nationalism.

I was born, raised, and spent most of my life in one of the largest cities in the United States. Despite its distance from Mexico, Chicago has a population of approximately a quarter of a million people of Mexican background. It is also the third most frequent U.S. destination of Mexican migrants after El Paso and Los Angeles. The greatest influx of Mexicans occurred during the first half of this century when the city required cheap labor for its factories, slaughterhouses, and steel mill industry.

In an effort to minimize their social and spiritual alienation, the Mexican communities there developed and maintained solid ties to Mexican culture and traditions. This was reinforced by the tough political patronage system in Chicago, which was dependent upon ethnically and racially divisive strategies to maintain its power. Thus I grew up perceiving myself to be Mexican despite the fact that I was born in the United States and did not visit Mexico until the age of ten.

Assimilation into dominant culture, while not impossible, was not encouraged nor desired by most ethnic groups in Chicago—Mexicans were no exception. We ate, slept, talked, and dreamed Mexican. Our parishes were Mexican. Small Mexican-owned businesses flourished. We were able to replicate Mexico to such a degree that the spiritual and psychological needs of a people so despised and undesired by white dominant culture were met in our own large communities.

Those who came up north to escape destitution in Mexico were, in general, dark-skinned mestizos. In the face of severe racism, it's no wonder we maintained such strong bonds to each other. But even those who were not as outwardly identifiably Mexican were usually so inherently Mexican by tradition that they could not fully assimilate. Not a few refused to "settle in" on this side of the border with the pretense that they would eventually return to their home towns in Mexico.

As I was growing up, Mexicans were the second largest minority in Chicago. There was also a fair size Puerto Rican community and a fair amount of Cubans and other Latin Americans. But in those years, before the blatant military disruption of Latin American countries such as Chile and El Salvador, a person with "mestiza" characteristics was considered Mexican. When one had occasion to venture away from her insulated community to, say, downtown, impressive and intimidating with its tremendous skyscrapers and evidently successful (white) people bustling about, she felt as if she were leaving her village to go into town on official matters. Once there she went about her business with a certain sense of invisibility, and even hoped for it, feeling so out of place and disoriented in the presence of U.S. Anglo, profit-based interests, which we had nothing to do with except as mass-production workers. On such occasions, if she were by chance to run across another mestiza (or mestizo), there was a mutual unspoken recognition and, perhaps, a reflexive avoidance of eye contact. An instantaneous mental communication might sound something like this:

I know you. You are Mexican (like me). You are brown-skinned (like me). You are poor (like me). You probably live in the same neighborhood as I do. You don't have anything, own anything. (Neither do I.) You're no one (here). At this moment I don't want to be reminded of this, in the midst of such luxury, such wealth, this disorienting language; it makes me ashamed of the food I eat, the flat I live in, the only clothes I can afford to wear, the alcoholism and defeat I live with. You remind me of all of it.

You remind me that I am not beautiful—because I am short, round-bellied and black-eyed. You remind me that I will never ride in that limousine that just passed us because we are going to board the same bus back to the neighborhood where we both live. You remind me of why the foreman doesn't move me out of that tedious job I do day after day, or why I got feverish and too tongue-tied to go to the main office to ask for that Saturday off when my child made her First Holy Communion.

When I see you, I see myself. You are the mirror of this despicable, lowly sub-human that I am in this place far from our homeland which scarcely offered us much more since the vast majority there live in destitution. None of the rich there look like us either. At least here we feed our children; they have shoes. We manage to survive. But don't look at me. Go on your way. Let me go on pretending my invisibility, so that I can observe close up all the possibilities—and dream the gullible dreams of a human being.[1]

At seventeen, I joined the Latino/Chicano movement. I went downtown and rallied around City Hall along with hundreds of other youth screaming, "Viva La Raza!" and "Chicano Power!" until we were hoarse. Our fears of being recognized as lowly Mexicans were replaced with socioeconomic theories that led to political radicalism. Yet our efforts to bring unity and courage to the majority of our people were short lived; they did not embrace us. Among the factors contributing to this were the ability of some to assimilate more easily on the basis of lighter skin color and the consumer fever that overrides people's social needs. The temptations of the rewards of assimilation and the internalization of racism by the colonized peoples of the United States were and are devastating. Society has yet to acknowledge the trauma it engenders.

The Hispanic population in the United States totaled 22,354,509, according to the 1990 U.S. Department of Commerce report; 13,495,938 of that total were of Mexican origin. (We can estimate therefore that when we are discussing the women of Mexican origin we are referring to a population of about 7 million women in the United States.) According to a 1989 report, immigration constituted half of the recent Hispanic population growth. I am personally glad to see the U.S. Department of Commerce gives this reason to explain the disproportionate growth of Hispanics as compared to non-Hispanics, as opposed to the 1987 Department of Labor Report, which states that there are so many Hispanics because Hispanic women tend to be more fertile than non-Hispanic women. These figures, of course, do not include the undocumented Latino population. The U.S. Immigration and Naturalization Service estimated 1.2 million apprehensions at the border in 1986.

"Hispanic" as the ethnic label for all people who reside in the United States with some distant connection with the culture brought by the Spaniards during the conquest of the Americas is a gross misnomer. The word promotes an official negation of people called "Hispanic" by implying that their ethnicity or race is exclusively European rather than partly Native American (as are most Chicano/as), or African American (as are those descendants of the African slave trade along the Caribbean coasts).

How can people from the Caribbean states, whose economies depended on slave trade, be generically called Hispanic? Is it because they are from states that are presently Spanish-speaking or were once colonized by the Spaniards, although they may presently be under another country's dominion? In the Caribbean, Hispanic includes Puerto Ricans, Cubans, and Dominicans. While Cuba's official language has remained Spanish since Spanish rule, many of its people are of African ancestry. Citizens of the Dominican Republic are considered Hispanic because they speak Spanish, but the residents of the other side of their island, Haiti, speak French (and more commonly, as I understand, patois). Are there enough major racial differences between these two nationalities on the same island to justifiably classify one as Hispanic but not the other? The Philippines were once colonized by Spain and now have English as a dominant language, but they are not classified as Hispanic. They are placed in another catchall group, Asian.

Hispanic gives us all one ultimate paternal cultural progenitor: Spain. The diverse cultures already on the American shores when the Europeans arrived, as well as those introduced because of the African slave trade, are completely obliterated by the term. Hispanic is nothing more than a concession made by the U.S. legislature when they saw they couldn't get rid of us. If we won't go away, why not at least Europeanize us, make us presentable guests at the dinner table, take away our feathers and rattles and civilize us once and for all.

This erroneous but nationally accepted label invented by a white supremacist bureaucracy essentially is a resignation to allow, after more than two hundred years of denial, some cultural representation of the conquistadors who originally colonized the Southwest. Until now, in other words, only Anglo-Saxons were legitimate informants of American culture.

To further worsen the supposition that we can be Hispanic—simply long forgotten descendants of Europeans just as white people are—is the horrific history of brutal and inhuman subjugation that not only Amerindians experienced under Spanish and other European rules in Mexico and throughout Latin America and the Caribbean, but all those of mixed blood. Indeed, shortly after the Conquest of Mexico, Spanish rule set up a complex caste system in which to be of mixed blood virtually excluded you from full rights as citizens and protection by the law. Jews and Moors in that Catholic society also experienced racist attitudes.[2] Just as with today's African Americans, among mestizo/as and Amerindians, the result of such intense, legislated racism throughout centuries is demoralization. As one historian puts it regarding the Mexic Amerindian people, "Trauma and neuroses linger still, and may not be entirely overcome. For the Spaniards, in Mexico, did not commit genocide; they committed culturcide."[3]

Among Latino/as in the United States today there is a universe of differences. There is a universe of difference, for example, between the experience of the Cuban man who arrived in the United States as a child with his parents after fleeing Castro's revolution and the Puerto Rican woman who is a third-generation single mother on the Lower East Side. There is a universe of difference between the young Mexican American aspiring to be an actor in Hollywood in the nineties and the community organizer working for rent control for the last ten years in San Francisco, although both may be sons of farmworkers. There is a universe of difference between Carolina Herrera, South American fashion designer and socialite, and a Guatemalan refugee who has hardly learned to speak Spanish but must already adapt to English in order to work as a domestic in the United States. Picture her: She is not statuesque or blonde (like Ms. Herrera). She is short, squat, with a moon face, and black, oily hair. She does not use six pieces of silverware at the dinner table, but one, if any, and a tortilla. There is a universe of differences among all of these individuals, yet Anglo society says they all belong to the same ethnic group: Hispanic.

A study by the University of Chicago shows that deep divisions based on race exist between black Hispanics and white Hispanics in the United States. The black/white dichotomy of the United States causes black Hispanics to relate more to African Americans than to non-black Hispanics. It is also revealed that "black Hispanics are far more segregated from U.S. whites than are white Hispanics."[4] *Color,* rather than saying simply ethnicity, in addition to class and gender, as well as *concientización,* all determine one's identity and predict one's fate in the United States.

Except for the historical period characterized by "manifest destiny," fate is not part of United States–Anglo-Saxon ideology. But the United States does have a fate.

Sir John Glubb in his book *A Short History of the Arab Peoples* suggests reviewing world history to see how frequently great empires reach and fall from their pinnacle of power, all within 200 to 300 years. According to Glubb, for example, the Greek Empire (330 B.C. to about 100 B.C.) lasted 230 years; the Spaniards endured for (1556 to 1800) 244 years; and the British Empire lasted 230 years (1700 to 1930). It is sobering to note that no great power simply lost its position as number one slipping into second or third place, nor has any former great power ever resumed its original, unchallenged position. They all have ceased to exist as a world power. After the fall of the Roman Empire, Italy has been little more than the home of the Pope for the past fifteen centuries. Moreover, Glubb tells us, "It is not desired to insist on rigid numbers, for many outside factors influence the fates of great nations. Nevertheless, the resemblance between the lives of so many and such varied empires is extremely striking, and it is obviously entirely unconnected with the development of those mechanical devices of which we are so proud."[5] "Mechanical devices" means military might.

Signs of the decline of the United States as the leading world power are most apparent in the phenomenal growth of the public debt in the 1980s: during the Reagan-Bush years, the public debt of the United States went from $907.7 billion in 1980 to over $3 trillion in 1990 (as reported by the U.S. Department of the Treasury).

The United States, being a relatively young, therefore resilient country, can and eventually will allow for the representation of people of color in the institutions that influence and mandate people's lives—government, private industry, and universities, for example. It will gradually relent with its blatant refusal to fulfill its professed democratic ideals and include the descendants of its slave trade, the Native Americans, mestizo/as, and Asians (who also come from a wide variety of countries and social and economic backgrounds, and who, due to various political circumstances, are immigrating to the United States at an exorbitant rate). It will do so because the world economy will not permit anything short of it. Nevertheless, most assuredly among those who will get further pushed down as the disparity between the few wealthy and the impoverished grows, will be our *gente*.

The largest movement in the history of the United States ever to force the government to reckon with its native Latino population was the Chicano/Latino movement of the late 1960s and 1970s. Because of its force there is today a visible sector of Latinos who have college degrees, who hold mortgages on decent houses, and who are articulate in English. (In Spanish, when a person has facility in a language to get by, we say we can "defend" ourselves; we now have a substantial number of Latinos who are defending themselves against Anglophile culture.) The generation that came of age in the 1980s was given the general message that acculturation can be rewarding. Yes, the status quo will always reward those who succumb to it, who serve it, and who do not threaten its well-being.

In 1980 when the Republicans and the Reagan administration came to office, their tremendous repression quashed the achievements of the Chicano/Latino movement, which has been based on collectivism and the retention of our Mexican/Amerindian culture. Community projects and grass-roots programs dependent on government funding—rehabilitation and training, child care, early education and alternative schooling, youth counseling, cultural projects that supported the arts and community artists, rehab housing for low-income families, and women's shelters—shut down.

In their place the old "American Dream"—a WASP male philosophy on which this country was founded at the expense of Third World labor—was reinstated. As in U.S. society before the civil rights movement, material accumulation equaled self-worth.

The new generation of Chicanos and Latinos who came of age in the 1980s had a radically different attitude from the collective mentality of the 1970s activists, believing that after two hundred years of racist and ethnic exploitation, the age of the "Hispanic" had finally come. Their *abuelos, tíos,* parents (some who had been in the Chicano/Latino movement) had paid the dues for the American Dream. Now they could finally claim their own place in society. They had acculturated.

Encouraged by media hype announcing our arrival in the 1980s as the "Decade of the Hispanic," for the first time in U.S. history, ad campaigns took the Latino/a consumer into consideration. Magazines, billboards, and even television commercials (Coors comes to mind) showed young, brown, beautiful Latina models in flashy wear reaping some of the comfort and pleasures of a democracy based on free enterprise. Also, there was the unprecedented tokenism of Latino/as in visible and high-level government posts and private industry that further convinced many among the new generation that each individual indeed had the ability to fulfill his or her own great master plan for material success. The new generation was not alone. The previous generation became more conservative, along with immigrating Latinos who also believed in the Republican administration and the trickle-down theory of Reagonomics.

It is difficult to generalize why so many Latino/as moved toward conservative, if not overtly right-wing, views. Personal disillusionment with leftist ideology may explain in part the change in attitude and goals for some. But for many, I believe it is basically a matter of desiring material acquisitions. It is difficult to maintain a collective ideology in a society where possessions and power status equal self-worth.

Unfortunately, the continuous drop of the U.S. dollar in the world trade market caused the economy to worsen each year. In the 1980s, jobs were lost, companies closed down and moved out of the country, banks foreclosed on mortgages, and scholarships and grants once available to needy college students in the 1970s were taken away. These were only a few of the losses experienced not only by Latino/as but by much of the population.

Simultaneously, the cost of living went up. The much coveted trendy lifestyle of the white yuppie moved further away from the grasp of the young and upwardly mobile Reagan-Bush generation. The nineties ushered in a new generation, cognizant of the white hegemonic atmosphere entrenched in colleges and universities and with a vigor reminiscent of the student movements of two decades earlier, which has begun protests on campuses throughout the country. The acceleration of gang violence in cities, drug wars, cancer on the rise, and AIDS continue to be the backdrop, while the new decade's highlights so far for living in these difficult times were the Persian Gulf War *Espectáculo* and the Rodney King riots that resounded throughout the world—sending out a message that this is indeed a troubled country.

El Movimiento Chicano/Latino saw its rise and fall within a time span of less than two decades on these territories where our people have resided for thousands of years. El Movimiento (or La Causa) was rooted to a degree in Marxist-oriented theory (despite the strong ties activists felt to their Catholic upbringings) because it offered some response to our oppression under capitalism. Socialist and Communist theories, which were based on late nineteenth-century ideas about the imminent mass industrialization of society, did not foresee the high technology world of the late twentieth century—one hundred years later—or fully consider the implications of race, gender, and sexual-preference differences on that world. Wealth accumulation no longer simply stays within the genteel class but our aristocracy now includes athletes, rock stars, and Hollywood celebrities.

The early feminista, as the Chicana feminist referred to herself then, had been actively fighting against her socioeconomic subjugation as a Chicana and as a woman since 1968, the same year the Chicano movement was announced. I am aware that there have been Chicana activists throughout U.S. history, but I am using as a date of departure an era in which women consciously referred to themselves as *feministas*.

An analysis of the social status of la Chicana was already under way by early feministas, who maintained that racism, sexism, and sexist racism were the mechanisms that socially and economically oppressed them. But, for reasons explained here, they were virtually censored. The early history of la feminista was documented in a paper entitled "La Feminista," by Anna Nieto Gómez, published in *Encuentro Feminil: The First Chicana Feminist Journal*, which may now be considered, both article and journal, archival material.[6]

The early feminista who actively participated in the woman's movement had to educate white feminist groups on their political, cultural, and philosophical differences. Issues that specifically concerned the feminista of that period were directly related to her status as a non-Anglo, culturally different, often Spanish-speaking woman of lower income. Early white feminism compared sexism (as experienced by white middle-class women) to the racism that African Americans are subjected to. But African American feminists, such as those of the Rio Combahee Collective,[7] pointed out that this was not only an inaccurate comparison but revealed an inherent racist attitude on the part of white feminists who did not understand what it was to be a woman *and* black in America.

By the same token, brown women were forced into a position in which we had to point out similar differences as well as continuously struggle against a prevalent condescension on the part of white middle-class women toward women of color, poor women, and women whose first language is Spanish and whose culture is not mainstream American. *This Bridge Called My Back*, first published in 1981, as well as other texts by feminists of color that followed serve as excellent testimonies on these issues and the experiences of feminists of color in the 1970s.

At the same time, according to Nieto Gómez, feministas were labeled as *vendidas* (sellouts) by activists within La Causa. Such criticism came not solely from men but also from women, whom Nieto Gómez calls Loyalists. These Chicanas believed that racism, not sexism, was the greater battle. Moreover, the Loyalists distrusted any movement led by any sector of white society. The early white women's movement saw its battle based on sex and gender, and did not take into account the race and class differences of women of color. The Loyalists had some reason to feel reluctant and cynical toward an ideology and organizing effort that at best was condescending toward them. Loyalists told the feministas that they should be fighting such hard-hitting community problems as police brutality, Vietnam, and La Huelga, the United Farm Workers labor strike. But white female intellectuals were largely unaware of these issues. While the Chicana resided in a First World Nation, indeed the most powerful nation at that time, she was part of a historically colonized people.

I am referring to the approximate period between 1968 through the 1970s. However, more than twenty years later, the Chicana—that is, a brown woman of Mexican descent with political consciousness, residing in the United States—is still participating in the struggle for recognition and respect from white dominant society. Residing throughout her life in a society that systematically intentionally or out of ignorance marginalizes her existence, often stereotypes her when she does "appear," suddenly represented (for example, by mass media or government sources), and perhaps more importantly, relegates her economic status to among the lowest paid according to the U.S. Census Bureau, the Chicana continues to be a countryless woman. She is—I am, we are—not considered to be, except marginally and stereotypically, U.S. citizens.

Nevertheless, according to las feministas, feminism was "a very dynamic aspect of the Chicana's heritage and not at all foreign to her nature."[8] Contrary to ethnographic data that portray Chicanas as submissive followers who are solely designated to preserve the culture, the feminista did not see herself or other women of her culture as such. While the feminist dialogue remained among the activists in el Movimiento, one sees in Encuentro Feminil that there indeed existed a solid initiative toward Chicana feminist thought, that is, recognition of sexism as a primary issue, as early as the late 1960s. Clarifying the differences between the needs of the Anglo feminist and the feminista was part of the early feminista's task.

And if the focus of the Chicano male-dominated movement with regard to women had to do with family issues, the feminista zeroed in on the very core of what those issues meant. For instance, the feministas believed that women would make use of birth control and abortion clinics if in fact they felt safe going for these services; that is, if they were community-controlled. Birth control and abortion are pertinent issues for all women, but they were particularly significant to the Chicana, who had always been at the mercy of Anglo-controlled institutions and policies.

Non-consenting sterilizations of women—poor white, Spanish-speaking, welfare recipients, poor women of color, women in prison among them—during the 1970s were being conducted and sponsored by the U.S. government. One third of the female population of Puerto Rico was sterilized during that period.[9] The case of ten Chicanas (Madrigal v. Quilligan) against the Los Angeles County Hospital who were sterilized without their consent led to activism demanding release of the Health, Education and Welfare (HEW) guidelines for sterilizations. During that period, HEW was financing up to 100,000 sterilizations a year.[10]

The feminista also wanted a bicultural and bilingual system of child care that would validate their children's culture and perhaps ward off an inferiority complex before they had a chance to start public school; traditionally, monolingual and anglocentric schools had alienated children, causing them great psychological damage.[11]

The early feminista understood the erroneous conceptions of the white woman's movement which equated sexism to racism because she was experiencing its compounding effects in her daily life. The feministas were fighting against being a "minority" in the labor market. According to Nieto Gómez, more Anglo women had jobs than did women of color. We must keep in mind that most women of color in this country have always needed employment to maintain even a level of subsistence for their families.

According to the 1991 U.S. Department of Commerce Census Bureau Report, income figures for 1989 show that "Hispanic" women are still among the lowest paid workers in the United States, earning less than African American women:

Weekly Income

Hispanic women	$269.00
Black women	301.00
White women	334.00
Hispanic men	315.00
Black men	348.00
All other women	361.00

The mestiza still ranks in the labor force among the least valued in this country. In Susan Faludi's best-selling *Backlash*, which focuses on the media's backlash against the white feminist movement, the only noteworthy observation of women of color refers to our economic status in the 1980s. Faludi states that overall income did not increase for the African American woman and for the Hispanic woman, it actually got worse.

We need not look very far back or for very long to see that we have been marginalized in every sense of the word by U.S. society. But an understanding of the U.S. economic system and its relationship to Mexico is essential in order that we may understand our inescapable role as a productive/reproductive entity within U.S./Mexican society for the past two hundred years.

The transnational labor force into which most of us are born was created out of Mexico's neocolonialist relationship to the United States.[12] Throughout the history of the United States, Mexicans have served as a labor reserve controlled by U.S. policy. Mexico encourages the emigration of this labor force to alleviate its own depressed economy, and the

United States all too willingly consumes this labor without giving it the benefits enjoyed by U.S. residents.

Contrary to the U.S. ideological claim which insists that all immigrants (which by legislature and action meant European) pay their dues before being able to participate fully in its melting pot economy, the underpaid Mexican worker is crucial to the survival of the profit-based U.S. system. The maquiladoras illustrate this point.[13]

Since the late sixties, U.S. production has undergone a transfer of manufacturing to less industrialized nations, such as Mexico.[14] The U.S.-Mexican border has been an appealing site for such assembly operations. Unskilled women pressed by dire economic necessity serve as a reserve for these industries. A continuing influx of labor from the interior of Mexico provides competition and keeps wages at a base minimum. Daily wage for a maquiladora *rose* to a mere $3.50 per day in 1988.[15] An unofficial border source told me that that figure had risen to $3.75 per day in 1992. The outrageously low wages for working in dangerous and unregulated conditions are among the strongest arguments against the free trade agreements between United States, Mexico, and Canada.

The cultural and religious beliefs which maintain that most Latinas on either side of the border are (and should be) dependent on their men for economic survival are not only unrealistic; evidence shows they do not reflect reality. On this side of the border, according to the 1987 Department of Labor Report, 1 million "Hispanic" households were headed by women. Their average income was $337.00 per week. Fifty-two percent of these households headed by women survive below poverty level.

Any woman without the major support of the father of her children and who has no other resources must, in order to survive, commodify her labor. Even most Chicano/Latino men do not earn enough to support their families; their wives must go outside the home to earn an income (or bring it home in the form of piecework). Furthermore, statistics show that many mothers do not live with the father of their children and do not receive any kind of financial assistance from him.

The majority of the populace, on either side of the border, in fact, is not actively devoted to real social change. That sense of inferiority, as when two people were confronted with their mexicanidad on the streets of downtown Chicago, permeates most Chicanas' self-perceptions. Lack of *conscientización* is what makes the maquiladora an ideal worker for the semi-legal, exploitative operations of multinational factory production.

At an early age we learn that our race is undesirable. Because of possible rejection, some of us may go to any length to deny our background.

But one cannot cruelly judge such women who have resorted to negation of their own heritage; constant rejection has accosted us since childhood. Certain women indeed had contact early on in their lives with Mexico and acquired enough identification with its diverse culture and traditions to battle against the attempts of white, middle-class society to usurp all its citizens into an abstract culture obsessed with material gain.

But many women born in the United States or brought here during childhood have little connection with the country of our ancestors. The umbilical cord was severed before we could develop the intellectual and emotional link to Mexico, to the astonishing accomplishments of its indigenous past, to its own philosophical and spiritual nature so much at odds with that of the WASP. Instead, we flounder between invisibility and a tacit hope that we may be accepted here and awarded the benefits of acculturation.

Looking different—that is, not being white nor black but something in between in a society that has historically acknowledged only a black/white racial schism—is cause for great anxiety. Our internalized racism causes us to boast of our light coloring, if indeed we have it, or imagine it. We hope for light-skinned children and brag no end of those infants who happen to be born *güeros,* white-looking; we are downright ecstatic if they have light-colored eyes and hair. We sometimes tragically reject those children who are dark.

On the subject of color and internal conflicts there are also those who, despite identification with Latino heritage, are light-skinned because of their dominating European genes or because one parent is white. For some this may be an added reason for internalizing racism, particularly when young (since it is difficult to explain the world to yourself when you are growing up). But for others, while their *güero* coloring may cause them to experience less racial tension in broad society, it may cause tension for a variety of reasons in their home, chosen communities, and when politically active against racism.

Let us consider for a moment a woman who does not necessarily desire marriage or bearing children, and works instead to attain a higher standard of living for herself. She must still interact with and quite often be subordinate to white people, and occasionally African Americans. I do not want to elaborate on the dynamics of her relationships with African Americans since it is understood here that institutionalized racism has not allowed either race to have real domination over the other. My own experience has been one of cultural difference rather than a racial one since there are also "black hispanos." But I will note that she will in all likelihood still feel "foreign" with African Americans who have an acknowledged history in the United States. Because of slavery, white people *know* why African Americans are here. They also *know* why Native Americans are here, yet they *assume* mestizos have all migrated here for economic gain as their own people did.

Compounding our anxiety over our foreignlike identity in the United States is the fact that Mexican Americans are also not generally accepted in Mexico. We are derogatorily considered *pochos,* American Mexicans who are either among the traitors or trash of Mexico because we, or previous generations, made the United States home. Unlike the experiences that many African Americans have had in "returning" and being welcomed in Africa, many U.S.-born mestizo/as have found themselves more unwelcomed by mexicanos than white gringos.[16]

Aside from skin color, language can add to the trauma of the Chicana's schizophrenic existence. She was educated in English and learned it is the only acceptable language in society, but Spanish was the language of her childhood, family, and community. She may not be able to rid herself of an accent; society has denigrated her first language. By the same token, women may also become anxious and self-conscious in later years if they have no or little facility in Spanish. They may feel that they had been forced to forfeit an important part of their personal identity and still never found acceptability by white society.

Race, ethnicity, and language are important factors for women who aspire to a decent standard of living in our anglocentric, xenophobic society. Gender compounds their social dilemma and determines the very nature of their lifestyle regardless of the ability to overcome all other obstacles set against them.

Feminism at its simplest has not ever been solely a political struggle for women's rights, that is, equal pay for equal work. The early feminista's initial attempts at placing women-related issues at the forefront were once viewed with suspicion by Marxist-oriented activists as the Woman Question was seen to be separate from or less significant than race and class issues by most activists, and along with gay issues, even thought to be an indication of betrayal to La Causa. Along those lines, in the 1990s, while issues of sexuality have come to the forefront—most recently with the national debate of permitting gays in the military—there remains a strong heterosexist bias among Chicano/Hispanic/Latino-based organizations and our varying communities.

With the tenacious insistence at integrating a feminist perspective to their political *conscientización* as Chicanas, feminist *activistas,* and intellectuals are in the process of developing what I call Xicanisma. On a pragmatic level, the basic premise of Xicanisma is to reconsider behavior long seen as inherent in the Mexic Amerindian woman's character, such as patience, perseverance, industriousness, loyalty to one's clan, and commitment to our children. Contrary to those not cognizant of what feminism is, we do not reject these virtues. We may not always welcome the taxing responsibility that comes with our roles as Chicanas. We've witnessed what strain and limitations they often placed on our mothers and other relatives. But these traits often seen as negative and oppressive to our growth as women, as well as having been translated as equal to being a drone for white society and its industrial interests, may be considered strengths. Simultaneously, as we redefine (not categorically reject) our roles within our families, communities at large, and white dominant society, our Xicanisma helps us to be self-confident and assertive in pursuing our needs and desires.

As brown-skinned females, often bilingual but not from a Spanish-speaking country (not a Mexican citizen yet generally considered not really American), frequently discouraged in numerous ways from pursuing formal education, usually with limited economic means, and therefore made to compete in a racist and sexist lower-skilled work force, we continue to be rendered invisible by society except as a stereotype. The U.S. women's movement, which in fact began long before the civil rights movement and the ensuing Chicano movement, is now incorporating a more expansive vision, which includes the unique perceptions and experiences of all peoples heretofore excluded from the democratic promise of the United States. Until we are all represented, respected, and protected by society and the laws that govern it, the status of the Chicana will remain that of a countryless woman.

■ ■ ▪

NOTES

1. As a young poet in 1974, I wrote something similar to this in "Our Tongue Was Nahuatl," in *New Worlds of Literature*, ed. J. Beaty and J. P. Hunter (New York: W.W. Norton, 1989).

2. T. R. Fehrenbach, *Fire and Blood: A History of Mexico* (New York: Bonanza Books, 1973), p. 234.

3. Fehrenbach, *Fire and Blood*, pp. 238 and 162.

4. Hispanic Link Weekly Report, Nov. 6, 1989.

5. Please refer to John Glubb, *A Short History of the Arab Peoples* (New York: Dorset Press, 1969).

6. *Encuentro Femenil: The First Chicana Feminist Journal* 1, no. 2 (1974): I can't recall how, but it seems fortuitously for me, this document came into my hands in Chicago around this time.

7. Please read their essay in *This Bridge Called My Back: Writings by Radical Women of*

Color, edited by Cherríe Moraga and Gloria Anzaldúa (Watertown, MA: Persephone Press, 1981).

8. Anna Nieto-Gomez, "La Feminista," *Encuentro Feminil: The First Chicana Feminist Journal* 1, no. 2 (1974): 38.

9. See Angela Davis, *Women, Culture and Politics* (New York: Random House, 1989).

10. Thomas Shapiro, *Population Control Politics: Women, Sterilization and Reproductive Choice* (Philadelphia: Temple University Press, 1985), pp. 91–93.

11. I am reminded of two stories I have heard from U.S.-born Spanish-speaking women who went to public schools in the United States. One was sent with her sister, upon starting school, to the class for the hearing impaired. Another, attending a school with a majority Chicano population, was sent to "girls' math" class. For further reading on the education of Chicanos please refer to Fernando Penalosa's *Chicano Linguistics*.

12. Marlene Dixon, "Chicanas and Mexicanas in a Transnational Working Class," in *The Future of Women* (San Francisco: Synthesis Publications, 1980).

13. Susan Tiano, "Maquiladoras, Women's Work, and Unemployment in Northern Mexico," *Aztlan* 15, no. 2 (1984): 341–78.

14. William C. Gruben, *Economic Review*, January 1990.

15. Figure quoted as of December 1988 by International Trade and Finance Association, Laredo State University, TX. I will also note that maquiladoras suffer exposure to deadly chemicals due to lack of health regulations. Please refer to "The Maquiladoras and Toxics: The Hidden Costs of Production South of the Border" by Leslie Kochan, published in a report by the AFL-CIO, 815 Sixteenth Street, N.W., Washington, DC, 20006.

16. Michael Jackson being crowned king in Africa comes to mind.

Where's the Revolution?

■ ■ ■

BARBARA SMITH

When I came out in Boston in the mid-1970s, I had no way of knowing that the lesbian and gay movement I was discovering was in many ways unique. As a new lesbian I had nothing to compare it with, and there was also nothing to compare it with in history. Stonewall had happened only six years before and the militance, irreverence, and joy of those early days were still very much apparent.

As a black woman who became politically active in the civil rights movement during high school and then in black student organizing and the anti-Vietnam War movement as the sixties continued, it seemed only natural that being oppressed as a lesbian would elicit the same militant collective response to the status quo that my other oppressions did. Boston's lesbian and gay movement came of age in the context of student activism, a visible counterculture, a relatively organized left, and a vibrant women's movement. The city had always had its own particularly violent brand of racism and had become even more polarized because of the crisis over school busing. All of these overlapping influences strengthened the gay and lesbian movement, as well as the political understandings of lesbian and gay activists.

Objectively, being out and politically active in the seventies was about as far from the mainstream as one could get. The system did not embrace us, nor did we want it to. We also got precious little support from people who were supposed to be progressive. The white sectarian left defined homosexuality as a "bourgeois aberration" that would disappear when capitalism did. Less doctrinaire leftists were also homophobic even if they offered a different set of excuses. Black power activists and black national-ists generally viewed lesbians and gay men as anathema—white-minded traitors to the race. Although the women's movement was the one place where out lesbians were permitted to do political work, its conservative elements still tried to dissociate themselves from the "lavender menace."

Because I came out in the context of black liberation, women's libera-tion, and—most significantly—the newly emerging black feminist move-ment that I was helping to build, I worked from the assumption that all of the "isms" were connected. It was simply not possible for any oppressed people, including lesbians and gay men, to achieve freedom under this system. Police dogs, cattle prods, firehoses, poverty, urban insurrections, the Vietnam War, the assassinations, Kent State, unchecked violence against women, the self-immolation of the closet, and the emotional and often physical violence experienced by those of us who dared leave it made the contradictions crystal clear. Nobody sane would want any part of the established order. It was the system—white supremacist, misogy-nistic, capitalist, and homophobic—that had made our lives so hard to begin with. We wanted something entirely new. Our movement was called lesbian and gay *liberation,* and more than a few of us, especially women and people of color, were working for a *revolution.*

Revolution seems like a largely irrelevant concept to the gay movement of the nineties. The liberation politics of the earlier era, which relied upon radical grass-roots strategies to eradicate oppression, have been largely replaced by an assimilationist "civil rights" agenda. The most visible elements of the movement have put their faith almost exclusively in electoral and legislative initiatives, bolstered by mainstream media cov-erage to alleviate *discrimination.* When the word "radical" is used at all, it means confrontational, "in your face" tactics, not strategic organizing aimed at the roots of oppression.

Unlike the early lesbian and gay movement, which had both ideologi-cal and practical links to the left, black activism and feminism, today's "queer" politicos seem to operate in a historical and ideological vacuum. "Queer" activists focus on "queer" issues, and racism, sexual oppression, and economic exploitation do not qualify, despite the fact that the majority of "queers" are people of color, female or working class. When other oppressions or movements are cited, it's to build a parallel case for the validity of lesbian and gay rights or to expedite alliances with mainstream political organizations. Building unified, ongoing coalitions that challenge the system and ultimately prepare a way for revolutionary change simply isn't what "queer" activists have in mind.

When lesbians and gay men of color urge the gay leadership to make connections between heterosexism and issues like police brutality, racial violence, homelessness, reproductive freedom, and violence against women and children, the standard dismissive response is, "Those are not our issues." At a time when the gay movement is under unprecedented public scrutiny, lesbians and gay men of color and others committed to antiracist organizing are asking: Does the gay and lesbian movement want to create a just society for everyone? Or does it only want to eradicate the last little glitch that makes life difficult for privileged (white male) queers?

The April 25, 1993, March on Washington, despite its historical importance, offers some unsettling answers. Two comments that I've heard repeatedly since the march are that it seemed more like a parade than a political demonstration and that the overall image of the hundreds of thousands of participants was overwhelmingly Middle American, that is, white and conventional. The identifiably queer—the drag queens, leather people, radical fairies, dykes on bikes, etc.—were definitely in the minority, as were people of color, who will never be Middle American no matter what kind of drag we put on or take off.

A friend from Boston commented that the weekend in Washington felt like being in a "blizzard." I knew what she meant. Despite the fact that large numbers of lesbians and gay men of color were present (perhaps even more than at the 1987 march), our impact upon the proceedings did not feel nearly as strong as it did six years ago. The bureaucratic nineties concept of "diversity," with its superficial goal of assuring that all the colors in the crayon box are visible, was very much the strategy of the day. Filling slots with people of color or women does not necessarily affect the politics of a movement if our participation does not change the agenda, that is, if we are not actually permitted to lead.

I had had my own doubts about attending the April march. Although I went to the first march in 1979 and was one of the eight major speakers at the 1987 march, I didn't make up my mind to go to this one until a few weeks before it happened. It felt painful to be so alienated from the gay movement that I wasn't even sure I wanted to be there; my feelings of being an outsider had been growing for some time.

I remember receiving a piece of fund-raising direct mail from the magazine *Outlook* in 1988 with the phrase "tacky but we'll take it" written next to the lowest potential contribution of $25. Since $25 is a lot more than I can give at any one time to the groups I support, I decided I might as well send my $5 somewhere else. In 1990 I read Queer Nation's manifesto, "I Hate Straights," in *Outweek* and wrote a letter to the editor suggesting that if queers of color followed its political lead, we would soon be issuing a statement titled, "I Hate Whiteys," including white queers of European origin. Since that time I've heard very little public criticism of the narrowness of lesbian and gay nationalism. No one would guess from recent stories about wealthy and "powerful" white lesbians on TV and in slick magazines that women earn 69 cents on the dollar compared with men and that black women earn even less.

These examples are directly connected to assumptions about race and class privilege. In fact, it's gay white men's racial, gender, and class privileges, as well as the vast numbers of them who identify with the system rather than distrust it, that have made the politics of the current gay movement so different from those of other identity-based movements for social and political change. In the seventies, progressive movements— especially feminism—positively influenced and inspired lesbians' and gays' visions of struggle. Since the eighties, as AIDS has helped to raise consciousness about gay issues in some quarters of the establishment, and as some battles against homophobia have been won, the movement has positioned itself more and more within the mainstream political arena. Clinton's courting of the gay vote (at the same time as he did everything possible to distance himself from the African American community) has also been a crucial factor in convincing the national gay and lesbian leadership that a place at the ruling class's table is just what they've been waiting for. Of course, the people left out of this new gay political equation of mainstream acceptance, power, and wealth are lesbians and gay men of color.

Our outsider status in the new queer movement is made even more untenable because supposedly progressive heterosexuals of all races do so little to support lesbian and gay freedom. Although homophobia may be mentioned when heterosexual leftists make lists of oppressions, they do virtually no risk-taking work to connect with our movement or to challenge attacks against lesbians and gays who live in their midst. Many straight activists whose politics are otherwise righteous simply refuse to acknowledge how dangerous heterosexism is, and that they have any responsibility to end it. Lesbians and gays working in straight political contexts are often expected to remain closeted so as not to diminish their own "credibility" or that of their groups. With so many heterosexuals studiously avoiding opportunities to become enlightened about lesbian and gay culture and struggle, it's not surprising that nearly twenty-five years after Stonewall so few heterosexuals get it. Given how well organized the Christian right is, and that one of its favorite tactics is pitting various oppressed groups against one another, it is past time for straight and gay activists to link issues and work together with respect.

The issue of access to the military embodies the current gay movement's inability to frame an issue in such a way that it brings various groups together instead of alienating them, as has happened with segments of the black community. It also reveals a gay political agenda that is not merely moderate but conservative. As long as a military exists, it should be open to everyone regardless of sexual orientation, especially since it represents job and training opportunities for poor and working-class youth who are disproportionately people of color. But given the U.S. military's role as the world's police force, which implements imperialist foreign policies and murders those who stand in its way (e.g., the estimated quarter of a million people, mostly civilians, who died in Iraq as a result of the Gulf War), a progressive lesbian and gay movement would at least consider the political implications of frantically organizing to get into the mercenary wing of the military-industrial complex. A radical lesbian and gay movement would of course be working to dismantle the military completely.

Many people of color (Colin Powell notwithstanding) understand all too well the paradox of our being sent to Third World countries to put down rebellions that are usually the efforts of indigenous populations to rule themselves. The paradox is even more wrenching when U.S. troops are sent to quell "unrest" in internal colonies like south-central Los Angeles. Thankfully, there were some pockets of dissent at the April march, expressed in slogans like "Lift the Ban—Ban the Military" and "Homosexual, Not Homicidal—Fuck the Military." Yet it seemingly has not occurred to movement leaders that there are lesbians and gays who have actively opposed the Gulf War, the Vietnam War, military intervention in Central America, and apartheid in South Africa. We need a nuanced and principled politics that fights discrimination and at the same time criticizes U.S. militarism and its negative effect on social justice and world peace.

The movement that I discovered when I came out was far from perfect. It was at times infuriatingly racist, sexist, and elitist, but also not nearly so monolithic. There was at least ideological room to point out failings, and a variety of allies willing to listen who wanted to build something better.

I think that homosexuality embodies an innately radical critique of the traditional nuclear family, whose political function has been to constrict the sexual expression and gender roles of all its members, especially women, lesbians, and gays. Being in structural opposition to the status quo because of one's identity, however, is quite different from being consciously and actively opposed to the status quo because one is a radical and understands how the system works.

It was talking to radical lesbians and gay men that finally made me decide to go to the April 25 march. Earlier in the month, I attended an extraordinary conference on the lesbian and gay left in Delray Beach, Florida. The planners had made a genuine commitment to racial and gender parity; 70 percent of the participants were people of color and 70 percent were women. They were also committed to supporting the leadership of people of color and lesbians—especially lesbians of color—which is almost never done outside of our own autonomous groupings. The conference felt like a homecoming. I got to spend time with people I'd worked with twenty years before in Boston as well as with younger activists from across the country.

What made the weekend so successful, aside from the humor, gossip, caring, and hot discussions about sex and politics, was the huge relief I felt at not being expected to cut off parts of myself that are as integral to who I am as my sexual orientation as the price for participating in lesbian and gay organizing. Whatever concerns were raised, discussions were never silenced by the remark, "But that's not our issue." Women and men, people of color and whites, all agreed that there desperately needs to be a visible alternative to the cut-and-dried, business-as-usual agenda of the gay political mainstream. Their energy and vision, as well as the astuteness and tenacity of radical lesbians and gays I encounter all over the country, convince me that a different way is possible.

If the gay movement ultimately wants to make a real difference, as opposed to settling for handouts, it must consider creating a multi-issue revolutionary agenda. This is not about political correctness, it's about winning. As black lesbian poet and warrior Audre Lorde insisted, "The master's tools will never dismantle the master's house." Gay *rights* are not enough for me, and I doubt that they're enough for most of us. Frankly, I want the same thing now that I did thirty years ago when I joined the civil rights movement and twenty years ago when I joined the women's movement, came out, and felt more alive than I ever dreamed possible: Freedom.

Rashomon Road:
On the Tao to San Diego

■ ■ ■

FRANK CHIN

My first novel is in the bookstores. My name and here and there my picture pops up in newspaper book reviews and Asian American weeklies.
"Are you famous?" Sam asks.

What is fame to a five-year-old kid? How am I, the almighty daddy-
isimo, to explain it to my son? Someday he's going to leave home—for
college, or to go to war, or take a job, or marry a woman out of state or
on the moon. If he grows up thinking I'm famous, he might not want to
go. And when the time comes for Sam to set off to fight the monsters on
his own, as it came for all the little boys in all the stories I told him, even
the little boy who was one-inch tall when the old couple found him, and
when he was five or six inches tall and it was time for him to take to the
river in a rice bowl for a boat, I want Sam to go. Short, skinny, fat, deaf,
dumb, or blind, when it's time for him to go, I want him to go. Till that
time, I can do my best to see he doesn't hit the road stupid.

I'm not famous. Yellow writers who get famous are afraid of offending
whites who buy their books and make them famous. They're overawed
by whites and their acceptance by whites. My first play was about to open

in New York. My name, the name of my play, the name of the theater about to open it were in the New York papers. Betty Lee Sung, the famous Chinese American author of the moment with her book of Christian white racist stereotypes cast in sociological jargon, *Mountain of Gold*, called me at the theater. More a preacher than scientist or teacher, she pounds away at the moral necessity for Chinese to lose their culture and *acculturate,* so they can be *accepted by the dominant society.* And as we are accepted, so shall we be *absorbed,* and once all absorbed we shall be *assimilated,* meaning racially extinct. American at last!

At the time she wrote, the majority of Chinese Americans alive were American-born. The old immigrants were very old or dead. The Gentlemen's Agreement of 1925 combined with the Chinese Exclusion Act to limit the number of Chinese entering the United States from any part of the world to 105. The number of new immigrants was insignificant. The white racist laws designed to accomplish the extinction of the yellow races in America made it possible for we Chinese Americans born after 1925 to become the adult majority by the seventies. To the generations of American-born, the acculturated Betty Lee Sung mounts the pulpit of the church of acceptance, absorption, and assimilation, and tells us to shut up and lie low, playing the role of the stereotypes and disappear from view until that great day of assimilation:

"Much to their credit, the Chinese view prejudice with a very healthy attitude. They were never overly bitter. They have gone into occupations which command respect and which lessen conflict from competition. The Chinese are not concentrated entirely in one section of the country. More dispersion away from the vortexes of San Francisco and New York should be encouraged. This ought to be the long-range goal of the Chinese because distribution reduces the degree of invisibility."

She's so positive and cheerful about showing her contempt for everything Chinese. The morality of despising the Chinese and cherishing the stereotype in the name of white acceptance got her published by a big publisher, and the book made her the queen of the Asian American Studies university programs and departments emerging around the country in the late sixties and early seventies.

The stage manager called me out of a rehearsal to take a phone call from Betty Lee Sung. She congratulated me on succeeding in getting a play mounted in New York, and said she expected I would now stop saying terrible things about her book, because "you're on my side now."

"Which side is that?" I asked.

"The Americans have accepted you. You are now in the mainstream."

"Huh?"

"We're famous."

I don't want to be famous, I tell Sam.

I'm well known enough among the American yellows to make the famous nervous and think I want their fame for myself. I don't want to be famous. Is fame the only reason yellows write in America? To be famous is to be TV, even if you're not on TV. The only way Asian Americans become famous is by ornamenting white fantasy. The only way yellows get to be on TV is putting their faces and bodies to Charlie Chan–Fu Manchu, Gunga Din cute, sissy, sexually repulsive men, and the sexually and personally unfulfilled pathological white supremacist women with an infinite number of weird, cute, and strange ways of saying, "Hey, sailor, wanna date?" over and over and over.

Grow up with the movies and TV as your storyteller and you can't blame a kid growing up believing yellow men are so unmanly they can't even play themselves in the movies. Television and Hollywood prove the point by giving us movies with Asian American actors playing the same Imperial Japanese naval officers; Japanese actors like Toshiro Mifune play in *Tora! Tora! Tora!*, the Hollywood-Japanese co-production that recreated the Japanese surprise attack on Pearl Harbor. Compare an admiral played by Toshiro Mifune to the same admiral played by James Shigeta. Case closed: Asian American men not only can't cut the mustard, they can't even lick the jar. That's Hollywood. That's TV. That's the most famous Asian Americans in the world. But TV is our friend. There are exceptions.

The actor George Takei does not play Sulu the helmsman of the *Starship Enterprise* as the stereotypical yellow kissass sissy, nor, thanks to genre fantasy science fiction, as either an Asian or American creature. It's not for nothing science fiction is called escapist. George Takei along with Pat Morita, of *Karate Kid* fame, and Mako, the definitive Hollywood Asian heavy, were exceptional among Asian American actors for lending their names to the Japanese American campaign to redress the constitutional damages that the Nikkei—people of Japanese ancestry—suffered in the American concentration camps of World War II. Other Asian American actors begged off. Their acting careers, their standing in the industry, their *fame* demanded they avoid controversy and stand for no greater cause than acceptance by the industry. Echoing the Betty Lee Sung tactic of not being overly bitter about racial prejudice, the actors in my plays with TV credits, and writers with book contracts, tell me they learned from the blacks that "anger doesn't work," as if blacks marched, went to court, went to jail, went to church, got out the vote to be famous and seen on TV. In the chicken-hearted world of Asian American Hollywood, George Takei, Pat Morita, and Mako were brave men, indeed.

Sam's seen him on *Star Trek* and knows he's famous. I can talk about George as if I know him, because I do.

He played the lead in a TV production of my second play, so he didn't bolt and run off with his dark glasses on when Sam and I happened on him in Little Tokyo, on a bright gray L.A. day. I introduced him to Sam. George Takei was gracious, famous, and leery of me. "That's the difference between being famous and well known," I told Sam. "He has to be gracious and bright. I can be sharp and nasty."

It was the first two weeks of the Chinese New Year. There were friends and bookstores up and down I–5 waiting for me to visit and read. It seemed like a good time to introduce Sam to the road. The Tao that Westerners found so mystical was just "the way," as in "path," as in "road." The Tao was nothing more and nothing less than the road. Jack Kerouac wrote about the road. His road. Robert Frost wrote about the Road Not Taken. Lao Tzu's notes on the road are no more and no less mystical than Kerouac or Frost or Paul Bowles or the AAA guide or any other book on the road. Everybody's road is different. The history of the Chinese in California is written in miles of old mining roads, and the railroad. My main road was Interstate 5, built along the Southern Pacific, and Union Pacific Railroad's mainline and old U.S. 99 from Bellingham, Washington, to San Diego, California. A Chinatown, a Japan Town, the remains and reminders of World War II concentration camps that interned Americans of Japanese ancestry in every town. Redbrick and granite stone buildings with cast-iron facades all the way. Pioneer Courthouse Square in Seattle, Old Town in Portland, the Gaslamp District in San Diego. All the windows of all the hotel rooms full of retired old seamen and railroaders in all these towns, around Christmas time, have the shades drawn up to little Christmas displays of lights and trees and plastic candy canes and snowmen. When it rains and the streets are wet and the brick and stone glow in the shadow of clouds, these places are beautiful, and I enjoy standing around and watching, and daydreaming.

The road was going to be an adventure with father and son discovering the deserts, valleys, mountains, volcanoes, birds, cities, and friends—especially the friends, some people I would like to take on the stature of heroes in Sam's memories, on I–5, the road. Asian American writers born and raised in America without feeling split between two incompatible cultures. That's the orphan in the boat, that's Momotaro, and the boy born from a lotus, and Moses. One reason we friends became friends was that the Asian American identity crisis didn't exist for us. We knew Chinese or Japanese culture and knew white American culture, and knew we were not both, nor were we the best of the East and the best of the West. We knew we were neither. Being neither did not mean we contemptuously ridiculed and stereotyped every culture we were not. We did not believe more than a century after the arrival and settling of our people that we, our generation, was the first to produce writers like us. We simply did not believe our people were that stupid for that long. The reason no one knew anything about Asian American literature was not that there was nothing to know. No one had bothered to look for Asian American writing before us.

For us, the adventure in Asian American writing was not just in the writing but in the study, the discovery, the history.

We had all published in small literary journals. Jeff Chan was teaching Asian American Studies at San Francisco State and had read my work when he found me hacking for a TV station in Seattle. Jeff Chan got me together with Shawn Wong, a poet protégé of Kay Boyle. Shawn Wong and I found Lawson Inada while thumbing through a collection of Fresno poetry at Cody's Books in Berkeley. Inada was teaching in the English Department at Southern Oregon State College in Ashland, Oregon, land of the fantasy Shakespeare Festival. All four of us met for the first time in San Francisco, at a party for Ishmael Reed's new book, an anthology of writings by Americans of many American races, colors, and cultures. Ishmael Reed's personality, his curiosity, his appetite, his mind was a multicultural, international marketplace.

Lawson Inada became the first Japanese American to publish a volume of poetry with a big publisher, in 1971, and together we dug through used bookstores, libraries, garage sales, old Japanese American newspapers and Chinese American magazines looking for writers and writing.

We learned about the Asian American identity crisis by reading the soul-searching sections of thirties Charlie Chan mystery novels. From Earl Derr Biggers's novel, *The Chinese Parrot* (1926):

> "It overwhelms me with sadness to admit it," Charlie answered, "for he is of my own origin, my own race, as you know. But when I look into his eyes, I discover that a gulf like the heaving Pacific lies between us. Why? Because he, though among Caucasians many more years than I, still remains Chinese. As Chinese today as in the first moon of his existence. While—I bear the brand, the label, Americanized."

Chan bowed his head. "I traveled with the current," he said softly. "I was ambitious. I sought success. For what I have won, I paid the price. Am I then an American? No. Am I then a Chinese? Not in the eyes of Ah Sing." He paused for a moment, then continued: "But I have chosen my path, and I must follow it."

Biggers's Charlie Chan exists in a Christian-Hollywood universe. In the Christian universe, all individuals are born sinners. Translated into Hollywood, all individuals are born losers. Both ideas are alien to Asian moral thought. In the Asian universe, all individuals are born soldiers. In Jeffersonian American thought, all individuals are born legislators. Those who suffer the stereotype of the dual identity crisis and enjoy the benefits of writing it in Christian autobiographies, and playing it on the screen, are playing ignorant of both Asian and American culture.

The identity crisis was the monster of Asian fairy tale to whom corrupt parents sold their children for the benefits of the good life.

The grand historian of the Han Szuma Chien, who set the grammar of the mandate of heaven in Chinese writing, said that Confucius' great accomplishment was the restoration of knowledge that was lost, and recovery of ways that had been abandoned.

And we found the yellow writers our own people had cast off and condemned because their grammar or their portrayal of Asian American life might offend whites, and pose a threat to the dream of acculturation, white acceptance, absorption, and assimilation.

Toshio Mori, John Okada, and Louis Chu embarrassed the Chinese and Japanese Americans of the fifties who craved to be assimilated by and disappear into whiteness. In the seventies we brought them back, and with them, a little history. The young Nisei writers and thinkers found Toshio Mori embarrassing because of his sweet and wilfully ungrammatical English. The World War II vet John Okada was embarrassing to the Japanese Americans for casting a No No Boy and draft resister as the hero of his novel *No No Boy*. Louis Chu wrote *Eat a Bowl of Tea* in a kind of literary Chinese accent that embarrassed Chinese American English majors of the sixties.

John Okada of Seattle died in California, and Louis Chu died in New York before we found their work, reprinted it, and saw thousands of copies of John Okada's *No No Boy* and Louis Chu's *Eat a Bowl of Tea* sell and become the first of Asian America's lost literature to return and be recognized. At a time when Asian American Studies was inventing itself on university campuses up and down I-5, *No No Boy* and *Eat a Bowl of Tea* became the first classics of Asian American literature. Their children, now in their childish forties and fifties, still have never read their fathers' work. Blame the East-West identity crisis. But the identity crisis is fake, it's phony. It's a belief, not a fact. All they have to do to prove that the cause of their self-contempt is a fraud is read their fathers' work. But they can't do that.

Where was Toshio Mori? Was he still alive? No one had heard from him in over ten years. His stories were set in Oakland and El Cerrito. We started with the obvious, looked him up in the phone book, found a number, and called him up. Toshio Mori was still alive.

Toshio Mori's son read his father's work and still Toshio Mori and his volume of stories, *Yokohama, California*, was forgotten. No one had gone looking for him till we found him in El Cerrito. Now, we who found Okada and Chu and Mori have children and books of our own. Our kids have grown up reading Asian American writing, and now I'd like Sam to learn the lessons of the road these old writers have taught me. Along this road we too can be read and forgotten. That's the mandate of heaven. That's the Tao. That's the Rashomon of I-5.

My friends—artists, writers, musicians, booksellers up and down the road—are like the loners, orphans, failed scholars, and the Monkey King who travel the road of life in the fairy tales. Being a stranger, an outcast, an outlaw, an immigrant does not make the boy born out of a peach, or Br'er Rabbit, a victim or a criminal. I tell Sam the stories from the heart of Asian and Western lit., the myth, folk and fairy tales of Asia, the Greeks, and Hollywood. If I don't, who will? The schools will teach him to feel incapacitated, inept, and morally constipated by the Asian American identity crisis, instead of teaching the stories Asian and American cultures tell their children while they're children.

So, before he can talk, I raise my boy Sam Chew Chin on a children's book version of *Momotaro*, published by Island Heritage of Hawaii. I like the pictures by George Suyenaga. They're well researched, well drawn, and dramatic. I show my baby the pictures and make sound effects to him, I point at the boy in the boat and say, "Momotaro," at the waves of the inland sea and make whooshing noises, point at the dog and bark at the pheasant, say "bird" and whistle, at the monkey say "monkey" and yip and whoop. Sam learns to whistle and whistles around the house before he learns to speak.

The peach is a boat, I tell him. In the story of the boy born inside a lotus, the lotus is a boat. Somebody, their mommy and daddy in another world, put their boys in the peach, in the flower, to escape the end of the world, the flood, the fire, the last war. The boat takes them to a world where the people have made a deal with monsters.

Life is war; we are all born soldiers. All behavior is tactics and strategy. All relationships are martial. Love is two warriors standing back to back fighting off the universe. That is as mystic as Asian culture gets; the rest is white Christian fantasy. Asia isn't mystic and static. It's martial and migrant. Not migratory, but migrant. Nah Jah and Momotaro and Monkey are orphans. They fit in exactly. They travel a lot. They cross borders.

The old couples who find the girl in the node of bamboo, the boy in the giant peach, the tiny boy inside the lotus in the new world promise to raise these children as their own. That promise is a military oath, a contract. In the course of the stories the oath will be challenged, and the adoptive parents will keep their word or break it.

In return for the monsters giving the people no flood, no famine, no drought, no disease, no crop failure, no tidal waves, no poverty, no crime, in short, the good life, the people give the monsters children. What do the monsters do with the children? They eat them. "This is a bad deal!" the boys say in their Chinese and Japanese stories.

"You don't understand politics, son," their parents say, but the boys insist on setting off to kill the monsters and free the children. Momotaro, the Japanese boy born out of a peach, goes with his parents' help. They keep their word. The Chinese Nah Jah's father, the commandant, sides with the monsters, ties his son up, and raises his sword to strike him down. Nah Jah breaks his bonds, snatches the sword out of his father's hand, says, "I give you back your flesh and blood," and cuts his own throat and dies. He turns into a lotus seed. A crane flies down from the mountaintop, picks up the seed, and carries it to the teacher on the mountain. The teacher plants the seed in his pond, out of the pond grows a new lotus, and out of the lotus is born a new Nah Jah with new powers and new weapons to fight the monsters. He has the power to sprout two extra heads and two extra sets of arms. With three heads and six arms he can fight in all directions at once, when he's surrounded. His new weapons include a red ribbon, hoops of heaven and earth, a tasseled spear, and fire-wheels under his feet to give him speed and flight.

The Japanese Momotaro instead of being reincarnated with new powers meets the dog. "Take me with you, Momotaro, and I'll help you fight the *oni*. Just give me a cookie," the dog says.

"No, I won't give you a cookie, but I'll share a cookie with you, dog."

Momotaro meets the Monkey and the Monkey says, "Take me with you, Momotaro, and I'll help you fight the *oni*. Just give me a cookie."

"No, I won't give you a whole cookie, but I'll share a cookie with you," Momotaro says, and splits a cookie and gives one half to the dog and eats the other half himself. The shared cookie is an oath of alliance.

Next he meets the bird. "Momotaro, take me with you, and I will help you fight the monsters, just give me a cookie."

"No, bird, but I will share a cookie with you," Momotaro says, and splits a cookie. The shared cookie is an oath of blood brotherhood. They are allies. Both boys kill the monsters and free the children. Momotaro and his allies go home and the people in this part of Japan have to keep their children and work for a living again.

Nah Jah, the boy born from a lotus, never goes home again. The man who had promised to raise him as his own broke his promise. Nah Jah is not the commandant's son. The commandant's son is dead. The moral of the stories: It is wrong to sell your children to monsters for the good life. The people who told these stories for a thousand years, even when the stories were banned, did not come to America to sell their children to monsters for the good life.

I hoped Sam would see that every stop we made on the road was like a trading post on the Congo River in a Discovery Channel documentary. The people who came out of the forest to trade by the river in the documentary might be at war with each other just out of sight, but here at the trading post they use a pidgin language of trade, a language of civil trade; they are here to do business, check each other's goods, and make a fair trade. Check your guns, your drugs, your prejudices and grudges at the door. All shootouts and fistfights off the premises. No exceptions.

The river in Africa was like Toshio Mori's Japanese American vision of America as a depot, and American Standard English as a pidgin language of trade in his short story "The Old Woman Who Makes Swell Doughnuts."

This modern Nisei story, published in the forties, appears to be a reminiscence of a childhood in a house in Oakland, near the Southern Pacific Railway passenger depot. In this house lived an old woman everyone in the neighborhood called "Momma." She deep-fried doughnuts and all the kids in the neighborhood liked the doughnuts so much they behaved with a natural civility and politeness in this house that shuddered whenever a Southern Pacific train moved by shifting its weight from one rail to another. William Saroyan, the Armenian American playwright and novelist who refused the Pulitzer Prize, both admired Mori's writing and flunked him in English. His Japanese American Nisei contemporaries were embarrassed by both Mori's English and his wistful, childish sentimentality.

★   ★   ★

In all the years since 1949 when Mori had published his collection of stories *Yokohama, California*, we were the first people to come looking for
him. And only now, years after he's died, do we discover that deep down
inside Mori's story lives a Japanese fairy tale. "The Woman Who Makes
Swell Doughnuts" is deeper, richer, more eloquent for being modeled on
a traditional Japanese story. "The Old Woman and Her Dumpling" is a
folk vision of civility born of the necessities of the road. I tell Sam the
story, on the road.

Old Japan: An old woman makes and sells dumplings at a crossroads
marketplace. One of her dumplings drops and rolls. She chases it down
the road. It rolls into a hole onto a road in another world and keeps on
rolling. A stone Jizo, the god of travelers and children who died in mis-
carriages, tries to hide the Old Woman from the demons known as *oni*.
The *oni* find her, take her across their river, give her a magic rice paddle
that fills an empty pot with rice merely by stirring, and make her their
cook. She steals the rice paddle and a boat to escape home to her world.
Halfway across the river, the *oni* arrive and start drinking the river water
up to the old woman's boat and capture her again. While the *oni* drink all
the water out of the river, the old woman stands in the boat and makes
faces and tells jokes, and the *oni* laugh, and as they laugh the water they've
drunk gushes out of their mouths. The more they laugh, the more water
gushes out of them, and they drown in the waters of their laughter. The
old woman gets to the other side of the river, returns home to the crossroads marketplace, makes rice with the magic paddle and dumplings, and
sells them.

Mori's inspiration for using this story may have come from an English
translation by Lafcadio Hearn, the American weirdo who became
Japanese enough to be accepted and respected by the Japanese as not
merely a Japanese, but a Japanese authority on the Japanese folktale. This
volume of Hearn's translations was in print and popular when Mori was
a young American-born Nisei writer with a sense of being the first of
his kind.

I wanted Sam to see that America was the road. America was a depot,
a marketplace. Everyone comes to America as a migrant, and has been
moving on, and sometimes forced to move on, but moving on ever since.
American culture was not a fixed culture. American culture was a pidgin
culture. American Standard English, the language of newspapers and TV
news, was a pidgin English, an ever-changing marketplace-depot language. What we called American culture, like the language, was a pidgin
marketplace culture.

*　　*　　✦

When we took to the road in our little red Honda CVCC, Operation Desert Shield in Kuwait had been going on a couple of weeks. We rolled down the Grapevine in our thirteen-year-old CVCC. Our ears popped. Then we were out of the clouds and on the flat valley floor. The light was different. All the shadows and shades and reflections of the mountains were gone. "What's that?" Sam asked and pointed to something out his side of the car. I was as surprised as Sam. A raggedy-looking coyote loped head down, tail down across a bare field. I had never seen a coyote from a car rolling on I–5 before.

The coyote is a character in stories that the people of many American Indian nations tell. Sam knows. Yeah, the trickster has nosed his way into American culture as known by TV. I take this opportunity to sing an old folk song, "The Buffalo Hunters." It's a long song about a young man hiring on a Buffalo hunt in Jacksboro, being armed and provisioned and crossing the Pease River to hunt the buffalo and be picked off by Indians. There's shooting the buffalo and skinning the buffalo, and smelling the skins of the buffalo and smelling worse than the buffalo in the song. At the end of the hunt, their boss, Crego, cheated them at cards and "we begged him, and we pleaded/But still it was no go./So we left his damned old bones to bleach/On the range of the buffalo."

The folksy old poet Carl Sandburg, known for saying, "Chicago! City of the big shoulders!" before anyone had gotten up the nerve to say the obvious, said that "The Buffalo Hunters" was American epic poetry, the *Odyssey* and *Iliad* of America. Sandburg was a collector of American folk songs and recorded them, and if he could sing 'em on record, in his scratchy old voice, I could sing 'em in the car in mine. Sam likes the song. We talk about the fur trade leading to the near extinction of the Native American races.

The scariest thing about a strange road or staying in a strange town is choosing a place to eat. No part of a man's body shows fear faster than the stomach. No, not even the swelling and shrinking dangling dangler shrivels up faster than the guts at the sight or smells of something strange in my food. But at the counter of Harris Ranch, at the junction of I–5 and State 198, Sam jumps on the Harris Ranch beef as soon as he smells it and sees I'm about to put a piece of it in my mouth.

"What's that!" he says. I'm glad. He hasn't shown an interest in eating meat till now.

"Steak," I say.

"Can I have a piece?" he asks. He has several. He also has his first baking powder biscuits here.

Sam's first soup and salad bar at his first truckstop first time out on the road isn't what I expect. A big man steps up to our booth wearing a white T-shirt with a red, white, and blue American flag over a map of Saudi Arabia, Iraq, and Kuwait, with the words "THESE COLORS DON'T RUN!" in red over the map. He sticks the shirt in my face. He points at his chest.

I think it best to act as if he is selling T-shirts and not picking a fight.

" 'These Colors Don't Run!' " I read out loud. "Amen to that, brother. Hand silkscreened on 100 percent cotton. I like that. A hundred percent made in America! Where can I get one these righteous T-shirts?"

In a truckstop near Medford I look up from my salad bar and sirloin into an American flag, red, white, and blue, on a black T-shirt, and in belligerent red across the chest the legend, *"Try Burning This One, Asshole!"*

I had an urge to introduce myself as an Iraqi cab driver on vacation from New York with my grandson, but chickened out and said, "Boss, T-shirt, brah! You think they got T-shirts like that in my son's size? Oooh, make my boy look sharp!" So, in order not to identify me and my boy as Iraqi I do a Don Ho, Hawaiian pidgin impression. Sun Tzu, the strategist, take note.

In Portland, the TV tells us the ground forces of Operation Desert Storm are moving fast. The ground war has started.

Portland is a beautiful little city. A collection of unmatching salt and pepper shakers, soy sauce bottles, steak sauce bottles, and ketchup bottles bunched together in a postmodern table setting downtown, along the Willamette River, glows jukeboxes in arcade machines at night. Off the road. Out of the world. Brick, stone. Cast-iron facades. Sam does a couple of drawings of a steel drawbridge over the river.

We are admiring the hollow bronze man with an umbrella in Pioneer Courthouse Square in Portland. Sam has discovered sculpted animals, beaver and ducks in the planter boxes. Now he counts the nails in the heel of the bronze man's shoe. I look forward to stopping in the coffeehut on the corner for a cappuccino.

Then a kid in a black leather jacket, earrings, and no hair walks by and grumbles something.

"What did he say?" Sam asks.

"I don't know," I say. I think back to the grumble. "I think he said '*foreigners,*' I say, "Poor kid doesn't know how to cuss." Then I see we're surrounded by these funny-looking white kids who mean to be offensive but don't know how to cuss. As with the college kid who'd sneered "Literary conservative!" at me for saying texts do not change, and the Marxist who'd meant "Cultural nationalist!" to wither me with contempt, I wanted to take the fuzz-headed boy aside and teach him how to swear. You want to provoke me, kid, you call me a *Chink!* Or you might call me *Jap!* I'm not a Jap, but I'll know what you mean. But *foreigner!* Come on! That's too intellectual to really get me on the proper emotional level."

Then I see we're surrounded by these Clairol kids in black leather. I forget about the cappuccino and say, "Let's walk on out of here, Sam."

I hate it. What am I teaching my kid, letting white racist brats who don't even know how to cuss like proper bigots run us out of a public park in the shadow of the federal courthouse? It's another story I tell Sam: Rumpelstiltskin. And we are the ugly little foreigner driven away by ugly visions of white idealism.

At a coffeehouse in Portland I read a section of the novel where the Chinese herbalist diagnosing the son of a Chinatown big shot says goofily the kid is suffering from a bad case of "Gotta dance!" And I burst into song, singing, "Gotta daaaance, gotta dance, gotta dance, gotta daaaaaaance!" The people sucking on espresso smile warmly and chuckle.

I don't expect to be ambushed by the fans of Maxine Hong Kingston, David Henry Hwang, and Amy Tan in Portland. They show up to vent their moral outrage and save my soul. They show up to whisper in my ear as I autograph books that Chinese culture doesn't deserve to survive, according to the Gospel of Kingston, Hwang, and Tan.

They know me only by word of mouth, by rep. They've never read a lick of me, only heard of me. What they've heard was enough to bring them grinning out of the West Coast night calling me a misogynist, a homophobe, a yellow macho maniac obsessed with Asian manhood. This is what they've heard, they said. "Oh," I say. They don't know what I wrote or said or when or where I said it, for other Asian American writers to call me those things. Maybe I know what they're talking about. "No," I say, "I can't talk about talk I haven't heard."

Instead of the heroic boys off to fight the monsters, the road is treating me like the Ugly Duckling going from bird to bird looking for acceptance.

This is my punishment for being a yellow man daring to call Maxine Hong Kingston, David Henry Hwang, and Amy Tan frauds, ornamental Oriental writers of the white racist stereotype of Orientals as ornaments of white supremacy. Chinese culture is neither as misogynist nor weird as they portray it.

People writing for the papers, interviewing me on the radio, ask me why I say such terrible things about the most accepted and most famous yellow writers in America. I tell them: Text. Text? What has text got to do with literature? Literature is text and the reading and comparison of text. Oh, is that so? What is text, then? Text is a specific arrangement of words on a page by an author. No magic, no mysticism. Text.

Text: Maxine Hong Kingston and David Henry Hwang claim that two popular works of Chinese children's literature celebrate and encourage abuse of women. *The Ballad of Mulan* and *The Romance of the Three Kingdoms*. I say the texts Kingston, Hwang, and Tan describe and quote do not exist. The titles are real, and every Chinese scholar and Chinese kid agrees the works bearing those titles have influenced Chinese culture for a thousand years, but the texts Kingston, Hwang, and Tan cite are fake. Amy Tan claims that "The worth of a woman is measured by the loudness of her husband's belch" is a common Chinese saying. I say she made up that saying herself and it cannot be found in any Chinese fairy tale, children's story, or book of sayings from the beginning of the Chinese language to the present. Text.

Amy Tan claims to have found a source of Chinese misogyny in the story of the Kitchen God and his wife. She asks why the Kitchen God's wife was not honored. The answer to her question is: She is! The Kitchen God is the Kitchen King, and his wife is the Kitchen Queen. It's a matter of text. Don't take my word for it. Just a little time in the library on your own will turn up the traditional pre–New York double poster of the Kitchen King and the Kitchen Queen. Amy Tan's question is phony, like asking, Why isn't water wet? It's a matter of text, not personalities, not interpretation, not philosophy. For asserting text, Amy Tan and Obie and Tony-winning playwright David Henry Hwang call me "a literary fascist."

"Don't take my word for it," I tell the Asian American journalists who wake me up to ask what right I have to say what is and is not Chinese. "This is common Chinese culture. You can find it for yourself in Chinatown." But there is no such thing as checking text, checking facts, in Asian American journalism. Whether or not Far Mulan, the girl warrior, is tattooed, or the Kitchen God's wife is honored as the Kitchen Queen, is not a matter of my word against theirs. It's a matter of text.

One yellow scholar-critic actually says that "texts change, even the text of the text of the Bible. . . ." These people teaching Asian American literature may actually know how to read and write, but they are preliterate. Texts don't change.

"Aren't you ashamed to be a Chinese man telling us what is and is not Chinese culture?" a white man, an editor of a literary review, asks me in Portland. It's a popular question. Sam hears people pop that question at me in Sacramento, San Francisco, Los Angeles.

"Why do you yell at people?" Sam asks in the car.

"I enjoy it."

"Why?"

"Good question," I say. "The point of reading is the reader can test the knowledge of a book without the knowledge or approval of the author. I write books. They're good or bad books because of the way I play with knowledge and language, not because people like my personality. I'm not famous. I'm not a star. I'm not going to act like I want to be famous, or a star—the famous, the star is the story. I am just a writer, not a divine visionary bearing higher truths, not a prophet, not a messiah, not a higher being or sacred cow. My writing is good because it stands up to all the testing and kicking around mere mortals with access to a library can devise. A writer is not the story. A star has to shine and dominate the scene. A writer has to fade into the shadows and watch the scene and write."

First stop in Seattle off the road is David Ishii, Bookseller, in Pioneer Square. Brick buildings. Brick alleys. Stone. Cast-iron facades. We're stopped at a light on Jackson Street, in sight of the two brick train railway stations, and the Wonder Bread factory Okada described in his novel. In my side-view mirror I see a biker in a faded Levi's jacket with no sleeves and patches and bullet holes in it, a bandana tied over his head, silvered shades, looking at my rear license plate and walking his personalized monster Harley toward me. "Oh, no," I say to baby Sam. "Seattle people don't like California people moving in and making crowds in their nice little city, and this guy knows we're from California because he just looked at our license plate and made a face."

The biker pulled up to my window, and looked in. "You really drive this thing all the way up from California?" he asked.

"Yeah," I said, trying not to show fear.

He dismounted his bike and walked around it while slipping his right hand out of its glove. "I want to shake your hand," he said.

David Ishii, Bookseller, is the model of the depot on the road. The books of mutual enemies are on his shelves of Asian Americana. Any writer of any race from anywhere knows when they're in Seattle that David Ishii the bookseller won't let you starve while you're in town. He used to show up at Tom Robbins's apartment in the University District with bags of groceries. He once bought ten pounds of clams in Pike Place Market, put them in a plastic bucket in his Porsche, and drove them ten hours south down I–5 to Ashland, Oregon, to cook them up in vermouth for poet Lawson Inada and his family, by way of introducing himself.

Writers as diverse and sometimes mutually repugnant as the late Barry Pritchard, a TV writer burned out writing episodes of *Run for Your Life* (the old Ben Gazzara—perhaps the only Ben Gazzara—series on TV); Garrett Hongo, poet and director of the Creative Writing Program at the University of Oregon; Leslie Marmon Silko, Laguna Pueblo author of *Ceremony* and *The Almanac of the Dead*; and Ishmael Reed, as well as writers I don't know, all speak of David Ishii with a certain affection and wonder.

At Powell's in Portland, the woman who invites me to read has the tattoo of a rose on her arm and matter-of-factly talks of tattoos elsewhere on her body. Tattoos are art. I heard that in Japan there is a museum where tattooed human skins are displayed as art. That's what I heard. I don't want to hear it again. Powell's is one of the three bookstores with a legitimate claim to being "the largest" in the nation. The bookstore takes up two stories of an entire city block. It feels like a bunker of books. Powell's is where books come to survive Armageddon.

The owner of Elliott Bay Books in Seattle's Pioneer Square wears a mustache and beard combo from King Arthur movies. Elliot Bay Books is redbrick walls and wooden staircases and wooden balconies of books. It's a mountain lodge resort for books and readers. At Elliott Bay, I pick up a copy of Carl Sandburg's collection of folk songs, *American Songbag*, for Sam.

A journalist, at Amy Tan's request, puts a question to me. What do I think of interracial marriages? This is a serious question? I'm no marriage counselor. I don't care who Amy Tan marries. Who she marries has nothing to do with her work. I don't think her work is white racist in form and content because she married a white man. I married a white woman and she is no less a Christian, nor I less a Chinaman for it. The young immigrants, the new generation of artists and writers—believing that their looks and talent and being unlike any Asians who have come before will make them famous—look on fame as a civil right. They look on all of the yellow writers who've married white not as racial traitors but literary cheats, as if the only reason Asian American writers as diverse and opposed as Amy Tan (*The Joy Luck Club*, *The Kitchen God's Wife*); Maxine Hong Kingston (*The Woman Warrior*, *China Men*, *Tripmaster Monkey*); Jeffery Paul Chan (*The Big Aiiieeeee!*); Jeanne Wakatsuki Houston (*Farewell to Manzanar*); Lawson Inada (*Before the War*, *Legends from Camp*); Bette Bao Lord (*China Moon*); Pardee Lowe (*Father and Glorious Descendant*); C. Y. Lee (*Flower Drum Song*); David Henry Hwang (*F.O.B.*, *M. Butterfly*); Fayenne Mae Eng (*Bone*); Diana Chang (*Frontiers of Love*); Hisaye Yamamoto (*Seventeen Syllables*); Milton Murayama (*All I Asking for Is My*

Body)—and the list goes on and on—are published is that we married white.

Statistically, yes, the rate of marrying outside one's race is growing and seems to be a fair indicator of racial extinction. The Japanese Americans came out of the World War II concentration camps encouraged by their government-approved leaders, the Japanese American Citizens League (JACL), to abandon all their Japanesey ways, become Americanized, and marry themselves out of existence by marrying white. Assimilation for the JACL was racial extinction. In the seventies, the Japanese Americans numbered almost a million and a half. They were also marrying out— both men and women—at the rate of 70 percent. Today there are fewer than 350,000 Japanese Americans—every one of them the product of a behavior modification program that worked. The proof that it worked is the fact that the JACL looks on the fade into extinction as a triumph of American patriotism. The object of the camps was to indoctrinate the Japanese Americans into hating their race, and everything that made them appear different from whites.

Whether or not Japanese America is culturally dead and historically lost won't be reflected in the marriage or census stats. How dead the history and culture is is revealed by the works of Japanese American writers and thinkers, not by their numbers or their husbands and wives.

Some are shocked to hear that my wife is white. They want a yellow man to hate whites so much that he would never be sexually turned on by a white woman and have a kid with a white woman. They thought they found satisfaction for that want in my work. No. I can be angry without hating whites.

Sam has always been taken for Chinese because he looks like me, and I'm Chinese. He looks like his Scots-English-Irish mom, too. But his skin is more my color than hers. Does Daddy the storyteller and TV pal teach his son to despise his mother's people? No, Mom's taken him to church. We watch documentaries about archeologists digging for the stories of the Bible. Charles Laughton, as the hunchback Quasimodo, swoops away with Maureen O'Hara into the belltowers of Notre Dame Cathedral and shouts, "Sanctuary! Sanctuary!" and Sam doesn't understand. So we talk about Christianity and the church state, state religion, and the separation of the church from the state as inventions and ideas of Western culture leading to Western democracy. Chinese morality was never founded on faith in a mysterious higher power; Chinese civilization was never founded on religion. Chinese politics never had the problem of separation of church and state. Church was an idea introduced to the East by whites. In Chinese, the word "atheist" exists only as a translation of the Western word. I want him to know everything before he leaves home. I don't want to set him loose, blinded by prejudice and unable to see the difference between the real and the fake in a fast marketplace. I don't want him to be an easy mark, a sucker for scammers, charlatans, and demagogues.

We all write from specific cultures, times, and places. And let's admit it. We non-whites are all ignorant of all cultures not white Christian European, or our own. That's why we do biz with each other in English. So, here we are, brilliant writers of variants and violations of American Standard English in all the depots and variants of the American marketplace, telling the world who we are, where we come from, how we see, how we do, what we live for, what we die for, what we tell our kids in our books and bookstores, and the books adopted for use as textbooks by their school districts.

Why should you take my word for it? And why should I take your word for what is and is not black, or Afro-American or Latino or Chicano, or Puerto Rican or Jewish or Native American? Who would you trust to tell stories of another culture to your children, in your home?

Like horse-trading in the marketplace, the value of any information we buy in the marketplace has to be independently corroborable. Cultures are bodies of knowledge, histories and their varied facts, artifacts and texts.

Shawn Wong reminds me that I found John Okada's novel *No No Boy* on a shelf in David's store. The book had lain in obscurity for years, condemned by the Japanese American Citizens League, the "JACL" the U.S. government had accepted as the leaders and representatives of Japanese American will without any form of Japanese American approval or consent in World War II "to lead Japanese America out of their homes on the West Coast into desert camps," as one leader of the JACL put it. This JACL leader called himself "Moses."

The Japanese Americans themselves saw that the racially selective evacuation and internment were violations of their constitutional rights. Why didn't the Japanese Americans resist the internment in court? For fifty years, everyone who asks the obvious and looks for answers goes to the JACL. And the JACL says Japanese America had no choice but to cooperate without protest or resistance because the U.S. army threatened to round them up with tanks and guns if they didn't. It wasn't so, but even if it were, that too is a violation of their constitutional rights.

The JACL idea of a Japanese American hero was a volunteer for the all-Nisei 442nd Regimental Combat Team. A Nisei who had proved his American loyalty with his blood. Their control of the public image of

Japanese America is obvious in the war movie *Go for Broke!*, the story of the not quite all-Nisei 442nd; true to the NACL vision, the 442nd was led by white officers. The movie starred Van Johnson as a prejudiced officer who learns in combat to respect and admire the Japanese American soldiers. Then Van Johnson teaches a fellow prejudiced Texan to call them "Nisei" and give the battle cry, "Go for broke!"

No one dared say the obvious: The heroism of the 442nd did not address the constitutional violations of Nisei civil rights. The 442nd won Japanese America a little good publicity that they parleyed into a movie, and nothing else.

Okada chose to explore the effect of the constitutional issues raised by the evacuation and internment with a Nisei protagonist who faced the issues directly. Okada's Nisei Everyman violates the obnoxious rules and laws to create a case in court to test those laws. Okada's novel led us to the discovery of an organized resistance movement inside the camps. The official histories of Japanese America by JACL writers such as Bill Hosokawa say nothing like an organized resistance existed. A close reading of the novel led inevitably to members of the resistance (now old men), who've lived as pariahs in Japanese America up and down the towns around I–5, and James Omura, the only Japanese American writer of the time, of any form, to write about the resistance movement as it spread inside individual camps and from camp to camp.

I wrote the story on the organized resistance at Camp Heart Mountain that emerged from a mass of FBI reports, army and naval intelligence reports, government documents from the camps, and the prolific pen of the master of the Japanese American public image, Mike "Moses" Masaoka. The *Rafu Shimpo* printed it with generous quotes from the documents. And year by year for fifteen years James Omura, Frank Emi— a leader of the resistance organized at Camp Heart Mountain—and a few others break loose from the silence of the despised and talk to me. Very gingerly, Frank Abe—a Sansei who entered journalism writing press releases and organizing events for the redress campaign—Lawson Inada, and I put together events with the Asian American Studies Association and Nikkei groups to restore the resisters to their hometown Japanese American communities in San Jose and Los Angeles.

Redress was won. The meetings of the men who resisted the draft to test the camps in court, and the community in San Jose and Los Angeles, were well attended; informative, feel-good family events ending in loud potluck suppers. Kenji Taguma, the son of a Japanese American who had resisted the draft from Camp Amache in Colorado, and his Asian

American Studies instructor, Wayne Maeda, put together a panel of resisters telling the history of their movement reading from contemporary documents, and the Presidential Proclamation of pardon, in Sacramento. At the end of the program, an old white man stood up. A cowboy. The stooped-over old man had to be helped to his feet by his daughter. He had a nice, freshly pressed cowboy shirt with pearl snaps instead of buttons. He wore blue jeans and boots. He had a big tooled leather belt and macho Cadillac bumper of a belt buckle covering his navel. "I was drafted in the war and I answered the call," he said. "I met the boys of the 442nd over there and I liked them."

I expected the rickety old vet to jitter us right into the JACL party line. The Nikkei owe the end of camp and everything they enjoy today to the all-Nisei 442nd, who threw themselves into battle to prove Japanese Americans worthy of the civil rights they'd been stripped of and imprisoned in concentration camps for. But, no, the old cowboy said something else. "I didn't know about camps till a long time after the war. And when I heard about them, I didn't believe it. I was shocked. I wanta tell ya I didn't fight in World War II to put you people in concentration camps. And what you boys did was right."

It was a rare moment. The resisters were stunned by acceptance. There were moments like that at every meeting of the resisters and the Japanese American community. But still the community is dominated by the JACL. And still the resisters are pariahs in the community. And still Japanese American art hasn't caught up with John Okada's *No No Boy* and Japanese American history.

The land war was declared won a couple of days before we left Seattle. It rained all the way out of Washington. The wheels of the big tractor trailers are taller than our little red Honda. In Oregon they roll two trailers and there's no seeing past the water spinning off their wheels. The wind whips the trailers slithering all over the road. Sam holds his bear.

Then, on the road home, we walk back into the real world, a crowded resort restaurant around Lake Mount Shasta in Northern California to get out of the nasty wind and rain.

"Did you tell them we're closed?" a middle-aged crinkled-up woman said to another, taller, less crinkled-up white woman.

"We're closed," the taller woman said. For an instant I didn't believe my ears. This hadn't happened to me since the South in the early sixties. Never in California.

"We're closed," the taller woman said again, and I could see she saw from the look in my eye I didn't believe they were closed at all. I wasn't about to punch either of these old white ladies in the face. I looked around for a customer to catch my eye, and none did. Then I remembered that Sam, my five-year-old boy about to start school, was with me.

"They're closed, Sam," I said, took his hand, walked out, and wondered what I was teaching my kid, letting skinheads and sixties-style white racists in California run us out of town. The winning of the Gulf War seems to have released an ugly brand of American patriotism that expresses itself as righteous white supremacy such as I have never seen before along the road between Seattle and L.A. I've called home for thirty years. I would have thought a nice cathartic victory would have released more winning sentiments on the road.

"It's like the story 'Rumpelstiltskin,' " I tell Sam, "except in this version, we're Rumpelstiltskin. I'm the one stamping my foot and angry. I'm the one run out of the place where I expected we'd be welcome. And those people in there laugh. Let this be a lesson to you, son: Do not spin straw into gold for a girl out to marry the prince, no matter what she promises you."

What has Sam learned from this trip? What will he remember?

I'm at a podium in Pasadena, at the Pacific Asia Museum, once again reading the herbalist diagnosing the opera master's son scene. "This boy has a bad case of Gotta Dance!" I read, and Sam jumps from his seat and onto the platform and sings "Gotta Daaaaance," and another song, "Make 'Em Laugh," from *Singin' in the Rain*.

And we come home to the story of L.A. cops caught in a home video camera beating up Rodney King.

It's five years later. Sam is nine going on ten. He's starting the fourth grade. I have a new book. It's time to hit the road, hawk the book, and make a moving target of myself again. I'm the Asian American writer other Asian American writers love to hate. I'd like to take Sam with me again, but he doesn't like seeing me yell at people. And I expect people I will enjoy yelling at to appear here and there, on what my publisher is calling "a ten-city tour."

I tell Sam a Cambodian story I heard recently. A pair of young parents are not doing well and have a son they don't like. They try selling the boy, but no one wants to buy him. They try giving him away, but no one wants him. They try to drive him away by making life at home tough, but he won't leave. So they take the little boy deep into the jungle and lose him. They leave him in the jungle and run out of the jungle, and after a while their life gets better. They have money. They have a nice house. They have everything they want, but they begin to miss their little boy.

They go into the jungle to find their little boy. After a long time in the jungle they find him. Long hair grows all over his body. He has become a wild beast. He doesn't want to leave the jungle. He wants nothing to do with his parents and runs deeper into the jungle. The parents leave the jungle and spend the rest of their lives in sadness. The story seems to me another, gentler, more melancholic way of saying that Momotaro and Nah Jah say: Do not sell your children to monsters for the good life.

San Francisco, Palo Alto, Bellingham, Seattle, Portland, Eugene, San Francisco, Berkeley. I wish Sam were on the road with me. The car my publisher rented for me is big and white. It's like driving my rich aunt's living-room couch. Sam would love it. But he has to start the fourth grade and two weeks on the road would blow his fourth-grade career.

The last stop before L.A., Capitola is a cute little scene out of Hitchcock's *The Birds*. Cute little cottages along the horseshoe lagoon. Yeah, Sam knows Hitchcock movies too. *The Birds*, *North by Northwest*, with the big fight on the big faces of Mount Rushmore, *Saboteur*, with the big fight on the outside of the Statue of Liberty. *Rear Window*, with the wall of windows by Norman Rockwell. A vignette in every window.

The bookstore's in a shopping center. There's a theater marquee over the bookstore. My name is up there with my book like a movie. "Frank Chin's terrific new *Gunga Din Highway*" up in lights. The illusion of fame. Stardom. If this were New York and not Capitola, I might be fooled. I've seen my name up in lights. I'm not a star. I am not famous. I'm glad it's Capitola.

My host at this bookstore wears a long-sleeved black turtleneck. He has a mustache. He treats me like royalty as soon as I walk in. He shows me to the café. He offers me a book as a gift for reading at his store. I see Lawson Inada's picture on the end of a bookcase facing the children's section. I take the collected Hans Christian Andersen and sit down to a cappuccino.

I am introduced as a writer other writers read for my licks and chops. I've never been introduced that way before. Don't be suckered by your own hype, the strategist says. But I can listen.

I come home again and Dana tells me a black kid pulled up the corners of his eyes with his fingers and went "Ching Chong" at Sam at school.

"What did Sam do?" I ask the obvious.

She tells me Sam asked the kid if he liked him. The kid said, Yes, Sam, I like you. Do you want to be my friend? Yes, Sam I want to be your friend. If you want to be my friend, you can't do that to me anymore. You should remember you were slaves and white people did to your people what you're doing to me. And your people didn't like it and didn't like being slaves. And you're not slaves now and you shouldn't do that to me. You should think about your history.

She asked Sam why he had said that, when the kid made a face at him.

Sam said he did what he thought Daddy would do. He learned something on the road besides baking powder biscuits and good steak.

Ethnic Conflict and Harmony Between African and Asian Americans in the United States

■ ■ ■

JOE CHUNG FONG

The Los Angeles upheaval in 1992 opened the public's eyes to the not so frequently discussed issue of inter-ethnic tension in the United States. It penetrated the American consciousness and shifted the public's understanding of White and Black interraction from majority/minority race relations to minority/minority race relations. The inter-ethnic confrontation between African American and Korean American brought national attention to this long-ignored problem of the conflict of the oppressed, and for a brief time overshadowed the accepted notions of White and Black race relations which concentrated on the oppressor and the oppressed.

Many pop theories offered to explain the reasons for this ethnic confrontation, but they only touched the surface of the problem. One popular explanation claims that the conflict arose from cultural differences. But this is too simplistic. An American from the South, for instance, may experience cultural differences if he chooses to live in the West Coast states. Such differences undoubtedly would not give rise to the level of tension directed at the Korean Americans during the Los Angeles riots.

The cultural differences argument also does not account for the experiences of other Asian Americans, such as the Southeast Asian refugees who reside near and in integrated African American communities across the United States. The Asian American communities in East Oakland and the Tenderloin district of San Francisco are two examples. Why have the Southeast Asians not faced a similar degree of ethnic tension? Why did African Americans single out Koreans and "consciously distinguish" the Koreans from the Chinese and Japanese Americans?

Among certain segments of the public, Korean Americans are perceived as petty capitalists, who have intruded into the Black community and taken money out without returning some profits. However, other Asian Americans—namely, Chinese and Japanese Americans—have historically opened businesses in the African American communities in California. Why are they not also perceived to be intruders who take money out of the community?

Placing sole blame on the system, or continuously recounting past injustices, will not produce the understanding needed in discussing racial friction between African Americans and Korean Americans. Instead, I want to attempt some rationalizations or alternative explanations for the causes of the inter-ethnic conflict.

Ethnic Formation

The formation of ethnic groups has by no means followed a single formula. In Stephen Steinberg's view, "Ethnic pluralism in America has its origins in conquest, slavery, and exploitation of foreign labor,"[1] while Thomas Sowell extols America as a land of opportunity in which "the peopling of America is one of the great dramas in all of human history."[2] These two positions epitomize the dichotomy of interpretative history and reflect radically divergent views of how people perceive ethnic America.

Even though each individual might have a slightly different interpretation of American history, historical records have conclusively shown how ethnic groups emerged and how they have been mistreated. Many social scientists and writers have developed theories about ethnic group formation with popular names such as "the melting pot" theory and "assimilation." John Ogbu's explanation of various types of American minorities provides a basis for discussion of some central issues.[3] Ogbu, one of the most prominent anthropological scholars, distinguishes various types of ethnic groups in the United States, and explains ethnic people's incorporation into this country in a historical context: He sees Africans, Mexicans, and Native Americans as involuntary minorities, or in a castelike situation; Asian Americans as voluntary immigrants; and Jews and Mormons as autonomous minorities.

Ogbu regards the Native Americans as a conquered people, whose homeland was taken from them, making them a people without a country. African Americans were brought to this country as slaves with limited choices. Mexican Americans were a defeated people, who were displaced from power and witnessed helplessly the partition of their country and land by the United States. The imposed incorporation by one dominant group over others robbed these people of their identity, culture, and way of life.

Once permanently incorporated, the Africans, Mexicans, and Native Americans became ethnic groups within the larger society. As social construct ethnic groups in white America, they were not kindly received. They were often denied full participation in the economic and political arena and were typically conferred what Ogbu terms castelike social status. Normally, castelike ethnic groups are relegated to a subordinate social role, in which their opportunity to advance themselves is cut short by legal means. In short, they will not enjoy the same rights as and be equal to the dominant group.

Ogbu considers Asian Americans to be voluntary immigrants, who did not confront historical and structural conditions or cultural forces emanating from the American social system and institutions. He maintains that there are differences between Asian Americans' perceptions of the dominant society and the incorporated groups' perceptions. According to him, Asian Americans came to the United States willingly and for economic opportunities. They did not perceive the American system to be oppressive, and if the social system and institutions did prove oppressive, Asian Americans rationalized that the situation was temporary.

As a consequence of this voluntary mentality, Asian Americans transplanted a set of methods, ways of doing things, and customs to America. Putting it plainly, they were not overtly forced into the white American way of life; they possessed a readymade set of cultural norms from their home country. Asian Americans were not relegated to a subordinate social status, like the incorporated ethnic groups. Asian American culture met American society on equal terms. Asian Americans did not feel threatened by, nor did they feel their culture was being robbed or undermined by, the dominant society. Instead, Asian American immigrants developed a "dual cultural frame of reference"—one derived from the host society and the other derived from their home country.

The autonomous minorities, such as the Jews and the Mormons, are ethnic groups primarily in a numerical sense.[4] "They may be victims of prejudice and pillory, but not of stratification," claims Ogbu. I will not address autonomous minorities in this essay because they are not confronting such great difficulties as other ethnic groups. But without diminishing Ogbu's contribution, I would contend that he has not fully and clearly addressed the Asian American minority.

Like many other social scientists and the public at large, Ogbu confuses Asian immigrants with native-born American Asians. Even his views on Asian immigrants are not clear in light of the fact that mid-nineteenth-century Chinese immigrants and early twentieth-century Japanese immigrants confronted adversity similar to that faced by other ethnic groups. In some places, particularly California, the Asian immigrants endured more.

The early Chinese and Japanese immigrants, the native-born American Japanese, and their offspring have faced, and shared, forms of oppression similar to those faced by other ethnic groups within the U.S. social, economic, and judicial systems. For instance, the 1849er pioneer Chinese were the only race ever to be denied entry to the United States. During the era from 1849 to 1965, Japanese and Chinese in this country viewed themselves as oppressed people. The hundred-year history in America of anti-Asian laws, overt violent acts, and blatant exclusion placed Chinese and Japanese on equal footing with other oppressed American minorities.

The year 1965 marked an important point in Asian American history: The 1965 Immigration and Nationality Act amendments allowed twenty thousand persons per country to emigrate from the eastern hemisphere and did away with the quota system for Asian countries.[5] Korean and other "new" Asian immigrants were allowed to come to the United States in significant numbers after 1965. The critical point here is that there remains a distinctive difference socially and culturally between the post-1965 Koreans and pre-1965 Asian immigrants.

In other words, "Asian American" is not a homogeneous group. Racially, Asian Americans are very similar as a collective group, but ethnically they are wide apart in terms of social and cultural orientation. These differences have not been addressed adequately in the academic community and have been misconstrued by the public at large. Asian Americans cannot be examined as an ethnic group without an understanding of the historical events that shaped the experiences of the different components within it.

For example, post-1965 Asian immigrants, such as the Koreans, did not experience overt violence, nor anti-Asian laws aimed specifically at them, nor flagrant exclusion from full participation by the dominant society. The hurdle of racism faced by Ogbu's four ethnic groups in the United States had been toppled by the time these post-1965 Asian immigrants set foot in this country. We can safely conclude that the post-1965 Korean and other Asian immigrants had no attachment, no shared history, no shared experience, and no link with African, Mexican, Native, and pre-1965 Asian Americans.

Thus it is fair to assume that ethnicity, ethnic solidarity, and ethnic pride did not take shape in the consciousness of these later Korean American and Asian immigrants. Due to their relatively new "American" status, they did not consider themselves to be an ethnic group. The fact of the matter is that the post-1965 Korean and other Asian immigrants such as the Southeast Asians have not yet been forcibly socialized into the American social system. In other words, the socializational process of discrimination, past blatant anti-Asian laws, and other structural impediments in this country did not impact as much as the post-1965 Korean immigrants' social, cultural, and economic development as did the earlier pre-1965 Japanese and Chinese immigrants. The socializational process is such that it creates two distinctive Asian American ethnic groups where the Japanese, Chinese, and Filipino Americans confronted many of the oppressions faced by the African and Mexican Americans while the post-1965 Asian immigrants did not.

Collective Structural Experiences

At one time or another, each ethnic group in the United States has combated social inequality and has acquired certain strategies to overcome systematic discrimination, based on their own historical, social, and cultural systems. For each clash between the dominant force and an ethnic people, even though the minorities have often been beaten, a part of that friction survives in the community. For each engagement, additional tactics used in that friction survive and are being internalized within the groups' social and cultural experience. Over time, these confrontations have shaped ethnic people's worldview of majority and minority relations.

Fortunately or unfortunately, depending on where an individual stands on this issue, the civil rights movement is considered the greatest accomplishment for all Americans. For American ethnic groups, the civil rights movement in the 1960s presented an opportunity for them to experience and to create a sense of common origin, and for them to be as one ethnic people. It was a time of cultural awakening. They no longer wanted to be part of the culture of the oppressed; rather, their collective efforts in the civil rights movement became each ethnic group's element of culture. Ethnicity was a strong unifying force with a multidimensional view.

The civil rights movement forced African, Native, Mexican, and pre-1965 Asian Americans to formulate a common ethnic history as well as a belief in the common cause to overcome oppression in the United States. That experience is such that the four ethnic groups conceived—whether unintentionally or intentionally—a collective identity as ethnic people and created a unique social culture in America.

The movement propelled the four groups to draw upon a common origin as a collective minority people. In their struggles against an oppressive social system, personal and group attachments emerged. One of the enduring legacies of the movement was this bonding and connecting among ethnic groups. In retrospect, they were creating history, a *shared* history in the United States.

The Koreans and other post-1965 Asian immigrants came after the height of the civil rights movement. "Ethnic solidarity" between Koreans and earlier ethnic groups was limited. The post-1965 Koreans and other Asian immigrants had no link and commonality with other involuntary ethnic groups. The bonding process and the ties were missing. At best, Koreans may have had some affinities with the pre-1965 Japanese and Chinese Americans. However, the gulf between Korean Americans and the African, Mexican, and Native Americans was too wide a canyon to overcome.

Korean Americans did not share the experience of overt and structural oppression as an ethnic group. As a matter of fact, the post-1965 Korean immigrants were much better received in this country than were the Japanese and Chinese pioneer immigrants. This ethnic experience is not unique. Cuban American community research in Miami by the leading "enclave economy" scholar Alejandro Portes confirms that Cuban immigrants enjoyed similar treatment, and that a similar analysis of structural contexts applies, including political support and lack of racial discrimination.[6] Consequently, Korean and Cuban immigrants apparently enjoyed the fruits of the earlier ethnic groups' struggles and political support from the U.S. government.

It would be unfair to ignore the later Korean immigrants' perspective. One must ask how could the Korean immigrants understand the experiences and the internalized feelings of other groups that suffered historical and structural oppression from an earlier time. How could they visualize the overt and legal oppression? Few anti-Korean laws existed for them to compare with other minority groups. And, most significantly, they had no shared "ethnic experience" with Africans, Mexicans, Native Americans, or the pre-1965 Asian Americans. There was no cultural and social basis to connect Korean Americans with African Americans as minority people who faced common oppression.

The Lack of Korean American Community Forces to Foster Ethnic Solidarity

Every society generates assumptions about people different from its own. Oftentimes, these generated assumptions reflect one's position in a given society. In America, where people of so many different racial backgrounds live, numerous assumptions about each other emerge. Popular literature frequently discusses and debates these assumptions. Unfortunately, most discussions about Korean and African American friction are measured, sadly, in contemporary comparative terms rather than in historical ones. History tells us that unlike African Americans, Korean Americans were never forced to incorporate into the social system. History also tells us that very limited shared experiences exist between Korean and African Americans.

It is no accident, then, that the African, Native, Mexican, and the pre-1965 Asian Americans look back at the civil rights movement era as their "classical period" in the United States. The movement symbolizes the "cultural renaissance" of their ethnic history. They stood up and were heard. They had spoken with a collective voice. The civil rights movement, with all its positive and negative aspects, affected the ethnic community and shaped cultural forces within it.

Assuming that the movement established and legitimized for the ethnic groups their cultural history, their collective cultural ethnicity, and their cultural awakening, it would be fair to infer that the next ethnic generation in America will be affected. Ethnic groups' involvement in the movement forms a history, a representation of the folkways of a people, which, like a story, will be told to the respective communities. The question is, does the Korean American community have such a story to tell?

Perhaps this could be one of the main causes of the friction between Koreans and African Americans. Decades after the civil rights movement, the four ethnic communities and their cultural forces persist to the extent that their leaders and people can relate to the bond of yesteryears' collective struggle and friendship. Such an enduring community force or aurally preserved story of a group nurtures its ability to instill in its people the sense of a common cause and a common struggle against the "Man," and to encourage ethnic solidarity.

This missing common experience with Korean people goes far to explain the existence of potential conflict. Since African American elders, aunts, uncles, relatives, and friends previously had minimum contact with the Korean people, misunderstandings among the two groups would be easily aroused. Unlike their view of Chinese and Japanese Americans, African Americans view Koreans in their community as "foreigners" rather than intruders. To them, Koreans represent not an ethnic invasion into their community but a "foreign" invasion.

On the other hand, Chinatown and Japantown are as American as apple pie: these two communities developed alongside urban centers within clearly identified boundaries that most Americans have come to recognize. Korean Americans did not have a community to speak of until after 1965. The number of Korean Americans involved in the civil rights movement was too small to convey a positive image of African Americans to the majority of Korean immigrants who came after 1965.

To a large extent, African Americans can identify with the overt structural oppression of the Japanese American internment during World War II and with the Chinese American "coolie" laborers who built the White Man's railroad. Such an identification does not exist for the African American with the Korean-American community. Conversely, Korean Americans do not identify with African Americans' historical and structural experiences. Their cultural forces still tend to reflect an "immigrants" worldview. The distinction is best demonstrated by four important observations of the psyche of the post-1965 Korean and other Asian immigrants: (1) they do not regard the United States and its white people as oppressors; (2) they do not view themselves as oppressed and their situation as oppressive; (3) they have yet to develop any bonds or connections with the four ethnic groups; and (4) Koreans had not been initiated as an ethnic group until the Los Angeles riots.

As much as the public wants to know the cause of the Los Angeles riots and the frantic attempt by some social scientists to find explanations for the upheaval, there are no easy available answers. Due to the nature of the riot which involved two ethnic groups, Koreans and African Americans, a more realistic suggestion needs to be addressed for Asian Americans.

What emerged from that experience is the necessity for Asian Americans to get their act together first. One must learn how to walk before he or she is able to run. During the Los Angeles riots, few Asian American communities supported Korean Americans. This fact, and the overt inaction of Asian Americans, has been lost intentionally within the "progressive" Asian American community at large. Such blatant inaction among Asian Americans reveals much about the problems and complexities of their community. As a matter of fact, as Elaine H. Kim's essay "Home Is Where the Han Is: A Korean-American Perspective on the Los Angeles Upheavals" indicates, Asian Americans overtly distance themselves from the issue and see the problem as a Korean predicament rather than an Asian American one.[7]

Instead of cultivating a dialogue of cooperation with the African American community, Asian Americans should develop a dialogue within. What we are talking about here is priorities. What is the priority of Asian Americans in such a charged crisis? Mere intellectualizing will not solve the problem. For the Asian American society at large, developing a dialogue within has three purposes: first, it will create a united front as Asian Americans; second, such a united front will give substance to the loosely intellectualized concept of Asian American; and third, it is politically sound and empowering for Asian Americans to speak with one voice. The unwilling public at large will heed that one loud voice.

Once the Asian American house is in order, cooperation with the African American community and other ethnic groups will be much more feasible. Cooperation, as an idea, is a two-way street. It is like a telephone: the phone rings both ways. But make sure your own house phone works well enough to receive calls.

■ ■ ▪

NOTES

1. Stephen Steinberg, *The Ethnic Myth: Race, Ethnicity, and Class in America* (Boston: Beacon Press, 1981), p. 1.

2. Thomas Sowell, *Ethnic America: A History* (New York: Basic Books, 1981), p. 3.

3. See John Ogbu, *The Next Generation: An Anthropology of Education in an Urban Neighbhorhood* (New York: Academic Press, 1974), and *Minority Education and Caste: The American System in Cross Cultural Perspective* (New York: Academic Press, 1978).

4. See John Ogbu, *Cultural Models and Educational Strategies of Non-Dominant Peoples* (New York: The City College Workshop Center, 1989).

5. Jack Chen, *The Chinese of America* (San Francisco: Harper & Row, 1980), p. 212.

318 · Joe Chung Fong

6. See Alejandro Portes, "The Social Origins of the Cuban Enclave Economy of Miami," *Sociological Perspective* 30, no. 4 (1987), 340–372, and Portes and Robert D. Manning, "The 'Immigrant Enclave' Theory and Empirical Examples," in *Competitive Ethnic Relations*, edited by Susan Olzak and Joane Nagel (New York: Academic Press, 1986).

7. Elaine Kim, "Home Is Where the Han Is: A Korean-American Perspective on the Los Angeles Upheavals," in *Reading Rodney King: Reading Urban Uprising*, edited by Robert Gooding-Williams (New York: Routledge, 1993).

Sexism in Asian America

■ ■ ■

HOYT SZE

I've been accused of sexism so many times lately that I'm almost starting to wonder if it's true.

I've been called "patriarchal" in my residence hall. Friends have told me that I criticized Asian American women with undue harshness when I came out with my column on interracial dating last semester. Strangers are surprised when I tell them that I don't consider myself a sexist.

It's not my fault if some people are a tad insecure about their relationships. I never said Asian American women couldn't go out with white men. There's a pretty clear difference with finding something counterproductive and trying to ban it.

Among Asian American men, I've heard a wide array of opinion on sexism within our community. I've seen some well-intentioned radicals bend over backwards—compassionate minds, already made weak by society's emasculation, made even weaker by their efforts to politically accommodate. And I've seen some Asian American men, in blind loyalty, adopt every sexist idea of their forefathers.

The right way lies somewhere in between.

★　　★　　★

Sexism is the greatest single problem within the Asian American society. Mail-order brides and thriving prostitution services are mirrored in this society by Miss Chinatown pageants and exotic "China Girl" media images.

In fact, sexism within the Asian American community is one of the chief reasons for "out-dating."

Think about it. An Asian American woman can choose, consciously or unconsciously, between Asian and white culture. The Asian culture devalues the woman, while the mainstream American culture puts her up on a sexual pedestal. Faced with such a seemingly unequal choice, it's hard to blame Asian American women for going outside of their culture.

But let me add some complexity to this picture.

First, the desirability of Asian American women is generally a deception. Will mainstream society treat Asian American women like human beings or sexual toys? Is white culture truly concerned with the Asian American woman's struggle, or is it diverted by a totally nonthreatening minority's experience?

Second, the comparison of Asian and Western society is unfair. Western nations are industrialized, and yet there's still rampant sexism beneath the shiny liberal surface. Most of our parents come from Third World, feudal Asian nations where sexism has never been challenged. From a cultural relativist view, we can't hold our parents responsible for their sexism.

There are some who won't even accept these modifiers. These so-called feminists have completely rejected issues of race for issues of gender. Again, that's an individual choice I disapprove of but cannot affect.

But let me warn those who ally themselves too closely with the feminist movement: Feminism is a white women's movement, originally designed to reduce the voting power of black men. Alice Walker and Amy Tan are fine writers. But once they attack their own race, they become the worst traitors to their communities.

Even white cultural colonialists can't get away today with portraying men of color as animalistic. When supposedly enlightened women of color so willingly backstab their culture, it's unforgivable

As Asian American men, the problem of sexism is a serious challenge. It's shortsighted to accept all of Asian culture and expect it will succeed in the United States.

We must be selective. From a purely humanist point of view, sexism and racism are inherently wrong. The days of provincial hatred and degradation of women are old-country memories which we should let go.

It is important, however, that we rectify our community rather than abandon it. It is important that we draw unity rather than divisiveness from the struggles against sexism and racism.

As Asian American men, though it is important always to fight against the old country's misogyny—to use fewer hastily coined comments like "Asian American women should stand by their men"—it is just as crucial that we never confuse alliance and deference with cowardice and silence.

6

IMAGE DISTORTION
DISORDER

Image Distortion Disorder

■ ■ ■

MICHAEL LeNOIR

In April 1994, four black youngsters were playing basketball in the largely black neighborhood of West Oakland.

The ball bounced over the fence into the yard of one of the few white residents living in that area. One of the boys climbed over the fence to retrieve the ball. Within minutes, he was dead. Killed by a man he did not know and who did not know him. Killed because of the distorted perception that young people of color pose a consistent physical threat to white Americans. This threat appears to be largely created by media, particularly television, and it leads to a societal anxiety that we call "image distortion disorder."

Image distortion probably affects every country with substantial multi-ethnic populations. When mixing of people within these groups is minimal, one group may have distorted perceptions about another. In the United States, the influence of the American media in distorting images has created a national crisis based on race. In America, white people fear all people of color, specifically black males. But statistics suggest crimes involving white Americans victimized by people of color are relatively rare. In fact, incidents like the one that occurred in Oakland are becoming increasingly more common. Young men of color are being killed or harmed because of the perception, real or imagined, that they pose a serious danger even in circumstances that are clearly non-threatening.

In America, there is relatively little mixing of ethnic populations. Most of the images that one ethnic group has of another are developed by the media. The incessant portrayal of African Americans as criminals and buffoons has been responsible for the success of many police programs and sitcoms. *Americans Most Wanted* and *Cops*, television programs about crime, have probably hired more black and Hispanic actors than almost any other programs on television.

Where do these perceptions about the danger posed to white society in America come from? The reality is that people of color pose little social, economic, or physical risk to them. Most people in America get their information about people of color from radio, movies, print, and especially television. In most instances, people of color are depicted as drug-addicted, homeless, child-abusing, welfare criminals. Our young athletes are portrayed as unintelligent, and spoiled if they do not iconize the sports media or management.

Every day the talk shows scour the country looking for people of color to represent themselves as buffoons and idiots. More importantly, there appears to be no balance, no apparent opportunities to show people of color in a positive light. Examples of the media's apparent intentional distortion of African Americans, Hispanics, and Asians are too numerous to mention here, but the end results have a devastating effect on every person in this country and undermine any attempt to bring us together as a people.

The portrait—particularly of young black men, who are especially popular as subject fodder for the corporate decision makers in the media—is never challenged by the more realistic images of our young people. Most of them graduate from high school, do not go to prison, and enter the work force in significant numbers. The perception painted by television of people of color becomes the reality, and it creates a background of anxiety and fear in America that is dangerous.

Consider two people walking down any street, anywhere in America. One person is white, the other is an African American or Hispanic male. The white person walks briskly, blanketed by a perception of African Americans stitched together night after night on television. Most are fearful that this other person poses a physical threat. What is seldom considered is the anxiety felt by any person of color in a situation like that. They realize that they are generally perceived as dangerous and threatening to white Americans. They know that they are likely to be blamed if anything happens on that street.

Treating image distortion disorder will not be easy. As long as the worst of what we are continues to entertain and improve ratings, people of color will continue to be depicted in this way. Changing the philosophy of the media is difficult, and people of color are not likely to own enough media outlets to significantly affect the message.

Those of us in America who are concerned about race relations must react to obvious distortions in the media by raising our voices in protest over the never-ending attempt to portray people of color in these caricatured, fragmented, and distorted images. African Americans must realize that the continuous depiction of people of color as criminals and buffoons can ultimately result in these images being incorporated into the psychological makeup of our children, leading to the deep, more pervasive problems of poor self-esteem and feelings of inferiority. We must encourage all children to read and seek other sources of information. And unfortunately, we must warn our children that those perceptions about the risk posed to white Americans by people of color create a climate that is dangerous to them in almost every social circumstance.

The American media seem to have no stake in the struggle to provide accurate representation of the style, families, and real values that we know represent the vast majority of people of color. We may never have the most effective resources to respond to these daily portrayals of our children and young people solely as deviants and criminals. But we must continue to try by writing letters to respond to distortions and by refusing to buy goods and services that support this kind of programming. Image distortion disorder is a real and expanding problem in America. It creeps subtly into our consciousness. Only by pointing out and acknowledging its existence do we begin to effectively deal with the end result. The death of the young man in Oakland over a misguided basketball is a tragedy to his friends and family. But the tragedy is compounded when we fail to see the larger issue it points to: the climate of racial fear that is perpetuated by the American media.

Crazy with the Heat

Conflict and Confusion in the Postmodern

African-American Psyche

■ ■ ■

NATHAN HARE

As a boy growing up under Jim Crow laws in the "blackjack hills and dales" of Oklahoma, I often heard the old folks telling each other they were "crazy with the heat." They appeared to mean that some designated individual wasn't outright (clinically) psychotic but was reflecting indisputable consequences of the sun or something in the environment hot enough to parboil his brains.

This notion of psychosis being caused by a source outside the individual alerts us to the verifiable probability that, if African Americans harbor higher rates of mental illness (such as psychosis, neurotic anxiety, depression, addiction, and homicidal compulsions), they are even more likely to suffer less malevolent difficulties (including the "healthy cultural paranoia" reported by psychiatrists William Grier and Price Cobb in *Black Rage*)—not to mention routine everyday psychological trauma, and dependency on mechanisms of defense such as denial and rationalization.

The transplanted African slave's experience of being uprooted and snatched from his biosocial habitat, his land, his memories, his language, his family, friends, lovers, parents, children, brothers, sisters, traumatized his psyche (or hers). The antebellum plantation itself comprised a "total institution," by any sociological measure, meaning that much in the way of a concentration camp, prison, or insane asylum, its inhabitants were totally restricted to its psychophysical grounds, completely confined to its territorial sphere of management and control, and stripped of familiar emotional attachments and associations. Once they were psychologically naked, they had to contend with alien attachments mandated by others, by their masters and their overseers.

For instance, the so-called Black Slave Codes robbed the slave of ordinary human access and the basic privileges of a full human interaction—from free and unrestrained daily personal movement to the right to marry or own property or weapons. African American slaves lost and missed the stability and continuity sometimes available to slaves, in that they could be abruptly sold "down the river" or elsewhere at their master's whim, with hardly any warning suddenly separated forever from their most rudimentary family and social groupings.

My own grandmother on my father's side, Grandma Betty, was sold away from her family at the early age of seven, never to hear tell of them again, though she would live to be 104. The full meaning of my grandmother's experience came home to me in the winter of 1985, when I was teaching a course on "The Afro-American and Western Racism" at San Francisco State. One day a coterie of white feminists brought up a point Angela Davis had made in *Women, Class and Race*, where she alleged that black slavewomen had been locked into their roles as women.

When I replied that the black slavewomen were, if anything, locked *out* of their role as women, often not allowed to be mothers to their children, forced to do the surrogate mothering chores of the white slavemaster's wife, the student feminists recoiled in outrage and indignation.

I went home and called my mother, who was then an octogenarian eighth-grade graduate living in a Kansas City senior citizens' complex. I asked her what her "Grandma Nancy" (the paternal grandmother she so often talked about around the living-room woodstove heater that warmed our family home in long winter months, or when we sat around smoldering smokefires under starry summer night skies) had told her that black women were concerned about when they were slaves.

For the first time, my mother told me moving stories of how both of her grandmothers had been sold away from their first set of children, not allowed to look back, made to wade through icy winter waters while their children stood crying on the other side of the river, lashed and beaten through the whole of their enforced separation.

History tells us that the brutal, dehumanizing restraints and deprecations of the Black Slave Codes persisted after emancipation in the forms of ritual segregation and white terror. A black person couldn't sit, had to stand, in the presence of any whites, couldn't eat in their company, couldn't enter by the front door or participate in ordinary human discourse.

Within such rigid rules and regulations of Jim Crow segregation, there was no need to tell black citizens they were inferior—though they *were* told, over and over again, in storybooks and later motion pictures, myths, and the routine observations of the lowly circumstances of themselves and other blacks, their roles, their status and relative social position. Many of these subliminal reminders continue to hover with punishing effect in the everyday life of a white-dominated world to this very day. Stark psychological and socioeconomic forces, including oppression and social rejection, also continue to fuel these compelling and subtle reminders—hammered into their minds through powerful high-tech machinery such as the continually cranking television screen, flashing routine and relentless psychological "karate chops" that bombard the unwary black viewer's psyche.

On some level, just about every time an African American ventures out of his residence, whether to walk into a store or try to flag a taxicab on mean inner-city streets, or encounters startled white individuals coming out of an elevator, or is inadvertently trapped in some alley, the black individual comes face-to-face with continual reminders of the white image of a black person as nothing more than a street thief, petty criminal, or other ominous assailant.

Indeed, it seems hardly necessary any longer to repeat the now rather hackneyed truism of social science that black people were kidnapped en masse from the continent of Africa and brought to America on rotten, rat-infested slaveships through the storm and sorrow of the Middle Passage; and that they suffered a brutal and indelible psychological shock, from which they clearly have not recovered to the present day. Yet it often seems easy for even the most enlightened (or endarkened) commentators gravely to understate the prolonged massive psychic trauma that continues to pummel the black mind-set in many deceptive, variegated, and multifaceted ways. This trauma may be all the more devastating and ruthless in its impact precisely because it appears to be benign, "unintentional," or "institutional."

Leaving aside the well-documented notion that the "ghetto" or "inner city" embodies the psychosocial characteristics of a concentration camp, a reservation, a cramped concourse of individual and collective captivity, we can see clearly now (from such accounts as Ulrich B. Philip's *The Slave Institution*, E. Franklin Frazier's *The Negro in the United States*, Stanley

Elkin's *Slavery*, John Blassingame's *The Slave Community*, and on, ad infinitum) very persistent and disturbing similarities between the mental sequelae of the plantation and the concentration camp. Ralph Turner and Lewis Killian in *Collective Behavior*, Frantz Fanon in *The Wretched of the Earth*, and contributors to a compendium on *Massive Psychic Trauma* edited by Henry Krystal have further analyzed these parallels.

Evidence that individuals, including African Americans, who have lived through and/or presently exist in a situation of extreme oppression or "massive psychic trauma," will frequently exhibit symptoms of Post-Traumatic Stress Disorder comparable to those who have confronted and survived disasters such as hurricanes, floods, and earthquakes, now inspires psychiatry's most conventional literature. It was in fact partly on this ground that the German government was moved to concede its obligations to World War II concentration camp survivors—and their descendants—as psychiatry has laid the claim that such symptoms of Post-Traumatic Stress can be visited upon the children, and even upon the grandchildren. These survivors may experience lifelong problems, which encompass a tendency to form pathological family units and other social attachments, including those born of overidentification with an aggressor, and sometimes turning that aggression upon the self, as in the case of individuals I once wrote about in *The Black Anglo Saxons*, who existed in the dark days of ultra-assimilationism that preceded the late 1960s black power movement.

However, a black person in a situation of oppression doesn't have to be a "Black Anglo Saxon," an "Oreo" or a "coconut"—needn't internalize self-deprecating attitudes from an oppressive society exhibited by many Jews in concentration camps—in order to take on the character of the "defeated male syndrome" also found in concentration camp victims, or to manifest concrete disturbances in the communication of affect and emotion, in which they lose most of their ability effectively to communicate anything but hostility and anger to intimates.

White observers will frequently stand amazed and even frightened by the spirited, seemingly recklessly hostile way in which African Americans interact on a regular basis, cursing one another routinely, even using curse words and pejoratives such as "motherfucker," "bitch," "nigger," and "ho" as superlative terms of endearment and admiration. We see this today in the way blacks and whites tend to respond to the 911 tape of O. J. Simpson arguing with Nicole.

I remember sitting in a fast-food restaurant having a casual luncheon meeting with a white businessman when several black boys in their late adolescence, whom I myself had barely noticed, started wolfing with one another just outside the see-through restaurant wall. All of a sudden the white businessman turned anxious and afraid, visibly squirming, as he tried to warn me that the black youths were on the verge of fighting. "Oh, they're just playing," I finally observed nonchalantly. But it was a long time before the alarmed white fellow could calm himself and return to his commercial considerations.

Reminiscent of concentration camp inhabitants, many black individuals have come to believe on some deep level that blacks as a group deserve their mistreatment. It is often said that "a nigger ain't shit," and "niggers this" and "niggers that," and it has become socially acceptable in many circles—and may even bring expressions of admiration from the black persons present—to cock your head and say, "You know, we're our own worst enemy," or, "We bring a whole lot of things on ourselves." This tendency appears to be fed in our time, to reflect and reinvent itself, in the contemporary fashion of civil rights fighters to focus on "self-help" as they help themselves at the leadership trough like modern-day Booker T. Washingtons, feasting on white foundation grants and multinational corporate remuneration.

Understandably, high levels of depression in blacks at large are being observed increasingly in psychiatric clinics as well as in the streets, where such depression is often masked by hostility and mock hostility, particularly in black males. You can see these young brothers slouching in the back of the bus or kicking back in college classrooms, presenting any powers that be or their representatives the hostile countenance of a defensive posture acquired in the many mean ghetto streets, where young black males are socioculturally compelled to "walk clean and look mean."

A U.S. Department of Mental Health examination of a random sample of black women found that they exhibited a level of depression equivalent to that of a sample of white female psychotics. This predicament feeds and is fed by the notion of the black woman as "bitch" and "evil" or both, churned into her by the constant displacement of rage between oppressed men and women, between acrid bouts of apathy and innumerable occasions of indiscriminate anger.

In this context, black males and females alike can, and do, suffer intense feelings of shame and unworthiness, and a level of apprehensiveness and insomnia matching that of concentration camp inhabitants and survivors. Restlessness, somatic complaints, headaches, stomachaches, and chronic fatigue are likewise as prevalent as are rampant ego dysfunctions during daylight waking hours. Future hopes and verbalized intentions may be hedged by ritualistic qualifiers such as "If it's the Lord's will and nothing happens." There is the constant expectation of unerring or automatic persecution, reinforced by the sad frequency of its occurrence.

Part of the difficulty of workaday black individuals—and the leaders and intellectuals who would liberate or correct them—is the way they see themselves and their place in the world, and the inability to reintegrate that concept with the collective African American image in the mirror held up to them by the white world. The black identity crisis is so pervasive it remains today uniquely problematic to call an African in America an African in the way that Asians in America are called Asians, Chinese are called Chinese, Italians are called Italians, Lebanese are called Lebanese, Irish Irish, Cubans Cubans, and so on. To call Africans in America "blacks" is tantamount to calling Asians in America "yellows," Indians "reds," or Latinos "browns," and it may be that Africans in America as a group will never quite begin to feel whole psychologically until they can feel comfortable calling and responding to themselves as merely Africans.

Not that other problems would immediately disappear. To begin with, Africans in America would doubtless continue to be stymied by the symptoms of a peculiar problem of identity which the great black sociologist W. E. B. Du Bois probably had in mind when he described the African American necessity of looking at the world through two lenses—one black and one white.

Today, Du Bois would have to add the problem of one-dimensionality (to paraphrase Marcuse) in the sense that black people look at themselves and are seen by whites as somehow white, as pseudowhites, parawhites, whites who just happen to be black, whites in black skin. They see themselves through the same lens white people use to see themselves (and to view black people), not to mention the same television network cameras. But black circumstances and experiences, and therefore black solutions, in reality will remain quite different and many times diametrically opposed to those of whites.

The result is the perennial subjugation of the black agenda, in almost every sphere, to white definition and direction, to a stupendous degree exceeding the bounds of simple dominance, or "institutional racism" or the collective unconscious. The one-eyed tendency of a white-dominated society may begin in part with the built-in goal of integration/assimilation for black people; but it is compounded by white expectations of black adherence to the ideals of ultra-assimilation (the "crossover" imperative), and it appears to persist as a potent driving force even in the minds of contemporary black intellectuals and leaders who profess ideologies of nationalism and separatism. These symbolic nationalists, or ritual nationalists, may cloak themselves in bounteous beads and dashikis, but they basically remain little more than Democrats in dashikis.

Admittedly this predicament may derive in part from the simple fact that such leaders and intellectuals tend to belong to the so-called black bourgeoisie, or at least are upwardly mobile individuals who take the middle class as their reference group. As members of E. Franklin Frazier's *Black Bourgeoisie*, they have tended to move out as they move up the black totem pole, coveting both physical and social distance from those they have left behind in the so-called underclass. In the process, they take from the black community the very people who—often by way of services to less fortunate blacks—have stood on their backs and moved up and out, resulting in a "brain drain," a dollar drain, a brawn drain, and an overall rape of the black community's talent, influence, affluence, resources, continuity, cohesion, basic orientation, and essential coherence.

Likewise, those who would trouble to lead the black race tend to be separated—if not to seek separation—from the psychological and social essence of the black condition. Even nationalist leaders of national prominence will not infrequently be the only black person in their residential neighborhoods. But this physical separation is minor compared to their separation in social empathy and political sensibility.

Indeed, this was a quandary that hounded the great Du Bois throughout his brilliant, marathon struggle to uplift and identify with the black race. Even the masterful Marcus Garvey, who is righteously revered for his preeminent success in capturing the collective imagination and allegiance of blacks by the millions with his projected vision of seceding from America and returning forever to the continent of Africa, never actually made it to the continent himself. By contrast, Du Bois, who helped a predominantly white coterie of organizers to found the NAACP and led the modern push for racial integration in America, eventually withdrew from America, renouncing his citizenship before dying in Africa, with citizenship in Ghana and Egypt.

Du Bois wound up far away from the African American condition to which he had devoted his long and brilliant life. At the august age of ninety-one, when he was honored as the pioneer organizer of the first Pan-African Congress, Du Bois confessed to a group of African leaders brought together by Kwame Nkrumah that he had been wrong in thinking that African Americans could lead Africans, when in fact, said Du Bois, "we African Americans couldn't even lead ourselves."

For their part, today's African American intellectual leaders are inclined to hold on to America, clinging to their citizenship with all their might while conspicuously casting their energy and enthusiasm on the physically remote continent of Africa. They thereby separate themselves in both time and mental space from the oppressive here and now, safely beyond Afro-America and its difficulties, while draping themselves in remote Africanity and symbolic Africanisms.

Thus, despite all the talk of "Afrocentrism" these days beneath the multiracial umbrella of "multiculturalism," on all major contemporary social matters or agendas other than the struggle for racial inclusion and acceptance (for instance, "the black image" or the search for bygone African glories and antecedents), whenever black intellectuals take a stand on major issues of the day, they invariably echo, mimic, and eventually join the social agendas of their white allies, even when public opinion polls show that the majority of black people differ from the majority of whites on a given problem or issue. This will be true of matters ranging from discipline in the home and school to abortion, prayer in the schools, busing, sexual harassment, child rearing, foster parenting related to the child abuse hustle, sex education, "voluntary sterilization," workfare, Mike Tyson, to O. J. Simpson (the most recent black male catalyst for a major white liberal social agenda—in his case, domestic violence).

While black intellectuals "make gains" and police the black image, the condition of the black underclass—riddled by drugs, drive-by shootings, street crime, delinquency, family decay, school failure, and paralyzing poverty—continues to deteriorate and disintegrate. When black intellectuals bristled thirty years ago over the so-called Moynihan Report's revelation of ensuing black family decay, the rate of single parenting was only 25 percent; today, 67 percent of black children are born to single mothers.

The very authority to rear and discipline our children increasingly is being relinquished to white dictates, policies, and regulations. The agents of nurturance and development (parents and teachers) are losing the authority to discipline the agents of punishment and rehabilitation (judges, lawyers, policemen, counselors, psychotherapists), typically directed and almost always defined by whites.

The drift toward institutionalism and the institutionalization of blacks (including children), males particularly, in jails, prisons, foster homes, group homes, boot camps, military service, and whatnot is now taking on the form of open public advocacy. Newt Gingrich is merely the latest to take center stage. For instance, the warehousing of pregnant adolescent girls in dormitories was advocated as early as the 1970s by the same

Charles Murray who recently clocked in with *The Bell Curve*. The late psychologist Bruno Bettelheim advocated the placing of disadvantaged children in dormitories in his *Children of the Dream*.

In the case of black boys, Bettelheim has now been joined by black educators such as Samuel Proctor and former Howard University president Franklyn G. Jenifer (now of the University of Texas at Dallas). The saxophone-tooting President Clinton may have simply echoed them in his early call for "boot camps." The social impulse to institutionalize black males will continue to be fed by our practice of placing drug addicts in prison instead of hospitals or treatment facilities. At the same time, a move is now afoot to continue to transfer the custody of black children rightly or wrongly believed to be abused or neglected to more affluent (increasingly white) adoptive parents.

Unable to tell the white world that if whites won't tell us how to raise our children, we won't tell them how to raise theirs; if they don't control the teaching of our children, we won't control and direct the education of their children; unable to assume any independent or holistic educational strategy or policy, we will continue to be thwarted in our hopes of solving black mental and social maladies.

It is this psychosocial impasse—the crisscrossed, checkerboard problem of black identity and identification—which blocks black progress as a social group in every realm. Forced to cross over in order to get over as a people, we remain chronically crossed-up, doomed to zigzag aimlessly, like chickens with our heads cut off, like we are crazy with the heat, in our search for psychological and social salvation.

Behind the "*Times*"

■ ■ ■

GERALD HORNE

The major news media is one of the most daunting obstacles faced by those seeking to build a progressive African American leadership that can keep abreast of rapidly changing developments in this global village, made even smaller by advanced telephone and computer communication.

The *New York Times* in particular, as perhaps befits an organ of what is considered to be the Eastern establishment, is consumed with "Afro-Eurocentrism" when it covers what it deems to be "racial matters." It not only reduces the complex question of race to "black-white," it also limits its scope to a circumscribed part of this nation. If this sounds inevitable and self-evident to you, check yourself: you, too, may be an Atlanticist masquerading as a universalist.

In the January 19, 1994, *New York Times*, after a daunting blitz of articles on the Nation of Islam and Khalid Abdul Muhammad, I tried to tell the paper of record gently that the destabilization of left-wing African American leaders like Paul Robeson, W. E. B. Du Bois, Shirley Graham Du Bois, et al., helped to prepare the way for the rise of the narrow nationalists they now so shrilly denounce. And, of course, if they examined their own newspaper morgue, they could find plenty of microfilmed evidence suggesting how the *Times* gleefully participated in this destabilization. It was, I suggested, not distant from how the Israelis cooperated with the rise of Hamas in order to undermine the secular Palestine Liberation Organization, and I could have added how this same process sparked the rise of "Islamic fundamentalism" from Algeria to Bosnia to Afghanistan to Iran to Indonesia—to New York's World Trade Center.

It is bad enough that the *New York Times* is consumed with Black-Jewish relations. What is worse is that they do such a poor job in writing about it. Real or apparent rifts between this nation's largest racial and religious minorities are of no small concern; the point is, however, that there are other rifts involving both the former and the latter that—for some reason—the "paper of record" apparently is not as concerned about; and this distorted perspective, too, is a product of a distorted perspective.

A truism of contemporary U.S. life is that trends begin in this nation's largest state, then sweep eastward toward the second largest state in population—Texas—then on to the third, New York. This was apparent by the 1960s when Berkeley in 1964 ignited a student movement and Watts in 1965 sparked a rise in Black nationalism and when Oakland gave birth to the Black Panther Party in 1966. The rise of "gangster rap," and the 1992 "civil unrest" that followed the acquittal of the officers who beat Rodney King, was further evidence, if any was needed, of this geographic transformation.

Also forgotten is that there has been a demographic transformation in the process. In California, the Chicano/Latino population is about 25 to 33 percent; and the Asia Pacific population, 12 percent, is larger than the African American, 8 percent—the latter disproportionately sited in the southern part of the state.

Though a number of Black and other commentators tried to portray the unrest of 1992 in terms more appropriate to 1965, we knew better out here. A plurality of those arrested during these tumultuous times were from the Latino community. This came in the wake of clashes in area high schools between Black and Latino youth. A prominent Chicano leader has charged that the post office, that familiar redoubt for African Americans even before *Hollywood Shuffle* raised the point, insufficiently hired in his community because of alleged favoritism to Blacks. Apparently, African Americans split down the middle during the November 1994 election over the controversial statewide initiative, Proposition 187, which proposed draconian measures targeting "illegal immigrants," who hailed disproportionately from Mexico and Central America generally. Some look at south-central L.A. as if it is another version of Watts in 1965, but times have changed. Like neighboring Compton, both communities—unfortunately—are wracked by tension between two poor working-class communities forced into friction, in part, because of the weaknesses of a labor movement debilitated by the same forces that did in Robeson and Du Bois.

Now, the supposed paper of record purports to be national in scope as it speaks authoritatively on what it considers to be the major concerns of African Americans. But the dearth of column inches it has given to the Black-Latino relationship—particularly when compared with its obsession with Black-Jewish issues and the Nation of Islam—suggests that the editors are misleading many who may think they can plot the future of Blacks confidently by relying on this paper. And if they were to confront the Black-Jewish question in Los Angeles, for example, they would have to consider the salient fact that one of the most prominent members of the Jewish community out here—Stanley Sheinbaum, who is married to an heir to the Warner fortune—was one of the biggest financial supporters of the presidential races of the much reviled Jesse Louis Jackson. They might have to consider the fact that the fabled Black-Jewish issue is not only not as relevant out here as Black-Latino relations, but the tensions that allegedly exist between the largest racial and religious minorities may be a product of the peculiar conditions obtaining on the Eastern seaboard, where African Americans, buoyed by certain affirmative action concessions, compete with Jewish Americans for diminishing opportunities in weakened unions, recession-burdened law firms, and a cutthroat publishing industry.

Most demographers claim that the Latino minority will be larger than the Black minority nationally at some point in the not too distant future, and undoubtedly, the entire nation will have to grapple with complications that California already is sifting through.

The Nation of Islam always seems to be at the center of the *Times*'s fixation. But even here this paper has been deficient, for one would think it would have paid attention to a Chicano group, the Nation of Aztlan, that resembles its Black counterpart in many ways—just as the "Brown Berets" resembled the Black Panthers. One would think that since reporters have tried to transform Khalid Muhammad and Minister Louis Farrakhan into the 1990s update of Hitler himself, the *Times* would spend a few of its precious column inches—often filled with less than riveting maunderings about the latest ephemeral fashion trends—providing perspective on the Nation of Islam.

One would think that today the *Times* would, again, simply examine its own morgue of microfilm in order to give its readers deeper insight into the Nation of Islam. But again, I'm afraid, the Atlanticist perspective of the *Times* is a hindrance. Ernest Allen pointed out in the *Black Scholar* in 1996 what some of us knew: Japanese nationalists were present at the creation of the Nation of Islam, and they collaborated until Pearl Harbor on a common platform of "anti-whiteness."

Given how Robeson and his crew were tarred so relentlessly by the *Times* for allegedly being agents of Moscow, one wonders why this paper has not briefed its readers on this Tokyo connection. Perhaps it is because the major media would then have to contemplate an eventuality that usually makes them shrink in horror—race is broader than "black-white," and the economic hegemony that has undergirded "white supremacy" is rapidly going the way of the dodo bird.

But actually one of the realities I have discovered—and here the *Los Angeles Times* is probably more sensitive than its New York counterpart—is that leading elites will usually view Euro-Afro relations through a racial lens, but are loathe to view Euro-Asian relations similarly; this is particularly true nowadays when even *The Economist* acknowledges that given prevailing trends, the economy of Japan, China, or both will surpass that of the United States at some point in the next decade.

Even when the admitted psychological pornography called *The Bell Curve* trumpeted that African Americans were genetically inferior intellectually to Euro-Americans, and (going one further) that Asians and Asian Americans are smarter than Euro-Americans, the *Times*, along with most of the U.S. media, cast the whole debate in the putatively comforting terms of "black-white." Not one writer argued in the *Times* that perhaps President Clinton should fire Mickey Kantor's staff, which is working so frantically to bring down the trade deficit with Tokyo, since everyone knows that this deficit is a simple reflection of higher IQs among Japanese management. No one informed Euro-American management that there are worse fates than being intellectually inferior, and that they should cultivate their admitted strengths—like downsizing an economy.

When the adventurous—and California-based—novelist Ishmael Reed tried to update the stale "Afro-Euro-centric" debate in his trailblazing *Japanese by Spring*, the *Times* and a good number of its bourgeois counterparts in the media did not pay sufficient attention or else dismissed the insights. Even when the November 4, 1994, *New York Times* carried the revealing words of MCA-Universal's Sidney Sheinberg, who complained that top brass at Tokyo's Matsushita treated him like a child and not an adult, the *Times* failed to point out how this comment resonated through the centuries for African Americans and, yes, other peoples of color.

In other words, race does matter; but if one seeks to understand some of its most weighty manifestations, one must transcend limitations narrowly imposed by the *Times* and much of the major news media. These limitations, sadly, hamper the ability of African American intellectuals and leaders to respond more effectively on the racial front. They are so tied down by incoming shelling from the *Times* and other organs that aggressively set the terms of engagement that, apparently, they barely have time to survey the entire landscape.

African Americans can best and most fruitfully be compared to the Muslim population of India or the Irish in the United Kingdom, or the Hungarian minority in Romania or the Romani or Gypsy population of Eastern Europe—actually the list is as endless as humanity itself. Inevitably, ruling elites fear that such minorities will align with the real or imagined enemies of the state and constitute the "enemy within." In the nineteenth century, notably after Britain abolished slavery in the 1830s, there was fear that Frederick Douglass and others would ally with London, which had come within a hair in 1814 of overthrowing Washington, or Port au Prince or Mexico City. In the 1930s and early 1940s, there was openly expressed fear about the Nation of Islam's ties to Tokyo and the ties of Robeson and other leftists to Moscow. This fear was fired by guilt that the mistreatment of African Americans would give them more than adequate cause and motivation to establish foreign alliances.

But after World War II began, pro-Nippon Black nationalists like Elijah Muhammad were jailed, and after the war Japan's alliance with Washington vitiated any hope of the Nation of Islam ruling this nation in league with Tokyo. The Cold War and Red scare not only marginalized Robeson but helped to turn many African American opinion molders into agnostics on global matters, apprehensive that the slightest interest expressed in the question would raise the centuries-old fear that Blacks would cut a separate deal with "foreigners."

So, when the eminent African American intellectual and president of Spelman College, Johnetta Cole, was mentioned as a possible cabinet nominee by then President-elect Bill Clinton, the *Times* and its acolytes—the *Washington Post* and the *Forward*—erupted in anger. They huffed and puffed about her alleged ties to the World Peace Council, still flayed as a "Communist front," though the Soviet Union had disappeared. They even objected to her supposed friendship with the Marxist historian Herbert Aptheker, although he was Jewish; one would think they would be heartened by such a relationship, since they are supposedly concerned with the state of Black-Jewish relations. The message sent to African American opinion molders was that you will be attacked if you are a nationalist and you will be attacked if you are an internationalist—

though the Cold War that supposedly had inspired this latter stricture had long since ended. Above all, the message sent was that African Americans should try to avoid stoking the none too latent fear of U.S. elites that we will make global alliances in this global village.

By setting the terms of debate so narrowly, the *Times* has ensured that only a certain kind of African American leader could emerge. Abiola Sinclair had a point when she argued in the October 8, 1994, *New York Amsterdam News* that Ben Chavis's personal peccadilloes were the immediate cause for his downfall from the leadership of the NAACP. But she also had a point when she suggested that the *Times* and other organs that called for his dismissal with blood in their eyes were upset—I would say hysterical, if one examines the analysis of *Commentary*—about his past and present ties to Angela Davis and, particularly, his press secretary, Don Rojas, who had held a similar job with Maurice Bishop in tiny Grenada before the U.S. invasion of 1983.

By hiring Rojas, they seemed to say, Chavis was straying from the approved path set in 1948 when the NAACP fired Du Bois after he sought to bring the United States before the United Nations for violating the human rights of African Americans. The Faustian bargain established was that the NAACP would retreat from the global front and civil rights concessions would flow.

The NAACP—until Chavis's administration—kept its end of the bargain, supporting wars in Korea, Vietnam, and elsewhere. But now, when affirmative action is in jeopardy and Supreme Court Justice Clarence Thomas is hinting that the Voting Rights Act of 1965 is unconstitutional, at least it can be said that U.S. elites are reneging on their end of the 1948 bargain, and it might be time to snatch back the potent quid pro quo of internationalism that we relinquished.

Yet the *Times* and the major media continue to define the terms of engagement narrowly; little wonder that the African American leaders and intellectuals who do emerge anointed in the *Times* have so much trouble maintaining credibility in their community. Folks suspect justifiably that if you make it through this draconian vetting process, there must be something wrong with you.

The *Times* supposedly is concerned with the rise of right-wing conservatism generally—at least, that's what its editorials say. But by continually squelching the left in the community where it is most likely to arise—among a predominantly working-class African American community—this paper is only serving to guarantee that various forms of right-wing conservatism will flourish among Blacks. And this will not only take the form of Black conservatives like Clarence Thomas and the two Black

Republican members of Congress, Gary Franks of Connecticut and J. C. Watts of Oklahoma; it will also take the form of a right-wing nationalism that subordinates women, accepts homophobia, and echoes the Islamic fundamentalism that is spreading like wildfire globally—in part because of the policies endorsed by the *Times*.

When will we be allowed to enjoy this "free marketplace of ideas" I keep reading about in ACLU mailings and law review articles? When will African American leaders be allowed to be internationalists? When will "race" be defined more broadly than "black-white"? When will Atlanticism cease to be the defining paradigm; more than this, when will even a limited Atlanticist outlook be pursued consistently and effectively?

Don't hold your breath waiting for these questions to be answered by the *New York Times* or by those that turn to them for answers to what's going on in the world. Yet, if we are finally to get ahead of the *Times*, somehow we must escape from the officially sanctioned and narrowly constructed channels to which race matters have been assigned.

An American
Multicultural Response

■ ■ ■

NICOLAS KANELLOS

It is ironic that a self-proclaimed descendant of Sephardic Jews expelled from Spain during the Inquisition would seek to expel from American literature—and presumably American identity—the writings of the descendants of non-European (also read non-white) Americans. But such is the real meaning and potential impact of Martin Peretz's sweepingly broad and erroneous declaration in his "Cambridge Diarist" column in the *New Republic* of June 5, 1989: Hispanic Americans, African Americans, American Indians, and Asian Americans are not represented by "substantial parities" in literature; "none exist," he claims. Peretz further asserts that to offer courses on these literatures at the University of California at Berkeley—and presumably at all American universities—is a "preposterous enterprise that marginalizes and Balkanizes the core of American civilization." If I understand him, his implication is that the non-European-stock citizens of the United States have not contributed substantially to American civilization. Thus would he not only expel us from the literary history books—something already accomplished by his ethnocentric and Eurocentric brethren—but he would also efface us from the multihued and multipatterned mosaic of "American" civilization, its history and culture.

Aside from the economic and historical determinants of racism, one can glean from Mr. Peretz's comments another ever present conditioner of racism, be it represented in the ranting of uneducated white supremacists or in the correct prose of the professors of eugenics: ignorance. It is obvious that Mr. Peretz did not take the time to research and evaluate the history and accomplishments of the non-white American ethnic people—traditionally the "other" in official American civilization. Had he done so, he would have found out, for instance, that Hispanic letters north of the Rio Grande date back to 1598, with an epic poem on the colonizing of New Mexico, and since then thousands of volumes have been written, mostly in Spanish, but also in English (since the nineteenth century).

Similar unbroken traditions exist for the other non-white ethnic literatures; and, of course, when we speak of the Native American, we can trace the origins to many centuries earlier.

The fact that these literatures—even the works written in English—have not been collected and safeguarded by American libraries, have not been published by the Eurocentric commercial presses of the Northeast, and have not been studied in our schools, may create the impression that they do not exist, that non-white American ethnics do not read, write, create art, or even think. But, of course, this too is the result of the self-promotion of Europeans and their civilization in the New World, and the self-fulfilling prophecies fomented by the institutors of colonialism, slavery, and nineteenth-century imperialist expansionism.

Oh, the volumes we could write, and have written!

It is surprising that a supposedly intelligent man, like Mr. Peretz, who has benefited from the tradition of the book since before the Inquisition, would burn our books and literary traditions with one unthinking and mean stroke of his pen. It is even more surprising that, writing from that seat of wisdom in Cambridge, he reveals his totally ingenuous acceptance of and obeisance to the cultural myth that the United States is an extension of Western Europe, even when in the light of day, all he has to do is walk the streets of Cambridge to be confronted with a mulitcolored, polyglot reality—and the cultural and literary traditions it represents.

The Berkeley professors, and others in our state-supported colleges, are also confronted with that reality in their classrooms. It simply is too difficult for them to continue to try to indoctrinate these descendants of non-Europeans in an exclusively Eurocentric curriculum; it is not just, honest, or humane. And in the late twentieth century, Mr. Peretz, it just won't wash anymore. Even the *Norton Anthology of American Literature*, another one of your bibles, has had to reform and become more inclusive and representative of the real American tradition, a New World tradition.

In his column Mr. Peretz quite obviously is joining forces with the William Bennetts, Lynne Cheneys, and Allan Blooms who are on the Western cultural heritage and "Great Books" bandwagon.

By exclusively identifying with Europe, education in the United States has denied not only the existence of its ethnic minorities but also of its own identity as a member of the New World, a hemisphere of mixed cultures and races. In fact, many of the great cultural contributions of the United States in the past, the present, and most certainly the future, derive from this country's cultural diversity, not from its self-conscious, awkward, and patently artificial mimicry of European civilization.

It is true that the Western tradition has informed life in the United States and the Americas, but the Western tradition has been transformed and enriched, not only by the new landscape and its indigenous people, but also by the thousands of other immigrants and mestizos who have participated in creating a new cultural landscape.

Rather than assuming its rightful role as Caliban—alongside the other New World cultures which fought to gain independence from the exploitative slavemaster Prospero—U.S. official culture has traditionally donned Prospero's garb and attempted to be his simulacrum vis-à-vis the other mestizos of the hemisphere.

"Great Books" are not to be used as graven images to be worshiped unquestioningly. They are great precisely because they can lead to and withstand all levels of discussion throughout the ages. Furthermore, all cultures have their own great literatures and their own canons. The canons of Western civilization were developed at the same time that Europe was solidifying its patriarchal order and colonizing—even enslaving—a sizable portion of humanity around the globe.

It is unfortunate that the protectors of the "Great Books" and the Western tradition cannot assimilate this into their consciences or their curricula, even when their classrooms are crowded with women and minorities. And the prognosis for further growth of minority enrollment at all levels of American education is extraordinary, especially given declining Anglo-American birth rates and high fertility and immigration rates among minorities.

As the scholars Charles Altieri, Arnold Krupat, and Robert Van Hallberg have shown at length: "Canons are recognized as the expression of social and political power," and they serve to maintain the prevailing social order. The writings of Allan Bloom and Edward Hirsch, the band-standing and rabble-rousing of William Bennett, and the quibbling of Mr. Peretz come at a time when they and many others perceive an impending change in the social order. Their voices are the academic equivalent of the reaction by American fundamentalist groups, the English Only movement, and, at the extreme, the book banners and burners (even of such canonical works as *Huckleberry Finn*).

In conclusion, multicultural literacy is as necessary for democracy as it is for the socialization process of tomorrow's citizens. It will, furthermore, be an important step in dealing humanely and humanistically with the other nations of the world, the result of an egalitarian orientation, nurtured domestically.

Hispanics and the Media

■ ■ ■

MARCO PORTALES

When we study the U.S. media's treatment of Hispanics in the 1990s, we find what unfortunately has to be characterized as brazen disregard for most things Hispanic. This neglect is damaging both to Hispanics and to the larger American population that is kept in ignorance, and it basically constitutes the same type of accusation that was leveled against American society by activists of the late 1960s and early 1970s. Succinctly phrased, the issue is that during the last twenty-five years the American media has made it too clear that it simply does not have the time, the space, or the inclination to focus attention on Hispanic matters. Whenever Hispanics are given a little news space or mentioned in the media, the issues are usually illegal immigration, crime, low educational attainment, or demographic projections. The last are either meant to or they nevertheless do tend to scare other Americans about the oncoming Brown Wave or the increasing population growth among Hispanics. Recently, two news items received some attention, and I would like to discuss some connections between the ways the media represent us and some Hispanic realities that could be improved, if the desire either commonsensically develops or is intelligently encouraged.

In May 1994, the National Council of La Raza made a media issue of the fact that the Smithsonian Institution does not and has not historically collected Hispanic materials and artifacts. As far as the Smithsonian has been concerned, until the summer of 1994 we Hispanics have not existed in the United States. Now that the Smithsonian has been made aware of our presence and has recognized and acknowledged the fact that Hispanics live in the United States, particularly in the Southwest, the current director told the press, the national museum devoted to the preservation of all things American will start to collect Hispanic materials.

So where have Hispanics been all of these years? Apparently during the length of the history of the United States, Hispanics have not officially existed in this country. We have not lived in Chicago, Philadelphia, Washington, New York, Florida, Texas, New Mexico, Arizona, Utah, California, and throughout all those other cities and towns of the Northeast, the Midwest, the West, and the South. It would be difficult to find another comparable case where a whole people, who have so willingly served the United States whenever called, have been so systematically *erased* from the national consciousness by the very agency commissioned by our government to preserve our past.

African Americans, for example, were enslaved, and, since Lincoln's 1863 Emancipation Proclamation, have experienced outright discrimination and all sorts of other objectionable human rights abuses. W. E. B. Du Bois's 1900 prediction that "the color line" would be the twentieth century's chief problem has been proven correct; so long as we do not properly educate people, race will continue to separate human beings. Native Americans, it would be unconscionable to forget, were historically decimated and consciously dispersed, breaking up community-centered lives. Asian Americans, everyone knows, were not historically welcomed, and, along with Hispanics, all four minority groups continue to labor in the country's more menial jobs.

Hispanics, the assertion needs to be made, have traditionally been ignored, and we continue to be disregarded, in spite of considerable talk of "cultural diversity" and "multiculturalism." If we look closely, we will observe that Hispanics are oddly missing or only tangentially included whenever "minorities" are being discussed. In referencing Hispanics, what we noticeably have—and one cannot soften the nature of the "oversight"—is a vast and pervasive national unwillingness to acknowledge nearly all things Hispanic. Worse, the concerted disregard that we see in American cultural life toward Hispanics—in advertisements, commercials, and in announcements and occasions of all kinds, the record amply shows—covers all facets of Hispanic existence in the United States.

That is why in the last twenty-five years, we Hispanics have developed our own media avenues and our own ways of publicizing our ventures and accomplishments. For we have had to create our own ways of building, asserting, and promoting the self-esteem and securing the attention that the larger American society has denied our communities and our individual men and women. Our efforts are only now beginning to be noticed, for we have long been most visible as the custodians and the gofers of the American world. Today, the people of the United States are seeing more Hispanics in the professions, but we are very far from meeting the current needs of our people, given our considerable demographic growth. Other things Hispanic, like our food, for example—though owned primarily by American entrepreneurs—are also making incursions into American life and culture. But, according to most scorecards, we lag sadly behind in virtually everything, and, it needs to be said, the resistance against our progress increases as soon as we venture out of our communities.

How has the American public media served us? The Center for Media and Public Affairs in Washington, D.C., in early September 1994 held a news conference to publicize what arguably may well be the most startling fact about Hispanics in the United States. The second news item that appeared innocuously here and there in the less prominent parts of some of the country's newspapers was that television quite blatantly ignores Hispanics. The rest of the news report said that when the little screen deigns to turn the cameras on us, invariably we are portrayed negatively, or most often very explicitly as downright criminals.

Consider for a moment what such coverage would likely do to a whole group of minority people who for nearly fifty years have been daily exposed to this type of national mirror. Why then do we wonder and, worse, how can some members of the larger population self-righteously blame the parents of Hispanic and other minority youths when they drop out of school? And why do we fault Hispanic adults for, in effect, refusing to participate in the highly touted competitive "American way of life" that so offensively excludes almost all of our people?

I saw this second news item in the local paper, and immediately went out quite elated to seek the better coverage that the *New York Times* usually reserves for such announcements. But there was nothing. The news conference did not make the country's most important paper that day, and I lost interest in seeing if that world-renowned paper covered this extremely significant item about Hispanics in America during the next few days.

Why should all Americans pay attention when television is characterized as a "vast wasteland" for Hispanic Americans?

The answer is that it is a little satisfying to hear that research centers and institutes are finally beginning to take note of what some Hispanics have been variously saying for years about the nature of Hispanic life in the United States. In different ways Hispanics have been requesting, perhaps too politely, more attention for our people for three or four generations. But not until this particular national study, which relies on the social science method of content analysis and quantitative analysis, has the official media been made aware of the fact that the nature of Hispanic reality in this country direly needs change if Hispanic Americans are going to be embraced as Americans instead of excluded as assumed foreigners. For Hispanic Americans, everything remains to be seen, and we are carefully watching both the rhetoric and the actions of the media and the American nation.

The Center for Media and Public Affairs found the following quantifiable facts:

- Hispanics comprise only 1% of all characters on entertainment TV today; forty years ago, in the 1950s, 3% of the characters on American television were Hispanic.
- 45% of Hispanic characters on "reality-based" TV programs commit crimes, compared to 10% of their white counterparts. The study found that "whites are shown enforcing the laws and minorities breaking them." Does this representation resemble reality too closely?
- Although very few Hispanics appear on TV, the few who do are portrayed negatively. 41% are portrayed negatively, compared to 31% of Whites and 24% of Blacks.
- 22% of Hispanics are represented as unskilled laborers, compared to 16% of Blacks and 13% of Whites.
- One out of every five Hispanics on TV is depicted as a criminal, as opposed to one out of every nine Whites and one of every fourteen Blacks.

That, say the numeral facts, is exactly the way that Hispanics are represented by television for all the world to see. And if we look at the other media and at the ways that other parts of the power establishment in this country depict Hispanics, we can see that the negative images that are everywhere widely disseminated shape and influence how Hispanics are treated and responded to everywhere in the world. Next to the malignant numbers done against Native Americans, how the media portrays America's Hispanics is the biggest case of communal traducement and mispresentation perpetrated against a people. In the case of other races in the United States, courageous representatives like Martin Luther King, Jr., have periodically spoken up against distorted misrepresentations; but Hispanics have not had similar champions, since Cesar Chavez spoke mainly for the migrant workers. Most Hispanics also tend to speak Spanish, and too many insensitive Americans simply assume that Hispanics can be ridiculed for the way we speak, and that we can be represented in all sorts of demeaning ways without consequences. But careless treatment of anyone has a way of affecting everyone.

Raul Yzaguirre, president of the National Council of La Raza, said of the long overdue media study:

> The toll it [misrepresentation] has taken on our population in terms of image and public goodwill has been enormous. Every day, we watch television programs that show we are not a part of the American community, that the only Hispanics visible to the mainstream population are drug lords, illegal immigrants, and criminals. Television exacerbates the stereotypes we face every day at work and throughout society; and it profoundly impacts the self-images our children develop.

The study I cite examined television programming in the United States from the 1950s to the 1980s, and it ended by focusing attention on television programming in the early 1990s. To drive home its conclusions, the study graded and filed report cards on the major television networks. ABC, for example, received a grade of F; CBS was rated C−; NBC earned a solid D; and FOX, the newest network, came in with an F. It is instructive to see that the youngest television company feels it can totally omit portraying Hispanics—the result, I suspect, of being blithely unaware of Hispanics in the United States, since we are clearly deemed inconsequential, having been so viewed for half a century on all the other American networks.

As I understand it, the Center for Media and Public Affairs will conduct another study in 1997 to see if the representation of Hispanics on television improves. I, for one, look forward to that report. I am interested in seeing, indeed, if this first report will make any difference to the television executives who plan the television programs and who unscrupulously tell us how to view the different age and ethnic groups in the United States. For the leading networks now know—even if the newspapers and much of the general public seems to have missed this important bit of news—that the growing awareness of ethnicity during the sixties, seventies, eighties, and nineties has completely bypassed Hispanics in television land.

What happens in television, to be sure, is extremely important for Hispanics, American society, and the world. Does reality mirror TV, or does TV mirror reality? The truth, of course, is that both TV and reality mutually shape each other, and the point that needs to be addressed is that Hispanics and the general population are not noticeably being helped by either television or reality as the situation now stands.

Could different television representation of Hispanics and other minorities help? Well, of course, Hispanics are starved for some models worth emulating, admiring, and holding in high regard.

The current state of the media's representation of Hispanics, as I suggested earlier, is the primary reason why both our adults and our young people are disaffected and uninvolved in American life. As a people, however, Hispanics are not uninvolved by choice. My personal view is that we Hispanics have been taught, very effectively, *not* to participate, not to feel that our views count. We have consequently learned, and very well, to walk away as we do, because we have traditionally been left out. For this reason, many of us are now disinclined to participate in many American activities, like voting, enrolling in local clubs, and joining and supporting educational groups. Some of us, to be sure, participate, but most Hispanics would rather not. Like other ethnic groups in this country, namely, African Americans and Native Americans, we Hispanics in fact have largely created our own worlds; and many of us are reluctant to involve ourselves with people who continue either to demean or to represent us in unattractive ways. Who enjoys being misrepresented all the time?

I believe I am correct in saying that Hispanic allegiance and respect for almost all things American is well known. Yet, if we were to base our sense of America according to the Smithsonian, according to the American media, and according to the advertising world, we would have to conclude that Hispanics virtually do not exist in the United States. For most of the time that Hispanics are allowed either visual or print presence in the media, it is generally to support Anglo-Americans who are invariably regarded as representing the more "American" positions or issues. Most Hispanics were also born in the United States or have become Americans; yet instead of being regarded and represented as such, too many of us are subtly or directly excluded, disregarded, or treated as inconsequential. Does this type of treatment make sense in the face of the fact that from all demographic projections Hispanics are expected to be the largest minority in the United States by the year 2010?

If this trend continues, if we continue to fail to make full use of the human resources of the United States, our country is going to be hopelessly enmeshed in the type of racial and social problems that we are already beginning to see.

The study conducted by the Center for Media and Public Affairs found that today, "Hispanics are less visible in prime time than they were in the 1950s." At that time we are supposed to be thankful that we had Ricky Ricardo, a Cuban entertainer, and Jose Jimenez, whose native background was never entirely clear to me. Did we then and have we ever had even one single Mexican American person, either male or female, that we Hispanics as a people can actually feel good about? Frankly, fellow Americans and, I hope, television executives, at this late date I cannot name one single TV person or personality. Can anyone? Did we, in fact, have other laudable, emulatable high-profile TV Hispanic characters who told us that we are part of America and that we have or can expect to have a future in this beautiful country? Again, frankly, nothing comes to mind. Oh, yes, there was Guy—what was his surname? was it Williams?—the actor who played Zorro and looked Hispanic, though likely he was a cousin of Errol Flynn, that other flamboyant swashbuckler who made amorous Casanovas out of all of us Hispanic kids at one time or another. I mean, don't too many of the images that we see on television begin to mirror and explain unattractive Hispanic realities? Like, who would be interested in imitating "My name's Jose Jimenez"?

As for women, I cannot honestly say that I remember even one Hispanic woman on the big or the little American screen. When I vaguely recall one, I see her as one of those morally loose, provocative vixens luring otherwise good men into disreputable actions or situations. I do, on the other hand, remember Marga Lopez, Lola Beltran, Sarita Montiel, Libertad Lamarque, Maria Felix, Flor Silvestre, and some other older women who peopled the Mexican films that we used to see in South Texas when I was growing up. But gone are those days and those films, and those more admirable types of actresses.

According to the Smithsonian, our Chicano childhoods never happened, since we have not ever really existed, though our kind have officially been living throughout the Southwest since the sixteenth century. Who knows, for example, that 1748 is the year that the Spanish land grants of Nuevo Santander opened up the South Texas area for settlement? But that, too, remains to be brought out, and soon will be by Professor Armando Alonzo, for here in Texas, history too often still tends to begin with the fall of the Alamo, despite the work of David Montejano, Gilbert Hinojosa, and other historians who have valiantly worked to give us scholarly books that should shape a history the school textbooks have ignored. Everyone knows the John Wayne Alamo story too well and what happened to the victorious Mexicans shortly after in San Jacinto. To this day, the events at San Jacinto are played out every year beside the San Jacinto Monument in southeast Houston, lest Mexican people forget. This celebration is as commonsensical as those where southerners continue to bring out the Dixie flag every chance they get, unmindful of how that symbol unjustly recalls for African Americans days of past slavery and continued oppression.

We need to undertake public discussions on the type of historical events and occasions that require reenactment, and we need to be clear about what we are commemorating. But that is another matter I will leave for another time. In this essay, I am more interested in how our Hispanic lives have been shaped by the type of images that television, the newspapers, and the film industry constantly transmit to the world. At the individual level, I will say that throughout my forty years in academic life, I have been met with a type of educated but nonetheless condescending curiosity that in effect subtly says again and again: What can a Mexican American think about? What could a Mexican American say that would be worth our attention and precious time? "Our," of course, refers to the media leaders and the highbrow professor types, who openly used to quip, "Oh, he's one of us"—those who, of course, said nothing if the person was not "one of us," since things have always been too visibly understood.

Nowadays, such people generally say less brazen things, especially since ethnic people have started to insist on our presence. But we have had to insist; and in too many quarters, we are seen as pushy, aggressive, and downright rude or crude when we stand our ground or assert our views. Some of us have had to be so, unfortunately—since little has been handed to us, and almost everything else that the dominant society naturally assumes is usually withheld or not sufficiently and effectively communicated. Life today is a little different, but the old biases tend to remain, altered, yet present nonetheless. The nature of the differences will elicit a variety of responses from what have become bifurcated political quarters, the conservatives and the liberals. Where are the Hispanics? We are lured by this group on this issue, and encouraged by the other group on other issues. The upshot of our progress, I need to say, is only as good as the next racist statement that may emerge from virtually anywhere. For Hispanics, like other minority groups, still encounter intolerance in one form or another almost anywhere. When we remember that the current generation has been educated by events since the passage of the 1964 Civil Rights Act, we have to note that racial consciousness is still too markedly ingrained in the supposedly educated American psyche.

Thirty years have not made as much of a difference as we thought and hoped they would.

People of different races are still quite noticeably uncomfortable when dealing with others who do not look like them. I do not personally know what can be done, especially since the majority of educators have chosen not to teach our youth about the beauties of learning to live across, among, and next to people from different cultural and racial backgrounds. Educators talk a good talk, but our youngsters are not taught how to like and how to appreciate people who differ from them. As a consequence, the racial divisions remain, and the discomfort felt with people of other races continues to sour our realities.

What we have continued to emphasize in our schools, neighborhoods, and communities is the insidious idea that each one of us is better than our neighbor. We continue to teach our young people that they need to learn to rely on themselves. Being taught in American schools, I essentially learned to rely on myself, and to need other people mainly when there was little choice. This notion is part of the American Creed. Yet, despite its proponents, I am convinced that the idea wreaks havoc on the development of our people, young and old, and on our way of life.

We can see the silly view at work almost everywhere we carefully look. Take a bus station, a restaurant, a ball game, to name a few of the places where people congregate. We tend to visit these places with friends, usually with people who look like us—unless, of course, we happen to be with fellow employees and thus are making the best of the situations under which we work. But when we have choice, we frequently choose to be with people with whom we feel comfortable, with people who could be our race and blood relatives.

What do we do with the rest of the world? Disregard it, largely because other people do not generally promote our interests, or because they do not directly affect us, except—should I say it?—as obstacles, nuisances, or as sources of inconvenience. The perspective is decidedly unChristian and unfortunately quite widespread. I am talking now even about educated people, about people who should have been taught otherwise and who supposedly know better. Which is also to say that the disregard and the lack of human consideration among others is even more noticeable. But what is the excuse of the educated who know better and yet continue to disappoint us as leaders and shapers of real life and public policies?

Where has education failed us? Everywhere, when it comes to human relations. Psychology, business, and a number of other disciplines have marked out "human relations" arenas, but how people deal with and treat other people cannot and should not be compartmentalized into specific disciplines and markedly ignored by other areas of study.

So, what do I see in contemporary postmodern America and as the twenty-first century approaches?

I see "human relations" classes or course components where African Americans, Whites, Hispanic citizens, Asian Americans, Native Americans, and people of many more ethnic groups sit incommunicado. Everyone is in his or her own separate world, supposedly respecting one another's privacy, but actually too carefully and actively engaged in disregarding the other. For, if we look closely, we can see that an enormous amount of human energy in such gatherings is invariably spent on cautiously ignoring each other without necessarily being impolite, though nowadays downright impoliteness is not out of order either.

When the professor or the class coordinator of our hypothetical class appears carrying the textbook for the class, it soon becomes clear that the objective of College Course 101 on "Human Relations" is to mix, to be human. The idea for this class, says the professor, is to treat other people who do not look like us as if they are actually human beings. The idea that needs to be communicated, expounds our imaginary professor, is that people need to feel comfortable about approaching others to discuss issues of supposed mutual concern. There is a basic common humanity that undergirds all of us, that minimizes the noticeable differences between us, that connects us to the human lot, and that brings out our common humanity. While the class or the lesson on "how to be human" lasts, interactions occur that are genuine or that may at least look genuine. But when the class or the situation ends and the student representatives of American culture filter back out into the streets of America and the world, the prevalent disregard for people of other races that we noted at the beginning of the class returns. That disregard essentially says, "I would prefer not to deal with you because you do not look like me. I don't feel comfortable talking to you, and, since I do not have to, I will instead talk to others who look more like me."

My point is that our education, since it is influenced and undermined by the images we constantly see on TV and in real life, is not real. Education is not meant to affect and to change for the better the real world that we all know and where we play out our days. What we teach in the schools and in the universities is not genuine. Our education does not consciously seek to change attitudes that are pernicious to the welfare of all human beings. Our educational materials do not attempt to change the souls of human beings. As educators, leaders, and parents, we do not try to transform the hearts of people who need to be taught that all human beings must be approached with respect if we are to build better relations with all other members of the human race.

What is to be done? There are no easy solutions to the human dilemma of desirable racial relations. But we need to begin to acknowledge widely that we have failed. We need to draw up local communal plans designed to transform the souls of people, so that we can all understand that true human relations do not consist of a course or two, but rather a full-time twenty-four-hour endeavor, that should be practiced everywhere we go.

We need to change the ways in which we visually and cognitively interpret and respond to people who are not like us. That is the bottom line when we consider how we really feel about people unlike us, about people who are different.

All-American Girl and Images
of Asians in the Media

■ ■ ■

K. CONNIE KANG

> Asians have never been accepted in America. Whether their ancestors have been here four or five generations, they are still held as foreigners.
>
> One of the great ironies of Asian American reality today is that the demography of Asians is overwhelmingly immigrant, but their spokesmen are predominantly American-born second, third, and fourth generations. The American-born spokesmen purport to represent immigrants even though their lives hardly cross each other.
>
> —*Conversations with K. W. Lee in 1994*

In Los Angeles, the capital for Koreans in America, vernacular language newspapers, television, and radio had hyped ABC's *All-American Girl* comedy series for weeks, as if it were the most important television program in years. By the time September 14, 1994, arrived, the sitcom and its star—Margaret Cho—were not only the talk of the town, but Koreans had planned their evening around the 9:30 P.M. show schedule.

I, too, was in front of the TV set that Wednesday night to catch this historic happening—the first time one of our own would play the central character in a prime network sitcom centered on a Korean immigrant family. I wondered how the Great American myth-making machine that had so often in the past misconstrued, stereotyped, garbled, and bungled the Asian American experience would handle it this time. Nationwide a million Koreans hung on eagerly, expectantly, hopefully, as did countless other Asians in America.

To my chagrin, what I saw was not a Korean immigrant family. Food, clothing, and home decor were a hodgepodge of what non-Asians might perceive to be generically Asian. Korean phrases and words spoken on the show were so mauled that they were unintelligible. Older members of the family—except for the father—spoke English with concocted Asian accents, stilted and very un-Korean. Try as I did, I saw nothing authentically Korean on the set.

Despite the dismal first episode, however, I watched the show periodically out of personal and professional interest. I wanted to see whether or not it was improving. Considerable criticism had been leveled by Asians, especially Koreans, from the start, and I had hoped that the producers and the writers of the sitcom would take these criticisms to heart. Apart from minor cosmetic changes here and there, *All-American Girl* remained a series that was not funny, failed to convey unique aspects of an immigrant Korean family life, and reduced cultural and generational gaps to a handful of silly, made-up situations.

It was hard to imagine a real-life twenty-two-year-old Korean American college student like Margaret, brash and loud, always sparring with her mother, hanging out in a mall, dating boys in leather riding motorcycles—even posing in the nude for a sculptor. Or the soft-spoken father, who stood a foot shorter than his wife and spoke perfect American English—"Oh, shucks" kind of American gestures and all. He didn't even come close to resembling Korean fathers. And the strong-willed mother, with her upswept hairdo and stilted Chinese accent and attire, hinted at the dragon lady image. In reality, Korean mothers are conciliators, who keep their families together. The grandmother came across as a nervous fool; Korean grandmothers are dignified and revered figures. And the cardiologist brother was so nerdy that it just confirmed the Asian stereotype that has dominated the image of Asian males in American movies and media for a century.

Too bad. *All-American Girl* had so much potential, had its creators tried even a little. The show could have been a ground-breaking entertainment that brought Asians into America's living rooms as real people. Instead, what the viewers got were eighteen episodes that failed to offer any insight into the dynamics of a Korean family. Chinese, Japanese, and Koreans were lumped together—their traditions mixed into a mishmash that grated on Koreans. For centuries Koreans have fought with their lives to maintain their culture in the face of foreign invasion and domination. Koreans rightfully don't like it when what isn't Korean is attributed as such. With half a million Koreans living in the Los Angeles area, even a cursory inquiry would have put the creators of *All-American Girl* in touch with real Koreans who know—not merely ones without historical or cultural memories who look "Korean."

Had there been other television shows about Koreans, one TV program would not have mattered so much. But *All-American Girl* was the only one out there, which is why a lot more than money and a network success or failure rode on it.

In the old days when there were relatively small numbers of Asians living in the country, Hollywood might have gotten away with this. But in the 1990s, coast to coast, there were almost 8 million Asians, their numbers growing at a faster rate than any other minority. Never before had there been as many Asians living in America engaged in so many different occupations and lifestyles. Though Asian Americans are renowned as senators, journalists, Nobel laureates, architects, and physicians, their image in the media continues to be stereotypical and one-dimensional. In California, Asians formed 10 percent of the population in the 1990 Census, surpassing African Americans as the second biggest minority, after Latinos. Nationwide, Koreans alone number 1 million. Until the late seventies, when America discovered Koreans running markets in inner cities, we Koreans were the most invisible among people from East Asia, living in the shadow of the more numerous Japanese and Chinese. Despite our long history in America, and our unique reason for coming here—America was one of three key areas from which Koreans waged an independence movement to rid themselves of Japan's colonial rule in the first five decades of the century—we never had a clear identity in America. We were considered Chinese or Japanese. Tell them we're "Korean" and people would ask, "What's that?"

K. W. Lee, a pioneering Korean American journalist, told me how he had changed his first name, Kyung Won, to the simple initials K.W. to accommodate Anglo editors who could not pronounce it. "Not only did I change my name but I became Chinese because no one knew what Korean was," he said. "Even during the height of the Korean War, people in the rural [American] South, where I worked, did not know what Korea was. They'd ask, 'Where are you from?' When I said, 'Korea,' they wanted to know, 'What part of China?' So I said I was from China to shorten the conversation." In the Tennessee of the 1950s, Lee was called "Chee-na-man."

That has been our history in America: a confusion of identities.

Likewise, a century and a half after their arrival on these shores, Americans of Asian ancestry still remain "foreigners" in their homeland.

"Asians have never been accepted in America," said Lee, an observer of Asian American life for half a century. "Whether their ancestors have been here four or five generations, they are still held as foreigners." It is as if you can never become a full-blooded American citizen as long as you have Asian features.

Moreover, our fate in America has been largely decided by forces beyond our control. We cannot escape fallout from political situations involving Asia—trade wars, immigration, and economic conditions. The impact of these various factors becomes pervasive and instantaneous today because of television. And the tendency of American news gatherers to accentuate the negative compounds the problem. The result is confused, half-baked images of Asians in America.

When the first Chinese came to California about the time of the Gold Rush, they were called "celestials"—meaning peculiar beings from another world. Later they were depicted as heathens who frequented opium and gambling dens. In the early decades of the twentieth century, American admiration of Japan's power tended to soften scapegoating—until World War II, when Japanese in this country became the "yellow peril," and California newspapers promoted the internment of Japanese Americans. In the early forties, when the United States supported General Chiang Kai-shek, Chinese here and abroad enjoyed a period of good feelings from Americans. But with the triumph of the Communist government on the mainland in 1949, the Chinese for the most part once again were seen as evil enemies. Pre-1970 portrayals of Asians in Hollywood were mostly negative: sly and sinister Fu Manchu; bumbling Charlie Chan, whose "Confucius say" fortune cookie aphorisms denigrated the great Chinese sage; exotic geisha images, and subservient women used as playthings for white males. The Korean and Vietnam wars contributed their share of negative images by making it appear as if Koreans and Vietnamese were less human than Americans, that their lives were worthless.

In *M*A*S*H*, the popular comedy series set in war-torn Korea, no attempt was made to endow Koreans with humanity. "When I watched *M*A*S*H*, I was often enraged by a supposedly Korean person wearing a Vietnamese-style hat wandering around in a Japanese-looking village mumbling nonsensical syllables that were supposed to be Korean," the Korean American attorney T. S. Chung told me. Like other Koreans, he was only too glad to see the show go off the air. "Americans may not think all this amounts to much. But let me ask this question: How would you feel if a Korean TV producer portrayed an American as a Mexican in a Canadian village mumbling sounds in German or French?"

With the great Asian migration to the United States in the 1970s and

1980s, the images began changing. The country's Asian population more than doubled, and new stereotypes arose. Popular portrayals cast Asians as model minorities who excelled academically and economically at the expense of others. But at the same time new perceptions distinguished some Asians as greedy inner-city merchants, or as uneducated and unskilled refugees who drain social services, or as vicious gangs who prey on their own people. These stereotypes continued to dominate the media and the public mind into the nineties. Along with them, Americans continued to cling to the intransigent tendency to confuse and conflate Asians from abroad with Asian Americans—a sore point exacerbated by movies like 1993's *Rising Sun*, which many activists criticized for failing to draw distinctions between American citizens of Asian descent and Japanese nationals. I am always amused when I peruse the so-called top American newspapers. They give more space to covering Asia and writing about Asians over there than Asians who live right here in their backyard. Asian American stories often are relegated to inside pages, thus continuing their invisibility instead of showing them as people with a range of experiences like everyone else. Like *sushi,* a trendy food for yuppies of the eighties, other Americans seemingly can only take just so much of things Asian.

It is against this backdrop that *All-American Girl* has to be considered. All along, the real problem with our misidentity had been the inclination of non-Asians to lump us all together, indistinguishable from one another. *All-American Girl* illustrated that propensity, and Hollywood's ignorance and indifference when it came to depicting an ethnic group about which it knew almost nothing. I can think of many sitcoms centered on cross-cultural journeys of Asians in America that would be both entertaining and informative. Time was more than ripe for a prime-time show featuring Asians. Koreans were a natural since they're the most visible Asians in urban centers, their presence having been blasted into the American consciousness during the 1992 Los Angeles riots. With Cho on the rise and on the scene, the ingredients for such a show were right at hand, making it seem all the more doable.

But the show's creators neglected some basic considerations. Instead, they simply superimposed Asian characters on a standard sitcom format. That's where they went wrong. Had they done a little research, they would have realized that you cannot simply substitute Asian faces for an Archie Bunker, or Cliff Huxtable, or any other previous television family. To depict an immigrant family is to know their history, their ethos, and the dilemma of their cross-cultural journeys. Judging by the end result, the family in *All-American Girl* could just as easily have sprung from the Midwest corn belt.

Had there been even one person on the show who spoke fluent Korean and knew the culture, it might have made a difference. Of the show's eleven writers, none was Korean. Margaret Cho, the only Korean in the cast, does not speak Korean, as is of course the case with many second-generation Korean Americans. In their press releases, its creators made a point of noting that there were two Asian American writers. Here again, they wrongly assumed that two Chinese American writers—merely because they looked like Koreans—would know about Koreans. Obviously they did not. An example: Chinese consider the color red good luck, but Koreans do not. Besides creating a hybrid Asian family and in the process failing to bring any semblance of accuracy or truth to the viewer, another major problem revealed by the *All-American Girl* gambit is the sitcom format itself. As it has evolved, it relies heavily for its humor on family members insulting each other, either aggressively or benignly. This formula, which characterizes most comedy sitcoms today, jars the Korean sensibility. Koreans esteem politeness; we do not find personal insults funny.

There may be some who would argue that even negative visibility is preferable to invisibility, and that the mere fact that the show was on television was an accomplishment. I don't agree. Judging from countless comments I have received from Koreans from Los Angeles to New York, I would have to say that almost all of them share my sentiment. It's interesting that the Koreans who were most critical of the show were Cho's contemporaries. They told me how "uncomfortable" they felt watching her poke fun at things that Koreans hold so dear, such as their relationship with their parents.

Certainly Asian Americans, including Korean Americans, need representation on TV, but not in the way of *All-American Girl*. We don't need more caricatures. What we need are depictions of Asians in our full humanity, be they Chinese, Japanese, or Korean. When people watch television sitcoms, they want to see reflections of themselves, something they can relate to. We are no different. Unless, of course, the aim of the show is to have the mainstream enjoy laughs at the expense of Koreans. Remember, Cho represents only herself—an ambitious stand-up comic determined to succeed. But cast in the role of a member of an immigrant family, she unfortunately appears to represent more than what she is to those who don't know Koreans and Korean family dynamics. Had she been more attuned to the Korean American community, she would have sought counsel from experts who would have been only too willing to help her and her show. Had that happened, we might not have seen these hokey, exaggerated characters, who didn't look or talk like Koreans, acting silly and looking foolish.

Cho isn't the first Korean American comedian to make it into the mainstream. Nearly two decades ago, Johnny Yune, a talk show host on Korean television in Los Angeles, dabbled in movies and TV shows. Henry Cho (no relation to Margaret Cho) is a popular stand-up comic who appears regularly on talk shows and in nightclubs. But Margaret Cho is the first highly visible female Korean American entertainer and the first one to receive such a high-profile venue. Unfortunately, she was not ready to meet community expectations surrounding such high visibility.

It's high time people in the entertainment industry accepted the reality that America is multicultural and diverse. I am well aware of the fact that few occupations are more segregated than TV and film writing, which is why most of what comes out of Hollywood is unacceptable not only to Asians but to other minorities as well. More than 95 percent of film and television writers may be white, but they must remember that in major American cities, minorities are the majority. It will have to be a rule for anyone contemplating a show like this in the future to retain someone more culturally knowledgeable about Koreans this time—not just a person with an Asian face. As K. W. Lee so aptly put it, a great irony of Asian American reality today is that while Asians are overwhelmingly immigrants, their spokesmen are predominantly American-born second, third, and fourth generations. The American-born spokesmen purport to represent immigrants, but they really can't and don't because they don't speak and read their ancestral language, which deprives them of a memory, and of understanding.

Multiculturalism and
the Media

■ ■ ■

JACK FOLEY

Multiculturalism is the point at which genetic inheritance becomes cultural inheritance. What deep information do we receive from our genes? What myths are possible in the light of that information? How do we connect with those generations whose histories we carry with us and whose choices influence ours?

I am half Irish and half Italian, but I was born and raised and shaped by America—first by east-coast America, then by west-coast America. What does it mean to be *Irish*-American? What does it mean to be *Italian*-American? What does it mean to be *white* American? Is an Irish-Italian-American a *white* American?

In the comic pages of the *San Francisco Chronicle* on Sunday, June 24, 1990, there appeared a strip which many of you probably saw. The name of the strip is "Funky Winkerbean" and its author is Tom Batiuk. The principal character of the strip was a fat man with a little mustache and curly hair. He is, evidently, the owner and only employee of Montoni's Pizza, and he is meant to impress us as Italian. The opening panel suggests that the minute Montoni goes to the bathroom, the telephone begins to ring. "It never fails," he remarks as we see the words "RIIING!" and "FLUSH!" written out in large letters. By the third panel he has answered the phone. He says, "You want a large pizza with everything except anchovies? Okay. . . . And who should we deliver this to?" Do you have any last names? Whatever you say. . . . Just Donatello, Raphael, Michelangelo . . ." The names are those of the Teenage Mutant Ninja Turtles as well as those of great Italian artists. But the point of the strip is that the little man (an Italian) does not seem to recognize the great names from his own cultural heritage any more than he recognizes the names of the turtles. In fact, the point of the strip is that such names have nothing to do with *his* cultural heritage. What relation has "Montoni," owner of a pizza parlor ("plus videos," says the sign), to the great artists Donatello, Raphael, and Michelangelo? If Montoni "looks Italian," as perhaps Donatello, Raphael, and Michelangelo did, his looks are deceptive. Montoni is an Italian *American,* a deracinated man, someone no longer in touch with the greatness of the Italian tradition. This, says the strip, is what it's like to be an Italian *here.*

But there is more to it than that. We the readers are not looking at works by great artists like Donatello, Raphael, and Michelangelo. We are looking at a *comic strip* by Tom Batiuk. It is true that the effect of the strip depends upon our recognizing the names of Donatello, Raphael, and Michelangelo, which is more than Montoni is able to do, but that is the extent of the cultural information required of us. We do not actually have to know anything about the works of these artists. The strip allows us to contemplate what might be called, in comparison to the work of the artists cited, a trivial art form and nevertheless to feel superior to the central character of the strip. But we can ask—who exactly is "deracinated" in this situation? We probably recognize Donatello, Raphael, and Michelangelo because we have read about them in high school or college texts. Are they in any way part of "our" cultural heritage, we who read comic strips? Who are "we" to feel superior to this man who, we discover immediately, goes to the bathroom, has bodily needs, and is ignorant of the art we have read about in books? Why do we laugh at Chico Marx, who spent his entire career playing a moronic Italian immigrant? Why do we not regard him as a vicious stereotype? Why do we not regard Montoni in the same way? Why do we not recognize the time-dishonored ploy of using great figures from the past in order to discredit living people? What does it mean, in our culture, to be Italian American? What do those turtles have to do with being Italian?

According to the *Oxford English Dictionary,* the first appearance in print of the word "white," meaning "a white man; a person of a race distinguished by a light complexion," was in 1671. The second was in 1726: "There may be about 20,000 Whites (or I should say Portuguese, for they are none of the whitest) and about treble that number of Slaves." The term "Caucasian" is even later: "Of or belonging to the region of the Caucasus; a name given by Blumenbach (*ca.* 1800) to the 'white' race of mankind, which he derived from this region."

"Through the centuries of the slave trade," writes Earl Conrad in his interesting book, *The Invention of the Negro,*

> the word race was rarely if ever used. . . . Shakespeare's Shylock uses the word tribe, nation, but not race. The Moor in *Othello* calls himself black and the word slave is several times used, but not race. The word does not appear in the King James version of the Bible in any context other than as running a race. The Bible refers to nations and says: "God made the world and all things therein; and hath made of one blood all nations of men for to dwell on all the face of the earth." The Bible, with all its violence and its incessant warfare between peoples, does not have racist references to tribes, groups, provinces, nations, men.

And again, on the subject of slavery:

> The traffic grew with the profits—the shuttle service importing human chattel to America in overcrowded ships.
> It was on these ships that we find the beginnings—the first crystallizations—of the curious doctrine which was to be called "white supremacy." . . .
> Among the first white men to develop attitudes of supremacy were the slaveship crews.

Hand in hand with what Mr. Conrad calls "the invention of the Negro" goes the invention of "the white man." My son Sean came home from school recently and told me that he had seen some T-shirts which had the equivalent of the phrase "Black Is Beautiful" on them. (I believe the phrase was in fact "Black By Popular Demand.") He complained that he couldn't wear a shirt saying, "White Is Beautiful" or "White By Popular Demand." I said, "That's true, but you *could* wear a shirt saying, 'Irish Is Beautiful' or, 'Italian Is Beautiful' or, 'Jewish Is Beautiful.' " The point is that *white is not an ethnic group*. It has no traditions, no culture, but if it isn't an ethnic group, what is it?

I think the answer is that white is an indication of dominance, that it is always involved at some level with what Kipling called "the white man's burden." "White" in this sense is always an indication of power, or of the struggle for power, or of power's lack. In the entry from 1726 which I quoted a moment ago, the opposite of "Whites" is not "Blacks" but "Slaves." To be white is to engage in dominance behavior. Insofar as one does not engage in dominance behavior, one is not white. But one remains Italian or Irish or German or Swedish or Jewish or whatever. *The only way for the "majority" to conceive of itself as a majority is to conceive of itself as white: without whiteness there are only "minorities."* To speak of multiculturalism, therefore, is to speak of a way of seeing the world *without whiteness*—though one has to admit that whiteness (power, dominance) is much in evidence. We create it daily in our interplay with others. To feel superior to another is to dominate him to some degree, and so part of the pleasure we feel in knowing the names of those artists which poor Montoni is ignorant of is the pleasure of dominance, the pleasure of "whiteness."

What does it mean to be Italian? What does it mean to be Irish? It is to create a deep and intricate fabric of mythologies rooted in the historical character of a people. It is to engage in the extraordinary pleasure of *fictionalizing,* though it is a fictionalizing which continually tests itself against the real. The idea of the "Negro" is indeed "invented," as Mr. Conrad puts it, as is the idea of the "Italian" or the "Irishman" or the "Swede." Only mythology can counter mythology, and if the mythologies we have are racist, sexist, or in some deep sense immoral, then it is necessary to create new mythologies. But mythologies are not created out of nothing. They are the deep expressions of the self-consciousness of a particular people who live in a particular place. It is in fact impossible to think without mythologizing, and mythologies abound in American culture. (What could be more mythological than "the news"?) But most fictions die as quickly as they spring up, and it is the work of the living artist to create mythologies we can live in, fictions which spring, not from the domineering behavior of Madison Avenue—an imperialism of the mind—but from the truth of the living heart. "Possible," wrote the poet Wallace Stevens, "it must be possible."

And of course it *is* possible, but it requires an effort not only of construction but of deconstruction. Only a mythology can counter a mythology, and it is only from the point of view of a new fiction that the inadequacies of the old fiction can be exposed. The matter is particularly complicated for writers because, for the first time in the history of writing, writing finds itself *in competition* with other forms of art. In another speech delivered to the Commonwealth Club, I spoke of, in Father Walter J. Ong's phrase, "the new orality of the electronic era." For many years writing was the only means of preserving what can now be preserved in many and different forms. For many years the only way to encounter the speeches of Thomas Jefferson was to find them in a book. But the speeches of John F. Kennedy? They are on film, on video, on phonograph records. Often the response of the literary community to this crisis of writing has been to denounce "the media," to complain, for example, of the baleful influence of television, though books, like television, are themselves an example of a highly sophisticated and successful mass medium. But surely a better response would be for the literary community to incorporate aspects of the media in order to compensate for some of the sensual limitations of books, and indeed this has already begun to happen. Young poets are producing poems for the page and for the cassette as well. It is here that multiculturalism and the media touch. Writing, like all mass media, continually creates fictions, but it is necessary to keep these fictions tuned to the continual demands and imperatives of multiculturalism. "You're a bigot," said one of the members of this panel to a poet I know. And she was right. A long time ago a friend of mine and I wrote a song called "There's No Man Like a White Man." I don't remember much of the song but the ending was,

> I once built a snow man
> And put him in the hall
> With a white man
>   there's no man
>   at all.

Multiculturalism implies a continual effort of construction and deconstruction. It allows us to test our concepts by bringing them home, taking them inside and seeing whether we end up with something more solid than a puddle of water. What does it mean to be Italian American? Did Columbus discover America or did he invade it? What does it mean to be Irish American? What does it mean to be white?

> I once built a snow man
> And put him in the hall
> With a white man
>   there's no man
>   at all.

7

■ ■ ■

WHAT'S AHEAD FOR ETHNIC STUDIES?

Ethnic Derivatives:
Tricksterese versus
Anthropologetics

■ ■ ■

GERALD VIZENOR

Almost Browne, that native savant of tricksterese, was invited by the student association to deliver the ethnic studies commencement lecture several years ago in Ishi Auditorium at the University of California.

Almost, you see, is almost brown; nearly, but not quite, an obvious trace of his native woodland ancestors. He bears the memories, the rush of native generations, the tease of wild shadows, the rue of heir and bone, in so many obscure stories. His traces are not terminal tragedies, his memories are not the strain of histories. The turn of his shadows must be *true,* but never borderline measures of civilization and reservations. His natural ties are chance, anything but the treason of absolutes. The native stories that overturn the burdens of the *real* are his beam.

Almost is an eternal brush of imagination, more than the real, but never the lonesome testimonies of mere victimry. The fealties of his house and motion are heard in the native tease of the seasons, and always in the summery solace of tricksterese.

Almost, in spite of his given name, derived, as you know, from a natal nickname, was the unconcerned choice of the students. The committee, more than eager to nominate a controversial speaker, had heard his wild lectures on reservation casinos at a recent conference. Tricksterese, his wise banter on cultural envy and "testcross sovereignty," or the sovereignty of native traces and natural motions, aroused the students at the time, but his otherwise natural contradictions and ironies at the commencement ceremonies were too much to bear in an hour, as he was bound to tease the dominance of ethnic nationalism at the university.

I was there, at the back of the auditorium, the last faculty in native studies, and not ready to sit on stage with my colleagues in ethnic studies. Not that we were at war; we were not, except in the sense of contentious promotions, associations, and resources at the university. But it would have been unbearable to be perched in a medieval gown on stage as the last crossblood native on the faculty.

The dominance of untrue histories caught me once more at the university, as ethnic studies advanced and the native presence waned in another trans-ethnic empire. We were burdened once more with historical ironies, those weary creases in our native remembrance. At the same time, our memories are sources of survivance, natural reason, and tricksterese. The auditorium, you see, was named in honor of Ishi, that obscure native other, who had been humanely secured in a museum, as the last of his tribe, by the anthropologist Alfred Kroeber at the University of California.

I sat next to a couple in the back row of the auditorium. They were handsomely dressed for an occasion that seemed to be more significant than the annual commencement ceremonies. The man wore a new suit, and bright black shoes. He told me they were refugees, and that their daughter was the first in their ancient families to be educated, to earn a university degree. I must have made my own family proud in a similar way, and now, by chance, we were the heirs who had overcome the cruelties of racialism and the contradictions of nationalism. The horrors of war were in their near memories, as the massacres of natives were in mine, but our presence at graduation was an assurance of survivance, not victimry, in a constitutional democracy.

Almost, my distant cousin from the reservation, had given me a copy of his lecture when he arrived on campus earlier in the week. He seldom ever said what he wrote in advance, as he would rather tease written words into an oral performance, and he wanted to tease me in that way at graduation.

The Vietnamese couple next to me could not, at first, appreciate the summary tease of native humor. Later, when the students protested, they were troubled, but they seemed to be pleased to hear that the speaker said

much more than he had actually written. Almost was always more eloquent in sound than in the silence of his written words.

The Vietnamese man turned and told me that his new name was much
the same, more than the words. His breath was scented with mint. "Gio
Nom, my nickname here, not my real country name," he said, as he
printed his name in capital letters next to the name of his daughter on the
program. "My name mean *south wind,* my freedom name." They were
honored, of course, by the achievements of their daughter, and, at the
same time, justly moved by the references to a constitutional democracy.

Almost was not so honored by the faculty of historians, literary theorists, social scientists, and others. They were curious, to be sure, and wary,
but that common academic pose soon turned to anger, accusations, and
summary evasion when he announced in tricksterese that academic evidence was "nothing more than a euphemism for anthropologism and the
colonial dominance over native memories and stories."

The "erstwhile ethnic identities," he shouted, "are fake because we are
tried, yes, *tried,* and feathered, by the racial evidence of invented cultures,
and the tricky trash, you heard me, tricky *trash,* of ethnic nationalism and
anthropologetics." He coined such words as "anthropologism," "anthropologetics," and "tricky trash" to underscore his notion that the practices
of cultural anthropology were, as he said at commencement, "colonial
doctrines, and the deistic rue of dominance."

Almost could not see the seven faculty members seated in a row
behind him on stage. Later he told me they were circus crows, "their
sickle feathers trimmed to the metal chairs." Nearly every sentence in his
lecture caused some bodily response in the faculty—a twitch, a frown, a
turn, a murmur, and at least the sound of their shoes on the hardwood
stage, the natural motion, as it turned out, to escape from the ceremonies.

"Listen to that trash," said a stout sociologist to a historian.

"What, the rue?" said the historian on stage.

"Who is this clown, an evangelist?"

"The student's choice," said the historian.

"Choice, indeed, he sounds like an aborted anthropologist."

"Surely, no more than an invented native."

"Not really, he's the choice of the students to get even with the faculty," said the sociologist. "He might crow their sermon, but not on my
time." Slowly he removed his gown and hood, folded them into a neat
bundle, and then walked out at the back of the stage.

Almost was always in motion, his natural fealty, and seldom troubled
by death or departures. Not much academic ever worried him either, but

he pretended otherwise in some of his stories. Natives, he said "are almost always in constant motion, even the spirit after death, and that's what native sovereignty means, motion, not the curses and causes of manifest manners at universities."

The very moment that he raised his arms over the podium, and opened his wide mouth over the microphone that morning in the auditorium, only a few students could remember, without evasions or apologies, why on earth he had ever been invited to lecture at the commencement ceremonies. Even the couple next to me had their doubts until he mentioned native sovereignty and the "tricky motion of constitutional democracies."

Almost leaned closer to the microphone. He was in constant motion at the podium, an assurance of his sovereignty. The faculty was trained to listen, but they were more practiced at other academic maneuvers, and made wry faces as they sat at the back of the stage in borrowed nests, circus crows in their black gowns, velvet hoods, and bright ribbons. The students, who were once his promoters, shunned the very sound of his voice early in his lecture. Not that he was a terrible speaker, almost never less than a memorable contradiction. He was timely, and the tone of his voice was rich and dramatic, but he turned and traced words and sentences in such an ironic manner of survivance that no one could be sure what he meant. No one was ever sure that native tricksterese ever meant anything at any time, anyway.

Almost teased the measures of civilization and the inventions of the native other, the abstruse other of dominance, as the extremes in his stories. Besides, he said, "manners are more extreme at universities." Those students on the committee who dared to stand by their nomination, and that out of mere courtesy, did not understand extremes either, but in the end many students, and most of their parents, wanted to learn how to stand and deliver a lecture in native tricksterese.

Some students insisted that his lecture was a learned satire, and for that, unwise, given the ethnic politics of the audience, but they too were taken with the tricky notion and motion of tricksterese. Nonetheless, his notions were evaded at the time, and since then his words have been twisted, revised, and terminated in hundreds of extreme comments and critiques at the university. The faculty never understood why he was invited in the first place, but no one ever forgot that he was there.

The hiss increased and rushed to the curtains on stage.

"What word, what's the hiss word now?"

The hiss circled the auditorium in harsh and uncertain waves.

"Incertitude, is that the hiss word?" shouted Almost.

The hiss seemed to weaken.

"Necromancy?"

The hiss heaved, rose louder, and became a demon wave.

"Victimry, how about pity, and tragic victimry?"

The demon hiss reached extreme overtones. The sound circled around and around and pierced every ear in the auditorium, but the intensities could not be sustained without some trace of humor. The hiss bounced, wavered, and weakened at last, and then the students laughed at their own hiss performance.

"The victims have it over the necromancers," said Almost.

"Never, never, never," chanted students at the back.

"Why the students do that?" asked Gio Nom.

"The great cultural hiss, no one really knows why."

"So much to hear," said Gio Nom. He was troubled by the want of manners, and, at the same time, he seemed to be amused by the hiss play. I could not understand what he said to his wife about the students.

"Stay out of those word museums," Almost had warned.

When his mood turned, the audience was silent. The students were uncertain and looked to each other for an answer. "So, who are you, the curator?" asked a student in the first row. No one was sure what he meant by "word museums," but it had to be an ironic storehouse of native stories. A double irony because he teased the very words that created the museum. The faculty on stage raised their hands, shrugged their shoulders in casual doubt, and then laughed, artfully.

"The museums that hold our bones and stories," shouted Almost.

"No bones here," said Gio Nom.

"Bravo, bravo," shouted Ishmael Reed. The novelist, who wore sports earphones, had arrived late and was standing at the back of the auditorium. As the audience turned to see who had shouted such bravos of approval, he walked down the center aisle toward the stage. Many children, the brothers and sisters, sons and daughters of the graduates, followed him and said their bravos in tune. "Tricksterese is the best street talk anybody ever heard at the university," said Reed. "We've heard too much from the tattlers, rattlers, and race talkers backlighted in museums, bank lobbies, and network news." The children chanced in the aisles, and they were amused by his gestures, tangled gray hair, and bright orange earphones.

"The converse histories of dominance rather than native survivance have been secured in museums and at universities by several generations of academic masters, and no one hissed about that," shouted Almost.

"Masters, who uses such a word?" said a woman in cultural studies.

"Who, indeed," said a political scientist out of the side of his mouth.

"I mean, the word is out, the ruins of colonialism, the essence of dominance, are at best an anachronism," she said, and tapped the heels of her shoes on the hardwood floor. "Who does he think he is, a candidate for the Senate?" She closed her backpack, raised her sunglasses in one hand, and left the stage.

Almost turned and saw one faculty member leave as another arrived. Ishmael walked on stage and sat in the empty chair next to the visiting faculty member. The children waved to him from the aisles. The audience was amused, and even the last of the faculty waved to the children.

"Now, that's a civilized way to bear commencement," said Roberta Peel, a visiting scholar from the University of Kent at Canterbury. "Please, what's on the orange radio?"

"O. J. Simpson trial," said Reed.

"Americans are so demonstrative about crime," said Peel.

"What was that?" said Reed.

"Natives are forever studied, invented as abstruse cultures, and then embodied in motion pictures as the simulated burdens of civilization," said Almost. "These adversities became more grievous and caused a turn in the notions, courses, and literary canons at universities, but the treacheries and dominance of *anthropologism,* the obsessive, unmerciful studies of natives by social scientists, have *not* been overturned in comparative ethnic studies at this great university."

That much brought the students to their feet in anger, because most students, ethnic or not, were eager consumers of native feathers, leathers, turquoise, photographs, and Mother Earth memorabilia. The students raised their arms to protest the speaker, and black gowns spread out like sails with their gestures. Many students marched in the aisles and chanted, "Natives are not unmerciful, never, never, never!"

Several faculty members removed their hoods and walked out of the commencement. No one was sure, then or now, what word or notion so tormented the students and so bored the faculty. One faculty member in education suggested that the students had no sense of what such words as "necromancy" meant and, rather than show their ignorance at the moment of their baccalaureates, the students protested, a common academic cover story.

"Almost, darn good on his feet," said Gio Nom.

"Now, back to anthropologetics," said Almost. He was unhurried. The faculty watched his every move, and they were much more critical in the end than the students. He wore no socks or tie, his shirt was too large, and his sports coat was stained on the sleeves and torn at the back.

"Johannes Fabian wrote in *Time and the Other* that 'anthropology's alliance with the forces of oppression is neither a simple nor recent one,' not simple here in ethnic studies, not recent anywhere," said Almost. "Ethnic studies is no exception to that oppression because the 'relationships between anthropology and its object are inevitably political,' and the 'production of knowledge occurs in a public forum,' such as this one, right here, the parents, students, and the last of the faculty on stage."

Almost paused to hear the hisses, but he seemed surprised, as the faculty and students were silent. So, he hissed at them. "Fabian, you know, argued as everyone must, that 'among the historical conditions under which our discipline emerged and which affected its growth and differentiation were the rise of capitalism and its colonial-imperialist expansion into the very societies which became the target of our inquiries.' So, the historical alliance with anthropology and the social sciences is evermore political in ethnic studies, and you might say that this graduation ceremony is a statement of that dominance."

"What does he mean?" asked Gio Nom.

"Anthropology is the natural enemy of natives."

Professor Simon Williams, a senior cultural anthropologist, one of the faculty members on stage, removed his black gown and walked toward the podium. A blush blotched his bald head and his face was double creased with rage. His shoes squeaked, and the moment of authoritarian surprise was lost to humor. Almost turned to the squeak and saluted the anthropologist.

"Browne, must you continue to malign everyone to make your point?" said the anthropologist. His wide mouth stretched back over his dark teeth, over the microphone, and his cheeks shivered as he spoke. "This is not the time to criticize the good work we have done to bring ethnic studies into the real world of the social sciences."

"Have you ever been in the military?" asked Almost.

"Have you ever been a professor?" countered Williams.

"Never, but we both know how to salute."

"Fabian is not relevant," said Williams.

"So, he's the squeaky name?" said Almost.

"He never wrote about ethnic studies anyway," said Williams.

"You mean, he never mentioned *your* name?"

"Almost, is that a traditional name?" asked Williams.

"Fabian wrote about the expansion of anthropologism, about the tragic curse of anthropologetics, and he almost wrote about your squeaky shoes and the end of natives in the social sciences," said Almost.

"Never mind the insults, nothing you've said makes any sense, and that's my major objection—not that you were the student's choice, with no credentials, not even a traditional name, but that you think you can tear down what we have taken so many years to build," said the anthropologist.

"You mean the alliance with dominance?"

"Yes, someone must preserve the standards, and the best part of that alliance, as the students, faculty, and parents have already demonstrated so clearly, is your absence, your silence," shouted Williams. The shivers turned into a weak smile, a pathetic figure. The audience was never on his side, and the students were more critical of his dominance than they were of the obscure traces of tricksterese.

"Anthropology's on the ropes," said Almost.

"We *are* the ropes," said Williams.

"You can say that again."

"I have never, in more than thirty years of teaching, been so humiliated and angry at a graduation ceremony," said the anthropologist. "You may have the right to speak at graduation, but you will never have the right to my attention as a listener."

"So, what are you saying, then?" asked Almost.

"You should be silenced," said the anthropologist. He waved his arms, and the sudden motion tossed his gown over his face. The students laughed, and with that he marched to the back of the stage and vanished between the curtains. His shoes squeaked in the distance.

Guess Who's Coming
to Academia?

The Impact and Current State of Black Studies

■ ■ ■

WILLIAM M. BANKS AND
STEFANIE KELLY

In 1967, Sidney Poitier was a *deus ex machina* on the social landscape and in the personal lives of Spencer Tracy and Katharine Hepburn, as well as in the mind's eye of many who watched the trio in Stanley Kramer's film classic, *Guess Who's Coming to Dinner*. The plot: Tracy and Hepburn's young daughter meets and falls in love with Poitier, and prior to soliciting parental approval, the two plan to be married. The film's primary focus, however, is not the couple's life together, but the puzzlement and discomfort of "lifelong" white liberals Tracy and Hepburn upon learning that their son-in-law-to-be is a Black man. In spite of Poitier's mainstream socialization—he is verbally articulate, highly educated, and thoroughly middle class—Tracy and Hepburn are at an unmistakable loss as they scrutinize their daughter's fiancé.

Some one hundred years after the Emancipation Proclamation conferred nominal freedom upon Black people in the United States, the problem of Black-white relations remained significant enough to be the subject of a major motion picture starring some of Hollywood's biggest names. *Guess Who's Coming to Dinner* was one articulation of the plight of Blacks who sought social integration, and of the anxieties of whites who were ill-prepared to deal with integration on a personal level. The era was a dynamic one for Black-white relations; if the fifties and early sixties saw Martin Luther King, Jr., and the integration-oriented civil rights movement garnering massive media attention, the late sixties saw the rise of the more radical black power movement, with the Black Panther Party becoming a new symbol of Black frustration over glacial progress toward social equality and justice in the United States. The March on Washington and King's famous "I Have a Dream" speech were supplanted by the strident voices of Fannie Lou Hamer and Malcolm X demanding a dignity that seemed to transcend the civil rights agenda.

Similarly, the somewhat defensive cry for integration was, to a large extent, replaced by the more (tactically) offensive assertion of Black power, Black beauty, and, if less explicitly than during the Harlem Renaissance, Black intellectual prowess. The leading figures of the black power movement—like so many of Black America's leaders throughout history—were not merely spokespeople but were vigorous thinkers and, frequently, philosophers, not to mention prolific writers.

With *Brown* v. *Board of Education* more than a decade old, its impact, though felt far and wide, had yet to be *seen* in terms of widespread school integration. Public schools, North and South, reflected the longstanding legacy of racial segregation, and even ostensibly liberal communities—like the Hepburn-Tracy household—carried on, unfazed by what they dismissed as the coincidental absence of Black faces in classrooms and communities. This was no less true of the country's overwhelmingly white colleges and universities, where Black activists sought to end a two-hundred-year legacy of racial exclusion.

With national attention focused on the struggle of Black students to gain entry into previously all-white schools at every level, the challenges faced by the tiny corps of Black intellectuals within academia were hardly on the front burner. Nonetheless, activists began reasoning that new intellectual forces were necessary if the institutional status quo was to be altered. African American faculty were seen as the agents—and Black Studies units as the outposts—of this intellectual revolution. Michael Thelwell was among those who challenged the academy's rather fantastic self-image as an oasis of liberal values, a sanctuary where all (qualified) individuals were free to pursue the truths they believed important. In many ways, the academy of the late sixties was not unlike the well-appointed residence of Sidney Poitier's future in-laws in *Guess Who's Coming to Dinner*, complete with its isolated Black staffperson.

However, activists—largely students—who were not content with tokenism, *or* with the confinement of Blacks to low-level administrative positions, disrupted the relative serenity of academia by taking up the cause of Black Studies in the university. Rather than settling for the standard menu and manners prescribed by members of the academic diners' club, Black activists invited themselves to the table and audaciously asserted their right to create their own menu, not to mention prepare their own food. Speaking to more general matters in 1964, Malcolm X prophetically asserted, "I'm not going to sit at your table and watch you eat, with nothing on my plate, and call myself a diner."[1]

Indeed, by the late sixties, documenting the historical failure of classrooms and research centers in higher education to recognize and make room within their agendas for the African American experience was a fairly facile exercise. And while energetic activism forced the majority of institutions to respond, rarely were their initial reactions substantial or sincere. Committees were set up to consider the concerns voiced by student activists, but these were little more than bureaucratic attempts to neutralize activist energy. Most often, universities sought to incorporate student demands into existing institutional parameters: If students wanted more attention paid to the social dynamics of race, professors (typically white) would add relevant readings and perhaps bring in a speaker. Slightly more impressive responses included establishing a course or two on Black history or literature, but on campuses like Yale, San Francisco State, and the University of California at Berkeley, such examples of mainstream-controlled incrementalism were rejected as inadequate. Black activists' sense of urgency clashed with the measured and bureaucratic traditions of colleges and universities to create a volatile atmosphere that demanded change.

At the earliest stages of the Black Studies movement, student activists and their supporters seemed to be gaining ground. Yielding to the logic/pressure presented by Black Studies advocates, campus after campus established Black Studies units. Sometimes these were "programs" comprised merely of an assortment of courses, but in other instances fullfledged "departments" were created, with the ability to confer degrees and recommend tenure. However, there were fundamental contradictions and limited resources built into many early Black Studies programs that escaped the notice of youthful protesters who were riding a rush of activist adrenaline. Among the problems plaguing many fledgling programs were non-tenured faculty, whose status precluded them from full or long-term participation in campus politics. As for funding, soft (i.e., temporary) money resources were tapped to support Black Studies, and in some instances (Berkeley, for example), Black Studies was set apart from the existing schools and colleges and reported directly to an administrator.

The fervor surrounding the Black Studies movement led many to expand the mission of Black Studies far beyond what was reasonable or practical. Forced to comply with student demands, administrators eagerly hoisted onto the shoulders of Black Studies personnel compound responsibility for cultural activities, academic support, campus racial politics, and community involvement. These structural problems indirectly led to the demise of many outposts of Black Studies. By the mid-seventies, when the momentum of the early activism had diminished significantly, administrators moved cautiously but resolutely to reorient Black Studies and establish hegemony. In maintaining but depoliticizing Black Studies, their liberal self-image, with Blacks on the "team," was enhanced.

More than twenty-five years have passed since Black students' demands for Black Studies convulsed American college campuses, and the present moment is ripe for beginning to assess the long-term impact of the Black Studies movement upon higher education and the American intellectual establishment. While we acknowledge that fields like sociology and philosophy were still embryonic at age twenty-five, we believe that the urgent and dynamic and explicitly political character of the Black Studies movement demands and deserves our early attention.

In the mid-eighties, Joseph Russell, director of the National Council for Black Studies, reported that there were approximately 525 programs in colleges and universities in the United States, and that the number was "holding steady."[2] Some programs offer only a few courses in history or literature, while others purport (sometimes naively) to address the "African Diaspora."[3] Some of this country's premier intellectuals are deeply involved in Black Studies programs: before leaving for Harvard in 1993, Cornel West helped to revitalize Princeton's Afro-American Studies program, where Nobel laureate Toni Morrison and a host of other impressive Black scholars currently reside; Sylvia Wynter teaches in African American Studies at Stanford University; Gerald Horne and Cedric Robinson have worked to bring respectability to Black Studies at the University of California at Santa Barbara; Patricia Hill Collins works in Afro-American Studies at the University of Cincinnati; Gerald Early leads African and Afro-American Studies at Washington University; and Harvard's Henry Louis Gates, Jr., was named the "new star" of Black Studies by the New York Times.[4] Some might consider it a sign of progress that Black Studies has the magnetism to attract some of the greatest thinkers of our day. Indeed, the presence of such eminent scholars in Black Studies programs lends a sort of credence to the Black Studies experiment.

High-powered scholars in Black Studies have made the field acceptable, in many respects, to the academic mainstream. The sense of "responsibility" or "commitment"—an imperative if often clumsily articulated concern—has been displaced by more traditional notions: obligation to "discipline," adherence to "professional standards," and priorities that further the careerist objectives of many academics. It is difficult to overstate how the absence of student protest has influenced what Black intellectuals and Black Studies departments do on campuses. Twenty years ago, Black students felt connected to the ideas and many concrete goals of the civil rights and/or black power movements. Consequently, when they fought for Black Studies, the expectation was that Black Studies would articulate some relevant intellectual link to the broader Black community. Today, however, with most Black students scrambling to make the connection between college and occupation, and with community activists reeling from the impact of economic and social repression, Black academic intellectuals are free to engage in flighty esoteric forays. They feel little pressure to serve concrete intellectual/political interests, and in this stance they are strongly supported by the Western academic tradition. Some scholars operate as if Black Studies exists solely to provide them with the same opportunities as the more traditional fields; but if this is true, what distinguishes Black Studies from its older curricular counterparts?

At a time when scholarship and scholarly publications have become absurdly specialized, it may be useful, in the spirit of C. Wright Mills, to question why a field that was launched out of a passionate concern over the "big picture" has lapsed somewhat dispassionately into "trivial pursuit" intellectuality, reifying the very fragmentation of knowledge that thoughtful scholars used to—and some still do—deride.

Russell Jacoby recently wrote of the demise of what he called "public intellectuals," persons who tackled big and important questions and did not hesitate to hurdle boundaries of "discipline." The fame and historical significance of persons like E. Franklin Frazier, Harold Cruse, and St. Clair Drake rests squarely in the public intellectual tradition. But today, in the name of sophistication, some of the most talented Black minds are hard at work shoving African American cultural products into European poststructuralist molds.

Jacoby attributed the decline of public intellectuals to the academization of intellectual life. Still, it was not completely naive to think that a generation of intellectuals whose very access to opportunity was born in the struggle for justice would continue the intellectual offensive on behalf of African Americans. The distance between institutions of higher education and the Black communities from which they pluck a fortunate few has become even greater than it was twenty-five years ago, when community activists were a visible presence on many college and university campuses. The breakdown of political activism in Black communities has created an atmosphere in which Black Studies on some levels can be seen as having been released of its accountability to its constituency outside of academia. This attitude, operating on both conscious and subconscious levels, in turn absolves individual Black intellectuals within the academy of their responsibility to be—and *do*—something different from their "mainstream" academic counterparts.

Obviously, Black intellectuals should not require pressure from without to motivate them to come out punching in public debates. Ample opportunities have arisen in recent years to inspire intellectual activism, among the most important of which was the debacle of President Clinton's aborted nomination of Lani Guinier to the post of Deputy Attorney General for Civil Rights. At a time when so many high-powered Black intellectuals have tenure, why was there such a deadening silence—at least in public forums where it mattered—with regard to the mistreatment of Lani Guinier by reactionary Republicans *and* timid Democrats? Guinier's own academic grounding, and the fact that her thoughtful and decidedly reality-based writings were labeled "radical" and cited as an excuse for her dismissal, should have brought the scourge of the Black intelligentsia. Recalling the powerful "African American Women in Defense of Ourselves" collective that took out a full page in the *New York Times* to protest the mishandling of Anita Hill's charges against Clarence Thomas, we wonder why there was not a similar and perhaps even grander outpouring over the Lani Guinier fiasco. Why was President Clinton not taken to task by individuals who rightly may be considered Lani Guinier's peers? Randall Kennedy of the Harvard Law School, editor of the intellectual journal *Reconstruction*, acknowledged that Guinier's peers were slow in responding to the distortions of her work. Kennedy honestly admits, "I was one of those unresponsive allies."[5] When one recalls his similar treatment of Johnetta Cole, who was considered but never nominated for a post in the Clinton administration, or Surgeon General Joycelyn Elders, who went from Clinton cabinet insider to pariah for merely *suggesting* that drug decriminalization be *considered*— and who ultimately was fired for speaking plainly about controversial public health issues—a disturbing pattern becomes apparent. We cannot help but wonder whether the very issues that caused Clinton to distance himself from Guinier did not also have an impact upon the folks who might have defended her. She was, after all, labeled dangerous precisely because her ideas challenge status quo interests, both white and Black. Her clearly articulated goal is to bring about changes in the big picture by encouraging more substantive dialogue about race, democracy, and power.

In general, though, academia is an ill-suited outpost for makers of social change. The self-contained, self-preserving nature of the academic world insulates it from public pressure in much the same way that Black Studies is divorced from the Black community. In fact, if we consider college and university curricula in a broad social context, they perhaps more than any other public institution historically have *resisted* change. We can look to traditional humanities programs like English and history to discover that, within the fields most deeply rooted in academic soil, stasis abounds. Nonetheless, this nation's institutions of higher education have mastered the tactic of coopting movements and swallowing up would-be social activists—students and faculty alike—and quickly distracting them from their dissatisfaction with the structure of society. In effect, political activism is rechanneled into and reduced to the kind of scholarship that is rewarded with tenure. And it is no secret that the dissemination and impact of such work is profoundly limited.

On the other hand, the emergence and tenacity of Black Studies have forced academia to rethink the organization of knowledge, thereby paving the way for fields such as Women's Studies, Asian American Studies, and Environmental Studies to ride its coattails into the academic arena. This process, of course, is paralleled by the host of domestic liberation movements that in the early seventies strode the trail blazed by the black power movement. But what real relationship do fields such as Black Studies bear to the academic mainstream? How much say do Black Studies personnel and students have in the larger academic context? More importantly, what connection does Black Studies maintain to the poor and working-class Black communities, where, generally speaking, conditions today are even more desperate than those that twenty-five years ago sparked the demand for Black Studies in the first place?

Many of the most powerful Black intellectuals who reside at colleges and universities across the United States tend to be positioned as social and cultural critics, regardless of their disciplinary training. Volumes of essays addressing various aspects of Black life in the United States have been published by Black professors of English, history, sociology, communications studies, American studies, and women's studies—not to mention Black Studies—and this trend promises to continue through the millennium. Indeed, such a proliferation of Black commentary and criticism, such frequent publication of Black writers, is an important development. However, when we consider the relatively narrow and almost exclusively academic readership these volumes appeal to and reach, we begin to wonder whether the work and energies of many leading Black intellectuals are not merely serving to fuel, if diversify, the academic treadmill on which they function. The same may be said of the many very exciting academic conferences that have been organized and largely attended by Black scholars in recent years; even when conscious efforts are made to ensure accessibility to the public, all too often these events culminate with the publication of a book—which takes us back to the top of this paragraph but, again, has little impact upon Black communities or the social policies that continue to marginalize them. Thoughtful people must consider why, at a time when Black intellectuals are the fad *du jour,* are the prospects for less privileged Blacks slowly eroding?

In addition to the questions we have raised above, we think it worthwhile to consider the impact of contemporary multiculturalism rhetoric upon Black Studies. The deleterious "melting pot theory" has been replaced by more "politically correct" references to a mixed salad, a revised conception of U.S. society in which individuals who previously (ideally) would have assimilated now have the purported opportunity to share in the American pie without compromising their culture, language, and so on. But discussions of diversity on college campuses and in society at large tend to obscure the centrality of the Black-white dynamic in American life.

In the sixties and early seventies, most Black scholars rejected the idea that the social experience of African Americans was just another immigrant odyssey. The long history of race-based discrimination in all American social and cultural institutions implied a different dynamic from the experience of other ethnic Americans. Yet today, scholars who elect to concentrate on this seminal aspect of American life are dismissed as "particularists." Analyses that blur or minimize distinctive aspects of African American history in favor of frameworks like "the other" or "people of color" find receptive audiences, but have the undesirable effect of impeding very important dialogues on Black-white relations in the United States. Thus, multiculturalists are thought to be the wave of the future, while so-called particularists are seen increasingly as backward in their thinking.

At the same time, the growing demand for interdisciplinary scholarship—which, by definition, Black Studies *is*—may be seen as suggesting that work on what once was called "the Negro question" (that is, how to eradicate the many problems Black people encounter living in the United States) must necessarily be in conversation with more traditional areas of theory, history, or literature in order to be valid or worthwhile. Many Black scholars respond to those pressures with a reluctance to focus exclusively on—or to specialize primarily in—Black Studies. They situate themselves within more traditional fields and then deal with African American subject matter, rather than rooting themselves firmly in Black Studies and redefining their scholarly approach altogether. Over twenty-five years ago Harold Cruse noted this trend and warned of the implications. But today a declining number of intellectuals seem unwilling to "marry our thought to the plight of the new poor and the environment."[6]

We believe, however, that to centralize Black-white relations—and to work exclusively in Black Studies—is not to dismiss the struggles of non-Black people of color or to turn one's back on other fields. Rather, it is to highlight and refocus attention upon the unique historical circumstances of African Americans and America's racial ordering hierarchy. Andrew Hacker perhaps overstates the case: "In many respects, [non-Black U.S. minority] groups find themselves sitting as spectators, while [Blacks and whites] try to work out how or whether they can coexist with one another."[7] However, in his landmark study *Two Nations: Black and White, Separate, Hostile, Unequal*, Hacker very effectively outlines the unmatched systematic oppression to which Black Americans historically have been subjected. On a related note, we further feel the need to point out that neither does what may seem a myopic focus on the dilemma of Black Americans necessarily signal a nationalist bent. This charge is a convenient excuse for dismissing discussions of the African American situation, and has been leveled at proponents of Black Studies for years. However, the intent of such focused discussions, as well as of Black Studies itself, is not to ignore, dismiss, or belittle the historic struggles of non-Black people of color, but to centralize African American life, culture, and history in one of the few institutional forums available for such activity.

One conclusion to be drawn from a prolonged reflection on the impact and current state of Black Studies is that the bottom seems to have fallen out of the historical legacy that gave birth to the field. In an era when distinctions between the political left and right are vague at best, a radical experiment like Black Studies seems to have landed somewhere in the center. Those scholars carrying out the radical/activist promise of Black Studies—those who have proven themselves to be public intellectuals—are the exception rather than the rule, and the enormous numbers of Black students who are being swallowed up in business programs (there remains a profound lack of African American students in math, sciences, English, etc.) suggest that something has gone awry. The societal reinforcement of incredulous messages like "What are you going to *do* with a degree in Black Studies?" is precisely what was being challenged when, shortly after Sidney Poitier came to dinner, Black Studies came to college campuses. Today, though, too many Black scholars, established and budding, are losing interest in the distinct flavors Black Studies has to offer, while at the same time the Black Studies menu is catering increasingly to an agenda of pious academic multiculturalism that is far removed from the reality of non-middle-class people of all ethnicities.

By all means, we celebrate the diversification of U.S. society and of student bodies across the country. However, as we all join hands and march toward a bright day, let us not fall back into the "melting pot" mentality that weakens the ongoing and ever crucial struggle for Black socioeconomic parity. The longstanding systematization of anti-Black racism in the United States has served as an effective model providing guidelines for the treatment of other so-called minority groups. For that reason alone, it is imperative that Black Studies scholars at every level—and from every ethnic or national background—refocus our attention and energy toward reconnecting Black Studies with Black communities and carrying on, with a vengeance, the work that began twenty-five years ago.

■ ■ ■

NOTES

1. George Breitman, ed., *Malcolm X Speaks*. 2nd edition (New York: Pathfinder, 1990), p. 26.
2. Joseph Russell quoted in "Black Studies Today" by Howard La Franchi, *Christian Science Monitor*, February 7, 1984, p. 23.
3. Phrases like "Diaspora Studies" tend to depoliticize the context of Black Studies, and invite abstract theorizing with little attention to historical realities.
4. See Adam Begley, "Black Studies New Star," *New York Times Magazine*, April 1, 1990, p. 24.
5. Randall Kennedy, "Lani Guinier's Constitution," *American Prospect* 15 (Fall 1993), p. 46.
6. Sylvia Wynter, "No Humans Involved: An Open Letter to My Colleagues," in *Knowledge for the 21st Century* 1, no. 1 (Fall 1994).
7. Andrew Hacker, *Two Nations* (New York: Ballantine Books, 1992), p. x.

Multinational, Multicultural America versus White Supremacy

■ ■ ■

AMIRI BARAKA

American culture, first of all, is hemispheric. When we say America, we are really saying Pan-America. Most of the people of Pan-America are brown and speak a Latino Spanish. Moreover, the official "Western" culture the rightist wags and academics speak of is Europe. But Europe is not the West. I have a poem that says, "Leave England/headed West/you arrive in Newark."

The Europe "cover" to Pan-American or even North American culture is merely the continuation of European colonialism and slavery. In fact, from its origins, the term "Western world" meant Europe in relationship to Asia and Africa, pre-Columbus's "discovery" of *el Mundo Nuevo,* the New World. And that discovery, we know from experience, certainly combines dis and cover. The rappers let us know what dissing someone means—to disrespect them. The biggest "dis" is that they can even make you dis/appear.

"Cover" is a record company term meaning that, for instance, when Big Mama Thornton or Big Joe Turner (or Duke Ellington, for that matter) put out a record, the white supremacist-oriented record industry immediately put out a "cover"—a version of the song by a white performer (in the first two cases, Elvis Presley and Pat Boone). Just as Vanilla Ice or Young Black Teenagers (a white rap group!) are beginning to do to rap.

It is very important to these corporate/government powers which control American society always to keep the musical lovers segregated. Like Confucius said, "If the people hear the wrong music, the Empire will fall." And for the broad multinational masses of the American nation to take up the sentiments and content of Afro-American music, in this case, is to disrupt the racist national oppression that is the fundamental philosophy of the American social system, reflecting its imperialist economic base.

When we say that American education must be as multinational and multicultural as the reality of American society, we are just saying that what is taught in the schools should be the whole culture of the American people.

Americans are still remarkably unconscious about the totality, the whole dimension, of their own culture. But that is because the powers that be are determined to maintain white supremacy as the philosophical justification for the exploitation and oppression of most of the world's peoples. Certainly, in relationship to all the variety of people inside the United States, the Eurocentric construct of so-called official Western culture America is a racist fraud. A fraud that has held the entire culture of the world—and certainly of the Pan-American world—as hostage.

The assertion that the very brief period of European hegemony in the world means that "European" culture (a term that could be disputed even in the nineteenth century since neither Germany nor Italy existed as states prior to this) is eternal, and the supreme measure and description of civilization, is, of course, Nazi diktat. There is no reality to it, except as a reflection of the rise of European hegemony in the world along with the rise of capitalism, the slave trade, colonialism, and modern imperialism.

The Greek Attic, like any culture, cannot be isolated from the whole context of its emergence and development. It is the result of what came before it, just like any other culture. But even more repressive is that since the majority of the peoples in the world are not European, this kind of thinking is just neo-Goebbels/ism, very fitting for our time, which has all the hallmarks of another Weimar Republic.

The very move to the right in the United States, for instance, particularly with the fall of the revisionist USSR, has seen the rise of extreme nationalism not only in the United States but around the world. The attempt to maintain a mainly Eurocentric and blatantly racist curriculum in public schools and colleges in the United States is an attempt to maintain old slavery while calling for new slavery.

Part of the stunning development of the retrograde trend in the United States of Negro academics, artists, politicians, as part of the whole reactionary period emerging in the eighties, shows how so-called integration into the racist academic and social curricula of these colleges has helped shape an entire new generation of Buppie Toms, who have profited by black struggle but who have been taught to disconnect themselves from the black majority, ideologically as well as socially.

One reason for the alienation of black and Latino students from the schools is the curriculum, which they begin to understand by the third grade has very little to do with their lives or history. The incorrectness of the teaching methodology comes from this as well, since these distortions and lies must be taught by rote, committed to memory rather than learned!

And even though the rubric of the Blooms and Schlesingers speaks of Western culture, and makes obeisances to the ancient Greeks and Romans, in their modern cultural assessment these same white supremacists dismiss both of these modern peoples as "degenerate." (More Goebbels!)

In fact, in the modern world, "Western culture" means mainly England, France, and Germany. Spain and Italy are always neglected, and the rest of the world plunges into silent oblivion.

When you speak to upholders of the status quo of undemocratic education and the culture of inequity, they will tell you that multicultural curricula are not possible because it's "technically impossible" to include all people's cultures, suggesting that only the distorted paper culture of national chauvinism is "normal" (a northern sickness).

It is simply that we want to include the real lives of the people of our world, the whole world. American culture is the creation, for instance, of all Americans. It is the combining of all the nationalities and cultures here that makes up the actual national character of American culture. And no one is belittling the accomplishment of European humanism. Actually, an authentically multinational and multicultural curriculum would revalidate the authentic masterpieces of all cultures, highlight their fundamental unity, and help diminish their conflicts.

The undeveloped material life of most Americans is justified by both the absence from U.S. school curricula of such cultures and the distortion of their lives in them. The racial chauvinism of the so-called Literary Canon justifies the military cannon that enforced colonialism throughout the Third World yesterday or the invasion of Panama, Grenada, the destruction of Iraq today. The academic or artistic chauvinism explains the economic and social exploitation.

But the very underdevelopment of the Northern Colossus itself, in real terms, with millions of Americans living under the poverty line—including the majority of the Afro-American nation's children—is tragic for black people. It also is an economic deprivation, a lack of development of the larger United States itself, since the lack of education and livelihood of the black masses subtracts from the whole of the U.S. livelihood and economic development. The old slavemaster continuum that Bush and U.S. imperialism favored generally has already been proven economically outmoded. The black and minority aspects of the U.S. market detract from the total prosperity, since black Americans constitute an important part of even U.S. monopoly capitalist market, whose potential cannot be tapped because of the low level of productive forces, including marginal education and high unemployment rates.

In the case of the almost neocolonial domination of English culture in the United States, it's as if the Tories at least won the cultural revolution. So you have huge English departments (even though "George Washington Won the War") and American Studies is tiny where it exists, and Black Studies, etc., are always under fire and in danger of being removed.

It is just this Eurocentric, white supremacist cover of the real American culture that issues like multicultural education seek to eliminate. The Jeffries/CCNY issue was not so much about what Professor Leonard Jeffries said. (The influence of the Jewish bourgeoisie in Hollywood has been well documented already by Jews, and the influence of organized crime, including the Mafia, has been equally publicly discussed. And no one of the slightest analytical capacity can doubt the caricature of black lives in American flicks. But then, to paraphrase a writer in *Cinéaste*, look at Hollywood's distortion of Jews and Italians as well.) Jeffries had been talking black cultural nationalism for years and nothing happened. It's just since he became a leading member of the group that put together New York's so-called Curriculum of Inclusion, that by attacking him dirt could be thrown which would cover that proposed new curriculum with much dis.

Remember, change of curriculum lessens the domination and influence of many vested interests within the schools, and even results in the expansion of certain curricula and teaching jobs within the education system. The development of a really democratic educational curriculum of "formal" U.S. culture would reflect a movement to create a more democratic United States and a more equitable relationship to the rest of the world.

Color at Cal

■ ■ ■

RUSSELL ELLIS

America has high hopes for its colleges and universities. We expect successful race and ethnic relations in them that have not been realized in any other of our institutional settings. Thus, there is great public disappointment in the much discussed tendency that has developed at all colleges or universities with multiethnic student bodies. This tendency inclines new undergraduates to inspect the merits of their ethnic identification before any other, including gender. The flagging attention of a front-line worker in the financial aid office now immediately fills the available interpretive vessel, "racism," when the new Asian, black, or Chicano student's palpable ache could easily be the usual homesickness, loneliness, or fear of failure.

As at any other college, Berkeley has its identity islands, onto which students climb for safety until they get their bearings. New college students remain nervously adventuresome yet conformist. What is new is the color coding. Once, Catholic, Protestant, Jew, and social class exhausted the main categories framing university students' campus identity. Otherwise, outside traditionally black colleges, almost everyone was "white." Campus life was meagerly larded with the occasional "Negro," "Mexican," or "Chinese" student that everyone knew and remembered. College graduates currently fifty, sixty, and seventy years of age can happily misremember being in classes rife with "colored" colleagues, but without all that ethnic or racial rancor that seems to characterize campus life today. So, why, now, is it like this? Why would university administrators allow something that looks like the dreaded "balkanization" of student sub-communities? Where will this all lead? Can it be any good?

During the 1980s, Chancellor Ira Michael Heyman successfully diversified the U.C. Berkeley undergraduate student body. His approach was simple. The California Master Plan in higher education obliges University of California campuses to select their freshmen students from the top 12.5 percent of the California high school graduating class, as measured by a combination of grades and test scores. At Cal, on average, 26,000 applications yield 4,800 new undergraduates each year. Being the most attractive U.C. campus for high-achieving students, Berkeley was able to admit the first 50 percent of its freshman class from the top 3 percent of California's high school graduating class, and to expand the range of qualities—including ethnicity—it looked for in the other half. Once this determination was made, the task was to recruit those eligible students to Cal. Heyman succeeded. As it happened, every successive entering class admitted under this policy since 1983–84 has, on raw numbers alone, improved. Each new class is the "best ever" on the numbers that pass for merit, i.e., gpa and SAT.

Now, what's interesting is that no decent college or university admits students on SAT scores or grade point averages alone. Not the elite privates. Harvard famously admits only 10 percent of its freshman class exclusively on a combination of gpa and test scores. Certainly not the public elites like Michigan, Virginia, Berkeley. You "build" a class. You have a notion, constrained by your public-ness, of how your mission as a university serves the larger public policy good. For the premier public university in a uniquely diverse state, Heyman sought and got ethnic diversity . . . on campus.

The kind reader will muffle his or her mocking laughter when I, a sociologist, report how little inter-ethnic mingling apparently takes place among the parents of our students. Roughly a third of our freshman class comes from households in which English is not the "first" language. This linguistic fact speaks as a proxy for ethnicity. Most students, even from ethnically concentrated urban schools, report some level of contact with teachers and students of other ethnicities or races. In general, students can even report with some certainty that their parents work with such others.

But, in over two decades of compulsive asking, it is the infrequent Berkeley student who can report that people of other ethnicities or races were close friends of their parents or, for example, were guests in their parents' homes for dinner.

As with the well-known segregated Sunday morning, dinner and after work friendships continue to happen, it seems, in white, Chinese, African-American, Chicano groupings. Nonetheless, we at the university continue to get beaten about the head and shoulders by the media arm of public opinion because of the perceived "balkanization" of the student body and the attendant "racial tension" the world believes must be the case on campus. It is easy to see why the world believes that.

In fact, our students are behaving like normal Americans. Actually, they're better behaved. Berkeley has one of the lowest incidences of student-on-student violence in the land. What inter-ethnic tension there is tends to come from idealistic students' frustrated attempts to realize the benefits of Berkeley's vaunted diversity or from clumsy attempts at intimacy ("How do you get your hair like that?"). One major and sobering exception to this relatively genteel negotiation of difference occurred after the Rodney King decision. It never erupted, but it was terrifying to stand between the "dissed" black students from L.A. and the L.A. Koreans who had lost face and property. As we speculate on post-black/white America, we should be prepared to hear a lot more about this one.

"When peoples meet, they may fight but they will definitely fuck."

1955: UCLA. The moment was shocking and indelible. The course was Cultural Anthropology. The professor's countenance bland and improbable. His topic, "enculturation." The only other thing I remember from that course was that I sat next to Elmira Schrogin. "Red diaper baby" had not entered the sociological lingo at the time, but Elmira was one. She was Jewish and I was "a Negro." Our connection seemed somehow natural and its implied fulfillment mildly illegal. The race and gender tension was delicious.

Forty years later, to the extent that Berkeley can be said to represent any tendencies, other magnetic ethnic, race, and gender intersections have displaced the old. Pushed firmly to the periphery of intense campus public debate on gender and ethnic relations is a large population of student couples. One typical version of this peripheral coupling is a white male and a Chinese female. They hold hands, eat sandwiches at noon quietly on quiet lawns. They study together. They seem small; not contending for the campus stage as actors or spectators.

Unlike the forties or fifties, those white students on campus who might worry out loud about "cross dating" are curiosities. An exception might be the traditionally high-status sorority women, who are quite explicitly disturbed by the new Asian competition. The current enforcers of ethnic romantic segregation today are the historically underrepresented groups, particularly black and Chicano students from modest socio-economic backgrounds and racially concentrated urban schools. Amazingly powerful intra-ethnic couples grow inside these walls, but such ideological constraints on the heart do not, of course, succeed. The new delicious illegality results in hidden liaisons of every conceivable permutation.

I visit an ex-student now in prison for failing—on three occasions—to understand the meaning of consent in sexual relations. An extremely bright, working-class, Catholic guy, I sometimes marvel at the worlds that now comprise the range of his social sophistication. He is a very competent prisoner, having earned a respected place with his fists and his reticence. But he fit infinitely better at Cal than he now does in prison, even though Cal's normative complications cost him his freedom. (Attractive, he could not negotiate the favors everyone around him seemed liberally to be trading.) Prison is simple, if you can turn your insight to behavior. Black, brown, and white are separate and formally hostile worlds. Class differences are minimal. At Cal, he had learned to negotiate a world where median annual family incomes of black and brown students were $40,000 lower than whites'. He had begun to understand and successfully manipulate literatures and concepts that seriously separated him from his friends and family. Sadly, prison is a brief break from the impossible tension.

In anticipation of his release, he asks me to send him literature on computer sciences and hotel management. He has the American job prospect scoped out. In that respect he is exactly like the parents of our prospective students. After nearly six years of managing U.C. Berkeley's admissions, I can safely aver that the growing contention over affirmative action is way less about race, ethnicity, or gender than it is about position, advantage, and jobs. Parents know that jobs are disappearing. They are hostile to anything that interferes with their children's place at the head of the line entering this next small occupational world of information and service management.

University officials like myself will spin elaborate developmental and pedagogic tales about why they appear to facilitate ethnicity-based student groupings on campus. There are really only two reasons. One reason is that it does seem successfully to ease student transition to more expansive participation in campus life. Participatory roles, once practiced, are exportable. The other reason is that we don't control it anyway. Despite our elaborate selection process, we work with what the world sends us. Within the groups that we receive, an extraordinary re-mixing of races and ethnicities is taking place among the students who will be holding leadership and authoritative positions in the coming economic and sociopolitical world. The nature and occupants of our coming prisons will be astonishing.

8

■ ■ ■

THE PARIAH SYNDROME

Black Male Perp: Interview with the Boogeyman

■ ■ ■

MICHAEL E. ROSS

It is a day like any other. He blinks and rises, scratches his ass and heads for the bathroom, starts breakfast and reaches for the newspaper, or the remote, to get the overnight news. Like anyone, he contemplates the day ahead, speculating on its likely velocities. He comes up with strategies for dealing with the egos he knows he'll encounter when he's at work, and the various chess moves he'll make just getting to work. He'll come up with the right coloration, the wardrobe the day recommends. And he'll turn the key in that front-door lock and inwardly or visibly take a deep breath and throw himself into another day in the bristling, cetrifugal world.

It starts the minute he walks outside. A neighbor, a young woman maybe halfway through college, freezes at the sight of him, then sprints past him with all the moves of a deer encountering headlights, her eyes trained on the ground but still revealing the edge of some discomfort, maybe even fear. Up the stairs with not so much as a glance backward.

And on the train he reads the papers but does it halfheartedly. He knows the big headline already. The verdict came in, the suspect was apprehended, the sentence was rendered, or the artist's composite of the probable perp was released. Whatever it was, it didn't sit right with anyone. All the day before, he could feel it from those around him in the office. Their stares, the stares he attracted from them, like iron filings to a magnet that could not reverse polarity. *This is all your fault*, they seemed to say without a word. *You did this*. And even now, on the train hurtling toward work, he hears things, senses things. The throat clearing going on around him is almost deafening. The tension he feels is almost palpable. The glares that he dodges are so unnecessary.

On the street above, there is not enough room on the sidewalk. People sense his drift, his loss of anchor. They're like sharks going after chum. And he is a target, buffeted and lashed, the grand booby prize, the bull in the ring.

In the office it continues. The thoughtless comment aimed at him indirectly, in the context of a conversation with someone else, almost daring him to respond. And sometimes he freezes, knowing he should respond, knowing that at some deeper level he must respond or freeze forever, a walking dead man waiting for the horizontal repose of the grave. And other times he fires back, sharp and clean and precise, his reply a razor of language and wit that settles the discussion before it's become a discussion. It is always this way, it seems, a constant keeping score, an assessment of little daily victories in a war that stretches out before him, perhaps indefinitely.

And at the end of the day, any one of ten thousand days of our time, he goes home inwardly exhausted and seeks his image, his likeness (or that of someone close to it) elsewhere, in the satellite forest of television or the magnifier of the movies, and finds it rarely done honestly, or rarely done at all. Most of the time he retreats to the old movie channels, and a handful of the classics in which he knew he would find a character he could relate to, somebody he could understand—*there,* in the flickering light of the oldies, the arcs of electricity snaking across the screen, the angry burghers following with pitchforks and torches and dogs straining at the leash, the lightning and thunder and somebody's scream. . . .

Yeah. He could always count on Frankenstein.

If you heard it on the grapevine or the evening news and you were black and male in America, it caught you momentarily unawares, taking your breath away for a split second. You were stunned at the arrogance, the sheer towering nerve of the facts of the case. But it didn't last long. You were off guard for only a moment. Then clarity—the clarity born of history and the real world—came roaring back. Friday, November 4, 1994, was just another black American day, another day when the unlikely became tangible, the abstract way too real.

That day, Howard Wells, the sheriff of Union, South Carolina, said at a hushed news conference that Susan V. Smith, a local mother of two young children, had confessed to murdering those children after leading the state's authorities, and much of America, on a frenzied nine-day pursuit of a mythical black carjacker in a Mazda Protegé—a man Smith had said kidnapped her children and stole her car at gunpoint while she idled at a stoplight in Monarch, a small mill town a few miles outside Union.

As she was driven from the courthouse after her arraignment, a consuming rage was directed at Smith, an anger from the people of Union, many of whom spent the previous eight days working the phones, reprinting pictures of the missing boys, getting the word out. Pain and tears were evident there—especially in the offers from some citizens to perform her execution—and, more poignantly, at the funeral, pain and tears for the two bright lives extinguished by drowning, strapped in child restraints, upside down in the eighteen feet of the water of Lake John D. Long.

Some similar attempts were made to close other wounds of this tragedy. One Union resident told the *New York Times*, perhaps a little defensively, that blacks and whites alike "prayed for and searched for those kids, and black and white feel bad about what has finally happened."

But black people, and especially black men, shuddered that day and in the months since the Susan Smith trial ended, nine months after the drownings. Black men continue to face down the other, parallel tragedy in the Union case, that tragedy of the living, that tragedy of misidentity that is America's most pernicious legacy. One black Union resident made it plain to the *Times*: "I'll forgive, but I don't think I will forget how they all believed for a time that a black person was responsible. Some of us would like to hear an apology, but I haven't heard one yet."

The Susan Smith episode has the stuff of a classic tragedy; the trajectory of its conclusion yielded a wider, uncomfortable truth, and suggested some scripted part being played out, not so much her story as the national willingness to believe it. The eagerness people exhibited in offering tips and descriptions to law enforcement officers was sadly astonishing. Perhaps not since Halloween eve 1938, when a fake radio broadcast reported the landing of Martians in a sleepy town in New Jersey, had so many fantasies run rampant. Perhaps not since then had so many public resources been enlisted in the search for a phantom, a ghoul of the imagination. Orson Welles might have been briefly amused.

Many black people weren't readily, cheerily dismissive of Smith's confession and its implications; nor were they assuaged by plans, revealed by her lawyers at trial, to invoke an insanity defense. Black people never had to go to court to know how insane this shit can get. As even a casual student of American history knows, we've been over this before.

Black men were similarly demonized in absentia in Boston in 1989, when that city's police force was similarly mobilized after Charles Stuart murdered his wife and blamed a nonexistent black assailant, only to commit suicide when his fabrication fell apart.

These were only two extravagantly imaginative examples of the presumption of black male guilt, an attitude with deep roots in the national life. It began in the earliest days of slavery with the diminution of spirit that comes when someone else thinks you're property. It persisted into this century, when black men were lynched throughout the country, and on to the present day, when young black men are marched daily before the cameras, the concretization of the national fear, the personification of evil on the evening news. For years before the current depiction in the panorama of the national despair, we were and remain the usual suspect, the Black Male Perp, the boogeyman, the tabula rasa onto which are etched the racial stereotypes and fears that have dogged this century, this century a handful of years from becoming another one.

There can be no denying the high numbers of young black men in American jails and prisons today, nor any way to deny the shattered state of the black family because of those numbers, and the pathologies arising from them. In September 1995, the Sentencing Project, a nonprofit research organization, reported, in a study based on Justice Department figures, that the number of black men in their twenties who are imprisoned or otherwise caught up in the criminal justice system was about one in every three. The study determined that about 32 percent of all black men in that age group—about 827,000 men—were either in jail, on probation, or on parole.

But prison population figures and mortality tables aside, the Susan Smith tragedy returned to center stage a fact central to the imposition of American justice, a fact that has held sway in America far longer than the recent dismal statistics: Black men have always had to bear a greater burden in the punitive calculus of American identity.

When whites commit crimes, the individuals are held accountable. There is, of course, an examination of the quirks of upbringing, a probing for historical reasons behind the acts in question. Nearly always, though, the white criminal is isolated from heritage, made to stand alone as his own cunning, monstrous creation, apart from the rest of society.

When blacks commit crimes, not only the individual is to blame; black people are often made to feel, through a rarely subtle imputation of like-mindedness, collectively responsible for the acts of one person. It is a furtherance of the dogged mind-set that black people are a monosyllabic, monolithic phenomenon in everything from politics to fashion to music. Black people are rarely afforded the luxury of deviations from the norm. Blacks are, far too often, presumed to be uniformly angry, reliably inarticulate, routinely less intelligent. The notion of a black person at a cocktail party being asked, "How do you people feel about that?" is far from dead. Despite the increasing diversity of Americans, the belief still persists that one black person is presumed to speak for the race; so it is thought, at some deeper, associative level, that one is presumed to think and act for the race, a representative of, a proxy for, the millions.

By looking at black people on such a one-dimensional level—as a singular and not as a plural experience—whites often fail to recognize their variety, fail to admit to a full visibility. That variety, for all practical purposes, is unseen.

Ralph Ellison said it plain in *Invisible Man*, articulating the alienation that blacks continue to feel in America, two generations after its first publication. In the novel's prologue, a stranger walks into our protagonist on a city street, a situation common to black men anywhere in Manhattan, and everywhere else in the country. It's the manifestation of a suspicion Ellison elaborates on with his special, timeless eloquence:

> You wonder whether you aren't simply a phantom in other people's minds. Say, a figure in a nightmare which the sleeper tries with all his strength to destroy. It's when you feel like this that, out of resentment, you begin to bump people back. And, let me confess, you feel that way most of the time. You ache with the need to convince yourself that you do exist in the real world, that you're a part of all the sound and anguish, and you strike out with your fists, you curse and you swear to make them recognize you. And alas, it's seldom successful.

This willful, aggressive blindness on the part of mainstream America is problem enough, but another kind of invisibility is at work today, a variable and selective mode of invisibility. Black men are invisible in a postmodern way, invisible in a manner that serves the needs and tastes of a visual culture. Black invisibility in the nineties is fleeting, transient. The black presence in certain parts of the cultural landscape can't be argued: Doo-wop blues and jazz are the music of the television commercial; Motown and rap are the staples of the motion picture soundtrack. Phrases that emanate from boomboxes on the street in one season are the slogans for corporate America in the next. Black singers make backup appearances for mainstream stars, lending a special signature, an emotional weight to what might otherwise be considered a white-bread enterprise. And as purveyors of strength and endurance and the act of levitation, in the physical world of sports, black dominance is undeniable. In the daily social diet of what America consumes, in the *lingua franca* of popular culture, blacks couldn't be more visible.

But in other ways, the invisibility Ellison explained has persisted, grown more insidious with the proliferation of television and other media, and the old cultural imprinting that persists there. TV, newspapers, and magazines have virtually edited blackness out of their reports, or they continue to frame the complexity of the black American experience primarily in narrow, monochromatic, pathological terms that foster the idea of Black Life as Problem and Little Else. The voices of black leaders and elected officials are heavily distilled in newscasts, their comments and context, unique to black dialect and expression, boiled down to the smallest sound bite. Even in the world of advertising, purportedly wide-open and receptive to new ideas, old second-class imprinting continues in a new way: The black male model is often the last in a visual series, lost in the crowd of faces on all sides, the one crouching while others stand at full height, shunted to the periphery, to the rear of the crowd shot, the edge of the frame—to the back of this new American bus.

Black men seem to achieve their fullest visibility in the context of the dangerous and the unpredictable. When things get out of hand. Like they did in June of 1994.

That was when Orenthal James Simpson, actor, charity golf fixture, Hertz pitchman, and running back for all time, was up and running again, this time as a prime suspect in the murder of his ex-wife, Nicole Brown, and a friend, Ronald Goldman, a waiter at a nearby restaurant, outside Nicole Brown's condominium in Brentwood. This run would be his longest run from scrimmage line ever: sixty miles, all over the freeways of California, from just north of El Toro to Simpson's home west of Beverly Hills; O.J., in the backseat of his own car, the celebrated white Ford Bronco, his homeboy Al Cowlings at the wheel; O.J. in flight from the linebackers of the justice system, only to surrender hours later before a national television audience that eclipsed any he had achieved in all of his past careers.

And almost immediately, on television and in the newspapers, there it was, another black male face, just possibly another black male perp, standing for a booking photo, O. J. Simpson, prisoner #4013970.

And if the rude shock of the booking photo released by the Los Angeles Police Department wasn't demonizing enough—all booking photos exhibit that flat, clinical quality of depiction—there was the media's continual use of perversely libelous shorthand, typified best by such towering imprecisions as preceding Simpson's name with the words "accused murderer," a technique of description used across the board, well before the trial's conclusion, on television and radio and in newspapers from the reliably breathless tabloids to the august *New York Times*.

What transpired for the next sixteen months could, perhaps, lay legitimate claim to being the so-called Trial of the Century, for better and for worse. By turns Shakespearean and Kafkaesque, a fashion show and a forensic Grand Guignol, the Simpson double-murder trial assumed the status of a daily numbing, day after day America comfortably numb to the sober theatrics of the longest trial in the history of the state of California.

The constant presence of his face exacerbated an already edgy racial climate. With the predisposition of his status already fixed in much of the media, it was another situation of presumptive guilt. There was much to compel such a predisposition. Some of the trial's more haunting moments were during the playbacks of 911 calls placed by Nicole Brown, calls in which the defendant is heard screaming at her in the background. Or when the prosecution displayed the photographs of a physically and psychically battered Nicole Brown, showing injuries inflicted by the defendant, O. J. Simpson.

But then came Mark Fuhrman, a man who, jury consultant Donald Vinson said, was "a godsend who dropped from the sky and exploded almost on cue."

In Mark Fuhrman, the defense had found the fulcrum, the basis for a defense strategy that, for all its posturing, effectively called into question presumptive black male guilt, while prosecuting a police department with a long and ragged reputation among its minority citizens. The N-word was the key; Fuhrman's documented use of the word contradicted his testimony on the stand. And the suspicions that were opened with the use of that word widened and deepened, festered in the mind of the jury, and the jury made its decision.

When O. J. Simpson was acquitted of murder on October 3, 1995, there was much speculation as to whether the jury was trying to "make a statement" or "send a signal," presumably implying that the jury had overstepped its bounds by ignoring the evidence at hand in rendering a verdict. And those people missed an underlying fact of the justice system:

Verdicts are not rendered in a convenient vacuum of isolation, or a bell jar of separation from the society in which they are made. Every verdict makes a statement; every verdict sends a signal. The verdict in the Simpson murder trial sent the message that the usual suspect would never be so conveniently arrived at again, that the black male perp could wield the leverage of reasonable doubt.

O. J. Simpson came back to the world, his image cleared if not rehabilitated. The photographs of Simpson post-trial lost the clinical hardness of a booking photo. In its special report on Simpson, *Time* magazine printed a grainy blow-up of his face, close up, unadorned, unmanipulated.

It was a far cry from the cover of *Time* magazine in June 1994, when Matt Mahurin, photographer and music video director, altered the booking photo, darkening and hardening Simpson's distinctive features, making a routine photograph unnecessarily provocative.

Mahurin's ghoulish photo-illustration is one example of the way the image of the black male has lately been worked on, and worked over. Another occurred in 1994, when the Whitney Museum of American Art launched "The Black Male," an exhaustive exhibition that examined the image of black men in various forms of artistic expression, mostly in paintings, sculpture, and video presentations by black American artists, male and female. The show was controversial in its scope and in the daring of the imagery of the artists exhibited. But for all the stylistic diversity in the show, one image lingers in the mind, not as an image of criminality but as a perpetuation of a stereotype reinforcing the boogeyman perception:

It is an image by the white photographer Robert Mapplethorpe, a shot of a black man's torso, his penis erect; it is a photograph whose reproduction in slightly larger than life size exacerbates the power of that other deep-seated American fixation: the black man not as criminal but as tireless stud, dangerous phallic champion, Superdick.

The Mapplethorpe image is a curious contradiction, a visible clash of intentions. His approach to viewing the black male in the photograph—updating a classical artistic expression, visually amputating heads, arms, and legs in the fashion of a Greek antiquity—is both icily ennobling and maddeningly impersonal. Chilly in its veneration of the subject, the photograph has a cold, formal symmetry that also affords little sense of the individual as an individual. In this photograph and others from the same series, we are offered a catalogue of body parts, the pieces of a mannequin, an arm, a foot, the outline of buttocks, penis de Milo, a clinical survey of still pictures of someone being inspected on a modern version of the auction block. Imparting no view of the black man as a whole being, the Mapplethorpe series is a brutally clear (if unintentional) metaphor for the lives of modern black American men. In the guise of being an artistic expression that purports to liberate the viewer from ancient mistaken notions of what art is, it imprisons both subject and viewer in equally mistaken notions of what black men are, shackling both to a misconception older than the republic.

Other images are less artfully contrived; the phallic presence need not be visible; the image of the black man in any sartorial guise is perhaps more than enough.

Consider the case of Edward L. Summers, a promising twenty-three-year-old premed student at South Carolina State University who was accused of shooting two teenagers in the head, one fatally, in the course of stealing their Jeep from a mall in Rockland County, New York, early in 1994.

In the course of his trial, Summers was requested by the prosecution at least twice to change his clothes—to exchange the traditional courtroom attire of suit and tie for the clothes he wore the day of the shootings: the gangbanger wardrobe of choice, a hooded sweatshirt, jeans, and, jammed in his waistband, a handgun.

Summers admitted to the shootings shortly after they occurred. He was convicted of the murder of one of the men in January 1995, after retracting his confession, alleging that it was coerced by the authorities. Due process was exercised; Summers had his days in court and did not prevail. But whether his confession was genuine or coerced, there is no ignoring one of the prosecution's methods of establishing guilt in the mind of the jury. It was a technique that went beyond the hard evidence presented at trial; it was a way of establishing guilt that resorted to provoking the imagination—presenting defendant Summers in clothes that a jury from upper-crusty Rockland County may have been all too ready to believe were the clothes of any black man intent on committing a crime. *This is the uniform of evil,* the prosecution seemed to say, these are the evil creatures you see on the TV news every night. *This is what black men look like*—not wearing suits and ties but wearing hooded sweatshirts and grimy jeans, the true vision of modern danger.

The notion of indictment by fashion has taken other twists before and since Summers's conviction, in New York City, in incidents further suggesting that black men are the standing examples of criminality no matter what they wear or who they are.

Ask Earl G. Graves, Jr., a senior vice president for *Black Enterprise* magazine and son of Earl Graves, the chairman and chief executive officer of *Black Enterprise* and a lightning rod for the cause of black entrepreneurship in America.

On May 1, 1995, the thirty-three-year-old Graves was minding his own, reading the morning paper on the 6:42 train from Chappaqua, Westchester, to Grand Central Station. Imagine his surprise at being restrained by two officers of the Metro-North transit police, an arm of the state Metropolitan Transportation Authority, the minute he got off the train.

Graves was stopped because the officers had been advised to be on the lookout for a man described (in an anonymous letter) as black, athletically built, well dressed, and carrying a gun in a briefcase. The agency said that the letter described the hypothetical man in question as about five feet ten inches tall, with a "trim or athletic build," and wearing a mustache. Graves is six feet four and cleanshaven.

The specificity of the letter's descriptions might have been useful to the officers, whom Graves said were looking for a black man with short hair. "Well, that narrows it down to about six million people," Graves said, in a *New York Times* article.

The mistake was quickly acknowledged—by Metro-North officials, but not by the officers themselves—after Graves *père* invoked some of the connections one comes by after twenty-five years in the publishing business. There were apologies all around, and advertisements, in the *Times* and other area papers, that expanded on the personal apologies of the president and police chief of the Metro-North utility. Still, understandably, the younger Graves, the victim of this misidentity, would have preferred a face-to-face.

"I want them to be able to look me in the eye," Graves told the *New York Times*. "They've got to look beyond black."

Joe Morgan can testify. The baseball Hall of Famer and sports broadcaster was waiting for a flight at Los Angeles International Airport in March 1988 when an LAPD detective approached him, accused him of being a drug courier, and threw him to the floor of the terminal. It was another example of mistaken identity, one that cost the taxpayers of Los Angeles a tidy six-figure sum as a way of settling the police brutality lawsuit Morgan brought against the department.

Al Joyner can testify, too. Joyner, a triple-jump Olympic Gold medalist, was pulled over for traffic stops in May 1992 and handcuffed not once but twice, both times in error. The officers said later they were investigating stolen vehicle reports and hit-and-run incidents; Joyner's suspicion was that he was stopped because he was a young black man

driving a good car, paid for, street legal, a short with no primer spots anywhere. If he'd been a low rider cruising South-Central, it might have
been a different situation (but more than likely the same situation in a different location). A judge basically sided with Joyner, ruling that the stop
by the police officers constituted an arrest without probable cause.

We come at last to that lovely phrase, engine of American justice:
probable cause, that legal catchall that by coincidence or design gives police
officers wide latitude in exercising the powers of arrest. Its scope has historically caused problems for black people, particularly black men, not
always but too often considered the presumptive suspects of a criminal act. Whether wearing jeans and Nikes or foulards and pinstripe
suits, whether driving showroom-sweet BMWs or Cadillacs with bad
shocks, we're too often the target of an automatic suspicion. Sometimes—often, even—it means inconvenience or embarrassment, another
deep bruise to the ego and the soul. But in some recent cases, the word
target has been only too appropriate for physical reasons.

On August 22, 1994, on the platform of the IND subway station at
53rd Street and Lexington Avenue in Manhattan, Desmond Robinson, a
black thirty-one-year-old undercover officer of the New York City
Transit Police Department, was seriously wounded—shot five times, at
least four times in the back—by white New York City police officer
Peter Del-Debbio, after numerous police officers responded to reports
there of two young subway passengers brandishing a shotgun on the train
platform. Confusion took over; conflicting accounts of the event surfaced
and resurfaced in the press for weeks; reconstructions of the lighting and
angles of fire at the scene assumed the tone of an assassination inquiry.

It has been suggested that one possible reason for the shooting may
have been Robinson's own brilliant disguise. Robinson, whom other
officers said tried hard not to look like a police officer, apparently went to
great lengths to blend into the scenery of a multicultural city, sometimes
wearing earrings, sandals, and shorts to work in the Manhattan underground. And it was reported that Robinson said he was not wearing the
color of the day—that color, rotated daily and worn on a bracelet or
headband, identifying him as a transit officer, a man empowered to bran-
dish a weapon, the weapon he had when he encountered Del-Debbio.

But one thing is undeniable—has to be, given the rigid loyalties that
arise between brother officers within a police department: For the seconds it took him to fire his weapon, Del-Debbio did not know the true
identity of his target. It was in that sliver of time that Del-Debbio entered
into his own presumption of guilt, a presumption whose components
possibly, if not probably, included the race of the armed man in front of

him. In those horrible seconds, Del-Debbio didn't see a fellow police officer, and wouldn't have known the color of the day if it were waved in his face. It didn't matter. He saw a criminal, first and foremost in his mind.

A grand jury did not concur with Del-Debbio's rush to judgment. In March 1995, Del-Debbio was indicted for first-degree assault, the grand jury concluding, with the state penal code, that Del-Debbio's actions constituted "a depraved indifference to human life." Del-Debbio was convicted of second-degree assault and was sentenced to five years probation.

Perhaps Del-Debbio wasn't thinking of human life when he fired. Perhaps he saw the same boogeyman seen by three white New York City transit police officers almost two years earlier, in November 1992, when they mistakenly fired at black plainclothes officer Derwin Pannell, who was rousting a fare cheat with his partner at a subway station in Brooklyn. Pannell, shot in the neck, survived his injuries, left the force, and became a father. But he no doubt learned again the brutal algebra of race, the indifferent math that presumes a black male is a black male perp until proven otherwise.

Reggie Miller can surely sympathize. In December 1992, while working a prostitution sting as an undercover officer for the Nashville Police Department, Miller was pulled over for driving a departmental vehicle with expired tags and beaten by five white officers—cops who worked every day in the same precinct as Miller. The young officer said it plain, speaking for black undercover operatives: "Even though he may be after a suspect, he's often a suspect himself."

Paul Mooney, a celebrated West Coast stand-up comedian, put the situation in terms black Americans can appreciate. In his blistering 1993 comedy album, *Race*, Mooney envisions another, parallel America where white customers guilty of some crime can make a phone call to a mythical agency and get fast, fast relief: "1-900-BLAME-A-NIGGER."

And so it is in our America, perhaps uncomfortably close to Mooney's ninth-circle-of-black-hell vision. Life goes on. After the incidents are forgotten, after police officers point guns, after Susan Smith points a finger, after such dramas are at least briefly resolved, black men return to the day-to-day process of living, putting one foot in front of the other, trying hard to let go of events whose outcomes say as much about America—its pride, its values, its hubris—as about the people involved.

But another event with another outcome spoke to what America is. On October 16, 1995, under a bright sky in Washington, D.C., the Million Man March consumed the public's attention span. The media fixed on the fact that the march was organized by Louis Farrakhan, the leader of the Nation of Islam; Farrakhan's odious comments about Jews resurfaced and threatened to dominate the spotlight on the march. But attention shifted on the day of the march, to its proper focus: the men who came from everywhere in America to be part of history. "Black men who were strangers greeted one another," Yusef Salaam said in the *New York Amsterdam News*. "We were Muslims, Christians, Five Percenters, nationalists, integrationists, socialists, dark-skinned, light-skinned, short, fat, tall, skinny, and didn't know each other from a man on the moon. Yet we did know each other's experiences in the U.S. as black men. We were sons of Africa who had survived enslavements, plantations, lynch ropes, mob violence, and had come together in D.C. to let an increasingly hostile government know that we were determined to continue to grow, develop, as men, as Americans."

On that day, some hypothetical threshold had been reached; within the hearts of many black American men, a clock of special purpose went off. You could see it in the faces of the men on the Mall and the Ellipse and the Capitol, men standing straight and tall, men of a common ancestral fiber, barely moving, seemingly hardly breathing, silent, no boomboxes, no crack sales, no gang colors, no weapons, no distractions, men quietly crying, strangers embracing each other, men perhaps not one hundred percent behind Farrakhan, the messenger of Islam, but still men fully awakened to the message of their presence, in that place and time, proud men, usual suspects no more, silently but powerfully sending the signal that black male self-perception would never be quite the same again.

Life goes on. While unofficial estimates from observers placed the crowd at at least one million strong—an estimate fortified by an ABC News investigation after the event—the National Park Service placed the crowd's size at about 400,000 people. Setting aside the difficulties in accurately gauging the size of a shifting, moving crowd, the suspicion of the Park Service's low estimate had justifiable origins. It struck some people as a new version of the three-fifths compromise; it prompted others to recall the reports of undercounting of black and minority faces in the 1990 Census.

And it made another black man think of other business as usual in America, where a black male professional wearing what's generally considered the prevailing wardrobe of the workaday world again finds himself the object of long and icy stares from people in the streets and on the subways, people who clutch for already-secure handbags or grope for wallets they know are safe, people who appear to be trying to place his face in some hypothetical post-office picture from the FBI's hit parade.

And as he rides to his floor, he's forced into momentary psychodrama, in an elevator with a lone white woman as a passenger, a lady suddenly given to fidgeting and foot-tapping and other manifestations of impatience, a woman mentally crawling up the walls of the car to escape this scaled-down real-life version of a scene from *Dutchman*.

And he knows, or is made to believe, that he is being demonized again. He knows that guilt by association obtains. He knows that he is sharing quiet company with countless other black men, innocent and guilty in the eyes of the law, men imprisoned, as are we all, in the windowless cells of a collective national tragedy, a free-floating mistrust that, left unchecked, could metastasize into the kind of sectarian hatred that has made Bosnia the worst kind of household word, a factionalism that may doom us, category by category, tribe by tribe, to become a nation of warring ethnic camps, a death of empathy that is killing our country before our very eyes.

The Criminalization
of Black Men

■ ■ ■

EARL OFARI HUTCHINSON

The sun broke through the gray morning clouds as I jogged along the streets near my home. When I stopped at an intersection to wait for the light to change, I caught the eye of a driver, a young white woman. She looked nervous and frightened. In a quick move, she snapped down the lock on her car door and sped off before the light changed.

This was not the first time I was the object of suspicion by fearful whites. I have been followed by security guards and clerks in stores. Women have clutched their purses when I approached. Cabdrivers have refused to pick me up. I've been stopped and questioned by police even though I wore a suit and tie and drove a late model car. Many black males tell the same tales. In fact, they've become so routine that they simply chalk them up to white America's deep fear of black males.

But there's more. A few months after the jogging incident, I was sitting in my car in the parking lot of an office building waiting for a business acquaintance to arrive. A young black man approached the car. He was neatly dressed. My first impulse was to lock the door and roll up the window. It turned out that he was only trying to locate another office building on the same street.

As he walked away, I thought of the woman who locked her door when she saw me. Her fear of black men had become my fear. The image of black criminality has been shoved so deep into America's collective psyche that no one is immune from fear. This includes many blacks.

In a way I can understand why. Crime is an intensely personal and emotional issue for those victimized. The trauma is deep and the memories cause perpetual pain for the victims and their families. It stirs the deepest human fears and vulnerabilities. But when racial and sexual stereotypes are mixed in, personal fear becomes public hysteria.

A study on reader perception of crime reported in the *Chicago Tribune* found that in several crime-related stories the paper mentioned that the suspect was a white male under age twenty-five. Many readers still identified the suspect as a black male under age twenty-five.

This was more than a case of warped perceptions of crime. Tal Mendleberg, a Princeton political scientist, analyzed the hidden racial content of political ads used in the 1988 presidential election. She zeroed in on the campaign ad used by George Bush on escaped black convict Willie Horton. The ad charged that Horton raped a Maryland woman while on furlough from prison in Massachusetts. Bush claimed that the ad was intended only to paint his opponent, Massachusetts Democrat Michael S. Dukakis, as soft on crime. Democrats charged that the ad pandered to racism. Bush denied it.

Mendleberg showed a group of participants campaign footage that included part of the Horton ad. She asked if they felt more threatened by crime, or perceived another message. The other message was race. The ad hardened the participants' attitude toward criminals. But it also hardened them to all blacks. Mendleberg concluded that they "decided they really didn't want more spending to aid blacks."

There is one exception: Americans are willing to spend more to lock them up. Crime has taken a tortured path to become America's number one fear. In February 1993, crime ranked nearly dead last on the list of issues that most troubled Americans; only 4 percent called it the major problem. Less than a year later, 19 percent said it was the number one problem facing America.

What happened? In California, the Assembly Commission on the Status of the African-American Male noted that four out of ten males entering California prisons are black. Less than half of lower-income black males under age twenty-one live in two-parent households. Black males with a high school education are twice as likely as white males to be unemployed. The national figures mirrored California's numbers.

President Clinton sensed the public fear and quickly moved to dislodge the Bush administration's $30 billion Federal Omnibus Crime Bill, which was bottled up in Congress for the three previous years. Congress procrastinated for a few months while engaging in the usual partisan political sparring. But the murder of twelve-year-old Polly Klass in California, shootings in Denver area fast-food restaurants, the attack on U.S. Olympic skater Nancy Kerrigan, and the murder of six and wounding of twenty commuters on a Long Island commuter train by an unemployed black handyman, Colin Ferguson, all in 1993, did it.

With the exception of Ferguson, these highly publicized crimes were committed by white men. Yet much of the public still saw crime with a young black male face. It was only a matter of time before the crime bill became law. A handful of critics, mostly civil libertarians and black leaders, warned that the provisions were too costly, racially discriminatory, and veered dangerously close to constitutional violations. They were brushed aside. Clinton and Congress congratulated each other when the bill passed in August 1994.

Crime was the hottest ticket item in America. States rushed to pass three-strikes and two-strikes legislation, hired more police and prosecutors, and stiffened sentences. The Department of Justice poured several million dollars into the development of *Star Wars*–type high-tech gadgetry: "smart" guns, anti-high-chase microwave devices, super-sticky foams, remote-control spikes, night-vision goggles, highway satellite systems, and remote-controlled robots.

The crime mania nearly doubled America's prison population, from 900,000 in 1987 to 1.4 million in 1994. The prison-industrial complex replaced the nearly defunct military-industrial complex as America's largest growth industry. In California, there would be plenty of new prison cells. State taxpayers would pay $21 billion over the next thirty years to build twenty-five new prisons. While they would pay $1.8 billion to run their eight campuses of the University of California system, they would spend $5 billion to run their prisons. Construction companies, contractors, architectural firms, and lobbyists would make billions. Wall Street would rake in a neat $35 million from the sale of California's $5.6 billion in lease revenue bonds the legislature floated without taxpayer approval.

What did this buy? The Rand Corporation claimed the money would reduce felonies by only 8 percent. The vast majority who would fill the new jail cells wouldn't be violent felons. They would be poor blacks and Latinos, who'd committed mostly property or drug-related crimes. Rand didn't state that if California taxpayers spent a fraction of the three-strikes budget on drug counseling, vocational job and skills training, and education and violence reduction programs, many of those people would not be in those cells.

The criminalization of black men perpetuated the dangerous cycle of arrest and incarceration. The cycle has trapped thousands. In 1992, one out of four young black men were in jail, or prison, on parole, or probation. Nearly half of America's 1 million prisoners were black. The top-heavy number of black men in jail reinforced the public view that they committed most of the major violent crime in America.

They didn't. In 1992:

- White males committed 54% of violent crimes in America.
- White males were 70% of the juveniles arrested nationally for criminal offenses.
- White males were 80% of America's drug users and abusers.
- White males committed 60% of the urban hate crimes.
- White males committed the majority of serial and mass murders.

This last point deserves special comment. I wondered why much of the media, the public, and sociologists weren't as obsessed with the serial murders committed mostly by white males as they were with black crime. I did a computer scan of four hundred academic journals between 1992 and 1994; there were 1,691 research articles published on crime. Forty identifiable research articles dealt specifically with black crime. Two identifiable research articles dealt with serial/mass murders. The one detailed article on serial murders was published in a small journal, *the Omega-Journal of Death and Dying*. The authors admitted that there was a "poverty of rigorous research in the area." It may stay that way.

I also closely monitored the press reports on the prison murder of mass murderer Jeffrey Dahmer in November 1994. The media spin was sympathy and compassion for Dahmer. His mother tearfully made the talk show rounds. In the *Los Angeles Times* account, Dahmer's prosecutor, psychologist, defense attorney, and relatives were quoted. They recast him as a tragic figure.

The prosecutor thundered that "this is not justice." The psychiatrist called him "pleasant, polite, free of prejudice and gentle." There was a brief quote from an attorney representing the family of one of his victims. There was only passing reference to the fact that fourteen out of seventeen of his known victims were black men; the other three were Hispanic or Asian. Ironically, Dahmer had no sympathy for himself. His mother told an interviewer that "he felt that he deserved anything he gets."

Suburban whites may have nightmares about being attacked by blacks, but their waking reality is that their attacker will be white. In 1990, 70 percent of violent crimes against whites were committed by other whites. However, many white offenders don't wind up behind bars. Their increasing absence from the prisons has become noticeable. A District of Columbia judge was curious to see what the jails were like that he sent defendants to. After he visited several, he was struck by the fact that most of those inside were black. He knew from his experience on the bench that many whites were charged with crimes. He wondered what happened to them.

There was a clue: 78 percent of the 580 white middle-class males convicted of defrauding savings and loans (and taxpayers) of nearly $8 billion went to prison during the early 1990s. Most didn't stay very long. Only 4 percent were sentenced to ten years or more. The average sentence was 36.4 months. The median time served was two years. A car thief spent 38 months in prison; a burglar, 55.6 months. In California, only one in four S&L fraud suspects was prosecuted. In Texas, one in seven was prosecuted. For those with the money, personal and family connections, and political clout to avoid prison, crime did indeed pay.

Despite the fears of many white and non-whites, few Americans really know how dangerous their streets are. Newsweek in 1994 still punched the murder panic button hard. It warned that murder was epidemic and the nation's streets had become free-fire zones. There were gruesome photos of mostly young black and Hispanic male victims. But a cursory glance at Newsweek's numbers showed that Americans were actually at less risk of becoming murder victims in 1990 (9.5 per 100,000) than in 1980 (10.2 per 100,000). In fact, Americans actually stood a better change of being murdered during the 1920s Prohibition era than in 1994.

The richer, older, and whiter a person, the less chance they have of being a crime victim. Older white women are the least victimized of any group in America. Those who earn more than $50,000 are two to three times less likely to be crime victims than the general population. For whites aged fifty to sixty-four, the victim rate dropped 35 percent. Whites are marginally at greater risk of being robbed by blacks. It has less to do with their color than their numbers and location. There are seven times more whites than blacks in America. Most of them aren't robbed in their homes or neighborhoods but rather on urban streets.

The arrest totals are further inflated by police saturation of black neighborhoods, gang sweeps, drug raids, and racially tainted "zero-tolerance" stop and search policies. Compton, a California city with a black and Latino majority, went one better. In 1993, it criminalized every youth in the city. The police department's database contained the names of

10,435 gang members in the city. It was a curious figure. The 1990 Census counted only 8,558 males aged fifteen to twenty-five in the city. There were three possible explanations: the database was faulty; the information was inputted incorrectly; or as one observer quipped, maybe there were gang members such as Crips moonlighting as Bloods, and vice versa.

During the past decade, drug-related arrests account for the sharp rise in America's jail and prison population. Some police officials publicly admit that these arrests are a tragic game of numbers that police and politicians play to calm a jittery public. Project housing dwellers can't hire pricey attorneys or make bail. They are easy to try, convict, or pressure into a plea bargain. A typical conspiracy investigation against white suburbanite drug dealers could last six months or more and in the end net fewer than six arrests. The white suburbanites could make bail and hire private counsel. They are not easy to try, convict, or pressure into a plea bargain. This wouldn't play well to the public; judges and prosecutors know this.

Former Reagan drug czar William Bennett laid it on the cost-effective line: "It's easier and less expensive to arrest black drug users and dealers than whites." The price is higher than he thinks. Bennett, much of the press, and lawmakers operate under the assumption that crack cocaine trafficking and abuse are solely black crimes. Congress responded to that public perception by making the minimum sentence longer for crack during the mid-1980s.

It's true that blacks are disproportionately more involved in crack dealing and are arrested more often. But many whites are also deeply involved in the crack trade and those arrested do have more serious criminal histories than blacks. Yet black crack traffickers still receive on average longer sentences than white crack traffickers.

If blacks did commit most of the violent crime in America, most whites still wouldn't be at risk. According to official figures, blacks commit nearly half the murders and robberies: 94 percent of their victims are other blacks. Blacks are mostly a menace not to society but to themselves.

The perception that they are a menace to whites has been magnified by the TV networks, which have spent the past twenty years honing tabloid-style reporting techniques. During the 1970s, the men who ran the ABC affiliates in Philadelphia and New York decided to rev up the ratings. They created *Action News*.

The concept was simple: Find crime, crime, and more crime. News teams roamed city streets looking for police car chases, crashes, gang shootouts, and drug busts. Most importantly, the city streets were in black neighborhoods. It was bloody. It was exploitive. It was racist. It was a smash success. The public loved it. Network profits jumped and their ratings soared. *Action News*, which began as a lead-in to the regular newscast, soon became *the* news. Local affiliates in every city copied it.

By 1990, 68 percent of Americans were hooked on the *Action News* nightly broadcast. The networks spun off legions of hybrid clones. These shows simulated live-action crime chases and busts. *Top Cops, Cops,* and *America's Most Wanted* often depicted whites as heroes and blacks as villains. This convinced even more Americans that violence-prone, drugged-out black men put their lives at great risk.

They didn't. But many Americans still exaggerate black crime even when the crimes are committed by others. In 1992 in Los Angeles, TV reporters stretched credulity to the limits during the civil disturbances. For three days the black and increasingly Latino inner city was judged by white, middle-class reporters, men and women. They lived far from the area, and in many cases needed maps to find the streets. They relentlessly tailored their reports to depict the violence as the handiwork of black rioters. Racism, poverty, alienation, and the indifference of the city's political power structure were barely mentioned.

The reporters couldn't ignore the abominable verdict in the state trial of the four LAPD officers who beat Rodney King. But they made no serious effort to analyze the criminal justice system, explain why the jury contained no blacks, or discuss the racism that motivated the jurors' decision. There was one passing reference in the *L.A. Times* to the negative remarks of white jurors about King's physical prowess and alleged aggressive actions.

One juror even made a borderline racially derogatory remark about him, and hinted that he got what he deserved. Hardly anyone second-guessed the inept and ineffectual prosecution strategy that practically tossed the case to the defense.

Instead, reporters stumbled over each other to stick microphones and cameras in the face and mouth of any black they could find on the streets. They framed questions to get sensational sound bites, and badgered their respondents to say something inflammatory. The networks repeatedly played the tape of the young blacks beating white truck driver Reginald Denny, further inflaming fear and anger in the white suburbs. The media's message to sympathetic whites was that the Denny beating canceled out the moral outrage over the King beating.

Reporters, news anchors, and in-studio talking heads gleefully milked the black-white conflict angle for all it was worth. But TV was an open mirror. Viewers could plainly see many of those doing the looting and burning were non-blacks. The streets at times looked like a microcosm of the United Nations.

A Rand Corporation study of the racial breakdown of 5,000 riot-related cases processed through Los Angeles municipal courts tallied these arrest totals: Latinos, 2,852; blacks 2,037; Anglos 601; and others, 147. Young men aged eighteen to thirty-four made up the highest percentage of those arrested (30 percent). They were young men of all categories, not exclusively black.

The number of whites arrested was nearly one third of the total black arrests. A Rand criminologist was puzzled by the fixation of the press on black rioters when the majority of those rioting weren't black. "This was clearly not a black riot. It was a minority riot." The report appeared as a news item in the back pages of the *L.A. Times*; the rest of the press ignored it. The media misrepresented the civil disturbances as a "black riot," and the effect was easy to equate: Blacks + violence = public fear.

America is a victim of its own warped reality. Many whites and some blacks in their rush to construct a national security state have swallowed their own myths about black crime and violence. They believe that young blacks kill because they enjoy violence, steal because they are part of a subculture of poverty, and join gangs and deal drugs because they have low self-esteem and aspirations.

The truth is much different. Crime and violence can't be separated from the ills of American society. Victims and victimizers come in all colors, classes, and genders. As long as many Americans are convinced that crime comes only with a young black male face, justice will always come in the form of a police nightstick and a prison cell.

Fifty Years in America:
Through Back Doors

■ ■ ■

ELENA CACERES

I arrived in America in 1945 as a child of five. It was a time when the sounds of war in the Pacific reverberated on California's shores and a time when Mexican immigrants came to the United States to fill the manpower shortage caused by the war. My mother, who helped the war effort by working in the San Pedro shipyards as a "Rosie the Riveter," was returning to America to marry a factory worker from Northern California. We were properly chaperoned, mother and I, by a maiden aunt who remained until after the civil marriage ceremony in El Paso, Texas.

My first impression of America was that it was bitterly cold. Icy winds cut into my legs with razorlike sharpness. Outfitted for the momentous occasion, I wore a wool coat, a knit dress, and a brand-new pair of black patent-leather shoes specifically purchased for Mother's American marriage ceremony. We traveled by train from the city of Chihuahua to Texas.

When we arrived at the El Paso border a cattle disease epidemic was raging, and in attempts to control it the U.S. government required every Mexican immigrant crossing the border to be disinfected by stepping through troughs of a sawdust and disinfectant mixture. To my child's eyes, it looked like muddy slush. The walk through was overseen by green-uniformed INS guards.

When it was our turn, Mother instinctively reached down to carry me across the trough, but one border guard, noting her action, immediately walked over to us and told her, in perfect Spanish, to put me down, that I, too, must walk through the disinfectant. I remember feeling myself go down from my mother's protective arms into the trough. The strong smell filled my nostrils and settled into my memory forever. The sensation of stepping and sinking into the mess frightened me, but Mother held my hand steadily. We would walk across together. I looked down at my black patent-leather shoes sinking into the ugly mixture. My socks got wet and dirty; my toes hurt from the cold. I felt very frightened and confused by this new experience but did not cry. My beautiful brand-new black patent-leather shoes were ruined.

That was my prophetic entrance into the United States of America.

America is a very interesting place. Mired in contradiction, it is as beautiful as it is ugly, as objective as it is closed. Many adjectives describe the America I know. America greets its immigrants in different ways: Some are received with open arms, jobs, and appreciation; others are not. America does not always blatantly display the type of policy that requires newcomers to walk through filth to get to their goal, but it does happen. I have learned much in my fifty years in America. My once beautiful, vivacious mother, who still lives in California's lush central valley, is dead. She did not survive America.

My mother's first and lasting advice on arrival to America was to "learn English and go to school." To please her I learned English rapidly, a language that escaped her because of its difficult pronunciation. She struggled with the hard Germanic sounds, so different from her lilting Spanish. As a result, I became the family interpreter at age seven, much as I now see other children becoming interpreters for their non-English-speaking parents. Communication, English and its sounds, became an important part of my new adaptation and survival. I learned early to exist between two languages, pressed between layers of unspoken meanings.

At thirteen I began to sense that I was somehow "different." Strong messages hung in the air radiating much uncomfortable information. The messages were beyond those of common adolescent experiences of discomfort and self-discovery. It was as if there were a secret in America that I was being perceived as undesirable and "different." The messages, imperceptible to others, weighed heavily on my thirteen-year-old self. I began to believe that *my* undesirability was related not simply to an awkward appearance but to something other.

Naively, I adopted a path to self-improvement, a true first American quest for perfection, and very fortunately experienced a great discovery at my high-insecurity phase. In the 1950s seventh-grade English class, I discovered something that was to affect me profoundly for the rest of my life. I discovered words. I discovered writing. I could write words that spellbound my restless classmates when I read to them. The ability to mesmerize with *my words* simultaneously cast an enchantment over me as the newly found word power aroused a wondrous sensation in my pubescent body. I immediately became a voracious reader who proceeded to swallow words whole like delicious little morsels. I wrote stories about gawky girls or remembered entire movies and rewrote them accurately. My sexual awakening, which occurred at about the same time as my word discovery, was less momentous. Sex on the printed page was more interesting.

As my English ability improved, my Spanish began to suffer. I symbolically pushed Spanish to the back of my brain because English was my preferred language. I began to "think" in English, which meant that Spanish words were being erased or supplanted by my English prowess. But it was wonderful. English allowed my exploration of America through the printed word, audio, and the beautiful but exaggerated images of the Hollywood screen. I developed a fascination for words. Glossy pages of print and photographs of beautiful "American" girls with perfectly straight teeth smiled at me from the pages of magazines like *Seventeen*. Oh, the agony and the ecstasy of those teeth! I flowered into puberty with pearly images of perfect American teeth and other American future perfects.

Perfect Americans. Imperfect me. How would I, a gawky misfit who had nothing of anything portrayed as American, possibly fit into America's high expectations of me? I hid my magnified adolescent imperfections, real or imagined, behind books and more words. I walked head down, shamed by my appearance and my "differentness." When I looked down at my feet, past my knobby knees and skinny legs, I saw only brown, ugly orthopedic shoes end-stopping my child-woman self like two silly commas in the middle of a sentence.

In high school I began the serious rejection of my undesirable self—that which signified my Spanish-speaking heritage. My adolescence was already being pounded by ominous forces carrying secret messages about "undesirability." I was forced to reject anything that might reveal who I *really* was, anything that might provide a clue to my undesirable "otherness." My first overt rejection was of language. I secreted my ability to speak Spanish behind my parents' doors. When anyone who visited the family did not speak English, I rejected them disdainfully, leaving the room where Spanish words might land on me and soil my English-speaking persona. I rejected the friendship of schoolmates who were not "American" (English-speaking). I also began instinctively to reject the "dark," understanding correctly that in America, skin color determined who you were and how you were treated. All the cheerleaders were white.

So, with *Seventeen* in one hand and Revlon in the other, I decided to become American. Assisted by that strange factor, light skin color, I pored over glossy magazines to transform my appearance into something American. As a result of that metamorphosis, I was mistaken for many nationalities—but never for Mexican. My speech was distinguished only as "California" English. I was on my way to becoming assimilated, a desirable "American."

I did not have the opportunity to develop my new Americanness to any degree. Asked whether I was going to "work in the canneries" after I graduated from high school, I was shocked into my American reality. It was 1956, and the Mexican destiny was to be systematically funneled into California's central valley agricultural and industrial labor force. I had not seen myself as merely another laborer in America's work force. I did not yet know about America's bigger plans for the many.

I had bright youthful dreams. I dreamed of tulle prom dresses as voluminous as those in the movies—and I dreamed of college. I dreamed of UCLA, of studying dramatic arts and becoming a beautiful, successful actress. I would leave the central valley nothingness forever. I noticed that my dreams weren't too different from those promised to American girls. Were they? Wasn't I entitled to those same dreams also? But my high school classes, held in postwar quonset huts in one-hundred-degree weather, seemed to offer only typing classes as an escape route. I became word-perfect, though I feared a future of typing endless, monotonous words in sterile offices. The canneries provided steady work, but I did not want to become an old, sick woman in one of those places, or in a factory performing mind-numbing tasks in endless shifts. Never did I want to be like my mother, a homemaker trapped by her culture and her social displacement, and frustrated by her inability to master the English language.

Pushed by a mother who held unrealizable dreams of her own, I briefly attended junior college, an experience that became a mere repetition of high school business courses. It presented no new or challenging options. Ironically, words came to my rescue in the form of shorthand skills. They saved me from the hard labor of canneries and factories. My first job at a local private college paid 90 cents an hour, a sum smaller than the 120 wpm I recorded. In that stuffy, dusty setting of admissions records and grade point averages I stopped dreaming about UCLA and drama. Another avenue, to pay the high tuition demanded by my employer for a college education, was impossible. I stopped. Frustrated by the invisible "thing" that contained me, I turned to my very fifties option: I bolted and married a handsome Latino with no morals and a serious drinking problem.

In 1986, exactly thirty years after my high school graduation, I enrolled at the University of California, Berkeley. I was liberated by the historical events of the sixties and seventies though the *significance* of the times escaped me. I possessed the confidence that comes from true political and social naïveté and genuinely believed that a college education, a final step, would transform me into an equal and fully assimilated American. I was an unfinished product in need of final packaging.

In the 1986 climate of political correctness and under the auspices of federal guidelines, I was the perfect reentry candidate. First and foremost, regardless of my academic achievements, I was an acceptable statistic. I was also a political pawn in America's education system. As a Mexican female over the age of forty, I was one of few Hispanic females at the university and the only older Mexican female at its prestigious English department. I do not remember seeing anyone like me. I was not expected to succeed and I sensed it. Undaunted, I moved ever forward and adopted complete Berkeley standards in order to be assimilated into the academic culture. My feet were shod in politically correct Birkenstock sandals.

I was admitted to Cal Berkeley because of my own political correctness, and to its acclaimed English department because I declared an intent to study literature "relevant to my cultural background." That specific curriculum was approved for someone sanctioned by the government to be there bodily. My mind was a separate entity, to be tracked appropriately. I was unaware of "tracking" or what it meant within the American education system, and how it would restrict future educational pursuits.

In order to achieve my academic goal, I purposely reidentified as "Mexican" on my college applications, though for all intents and purposes I considered myself devoid of Mexican ethnicity. Having waited thirty years for my wonderful college education, I willingly submitted to the state's definition of me by overlooking its idiosyncratic forms and classifications. Admission to Cal Berkeley would finally correct all wrongs and any incompleteness required for Americanization.

Enamored with the idea that is Berkeley, I reverted to the role of submissive Mexican woman, grateful for any educational bit thrown to me. Something, however, alerted my recognition of glaring inequalities that particularly affected those of us classified as "minority students." I remained silent and uninvolved because I wanted my Cal college degree. I focused on books and words, and rejected the sights and sounds of painful experiences, my own and those of others. Berkeley soon began to provide more than the usual "Berkeley" experiences. Cal's illumination symbol finally proved real. I saw that Cal Berkeley was a brutal place.

Discrimination raged rampant in that most liberal of all campuses. Discriminatory practices ranged from insults hurled at minority students standing in the cafeteria lines to admitted administrative racism. "Yes," one administrator said to me informally, "we know everything about every student here, down to their eye color. This university is a microcosm of the state, where we test policy later implemented at large. If it works here, it will work statewide." In 1989, several hundred slots reserved for Hispanic applicants under supposed affirmative action guidelines were transferred to Asian applicants, who were overwhelming Cal with their high scores and demands for admission. The Hispanic contingent made no protest. The wide-sweeping action proved once again that Hispanics could be manipulated, if necessary, within the state's demographics. In 1995, California Hispanics were being summarily targeted by Governor Pete Wilson's racist Proposition 187, which denies health care and education to "illegal immigrants," meaning Hispanics who comprise the bulk of California's undocumented cheap labor force.

Cal Berkeley's unwritten discriminatory policies became more than clearly apparent. The English department's ethnic professors were not exempt, either, from a policy that paid the salary, then expected invisibility. As a group, we minority students discovered our complaints to be very similar. Teaching assistants did not "assist" us as they did other students. Ethnic slurs as embedded forms of American English were used freely both in and out of the classrooms. Everyone not ostracized as minority apparently believed they were "sacrificing" in allowing our collective stupidity within their hallowed halls. They seriously believed we could not distinguish their sometimes mildly amusing institutional terrorism.

The outrages varied. Professors literally slammed doors in our ethnic faces. I used the term "downgrading" to explain the widespread custom of lowering the grades of ethnic students. This practice was not often challenged by students, who did not dare to question the power of the institution. No one wanted to lose their "slot." Although the university's "door" opened to us symbolically, it was in fact closed.

Minority students failed, yes. In a hostile climate, defeat was part of the intended curriculum. Students who opted to transfer to other institutions were probably classified under that infamous statistic—"dropout." Most importantly, as a socioeconomic group we were not realistically *prepared* to compete on an equal level in a world-class university setting. Extensive remedial instruction blocks served as unassailable proof that minorities with their inferior brains did not belong at the university. As non-members of that privileged group who came from backgrounds of private schools and expensive tutors, we were only education's props. We satisfied statistical demands. Many left the idyllic campus because it was an American hell.

It was at Cal Berkeley that I first heard the most racist phrase in the English language directed to me: "You can pass for white." Once, I might have been elated by the culture blurring, but the myth of American equality had been clarified. I had naively existed inside an American Dream found nowhere but in my head. What my Berkeley experience taught me was that our immigrant ideas of America were only vacuous messages. In reality, mega-AMERICA with its wonderful paper-thin philosophies was only a bundle of scrap-paper promises. I was unequivocably, irrevocably, the dreaded "other." Passing for white (assimilation?) was *not* the answer.

My next metamorphosis occurred through one final Berkeley incident that left me, literally, wordless. Though my adviser counseled that I apply to "Hispanic-friendly" universities—suggesting New Mexico, Texas, or Arizona for a Ph.D. in English literature—I persisted at Cal's door. I learned survival tactics of my own and through some maneuvers changed my course of study to medieval English literature, an area of study apparently reserved for only a few, preferably non-minority students. If traditional English literature was sealed off to me, what other knowledge might also be out of my ethnic reach? I knew that I was being tracked for specific university programs designed for minority students, and I objected. My adviser continued, "Of course, you are *welcome* to apply to Berkeley, but I will tell you now, you will never be admitted here." I did not know of any student's rejection prior to application, but then, I was the department's literary thorn in the side. Burning with idealism, I rejected state-imposed tracking, demanding admission to the pristinely white ivory tower where "white" and "tower" carried dual interpretations.

The adviser who with a few cold words ended my dreams of entering the Ph.D. program at Cal then charmingly commented on my "Mexican-ness" and how well I "wore" it. Her words roused a strange anger within me and a stronger sense of determination. The Germanic passion for clas-sification surrounded me. Fortunately, I had learned my lessons well about both language and classification. Standing in the middle of the Wheeler Hall corridor, I looked down at my feet. I was not wearing the *huaraches* of a Mexican peasant tending a cornfield.

The incident that finally silenced me was not the rejection of admis-sion to the English Ph.D. program but something more devastating. I persisted, applied to the master of arts program, and began preparing by undertaking further rigorous studies. Then, I was stunned by one of the hardest blows ever received by a much battered psyche. In a medieval his-tory class, I became the object of derision and humiliation by yet another elitist professor, whose attack took place in the presence of an entire crowded classroom. My words, and therefore my "self," were viciously attacked to vent some deep-seated feelings about race and gender. Like printed text, I was deconstructed. I was the victim of intellectual rape. The emotional trauma is something that leaves you a sterile non-being. I was effectively silenced by a master.

I remained in total silence for several weeks. Words left my head floating out into the atmosphere as easily as they had floated in. I could not *think* of any of the thousands of English words that were the sum total of my American college education and of my assimilated self. My elderly mother nursed me, a silent object, in my sickbed. She fed my body chicken soup. She fed my fevered brain soft Spanish words. Ironically, in the midst of the volumes of silence, a letter printed with many words arrived from the university: It was my admission to the M.A. program in English literature. I saw the words and felt strangled. Unable to speak, I had been admitted to a program that required words, words, words. As in my medieval sto-ries, I had been effectively numbed by a powerful sorcerer who laughed at my Mexican fate.

When language finally returned to me, it was in the form of Spanish words. Spanish words and comfortable images began to flood my memory with pleasant sounds and remembrances. I heard inside my head the mellifluous sounds of my childhood. Words suddenly appeared in my consciousness bright and sharp like children's color-building blocks. Words supposedly lost by my American assimilation reappeared from their secret hiding places. Words that I had disdained for their ability to define the real me reappeared to save my American self. I flailed about, reaching out for the evanescent words whirling around me and clinging to them passionately. Their forms and sounds revitalized my exhausted brain. Truth time. In America I could not shed my Mexican skin by learning a new language or by adopting an American posture. More importantly, no longer did I want to.

It has taken five years to recapture the "English" that I lost from the traumatic Berkeley experience. I have since singed the edges of American literature with some minor writing successes. My Berkeley education has meant not a thing in the America that was supposed to receive me with many equal opportunities after a rigorous college education. As a fringe spectator, I have now watched my non-minority fellow classmates, degreed or not, enter the world of publishing as editors, writers, readers, or any other occupation dear to an English major's heart. My English degree experiences have been very different. When I teach, I am inevitably placed, or offered, bilingual English positions. When I write, editors either angrily reject my work ("You will *never* be accepted by this publication") or request articles that I refer to as my "tortilla stories." My Mexicanness appears to limit my writing parameters. With one particularly crude editing experience I learned well the depth of the "power of the press." But then, my work is not easy, palatable reading. My words, once compared to those emanating from apartheid South Africa, question how it is that in free America I have something in common with millions in South African bondage.

Suppression succeeds only temporarily. Suppression contradictorily creates greater courage and determination, though that may not be immediately apparent. It takes courage to live invisible lives. While the young explode into fire and rage, the rest of us who have lived and borne outrage in measured silences simply wait. I know. I write words that are sealed away in silent boxes.

It is summer 1995. I look down now and see old, worn slippers on my tired feet. I have walked countless American miles in search of the equality and opportunity that I was told reside in America. My wanderings invariably led me to America's back doors. On my cluttered desk is a piece of crisp, white paper with printed black words. It is a letter of admission to Columbia University. Once again, expectations high, I have been admitted only through a great institution's back door. Words. Words on paper. My bane and my energy. I am words. One day America will permit my words through its front doors.

The Border Patrol State

■ ■ ■

LESLIE MARMON SILKO

I used to travel the highways of New Mexico and Arizona with a wonderful sensation of absolute freedom as I cruised down the open road and across the vast desert plateaus. On the Laguna Pueblo reservation, where I was raised, the people were patriotic despite the way the U.S. government had treated Native Americans. As proud citizens, we grew up believing the freedom to travel was our inalienable right, a right that some Native Americans had been denied in the early twentieth century. Our cousin, old Bill Pratt, used to ride his horse three hundred miles overland from Laguna, New Mexico, to Prescott, Arizona, every summer to work as a fire lookout.

In school in the 1950s, we were taught that our right to travel from state to state without special papers or threat of detainment was a right that citizens under Communist and totalitarian governments did not possess. That wide open highway told us we were U.S. citizens; we were free. . . .

Not so long ago, my companion Gus and I were driving south from Albuquerque, returning to Tucson after a book promotion for the paperback edition of my novel *Almanac of the Dead*. I had settled back and gone to sleep while Gus drove, but I was awakened when I felt the car slowing to a stop. It was nearly midnight on New Mexico State Road 26, a dark, lonely stretch of two-lane highway between Hatch and Deming. When I sat up, I saw the headlights and emergency flashers of six vehicles—Border Patrol cars and a van were blocking both lanes of the highway. Gus stopped the car and rolled down the window to ask what was wrong. But the closest Border Patrolman and his companion did not reply; instead, the first agent ordered us to "step out of the car." Gus asked why, but his question seemed to set them off. Two more Border Patrol agents immediately approached our car, and one of them snapped, "Are you looking for trouble?" as if he would relish it.

I will never forget that night beside the highway. There was an awful feeling of menace and violence straining to break loose. It was clear that the uniformed men would be only too happy to drag us out of the car if we did not speedily comply with their request (asking a question is tantamount to resistance, it seems). So we stepped out of the car and they motioned for us to stand on the shoulder of the road. The night was very dark, and no other traffic had come down the road since we had been stopped. All I could think about was a book I had read—*Nunca Más*—the official report of a human rights commission that investigated and certified more than twelve thousand "disappearances" during Argentina's "dirty war" in the late 1970s.

The weird anger of these Border Patrolmen made me think about descriptions in the report of Argentine police and military officers who became addicted to interrogation, torture, and the murder that followed. When the military and police ran out of political suspects to torture and kill, they resorted to the random abduction of citizens off the streets. I thought how easy it would be for the Border Patrol to shoot us and leave our bodies and car beside the highway, like so many bodies found in these parts and ascribed to "drug runners."

Two other Border Patrolmen stood by the white van. The one who had asked if we were looking for trouble ordered his partner to "get the dog," and from the back of the van another patrolman brought a small female German shepherd on a leash. The dog apparently did not heel well enough to suit him, and the handler jerked the leash. They opened the doors of our car and pulled the dog's head into it, but I saw immediately from the expression in her eyes that the dog hated them, and that she would not serve them. When she showed no interest in the inside of our car, they brought her around back to the trunk, near where we were standing. They half-dragged her up into the trunk, but still she did not indicate any stowed-away human beings or illegal drugs.

Their mood got uglier; the officers seemed outraged that the dog could not find any contraband, and they dragged her over to us and commanded her to sniff our legs and feet. To my relief, the strange violence the Border Patrol agents had focused on us now seemed shifted to the dog. I no longer felt so strongly that we would be murdered. We exchanged looks—the dog and I. She was afraid of what they might do, just as I was. The dog's handler jerked the leash sharply as she sniffed us, as if to make her perform better, but the dog refused to accuse us: She had an innate dignity that did not permit her to serve the murderous impulses of those men. I can't forget the expression in the dog's eyes; it was as if she were embarrassed to be associated with them. I had a small amount of medicinal marijuana in my purse that night, but she refused to expose me. I am not partial to dogs, but I will always remember that small German shepherd.

Unfortunately, what happened to me is an everyday occurrence here now. Since the 1980s, on top of greatly expanding border checkpoints, the Immigration and Naturalization Service and the Border Patrol have implemented policies that interfere with the rights of U.S. citizens to travel freely within our borders. INS agents now patrol all interstate highways and roads that lead to or from the U.S.-Mexico border in Texas, New Mexico, Arizona, and California. Now, when you drive east from Tucson on Interstate 10 toward El Paso, you encounter an INS check station outside Las Cruces, New Mexico. When you drive north from Las Cruces up Interstate 25, two miles north of the town of Truth or Consequences, the highway is blocked with orange emergency barriers, and all traffic is diverted into a two-lane Border Patrol checkpoint—ninety-five miles north of the U.S.-Mexico border.

I was detained once at Truth or Consequences, despite my and my companion's Arizona driver's licenses. Two men, both Chicanos, were detained at the same time, despite the fact that they too presented ID and spoke English without the thick Texas accents of the Border Patrol agents. While we were stopped, we watched as other vehicles—whose occupants were white—were waved through the checkpoint. White people traveling with brown people, however, can expect to be stopped on suspicion they work with the sanctuary movement, which shelters refugees. White people who appear to be clergy, those who wear ethnic clothing or jewelry, and women with very long hair or very short hair (they could be nuns) are also frequently detained; white men with beards or men with long hair are likely to be detained, too, because Border

Patrol agents have "profiles" of "those sorts" of white people who may help political refugees. (Most of the political refugees from Guatemala and El Salvador are Native American or mestizo because the indigenous people of the Americas have continued to resist efforts by invaders to displace them from their ancestral lands.) Alleged increases in illegal immigration by people of Asian ancestry means that the Border Patrol now routinely detains anyone who appears to be Asian or part Asian, as well.

Once your car is diverted from the Interstate Highway into the checkpoint area, you are under the control of the Border Patrol, which in practical terms exercises a power that no highway patrol or city patrolman possesses: They are willing to detain anyone, for no apparent reason. Other law enforcement officers need a shred of probable cause in order to detain someone. On the books, so does the Border Patrol; but on the road, it's another matter. They'll order you to stop your car and step out; then they'll ask you to open the trunk. If you ask why or request a search warrant, you'll be told that they'll have to have a dog sniff the car before they can request a search warrant, and the dog might not get there for two or three hours. The search warrant might require an hour or two past that. They make it clear that if you force them to obtain a search warrant for the car, they will make you submit to a strip search as well.

Traveling in the open, though, the sense of violation can be even worse. Never mind high-profile cases like that of former Border Patrol agent Michael Elmer, acquitted of murder by claiming self-defense, despite admitting that as an officer he shot an "illegal" immigrant in the back and then hid the body, which remained undiscovered until another Border Patrolman reported the event. (In September 1994, Elmer was convicted of reckless endangerment in a separate incident, for shooting at least ten rounds from his M-16 too close to a group of immigrants as they were crossing illegally into Nogales in March 1992.) Or that in El Paso, a high school football coach driving a vanload of his players in full uniform was pulled over on the freeway and a Border Patrol agent put a cocked revolver to his head. (The football coach was Mexican American, as were most of the players in his van; the incident eventually caused a federal judge to issue a restraining order against the Border Patrol.) We've a mountain of personal experiences like that which never make the newspapers. A history professor at UCLA told me she had been traveling by train from Los Angeles to Albuquerque twice a month doing research. On each of her trips, she had noticed that the Border Patrol agents were at the station in Albuquerque scrutinizing the passengers. Since she is six feet tall and of Irish and German ancestry, she was not particularly concerned. Then one day when she stepped off the train in Albuquerque, two Border Patrolmen accosted her, wanting to know what she was doing, and why she was traveling between Los Angeles and Albuquerque twice a month. She presented identification and an explanation deemed "suitable" by the agents, and was allowed to go about her business.

Just the other day, I mentioned to a friend that I was writing this essay and he told me about his seventy-three-year-old father, who is half Chinese and had set out alone by car from Tucson to Albuquerque the week before. His father had become confused by road construction and missed a turnoff from Interstate 10 to Interstate 25; when he turned around and circled back, he missed the turnoff a second time. But when he looped back for yet another try, Border Patrol agents stopped him and forced him to open his trunk. After they satisfied themselves that he was not smuggling Chinese immigrants, they sent him on his way. He was so rattled by the event that he had to be driven home by his daughter.

This is the police state that has developed in the southwestern United States since the 1980s. No person, no citizen, is free to travel without the scrutiny of the Border Patrol. In the city of South Tucson, where 80 percent of the respondents were Chicano or Mexicano, a joint research project by the University of Wisconsin and the University of Arizona concluded in 1994 that one out of every five people there had been detained, mistreated verbally or non-verbally, or questioned by INS agents in the past two years.

"Manifest destiny" may lack its old grandeur of theft and blood—"lock the door" is what it means now, with racism a trump card to be played again and again, shamelessly, by both major political parties. "Immigration," like "street crime" and "welfare fraud," is a political euphemism that refers to people of color. Politicians and media people talk about "illegal aliens" to dehumanize and demonize undocumented immigrants, who are for the most part people of color. Even in the days of Spanish and Mexican rule, no attempts were made to interfere with the flow of people and goods from south to north and north to south. It is the U.S. government that has continually attempted to sever contact between the tribal people north of the border and those to the south.*

Now that the Iron Curtain is gone, it is ironic that the U.S. government and its Border Patrol are constructing a steel wall ten feet high to

*The Treaty of Guadalupe Hidalgo, signed in 1848, recognizes the right of the Tohano O'Odom (Papago) people to move freely across the U.S.-Mexico border without documents. A treaty with Canada guarantees similar rights to those of the Iroquois nation in traversing the U.S.-Canada border.

span sections of the border with Mexico. While politicians and multi-national corporations extol the virtues of NAFTA and "free trade" (in goods, not flesh), the ominous curtain is already up in a six-mile section at the border crossing at Mexicali; two miles are being erected but are not yet finished at Naco; and at Nogales, sixty miles south of Tucson, the steel wall has been all rubber-stamped and awaits construction. Like the pathetic multi-million-dollar "antidrug" border surveillance balloons that were continually deflated by high winds and made only a couple of meager interceptions before they blew away, the fence along the border is a theatrical prop, a bit of pork for contractors. Border entrepreneurs have already used blowtorches to cut passageways through the fence to collect "tolls," and are doing a brisk business. Back in Washington, the INS announces a $300 million computer contract to modernize its record-keeping and Congress passes a crime bill that shunts $255 million to the INS for 1995, $181 million earmarked for border control, which is to include seven hundred new partners for the men who stopped Gus and me in our travels, and the history professor, and my friend's father, and as many as they could from South Tucson.

It is no use; borders haven't worked, and they won't work, not now, as the indigenous people of the Americas reassert their kinship and solidarity with one another. A mass migration is already under way; its roots are not simply economic. The Uto-Aztecan languages are spoken as far north as Taos Pueblo near the Colorado border, all the way south to Mexico City. Before the arrival of the Europeans, the indigenous communities throughout this region not only conducted commerce, but the people also shared cosmologies, and oral narratives about the Maize Mother, the Twin Brothers and their Grandmother, Spider Woman, as well as Quetzalcoatl the benevolent snake. The great human migration within the Americas cannot be stopped; human beings are natural forces of the earth, just as rivers and winds are natural forces.

Deep down the issue is simple: The so-called Indian Wars from the days of Sitting Bull and Red Cloud have never really ended in the Americas. The Indian people of southern Mexico, of Guatemala, and those left in El Salvador, too, are still fighting for their lives and for their land against the "cavalry" patrols sent out by the governments of those lands. The Americas are Indian country, and the "Indian problem" is not about to go away.

One evening at sundown, we were stopped in traffic at a railroad crossing in downtown Tucson while a freight train passed us, slowly gaining speed as it headed north to Phoenix. In the twilight I saw the most amazing sight: Dozens of human beings, mostly young men, were riding the train; everywhere, on flat cars, inside open boxcars, perched on top of boxcars, hanging off ladders on tank cars and between boxcars. I couldn't count fast enough, but I saw fifty or sixty people headed north. They were dark young men, Indian and mestizo; they were smiling and a few of them waved at us in our cars. I was reminded of the ancient story of Aztlán, told by the Aztecs but known in other Uto-Aztecan communities as well. Aztlán is the beautiful land to the north, the origin place of the Aztec people. I don't remember how or why the people left Aztlán to journey farther south, but the old story says that one day, they will return.

9

■ ■ ■

THE FUTURE: NATIONALISM
OR INTERNATIONALISM?

Cultural Work: Planting New Trees with New Seeds

■ ■ ■

HAKI R. MADHUBUTI

In America, people of African descent are caught between a hurricane and a volcano when it comes to the acquisition of life-giving and life-sustaining knowledge. Too many of our children are trapped in urban school systems that have been "programmed" for failure. All too often, the answer to what must be done to correct this injustice is left in the hands of those most responsible for creating the problem. If your child is sleeping and a rat starts to bite at his/her head, you don't ask the rat to please stop biting at your child's brain. If you are a sane, normal, and loving parent, you go on the attack and try your damnedest to kill the rat.

When it comes to the education of African American children, rats are biting at the doors, floors, desks, and gym shoes of the nation's public schools. Jonathan Kozol, in his heartfelt book *Savage Inequalities* (1993), documents the near collapse of urban public education. He writes of young people who "have no feeling of belonging to America." If public education is the first formal, state-sponsored orientation into becoming a productive citizen, the country is in deep, deep trouble. If public schooling is supposed to stimulate the nation's children into becoming poets, doctors, teachers, scientists, farmers, computer experts, musicians, entrepreneurs, carpenters, professors, etc., get ready to throw in the towel. This is the eleventh round and the major answer that is offered by most urban school systems is simply to change the superintendent. Rather than look at the system, we personalize the problem as if one man or woman can affect real change. For example, in a city like Chicago where sixty years of "boss" politics control a $2.7 billion school budget, change and child-centered education takes a backseat to economics and patronage. To bring an "unschooled" outsider in as superintendent is like a chicken prescribing chicken soup for a cold.

Why is it that in 1996 we still lie to ourselves? Some of the most intelligent advocates of public school education continue to blame the victim as if our children have the capacity to educate themselves. They overlook the ever present political, racial, and economic realities of the major consumers of public education: Black and Latino children. They overlook the all-consuming cultures of defeat and poverty that blanket large portions of the Black community. The metaphorical "rat" I speak of is white supremacy (racism), which manifests itself freely in the structured and systematic destruction of millions of unsuspecting children and their parents.

It is argued in some quarters in the Black community that a public school education can be a handicap to one's survival. Young brothers seen too often with books (without pictures) are categorized as unmanly. However, this view is unenlightened and represents a small slice of the miseducation that is accepted and encouraged by a growing number of people with enslaved minds enclosed in short-circuited memories. On the other hand, white supremacist ideology has a way of making another type of enslaved mind think that by acquiring pieces of paper (degrees), he/she is indeed free. Yet, the one freedom that is openly accessible to all Black folks in America is the freedom to self-destruct.

Memory is instructive here. Africans did not swim, motor-boat, or free fly to America. There is a horrible connection between Africans and Europeans that must not be forgotten, negated, or minimized. The African holocaust is seldom explored or taught in our schools. This relationship of white slave trader to enslaved African has been the glue connecting us for over a millennium.

There are over 100 million people of African descent in the western hemisphere, and we all face similar problems. Whether one is in Canada, the United States, or Brazil, the fight for self-definition and self-reliance is like using a shovel to dig a hole in steel-enforced concrete. There are over 69 million people of African descent in Brazil who speak Portuguese, there are over 35 million people of African descent in the United States who attempt to speak English, and we Africans don't talk to each other. I maintain that this is a learned activity and acutely cultural. Over 100 million Africans moving and working for the same goals in the same hemisphere is a threat to anyone's rule. Our clothes, names, street address, employment, and articulations in their languages have changed, but the basic relationship has remained the same: Black folks are still dependent upon white folks in America. To Africanize or to liberate this system from its exclusive Euro-American model is indeed a progressive and often revolutionary act.

Another memory. I'll never forget a trip I made to Tanzania in the 1970s to attend an international conference. After the day's work, I walked alone in the city of Dar es Salaam. As the sun set and the street lights illuminated the city, I noticed three children about a block away huddled close together under a lamppost. As I approached them, I noticed that my presence was not important to them. I smiled at the reason why. The three of them, two boys and a girl, were deeply engrossed in reading and discussing a book. I walked on without disturbing them in their obvious joy. These were poor African children using the only light available at that time. Their enthusiasm for learning was at one time the reality for the great majority of African Americans.

The history of the fight to educate African Americans is one that is rarely told in this age of integration. In fact, if the truth was ever unshackled, it would reveal that students in Black schools along with Black church members led the modern fight for full educational and political equality in the United States. This fight was never a battle to sit next to white children in a classroom. It was and still is a struggle for an equal and level playing field in all areas of human endeavor: finance, law, politics, military, commerce, sports, entertainment, science, technology, and education.

Many believed that if we had first-rate facilities, buildings, supplies, environment, teachers, and support personnel, a quality education would follow. This is obviously not true. We now understand that there is a profound difference between going to school and being educated. We know that close to a half-million children frequent the Chicago public schools each day and that less than 20 percent are truly receiving a first-class education that could stand remotely close to that offered by the best private schools.

For the last twenty-five years, I have been involved in the Independent Black School movement. This movement grew out of the Black empowerment struggles and initiatives of the 1960s and has developed African-centered schools around the country. It also has established a national professional organization, the Council of Independent Black Institutes

(CIBI). The great majority of persons involved in the first generation of this movement were products of the public school system. We knew first-hand the type of school not needed. From the beginning, we were (and continue to be) cultural workers who had been tremendously influenced by Black struggle and the works of W. E. B. Du Bois, Carter G. Woodson, Frantz Fanon, Paulo Freire, Marcus Garvey, Harold Cruse, Chancellor Williams, E. Franklin Frazier, Mary McLeod Bethune, and others.

The critical examination of schools and education always has been central in our analysis. The development of our school in Chicago, New Concept Development Center (NCDC), has indeed been a labor of love. Also, I can assure you that it has been a love of that type of labor. Because if the love was not there, we would not have a school. Our twenty-three years of developing NCDC have been extremely difficult and have taxed us both physically and emotionally. The question of schools versus education is not a question of becoming an "educated fool"; the fear of book learning disconnecting one from community development has a long tradition in the Black community. In fact, in our community a distinction has always been made between schools and education. Since we had to fight so hard to get a foot into the schoolhouse door, the struggle to go to school has, in itself, meant to most Africans in America that a quality education would not necessarily be the results of such an endeavor.

James D. Anderson, in his brilliant book *The Education of Blacks in the South 1860–1935*, makes it clear that Africans in America viewed education as a birth right in the same light as freedom. The first two types of institutions that Africans built from the ground up with their own hands and resources were schools and churches. Therefore, our continued inquiry into the state of Black education must be an insightful and informed one. Such an examination must be one that asks the difficult questions:

1. What is more important than the enlightened education of our children? Should one's children have any obligation to their own people and culture? Who is ultimately responsible for providing education: the family, the state, or others?
2. Education in the past has been used politically against the advancement of African Americans. Is it any different today? Will African-centered studies connect education to the political, scientific, economic, and racial realities of today's world?
3. The European-American centeredness or Western focus of today's education continues to place conscious Blacks on a collision course with its basic premise: that European culture stands at

the center and is pivotal to one's understanding of the world. Is European culture universal? Will the introduction of African-centered thought and pedagogy broaden our students' minds or pigeonhole them into a false sense of security and narrow nationalism? Is African-centered studies a new form of ethnocentrism or exclusivity masked in new terminology and contexts?

4. All education is value-based. Whose values are our children learning? Will African-centered studies teach a value base that will encourage and allow competition at a world level and cooperation at a local one?

An educated Black person must not only be aware of the core curriculum of his or her school but must also have a core understanding of his/her own people's contributions to local, national, and world civilization. When we argue for an African-centered education, it is not at the expense or exclusion of an enlightened Western education; rather, it is an important addition to this knowledge base. Dr. Wade Nobles and his staff have instituted an African-centered curriculum at the McClymonds International Science, Culture and Technology High School in Oakland, California. His program defines African-centered education in the following ways:

"Afrocentric, Africentric, or African Centered" are interchangeable terms representing the concept which categorizes a quality of thought and practice which is rooted in the cultural image and interest of people of African ancestry and which represents and reflects the life experiences, history and traditions of people of African ancestry as the center of analyses. Afrocentricity is therein the intellectual and philosophical foundation upon which people of African ancestry should create their own scientific and moral criterion for authenticating the reality of African human processes. It represents the core and fundamental quality of the "Belonging" of people of African ancestry.

In terms of education, African centered education utilizes African and African American cultural precepts, processes, laws and experiences to solve, guide and understand human functioning relative to the educational process. In essence, Afrocentricity represents the fact that as human beings, people of African ancestry have the right and responsibility to "center" themselves in their own subjective possibilities and potential and through the recentering process reproduce and refine the best of themselves.

We must never lose sight of the fact that Black people in America must function and excel in the cultures in which they live. This means essentially that we must tackle, absorb, decipher, reject, and appreciate European American culture in all of its racism, complexity, contributions, liberating ideas, and models. However, if one is to become and remain a culturally whole African (Black) person, he or she must be first and foremost concerned about the culture of his or her people. To quote Dr. Nobles again,

> African centered multicultural education is driven by truth, respect for knowledge, desire to learn and a passion for excellence. In regards to "centric" education, the importance of culture is not simply relegated or minimized to the task of being sensitive to cultural differences or superficially appreciating or exploring the common ground of different people. As the foundation for multi-cultural education, culture, as both the process and the subject of eduction, will serve as the medium and mechanism for teaching, learning, counseling and educational management/administration.

The logic behind this is that in most cases a person's contribution to society is closely related to his or her understanding and perception of himself or herself in relation to the culture in which he or she functions and lives. Such a culture can be one that either enslaves and shortens life or that liberates and gives life. The best protection for any people can be found in culture that is intellectually and psychologically liberating. We should be about the development of whole persons, and should begin that wholeness with an accurate understanding and assessment of our own involvement in our community, city, state, nation, and world.

For example, the normalization of Malcolm X, psychologically and intellectually, came about when he was a young man locked up in prison. I say that Malcolm X was normalized rather than radicalized because he was introduced to ideas that challenged and liberated his mind. Ideas that put his people close to the center of civilization. He saw in the teachings of Elijah Muhammad and others a self-protective shield as well as the core wisdom for the making of a new Black person in America. From that point on, Malcolm X prepared himself to go on the offensive, to be proactive and combative in a self-reliant and self-protective manner. Any person, from any culture, functioning *sanely* would have acted the same way.

My own development, or should I say misdevelopment, was not unlike that of millions of Black people in America. I was born into acute poverty, educated in public schools by insensitive and uncaring teachers, and dependent upon a welfare system that was demeaning, inadequate, and corrupt. I was nurtured in a single-parent family where my mother was ill-equipped to navigate the economic, social, and political pressures of our world. All of this drove her to alcohol, drugs, and death at the age of thirty-six. My own transformation came about as a direct result of being introduced to African (Black) ideas that did not insult my own personhood, but guided me, invigorated me, and lifted me beyond the white supremacist theories that confined me and my people to the toilets of other people's promises and progress.

All education must lead to deep understanding and mastery. The crucial question is, deep understanding and mastery of what? Introduction to many forms of knowing is absolutely necessary. However, most of the understandings about life that are being taught to our children have ceased to be life-giving and life-sustaining, and do not lend themselves to self-reliance or deep reflection on the state of one's self and one's people in a highly charged, competitive, and often oppressive world. One must be anchored in one's self, people, history, that is, culture, before one can truly be a whole participant in world culture or multiculturalism; we must always start local in order to appreciate and incorporate the positive agents of the universal. One cannot achieve the multi-anything if one has not explored the singular inside one first.

African-centered cultural studies must lead, encourage, and direct African American students into the technologies of the future. This is where the new statements about power, control, and wealth are being made in the world today.

Black students must have deep understandings of the political, racial, economic, scientific, and technological realities that confront the very survival of African people locally, nationally, and internationally. They must be grounded in a world view that promotes cross-cultural communication, understanding, and sharing; yet they must be self-protective enough to realize that the world is not fair and that one's own interests often come into conflict with the interests of others, especially when race is involved. Therefore, if we want our children to achieve significantly, they must:

1. Possess a deep understanding of the world in which they will have to function. However, the foundation of their knowledge must be anchored in positive self-concept and taught in an environment that encourages growth. If one is secure in one's self, that which others project—in all areas—will be less appealing, confusing, or threatening.

2. Realize that all education is foundational. The values we practice are introduced early and often in school and non-school settings such as family, media, church, entertainment, sports functions, etc., and can either work for or against development.

3. Understand that successful development is difficult with a quality education, but almost impossible without one. Further, education can be fun, but it is often hard and boring work and requires a commitment far beyond picking up a basketball or learning a new dance or handshake. It demands deep study and quiet time.

4. Understand that multiculturalism, if it is to mean anything, must exist among enlightened cultures who bring their best to the table for discussion. If all people of African descent have to contribute is that from Europe, what does that say about us? How are we any different—in cultural substance—from the ethnic groups of Europe and the United States?

Too Much Schooling, Too Little Education, edited by M. Mwalimi Shujaa, and Useni Eugene Perkins's *Harvesting New Generations* are must reading if we are to completely understand the urgency of this task. Other critical works to study and absorb are Janice Hale-Benson's *Black Children: Their Roots, Culture and Learning Styles*; Nsenga Warfield Coppock's *Transformation: A Rites of Passage Manual for African American Girls*; Carter G. Woodson's *The Miseducation of the Negro*; Amos Wilson's *The Developmental Psychology of the Black Child*; and Wade Nobles's *Africanity and the Black Family*.

Our children are our priority and the only thing more important than their care is the care of ourselves—their parents and teachers—in a way that does not diminish our ability to provide them with the best education in all the life-giving and life-saving areas. To do less is a profound comment on our own cultural education.

Toward a Non-Racial, Non-Ethnic Society

■ ■ ■

ORTIZ MONTAIGNE WALTON

A few years ago I was asked to appear on the *Mort Downey Show*, one of our nation's first television talk shows featuring audience participation. The topic of discussion was a growing usage of the term "African American," which had begun to replace the term "black." In this essay, I shall endeavor to demonstrate that the confusion and sometimes chaos resulting from those labeled by racial terms is a general phenomenon rather than particular to those bearing certain phenotypical characteristics.

When I began my research on color, race, and ethnicity in the 1970s, the topic seemed a very straightforward concern, akin to a proposition that the earth was round rather than flat. But the Zeitgeist did not favor intellectual interest along these lines. However, there has been an increasing interest in the subject since the emergence of South Africa as the first non-racial society, and a greater awareness that the overall population of those given formal classification as "whites" comprise a minority. Although interest in this subject has increased and a number of books have been published, none of the research effort has resulted in coherent social theory. Even former U.S. President Ronald Reagan has "gotten into the act." Patti Davis, Reagan's daughter, comments on her father's perspective:

> That fall, I invited my parents to my house for dinner. My brother, Ron, his wife, Doria, and a friend of mine were also there. I can't recall exactly how the subject came up, but I vividly remember my father discussing his feelings on the subject. He pointed out that America is a "melting pot" and there really are no pure races left. We're all a mixture of various races and ethnic backgrounds. That fact alone, he said, should be enough to make us all strive for harmony. I thought of Rodney King saying, "Can't we all just get along." My father went on at length about how races had crossed lines and melted into one another, so there was no reason for violence and hatred on racial differences. . . . And I couldn't help speculating what could have happened if Ronald Reagan had stood in front of the American public while he was President and said the same things that he was saying at home that night. As appealing as that fantasy is, that's not what happened.[1]

The quotation begs the question whether indeed there were ever "pure races" in America or anywhere else, with the possible exception of the world's first inhabitants residing in Central Africa's Lake Tanganyika region. Sociologist Robert Merton argues that intermarriage, the antecedent of ethnic and racial mixture, becomes salient only with variation in pigmentation.[2] On the other hand, it seems to me that racial and ethnic classifications are more ideological than scientific and frequently utilized by politicians and demagogues for the purposes of divisiveness. Concerning matters of genealogy—how many of us can validly trace our ancestry beyond a few generations? One would be extremely suspect in arguing a "racially pure" background over eons of time. When the matter of race and pigmentation is considered in strictly physical terms, another *reductio ad absurdum* results, given white as the combination of all color, and black as its absence.

Let us return to my opening comments about the *Mort Downey Show.* An air of excitement filled the Secaucus, New Jersey, studio the night of the filming. I recognized a number of familiar faces in the crowd, folks who had appeared as "regulars" on many of his shows. One was a loud, vexatious person who had usually played the role of devil's advocate. In response to a question by Downey about his national origins (the fellow having repeatedly denied being an American), he uttered something about Africa. Downey corrected him by arguing that Africa was not a country or nation but a continent. Soon thereafter, I was asked whether the use of the term "African American" would have eased my entry and tenure with the Boston Symphony Orchestra. I explained that to the best of my knowledge I was awarded the position not because of my so-called racial background, but because I was the best contrabassist in the world as judged by the color-blind European conductor Charles Munch (for my audition I performed Mozart's Violin Concerto No. 3 on the double bass, a feat never before or since accomplished).

The loud, vexatious fellow immediately became livid and retorted in a thinly disguised effort to undermine my statement: "There are those who are light enough to pass for white. . . ." The ruckus continued with Downey's sobering reflection on the political career of Adam Clayton Powell, Sr., who had also been light enough to pass for white but had early in his career forsaken the perquisites of putative identity as white to become a vigorous spokesman for civil rights for so-called blacks and human rights for human beings.

Now that we have entered the Hobbesian age—the war of every man against Everyman, with virtual genocide taking place right before our eyes in what was formerly Yugoslavia (please note the impermanence and relativism of ethnicity here), mass homicide in Oklahoma, neo-Nazism in Germany and throughout much of the European continent, the inter-ethnic slaughter of more than a million people in Rwanda, and a new wave of fascistic ideology rapidly enveloping America and throughout the world—are we yet at the point of just becoming human beings sans eth-nicity and race? I rather doubt it. Perhaps we await the Day of Judgment, or "Doomsday," that final day on earth when no doubt our politicos will announce begrudgingly that we once lived in a beautiful world that is now dead.

■ ■ ■

NOTES

1. Patti Davis, "My Father's Gift," *San Francisco Examiner*, April 23, 1995.
2. See Robert K. Merton, "Intermarriage and the Social Structure," *Psychiatry* 4 (August 1941), pp. 361–374.

Beyond Multiculturalism: Surviving the Nineties

■ ■ ■

BHARATI MUKHERJEE

In these times of serious, often violent, cultural and ethnic identity crises that are tearing apart many nations, I am particularly thankful to have this opportunity to share with you—who are mostly second-, third-, and fourth-generation descendants of European immigrants—my experiences as a non-European pioneer, and my hopes for the future of the country you and I have chosen to live in.

The United States exists as a sovereign nation with its officially stated Constitution, its economic and foreign policies, its demarcated, patrolled boundaries. "America," however, exists as image or idea, as dream or nightmare, as romance or plague, constructed by discrete individual fantasies, and shaded by collective paranoias and mythologies.

I am a naturalized U.S. citizen with a certificate of citizenship; more importantly, I am an American for whom "America" is the stage for the drama of self-transformation. I see American culture as a culture of dreamers, who believe material shape (which is not the same as materialism) can be given to dreams. They believe that one's station in life—poverty, education, family background—does not determine one's fate. They believe in the reversal of omens; early failures do not spell inevitable disaster. Outsiders can triumph on merit. All of this happens against the backdrop of the familiar vicissitudes of American life.

I first came to the United States—to the state of Iowa, to be precise—on a late summer evening nearly thirty-three years ago. I flew into a placid, verdant airport in Iowa City on a commercial airliner, ready to fulfill the goals written out in a large, lined notebook for me by my guiltlessly patriarchal father. Those goals were unambiguous: I was to spend two years studying Creative Writing at Paul Engle's unique Writers Workshop; then I was to marry the perfect Bengali bridegroom selected by my father and live out the rest of a contented, predictable life in the city of my birth, Calcutta. In 1961, I was a shy, pliant, well-mannered, dutiful young daughter from a very privileged, traditional, mainstream Hindu family that believed women should be protected and provided for by their fathers, husbands, sons, and it did not once occur to me that I might have goals of my own, quite distinct from those specified for me by my father. I certainly did not anticipate then that, over the next three decades, Iowans—who seemed to me so racially and culturally homogeneous—would be forced to shudder through the violent paroxysms of a collective identity in crisis.

When I was growing up in Calcutta in the fifties, I heard no talk of "identity crisis"—communal or individual. The concept itself—of a person not knowing who she or he was—was unimaginable in a hierarchical, classification-obsessed society. One's identity was absolutely fixed, derived from religion, caste, patrimony, and mother tongue. A Hindu Indian's last name was designed to announce his or her forefathers' caste and place of origin. A Mukherjee could *only* be a Brahmin from Bengal. Indian tradition forbade inter-caste, inter-language, inter-ethnic marriages. Bengali tradition discouraged even emigration; to remove oneself from Bengal was to "pollute" true culture.

Until the age of eight, I lived in a house crowded with forty or fifty relatives. We lived together because we were "family," bonded by kinship, though kinship was interpreted in flexible enough terms to include, when necessary, men, women, children who came from the same *desh*—which is the Bengali word for "homeland"—as had my father and grandfather. I was who I was because I was Dr. Sudhir Lal Mukherjee's daughter, because I was a Hindu Brahmin, because I was Bengali-speaking, and because my *desh* was an East Bengal village called Faridpur. I was encouraged to think of myself as indistinguishable from my dozen girl cousins. Identity was viscerally connected with ancestral soil and family origins. I was first a Mukherjee, then a Bengali Brahmin, and only then an Indian.

Deep down I knew, of course, that I was not quite like my girl cousins. Deeper down, I was sure that pride in the purity of one's culture has a sinister underside. As a child I had witnessed bloody religious riots between Muslims and Hindus, and violent language riots between Bengalis and Biharis. People kill for culture, and die of hunger. Language, race, religion, blood, myth, history, national codes, and manners have all been used, in India, in the United States, are being used in Bosnia and Rwanda even today, to enforce terror, to "otherize," to murder.

I do not know what compelled my strong-willed and overprotective father to risk sending us, his three daughters, to school in the United States, a country he had not visited. In Calcutta, he had insisted on sheltering us from danger and temptation by sending us to girls-only schools, and by providing us with chaperones, chauffeurs, and bodyguards.

The Writers Workshop in a quonset hut in Iowa City was my first experience of coeducation. And after not too long, I fell in love with a fellow student named Clark Blaise, an American of Canadian origin, and impulsively married him during a lunch break in a lawyer's office above a coffeeshop.

That impulsive act cut me off forever from the rules and ways of upper-middle-class life in Bengal, and hurled me precipitously into a New World life of scary improvisations and heady explorations. Until my lunchtime wedding, I had seen myself as an Indian foreign student, a transient in the United States. The five-minute ceremony in the lawyer's office had changed me into a permanent transient.

Over the last three decades the important lesson that I have learned is that in this era of massive diasporic movements, honorable survival requires resilience, curiosity, and compassion, a letting go of rigid ideals about the purity of inherited culture.

The first ten years into marriage, years spent mostly in my husband's *desh* of Canada, I thought myself an expatriate Bengali permanently stranded in North America because of a power surge of destiny or of desire. My first novel, *The Tiger's Daughter*, embodies the loneliness I felt but could not acknowledge, even to myself, as I negotiated the no-man's-land between the country of my past and the continent of my present. Shaped by memory, textured with nostalgia for a class and culture I had abandoned, this novel quite naturally became my expression of the *expatriate consciousness*.

It took me a decade of painful introspection to put the smothering tyranny of nostalgia into perspective, and to make the transition from expatriate to immigrant. I have found my way back to the United States after a fourteen-year stay in Canada. The transition from foreign student to U.S. citizen, from detached onlooker to committed immigrant, has not been easy.

The years in Canada were particularly harsh. Canada is a country that officially—and proudly—resists the policy and process of cultural fusion. For all its smug rhetoric about "cultural mosaic," Canada refuses to renovate its national self-image to include its changing complexion. It is a New World country with Old World concepts of a fixed, exclusivist national identity. And all through the seventies when I lived there, it was a country without a Bill of Rights or its own Constitution. Canadian official rhetoric designated me, as a citizen of non-European origin, one of the "visible minority" who, even though I spoke the Canadian national languages of English and French, was straining "the absorptive capacity" of Canada. Canadians of color were routinely treated as "not real" Canadians. In fact, when a terrorist bomb, planted in an Air India jet on Canadian soil, blew up after leaving Montreal, killing 329 passengers, 90 percent of whom were Canadians of Indian origin, the prime minister of Canada at the time, Brian Mulroney, cabled the Indian prime minister to offer Canada's condolences for India's loss, exposing the Eurocentricity of the "mosaic" policy of immigration.

In private conversations, some Canadian ambassadors and External Affairs officials have admitted to me that the creation of the Ministry of Multiculturism in the seventies was less an instrument for cultural tolerance, and more a vote-getting strategy to pacify ethnic European constituents who were alienated by the rise of Quebec separatism and the simultaneous increase of non-white immigrants.

The years of race-related harassments in a Canada without a Constitution have politicized me, and deepened my love of the ideals embedded in the American Bill of Rights.

I take my American citizenship very seriously. I am a voluntary immigrant. I am not an economic refugee, and not a seeker of political asylum. I am an American by choice, and not by the simple accident of birth. I have made emotional, social, and political commitments to this country. I have earned the right to think of myself as an American.

But in this blood-splattered decade, questions such as who is an American and what is American culture are being posed with belligerence and being answered with violence. We are witnessing an increase in physical, too often fatal, assaults on Asian Americans. An increase in systematic "dot-busting" of Indo-Americans in New Jersey, xenophobic immigrant-baiting in California, minority-on-minority violence during the south-central Los Angeles revolution.

America's complexion is browning daily. Journalists' surveys have established that whites are losing their clear majority status in some states, and have already lost it in New York and California. A recent *Time* magazine poll indicated that 60 percent of Americans favor limiting *legal* immigration. Eighty percent of Americans polled favor curbing the entry of undocumented aliens. U.S. borders are too extensive and too porous to be adequately policed. Immigration, by documented and undocumented aliens, is less affected by the U.S. Immigration and Naturalization Service, and more by wars, ethnic genocides, famines in the emigrant's own country.

Every sovereign nation has a right to formulate its immigration policy. In this decade of continual, large-scale diasporic movements, it is imperative that we come to some agreement about who "we" are now that the community includes old-timers, newcomers, many races, languages, and religions; about what our expectations of happiness and strategies for its pursuit are; and what our goals are for the nation.

Scapegoating of immigrants has been the politicians' easy instant remedy. Hate speeches fill auditoria, and bring in megabucks for those demagogues willing to profit from stirring up racial animosity.

The hysteria against newcomers is only minimally generated by the downturn in our economy. The panic, I suspect, is unleashed by a fear of the "other," the fear of what Daniel Stein, executive director of the Federation for American Immigration Reform, and a champion of closed borders, is quoted as having termed "cultural transmogrification."

The debate about American culture has to date been monopolized by rabid Eurocentrists and ethnocentrists; the rhetoric has been flamboyantly divisive, pitting a phantom "us" against a demonized "them." I am here to launch a new discourse, to reconstitute the hostile, biology-derived "us" versus "them" communities into a new *consensual* community of "we."

All countries view themselves by their ideals. Indians idealize, as well they should, the cultural continuum, the inherent value system of India, and are properly incensed when foreigners see nothing but poverty, intolerance, ignorance, strife, and injustice. Americans see themselves as the embodiments of liberty, openness, and individualism, even when the world judges them for drugs, crime, violence, bigotry, militarism, and homelessness. I was in Singapore when the media was very vocal about the case of an American teenager sentenced to caning for having allegedly vandalized cars. The overwhelming local sentiment was that caning Michael Fay would deter local youths from being tempted into "Americanization," meaning into gleefully breaking the law.

Conversely, in Tavares, Florida, an ardently patriotic school board has legislated that middle school teachers be required to instruct their students that American culture—meaning European-American culture—is inherently "superior to other foreign or historic cultures." The sinister, or at least misguided implication is that American culture has not been affected by the American Indian, African American, Latin American, and Asian American segments of its population.

The idea of "America" as a nation has been set up in opposition to the tenet that a nation is a collection of like-looking, like-speaking, like-worshiping people. Our nation is unique in human history. We have seen very recently, in a Germany plagued by anti-foreigner frenzy, how violently destabilizing the traditional concept of nation can be. In Europe, each country is, in a sense, a tribal homeland. Therefore, the primary criterion for nationhood in Europe is homogeneity of culture, and race, and religion. And that has contributed to blood-soaked balkanization in the former Yugoslavia and the former Soviet Union.

All European Americans, or their pioneering ancestors, gave up an easy homogeneity in their original countries for a new idea of Utopia. What we have going for us in the 1990s is the exciting chance to share in the making of a new American culture, rather than the coerced acceptance of either the failed nineteenth-century model of "melting pot" or the Canadian model of the "multicultural mosaic."

The "mosaic" implies a contiguity of self-sufficient, utterly distinct culture. "Multiculturism" has come to imply the existence of a central culture, ringed by peripheral cultures. The sinister fallout of official multiculturism and of professional multiculturists is the establishment of one culture as the norm and the rest as aberrations. Multiculturism emphasizes the differences between racial heritages. This emphasis on the differences has too often led to the dehumanization of the different. Dehumanization leads to discrimination. And discrimination can ultimately lead to genocide.

We need to alert ourselves to the limitations and the dangers of those discourses that reinforce an "us" versus "them" mentality. We need to protest any official rhetoric or demagoguery that marginalizes on a race-related and/or religion-related basis any segment of our society. I want to discourage the retention of cultural memory if the aim of that retention is cultural balkanization. I want to sensitize you to think of culture and nationhood *not* as an uneasy aggregate of antagonistic "them" and "us," but as a constantly re-forming, transmogrifying "we."

In this diasporic age, one's biological identity may not be the only one. Erosions and accretions come with the act of emigration. The experiences of violent unhousing from a biological "homeland" and rehousing in an adopted "homeland" that is not always welcoming to its dark-complected citizens have tested me as a person, and made me the writer I am today.

I choose to describe myself on my own terms, that is, as an American without hyphens. It is to sabotage the politics of hate and the campaigns of revenge spawned by Eurocentric patriots on the one hand and the professional multiculturists on the other, that I describe myself as an "American" rather than as an "Asian-American." Why is it that hyphenization is imposed only on non-white Americans? And why is it that only non-white citizens are "problematized" if they choose to describe themselves on their own terms? My outspoken rejection of hyphenization is my lonely campaign to obliterate categorizing the cultural landscape into a "center" and its "peripheries." To reject hyphenization is to demand that the nation deliver the promises of the American Dream and the American Constitution to *all* its citizens. I want nothing less than to invent a new vocabulary that demands, and obtains, an equitable power-sharing for all members of the American community.

But my self-empowering refusal to be "otherized" and "objectified" has come at tremendous cost. My rejection of hyphenization has been deliberately misrepresented as "race treachery" by some India-born, urban, upper-middle-class Marxist "green card holders" with lucrative chairs on U.S. campuses. These academics strategically position themselves as self-appointed spokespersons for their ethnic communities, and as guardians of the "purity" of ethnic cultures. At the same time, though they reside permanently in the United States and participate in the capitalist economy of this nation, they publicly denounce American ideals and institutions.

They direct their rage at me because, as a U.S. citizen, I have invested in the present and the future rather than in the expatriate's imagined homeland. They condemn me because I acknowledge erosion of memory as a natural result of emigration; because I count that erosion as net gain rather than as loss; and because I celebrate racial and cultural "mongrelization." I have no respect for these expatriate fence-straddlers who, even while competing fiercely for tenure and promotion within the U.S. academic system, glibly equate all evil in the world with the United States, capitalism, colonialism, and corporate and military expansionism. I regard the artificial retentions of "pure race" and "pure culture" as dangerous, reactionary illusions fostered by the Eurocentric and the ethnocentric empire builders within the academy. I fear still more the politics of revenge preached from pulpits by some minority demagogues.

People who choose to reside permanently in the United States but who refuse to share the responsibility entailed in taking out American citizenship should not presume to speak for, let alone condemn, those of us who have accepted the psychological, social, political transformations and responsibilities necessitated by naturalization.

As a writer, my literary agenda begins by acknowledging that America has transformed *me*. It does not end until I show that I (and the hundreds of thousands of recent immigrants like me) am minute by minute transforming America. The transformation is a two-way process; it affects both the individual and the national cultural identity. The end result of immigration, then, is this two-way transformation: that's my heartfelt message.

Others often talk of diaspora, of arrival as the end of the process. They talk of arrival in the context of loss, the loss of communal memory and the erosion of an intact ethnic culture. They use words like "erosion" and "loss" in alarmist ways. I want to talk of arrival as gain. Both Salman Rushdie and I see immigration as a process of self-integration.

What excites me is that we have the chance to retain those values we treasure from our original cultures, but we also acknowledge that the outer forms of those values are likely to change. In the Indian American community, I see a great deal of guilt about the inability to hang on to "pure culture." Parents express rage or despair at their U.S.-born children's forgetting of, or indifference to, some aspects of Indian culture. Of those parents, I would ask: What is it we have lost if our children are acculturating into the culture in which we are living? Is it so terrible that our children are discovering or inventing homelands for themselves? Some first-generation Indo-Americans, embittered by overt anti-Asian racism and by unofficial "glass ceilings," construct a phantom more-Indian-than-Indians-in-India identity as defense against marginalization. Of them I would ask: Why not get actively involved in fighting discrimination through protests and lawsuits?

I prefer that we forge a national identity that is born of our acknowledgment of the steady de-Europeanization of the U.S. population; that constantly synthesizes—fuses—the disparate cultures of our country's residents; and that provides a new, sustaining, and unifying national creed.

One More Time

■ ■ ■

JOHN A. WILLIAMS

There is absolutely no reason why anyone should expect a new period of enlightenment with the onset of a multicultural society; we are now and always have been such a society. Another name does not necessarily mean a new or even better product. Usually all it has ever meant is old snake oil in new bottles. "New" has been the most abused adjective in the American language.

Earlier, when our society, formed along rigid class and race lines, began to push at the limitations, we were urged to embrace a melting pot society, then one that was desegregated, beyond the melting pot or integrated; then it was a rainbow society; and now it is a multicultural society that blows across the land scattering seeds of diversity (which has yet to be precisely defined). But desegregation is still in the courts, seesawing over busing and school districts, and trying to reverse, at least in school attendance, white avoidance of non-white populations. The pot never melted its contents, and there was no gold at the end of the rainbow. In short, racism is proving to be an immovable force.

The power struggle—for that's what it is—continues, although on lesser, more personal levels, the battle to be Americans free of hyphen or prefix has been successfully settled. Not, however, in numbers that have had any influence or meaning upon the entrenched attitudes of most other Americans.

Multiculturalism should reject the practice and theory that every society possess a collective goat to blame when things are going badly. What's going badly isn't anything new, just more of the same: corruption and collusion in high places, crime, burgeoning welfare costs, Hippocratic pilfering of medical monies, dangerous, deteriorating confinement areas called "neighborhoods," and the frantic but failing struggle of the cops to maintain a class structure where few control many on the premise that those few people are better than others. But in a society where true equality exists, it would be difficult to discern one goat to take the fall from another. People like Pat Buchanan are frightened by this possibility; that is why he exhorts whites to "take back our country," suggesting that it has already been lost, to multiculturists, perhaps. But, in fact, multiculturalism is being fought at all levels of this society with the same doggedness that continues combat with affirmative action in the academy, in social exchange, in the workplace, and with the very government that instituted it.

What we are now witnessing is a kind of multiculturalism in its sleaziest, economic form, where everyone, everywhere is used and abused equally. A trade agreement such as NAFTA, for example, sanctions the multicultural slavery of peoples of color and whites of the working class— the usual suspects—as jobs zip out of the nation to the limitless sources of cheap colored labor abroad. NAFTA, furthermore, ultimately must spawn wars between the trading blocs of Europe, North and South America, and Asia, each with its own ethnic, nationalist, and economic visions of the future, because all wars derive from the desire to control trade and thereby accumulate wealth.

As is always the case, each new dream gathers adherents who struggle to be heard, and today it is the multiculturalists whose outward thrusts seem to be moral. But democratic capitalism, which has evinced few moral concerns and whose modus operandi is accumulation through someone else's loss, only mimes attention to these dreams. Its basic concern is that the dreams don't rattle reality. We see rampant multiculturalism in the pools of cheap labor, and in the televised productions of sports; what we don't see in sports is what happens between black, brown, and white teammates after the games: not much. Multicultural television commercials are wonderful; they sell products to all consumers. Bill Clinton follows this very transparent program with his multicultural symbols splattered throughout an administration that goes into a rapid wilting before each opportunity to do the right thing. He has no product that doesn't vanish under the shell of a pea or the withering scowl of Bob Dole.

Yet, real concerns like acknowledging that we live in a multicultural society and could, if we wished, draw moral and intellectual instruction from it, not to mention domestic tranquility instead of tension, must be supported at the top. We have had few leaders dedicated to creating the instruments for domestic soothing; where they have, their successors have expeditiously removed them. Some at times have talked a good game; others have disdained even this feint at ethnic amelioration. Multiculturalism cannot travel far without real sustenance from whoever inhabits the White House and/or Capitol Hill.

We may think the academy, therefore, can be the podium, or should— and many university administrators do, too. The academy, however, can be a treacherous arena, as Richard Wright suggested in a letter to his daughter in 1960: "A university," he wrote, "is a social club designed to condition people to help maintain a given social order." That order does not include teaching the Periodic Table of Equality. Every teacher knows other teachers who steadfastly resist usage of multicultural textbooks; they have also noted student resentment at having to read works by writers of color, American and not, whether this harms their grades or not.

A "post–Black White America" is a situation one can hardly envision from the contemporary perspective, not with one hundred thousand more cops and a $22.3 billion crime bill aimed precisely at black and Hispanic America, the denials be damned; ethnic cleansing, always at a deliberate slog, has picked up the pace.

But if there is a greater danger, it is the assumption that multiculturalism means all the many cultures in the nation will be equally respected. Given the history of humankind, the assumption is false on its face. Every culture extant has battled for supremacy (though they may have had to settle for parity, which seems to be anathema in the United States) over others. Each culture group has felt itself to be superior to others, and some have been quite honest about this; others have attempted to keep it to themselves. The "They are not like us" (read: "We are better than they are") syndrome haunts all our efforts, with the bottom line being that cultural respect need only be paid until certain ends, having little to do with cultural respect, are attained. This is not at all a secret to the white managers, many of whom were earlier engaged in the same struggle with each other. But now it is they in concert who grant this or that group of color certain favors while denying other colored groups the same favors, thus creating antagonisms and diversions between these groups so that no collaborative effort can be mounted against the white majority that seeks to maintain its superior status over all of them. This represents a consolidation of power. Arguments to the contrary can hold no water when we witness, daily, the practically unchecked mayhem of racist gangs, the push and pull of redistricting, the proportional absence of people of color in Congress, the racist acts and attitudes of police officials from the elites in government down to the county sheriffs, and the absolute refusal to permit the entrance of people of color into the decision-making levels of the media.

No immigrant, white or of color, would have responded to the democratic slogans broadcast by the United States if he or she knew they would immediately be relegated to the status of the black American, because they *knew* that would not be their position when they came—which is only common sense, but also an immutable fact when considering the possible success or failure of a multiculturist society. There is no culture group of color that has not at some time felt, or continues to feel, the powerful backhanded slap of white Americans who have now been subsumed into the dominant group as honorary members.

Having all felt the lash, the betrayals, the ugly contradictions, we ought to try harder to get it right this time. We can began at the roots by exercising intracommunal support in all things that benefit all of us. We can stop pretending to do the things we really don't want to, and being the culturally respectful people we really aren't. Let's be for real. Let's acknowledge our differences, iron them out, and do what they don't want us to do—pull together, not apart. White America recognizes that unless some things are changed drastically, this country cannot remain majority white. The critical pro-life groups seem to be not so much concerned with life as with white life. The recent emphasis on the care and feeding of infants appears to be, if one can make a judgment based on television and the photos in the papers, on the care and development of white infants. We are always late with help to the regions of the world where children of color are starving. The suspicion that certain Western-created viruses were spawned in Asia and Africa and are now decimating the U.S. population is not unrelated to the perceived notion that powerful white Americans want the United States to remain powerful and mostly white. These may be tactics of a grand strategy.

Of course, a united front diminishes the apparent power that may be vested in a single group—which may be the design of some who pretend multiculturalism is a great movement. Care must be exercised, therefore, in considering motive, means, and ends. Studying the power of conservative politics in this country today, one may easily conclude that multiculturalism is the last best hope to alter that situation.

BIOGRAPHICAL NOTES

■ ■ ■

Miguel Algarin is a recipient of three American Book Awards and an Obie for his work in the theatre. He is also the editor of *Aloud!*, a poetry anthology, and the author of *Love Is Hard Work*, a book of poetry.

Rudolfo Anaya is the author of the novels *Bless Me Ultima* and *Albuquerque*. He is a professor of English at the University of New Mexico.

William M. Banks is a professor in the African-American studies department at the University of California at Berkeley. He is the author of *Black Intellectuals*.

Amiri Baraka is a prolific poet and playwright. He is the author of the Obie Award–winning *Dutchman* and one of the true originals among American writers.

Helen Barolini is the editor of *The Dream Book: An Anthology of Writings by Italian-American Women*.

Lucia Chiavola Birnbaum won the American Book Award for her book *Liberazione della donna: Feminism in Italy*.

Karla Brundage is a Vassar graduate. She teaches school in Hawaii and has been published in *Konch* magazine.

Elena Caceres is a freelance writer currently living in the California Central Valley. She is completing her autobiography, *Fifty Years: My Life and Education in America*.

Ana Castillo is the author of the 1987 American Book Award winner *The Mixquiahuala Letters*. Her most recent book is *Massacre of the Dreamers*.

Frank Chin is the author of *Gunga Din Highway* and *Donald Duk*.

Lawrence Di Stasi is the author of *The Big Book of Italian American Culture*, and is project director for Una Storia Segreta, a traveling exhibit about the restrictions on Italian Americans during World War II.

Russell Ellis is the former vice chancellor for undergraduate affairs at the University of California at Berkeley.

Jack Foley is the radio host of *Cover to Cover*, a program about books and authors, on KPFA in Berkeley, California. His most recent book is *Exiles*.

Joe Chung Fong is a Ph.D. candidate in anthropology at the University of California at Berkeley.

Robert Elliot Fox is a professor of English at Southern Illinois University at Carbondale. He is the author of *Conscientious Sorcerers* and *Masters of the Drum*.

Allison Francis is an advanced Ph.D. candidate in English at Washington University in St. Louis. Her poems have been published in *Konch* magazine.

Daniela Gioseffi won the American Book Award for *Women on War*, and the short story *Daffodil Dollars* received a PEN fiction award in 1990.

Nathan Hare is the president of The Black Think Tank. He is the author of *The Black Anglo Saxons*.

Calvin Hernton is a professor of English at Oberlin College. Among his works are *Sex and Racism in America* and *Medicine Man*.

Juan Felipe Herrera is a prolific poet whose latest work is *Night Train to Tuxtla*. His play, *I Don't Have to Show You No Stinking Badges!*, was performed at California State University at Fresno.

Gerald Horne is a professor in the black studies department at the University of California at Berkeley. His latest book is *Fire This Time: The Watts Uprising and the 1960s*.

Earl Ofari Hutchinson is a television commentator and author of *The Assassination of the Black Male Image*.

Yuri Kageyama is a correspondent for Associated Press in Tokyo. She is the author of *Peeling*.

Nicolas Kanellos is the founder and director of *Arte de Publico Press*, the oldest and largest publisher of United States Hispanic literature, as well as the *Americas Review* (formerly *Revista Chicano-Reguena*). He is a full professor at the University of Houston.

K. Connie Kang is a reporter for the *Los Angeles Times* and the author of *Home Was the Land of Morning Calm: A Saga of a Korean-American Family*.

Maulana Karenga is professor and chair of the department of black studies at California State University, Long Beach. Among his books is *Introduction to Black Studies*. He is the founder of *Kwanzaa*.

Stefanie Kelly is an honors graduate in English from the University of California at Berkeley.

Martin Kilson is the Frank G. Thomson Professor at Harvard University and a regular contributor to *Dissent* magazine.

Elaine H. Kim is a professor of Asian American studies and the chair of ethnic studies at the University of California at Berkeley. Her most recent book is *Korean American Life Stories*.

A. Robert Lee is the Reader in American Literature at the University of Kent at Canterbury. Among his books is *Shadow Distance: A Gerald Vizenor Reader*.

Michael LeNoir is a distinguished Oakland physician and television producer. He is the executive director of the Ethnic Health Institute.

Lloyd is a professor of English and Irish studies at the University of California Berkeley.

R. Madhubuti is the author of *Black Men: Obsolete, Single, Dangerous?* and *Claiming Earth: Race, Rage, Rape, Redemption: Black Seeking a Culture of Enlightened Empowerment.*

Lois Mätt-Fässbinder is a professor of sociology at Canada College.

Bharati Mukherjee is a professor at the University of California at Berkeley. Among her novels is *Jasmine.*

Ngozi O. Ola is a Harvard graduate who now works for German television.

Brenda Payton, columnist for the *Oakland Tribune*, recently received an award from the California Newspaper Publishers Association.

Marco Portales is a professor of English at Texas A&M University and executive assistant to the president.

Tennessee Reed is a sophomore at Oakland's Laney College. Her most recent book is *Airborne.*

Roberto Rodríguez and **Patrisia Gonzales** are columnists for *Chronicle Features.*

Danny Romero is the author of *10 Calle*, a novel.

Michael Ross is the author of *As Soon as the Weather Breaks*, a novel, and *Black and Blue in America.* He has worked for the *New York Times* and the *San Francisco Chronicle.*

Leslie Marmon Silko is the author of *Almanac of the Dead*, *Ceremony*, and *Yellow Woman and the Beauty of the Spirit.*

Amritjit Singh is a professor of English and African American studies at Rhode Island College. He is the author of *The Novels of the Harlem Renaissance.*

Barbara Smith is the editor of *Home Girls: A Black Feminist Anthology* and the publisher of *Kitchen Table: Women of Color Press.*

Werner Sollors teaches Afro-American studies and English at Harvard University. His most recent book is *Neither Black Nor White Yet Both.*

Gundars Strads is the executive director of the Before Columbus Foundation and editor of *California Management* magazine. He has contributed to the *Nation* magazine.

Hoyt Sze is a former columnist for the *Daily Californian.*

Kathryn Waddell Takara is a professor in the ethnic studies department at the University of Hawaii.

Gerald Vizenor teaches at the University of California at Berkeley. His most recent publications are *Manifest Manners* and *Shadow Distance: A Gerald Vizenor Reader.*

Ortiz Montaigne Walton is the author of *Music: Black, White, and Blue.*

Robin Washington is an Emmy Award–winning television producer and a three-time honoree of the National Association of Black Journalists.

John A. Williams has published many distinguished works, including *The Man Who Cried I Am* and *(!) Click Song.*

William Wong is a freelance journalist who has worked for the *Wall Street Journal* and the *Oakland Tribune.* He is also a regular commentator on *The Jim Lehrer NewsHour.*